Taking SIDES

Clashing Views on Controversial Issues in Crime and Criminology

Fifth Edition

Edited, Selected, and with Introductions by

Richard C. Monk
Coppin State College

Dushkin/McGraw-Hill
A Division of The McGraw-Hill Companies

To the memory of my father, Daniel R. Monk (April 29, 1913–March 17, 1995), and to my mother, Elsie M. Monk, who first taught me the importance of debating controversial issues.

Photo Acknowledgments

Cover image: © 1995 by AP-Wide World Photos/Kevork Djansezian

Cover Art Acknowledgment

Charles Vitelli

Library of Congress Cataloging-in-Publication Data

Main entry under title:
   Taking sides: clashing views on controversial issues in crime and criminology/edited, selected, and with introductions by Richard C. Monk.—5th ed.
   Includes bibliographical references and index.
   1. Crime and criminals. I. Monk, Richard C., *comp.*

0-697-39109-4

364
ISSN: 1098-5379

Printed on Recycled Paper

PREFACE

To those who share the age-old hope that man's inhumanity to man can be diminished.

—Harry Elmer Barnes and Howard Becker

Comprehension without critical evaluation is impossible.

—Hegel

It was my fate to be a scholar for a while.

—Nietzsche

This volume contains 38 essays presented in a pro and con format. A total of 19 different clashing issues within crime and criminology are debated. The issues are arranged in four broad topical areas that touch upon some of the most important and interesting aspects of criminology and criminal justice.

I have included a mix of fundamental issues and newly emerging ones. Some of the authors unabashedly write for a popular audience primarily to grind their own axes or to arouse public sentiment. Other selections are written by some of the most profound thinkers within the social sciences and deal with vital theoretical issues in crime and criminology (for example, the functionality of crime). I have not shirked my obligation to provide you with the best discussions on relevant issues available, even if the discussions are sometimes technical or theoretical and require you to think deeply about the issue at hand before making up your mind.

In order to assist you in your voyage into controversial criminological issues, I have supplied you with an *introduction* to each issue and an issue *postscript*, which follows the "yes" and "no" readings. All the postscripts have detailed suggestions for further reading should you want to pursue the topics raised in an issue. While my primary concern was to get the authors' ideas up front so that you could be immersed in them, fight with them, embrace some of them, than make your own decisions, I have not been averse to "editorializing." Now and then my own disdain (or support) for certain ideas will be more manifest than on other occasions. Do not be bashful about debating the authors and their ideas, or your editor as well. I definitely could be wrong and may need your critical evaluation!

I feel strongly that the only way that irrationalities and cruelties among men and women can be reduced is through critical evaluation of the issues at hand. I hope that this volume can assist you and your generation in keeping criminology and criminal justice vital areas of study. I feel that one realistic way to achieve this goal is through reintroducing the necessary art of systematic and informed debate over clashing issues in crime and criminology.

Changes to this edition In response to the rapidly changing world of crime and criminal justice, and on the strength of the recommendations that have come from professors who have used the book, I have made considerable changes to this edition. There are 11 completely new issues: *Does IQ Significantly Contribute to Crime?* (Issue 3); *Should the Federal Government Have a Major Role in Reducing Juvenile Crime?* (Issue 6); *Are the Dangers of Internet Child Pornography Exaggerated?* (Issue 7); *Are the New Sex Offender Laws Rational?* (Issue 8); *Does Arresting Batterers Do More Harm Than Good?* (Issue 9); *Are Blacks Helped by the Drug War?* (Issue 10); *Should Jury Nullification Be Used to Reduce Ethnic and Racial Inequities?* (Issue 11); *Does Three Strikes and Other Tough Approaches Work?* (Issue 13); *Should Partial Identifications Be Accepted in Police Lineups?* (Issue 14); *Does Increased Crime Control Make New York Safer?* (Issue 17); and *Does the International Drug War Encourage Human Rights Violations?* (Issue 19). In addition, for the issue on euthanasia (Issue 16), both selections have been replaced, so the issue should be considered new. In all, there are 23 new readings in this edition. Issue introductions and postscripts have been revised and updated where necessary.

A word to the instructor An *Instructor's Manual With Test Questions* (multiple-choice and essay) is available through the publisher for the instructor using *Taking Sides* in the classroom. And a general guidebook, *Using Taking Sides in the Classroom*, which discusses methods and techniques for integrating the pro-con approach into any classroom setting, is also available. An online version of *Using Taking Sides in the Classroom* and a correspondence service for *Taking Sides* adopters can be found at www.cybsol.com/usingtakingsides/. For students, we offer a field guide to analyzing argumentative essays, *Analyzing Controversy: An Introductory Guide*, with exercises and techniques to help them to decipher genuine controversies.

Taking Sides: Clashing Views on Controversial Issues in Crime and Criminology is only one title in the Taking Sides series. If you are interested in seeing the table of contents for any of the other titles, please visit the Taking Sides Web site at http://www.dushkin.com/takingsides/.

Acknowledgments Many people contribute to any worthwhile project. Among those more directly involved in this project whom I would like to thank are the authors of these excellent and stimulating selections. Also, my thanks to my many students over the years who have contributed to the criminological dialogue. At Coppin State College, these students include Jodi Buckson; Heather M. Allen; Ray Hollander; Derrick Eleazer; John Hamilton, whose discussions about the Internet were very helpful; and Dayna S. McCain. I remain honored to have been the teacher of the brave writers and researchers of the student journal *Kaleidoscope*, now no longer published, at

Valdosta State University. Their courageous work remains a beacon illuminating the surrounding land.

Several colleagues, scholars, and administrators provided comments and support that were immensely helpful and greatly appreciated. Thanks are extended to Coppin State College president Calvin L. Burnett; T. J. Bryan, dean of Arts and Sciences at Coppin State College; Elizabeth C. Gray, chair, and Shaun L. Gabbidon of the Department of Criminal Justice at Coppin State College; Kurt Finsterbusch of the University of Maryland; Alex Hooke of Villa Julie College; Nijole V. Benokraitis and Ben Wright of the University of Baltimore; Maurice St. Pierre of Morgan State University; Vincent Schiraldi, executive director of the Center on Juvenile and Criminal Justice; Joel Henderson and Tom Gitchoff of San Diego State University; George Rush of California State University, Long Beach; Paul A. Wortman of New York City Public School 252; Horst Senger of Simi Valley, California; O. Elmer Polk of the University of Texas at Arlington; Harv Greisman of West Chester State University; Mike Lynch of the University of South Florida; Rudy Faller of the Inter-American Development Bank; Frank Cullen of the University of Cincinnati; George T. Black of Longwood, Florida; Daniel B. Monk of Arlington, Virginia; Stacey Graham, library assistant at Coppin State College; and Carole Mason, library assistant at the University of Baltimore.

I also received many helpful comments and suggestions from professors across the United States and Canada. Their suggestions have markedly enhanced the quality of this edition. Special thanks to those professors who responded to the questionnaire with specific suggestions for the fifth edition:

David L. Carlson
Concordia College

Raymond D'Angelo
St. Joseph's College

Robert Dunn
St. Joseph's College

Elaine Ellington
Texas A&M University

Patricia W. Gavin
Anna Maria College

Evan Gorelick
Marist College

Danny Hobbs
Southwest Baptist University

Finn Hornum
La Salle University

David M. Horton
St. Edward's University

Karim Ismaili
Radford University

Lynnette L. James Callender
Florida Community
  College–Jacksonville South

J. A. H. Keyes
Shaw University

Richard G. Kiekbusch
University of Texas–Permian
  Basin

Gregory Osowski
Henry Ford Community
  College

Cynthia Shelmidine
Jefferson Community
College

Richard Stempien
Mohawk Valley Community
College

Finally, someone must have once said that an author or an editor is only as good as his or her publisher. Without doubt, this *Taking Sides* would not have seen the light of day without the professional assistance and ingenious prodding of David Dean, list manager for the Taking Sides series, and the work of the staff at Dushkin/McGraw-Hill. Naturally, I remain solely responsible for errors.

Richard C. Monk
Coppin State College

CONTENTS IN BRIEF

CONTENTS

Classic sociologist Emile Durkheim (1858–1917) theorizes that crime reaffirms moral boundaries and helps bring about needed social changes. U.S. senator Daniel Patrick Moynihan (D-New York) argues that Durkheim does not address deviancy as a serious societal problem and that modern crime has gone way beyond the point of being functional.

Dennis R. Martin, president of the National Association of Chiefs of Police, theorizes that rising racial tensions and violence can be attributed to rock music's promotion of "vile, deviant, and sociopathic behaviors." Criminologists Mark S. Hamm and Jeff Ferrell charge that Martin's theory is based on racism and ignorance of both music and broader cultural forces.

The late psychologist and criminologist Richard J. Herrnstein and Charles Murray, a fellow of the American Enterprise Institute, argue that a significant cause of crime is low IQ. Indeed, criminological theories and policies ignore this at great peril, they contend. Criminologists Francis T. Cullen, Paul Gendreau, G. Roger Jarjoura, and John Paul Wright assert that Herrnstein and Murray utilize faulty data, ignore the many significant environmental factors related to both crime and intelligence, and derive mean-spirited and repressive policy conclusions.

Professor of management and public policy James Q. Wilson and the late psychologist Richard J. Herrnstein argue that the focus of crime study ought to be on street criminals. Professor of philosophy Jeffrey Reiman contends that pollution, medical malpractice, and dangerous working conditions that go uncorrected are far more serious than street crime.

Criminologist Charles R. Tittle insists that criminology will remain stagnant unless it promotes general theory building. Professors Michael J. Lynch and W. Byron Groves argue that it is better to develop specific, grounded theories and to engage in careful comparative criminology.

The U.S. Department of Justice's Office of Juvenile Justice and Delinquency Prevention (OJJDP) contends that with rising juvenile violent crime rates, federal help is needed to identify the best strategies for dealing with juveniles, coordinating states' efforts to reduce crime, and providing technical assistance and training. Patrick Fagan, a William H. G. FitzGerald Senior Fellow in Family and Cultural Issues at the Heritage Foundation, argues that the government has made matters far worse by promoting false explanations of crime and by ignoring the vital role of the local trinity of family, school, and church in reducing crime.

Julia Wilkins, a writer of books and articles on educating children, argues that claims of Internet dangers are simply an example of "moral panic" causing otherwise sensible people to overreact. Magazine writer Bob Trebilcock contends that the Internet is a real danger to children because it provides easy access to pornography, encourages the creation and dissemination of child pornography, and provides pedophiles with a new crop of children to prey upon.

Journalist Bruce Fein contends that community notification laws of convicted sex offenders is necessary in lieu of increasing rage at violent child sex offenders, which could result in demands for excessive prison sentences if something is not done. Edward Martone, an American Civil Liberties Union activist, acknowledges community rage but maintains that the new laws create vigilantism, unfairly punish offenders, and contribute little to solving the problem of compulsive sex offenders.

Janell D. Schmidt, supervisor of the Milwaukee County Child Protective Services, and professor of criminology Lawrence W. Sherman argue that arresting batterers in many cases does more harm than good, and they advocate alternatives to mandatory arrest. Associate professor of public administration and social work Evan Stark contends that arresting batterers is a vital step for female empowerment and for women's achieving full citizenship status.

James A. Inciardi, director of the Center for Drug and Alcohol Studies at the University of Delaware, surveys several arguments supporting the legalization of drugs and rejects them all, insisting that blacks and others would be hurt by legalization. Psychiatrist and psychoanalyst Thomas Szasz maintains that the current drug war harms almost all people, especially blacks, and that its main function is to increase the power of the medical and criminal justice establishments.

Paul Butler, an associate professor at the George Washington University Law School, argues that black jurors should acquit black defendants of certain crimes, regardless of whether or not they perceive the defendant to be guilty, to make up for inequities in the criminal justice system. Randall Kennedy, a professor at the Harvard Law School, in examining the acquittal of O. J. Simpson, finds it tragic that black jurors would pronounce a murderer "not guilty" just to send a message to white people.

David Von Drehle, a writer and the arts editor for the *Washington Post*, examines specific capital punishment cases and statistics and concludes that capital punishment is bad policy. Ernest van den Haag, a professor of jurisprudence and public policy (now retired), rejects claims that capital punishment is unfair and barbaric, and he insists that the death penalty is just retribution for terrible crimes.

Eugene H. Methvin, senior editor for *Reader's Digest*, contends that a very small number of juveniles and adults commit the majority of serious crimes. The main solution to the crime problem, then, is to identify them as early as possible and increase the punishments each time they offend, eventually incarcerating the repeat offenders. Professor of criminal justice David Shichor argues that the "three-strikes" policy is costly, inefficient, unfair, and does little to reduce crime.

A. M. Levi and Noam Jungman, of the Division of Identification and Forensic Sciences at the Israel Police Headquarters in Jerusalem, identify several serious flaws in existing police lineup procedures and propose novel remedies, including the allowance of partial identifications. Psychological researcher

Michael R. Leippe and psychologist Gary L. Wells reject key aspects of the proposal as being unrealistic and untested.

Josh Sugarmann, formerly with the National Coalition to Ban Handguns, identifies several problems with legal handguns, including what he describes as unacceptably high rates of suicides with guns, family homicides, and accidents. Sociologist James D. Wright offers ten "fundamental truths" about guns. While he acknowledges that there is widespread disagreement over interpretations of the facts, he concludes that most gun control laws are unfair and ineffective.

Paul R. McHugh, director of the Department of Psychiatry and Behavioral Sciences at the Johns Hopkins University School of Medicine, contends that many patients who indicate that they want to die are actually mentally depressed individuals who should be counseled, not helped to die. Professor of jurisprudence Ronald Dworkin and five fellow moral philosophers, in a brief filed in two cases before the Supreme Court, maintain that individuals have a moral and constitutional right to determine their own life's value.

Writer Paul Ruffins traces the "miracle" of New York City's crime reduction to efforts in the late 1980s to increase community policing and to halt petty street crimes. Former New York mayor David N. Dinkins maintains that crime control in the city has gotten out of control, making the streets unsafe for citizens, especially citizens of color.

Sociology professor Rhoda E. Howard argues that justice largely depends on a general acceptance of basic human rights. Vinay Lal, a professor of humanities, dismisses human rights as a tool used by Western nations to legitimize brutal tactics that maintain their power over weaker nations and regions.

Eyal Press, a writer and journalist, contends that expanding U.S. support of drug control in Latin America serves only to curry political favor with conservatives and allow other countries' militaries to terrorize and repress their people. General Barry McCaffrey, director of the Office of National Drug Control Policy, argues that hemispheric drug control is a vital example of historical and economic linkages between North and South America to solve mutual problems.

INTRODUCTION

The Changing Study of Crime and Criminology

Richard C. Monk

By almost any measurement of "what is important," crime continues to rank at or near the top of America's priorities and concerns. Local, state, and federal crime fighting and crime control budgets often involve the highest expenditures—typically numbering in the billions of dollars—for the police, courts, and prisons. The losses from crime in lives and in dollars are equally high. The perception of crime expressed as fear is very high among most Americans. For instance, a recent Gallup Poll reveals that some 62 percent of all women and over 25 percent of all men state that there are areas within a mile of their home in which they would be afraid to walk at night.

Ironically, the fear of crime is often highest among those who are least likely to be victimized, such as women and the elderly. Those who run the greatest risk of being assaulted or killed—young, male racial minorities—are much less concerned about crime.

Since the 1960s, following the Omnibus Safe Streets Act, billions of federal dollars have been spent to create law enforcement training programs, to buy equipment for local police, to fund hundreds of massive research studies, and to create new state and federal crime control agencies and research centers (for example, the Bureau of Justice Statistics). Unfortunately, many politicians and criminal justice administrators, most of the public, and a growing number of criminologists view these efforts as dismal failures.

The United States now has the greatest number of citizens behind bars than at any other time in its history. It also has more citizens in prison than any other nation on Earth. California alone has more prison inmates than all other nations except Russia and China. In some states, such as California, spending on prisons has for the first time surpassed spending on education. In many urban areas young, black males are more likely to go to prison than to attend college.

Intellectually, one can also discern a definite shift in scholarly attitudes toward crime, criminals, and crime control. In the early years of the twentieth century, criminologists registered optimism about conquering crime. The assumption was that if we simply started to research crime systematically, utilizing the cognitive tools of science, based upon rationality and empirical investigations free of sensationalism and biases, then significant advances would follow.

John Lewis Gillin, in his popular 1926 criminology text, said:

> Criminal statistics are becoming more reliable every year.... It is time that calm, scientific study, rather than sensational journalistic methods be devoted to the problem of crime and criminals. Only so can popular fallacies concerning what makes the criminal and how to treat him be exploded, and a sound program for the treatment and the prevention of crime be established.

A short time later, the preeminent criminologist Thorsten Sellin, as cited by F. Zimring and G. Hawkins in *Capital Punishment and the American Agenda* (Cambridge University Press, 1986), wrote what might be considered the basis of the modern scientific research approach to crime:

> [It] is characteristic of modern man, reared in an age of scientific orientation, that he wishes to use scientific thoughtways in the approach to his problems. He does not like to be considered irrational. When he formulates public policies, he wants to think that such policies are based on scientific facts.

Disputations over what the "scientific facts" are and what they mean remain acrimonious. For instance, some criminologists enthuse that the past few years have witnessed an important decline in serious crime. However, as Elliott Currie points out in *Crime and Punishment in America* (Metropolitan Books, 1998), these seemingly bright statistics are based on comparisons with the years 1990–1993, which were especially high violent crime years. Furthermore, if crime in 1996 were compared with crime in 1984, it would reflect a 13 percent *increase*.

Even if crime is "getting better," criminologists explain this finding with several different theories. One explanation is that crime has been reduced because there is better social control—more police work being done and more people being incarcerated. However, some claim that increased crime control has had terrible, unanticipated, negative results, such as racial discrimination, the creation of a police state, and the alienation of an entire generation of young people.

Other criminologists argue that the decline in crime (if it exists) reflects the current demographic decline in young people and is therefore only temporary. They predict that the United States will soon experience an explosion in crime as the number of young people entering their teens increases. These are only a few of the competing descriptions of the "facts" of crime and their explanations. The five issues on crime theories in Part 1 further illustrate the sharp disagreement among criminologists.

It appears that current criminologists are imbued with a more realistic understanding of both the complexities of the twentieth century and crime and criminals. In the words of noted sociologist Peter Berger, in his book *The Heretical Imperative* (Doubleday, 1979), current academic thinking is probably more likely to be influenced by an awareness that

> the institutional pluralization that marks modernity affects not only human actions but also human consciousness: Modern men and women find themselves

confronted not only by multiple options of possible courses of action but also by multiple options of possible ways of thinking about the world.

This volume attempts to assist you in examining possible options for action and possible ways of thinking about crime, criminals, and criminology.

CRIME: DEFINITIONS AND CAUSES

Ideological Issues

Any theory or explanation of crime obviously has several dimensions built into it from the start. First, even the most "scientific" or "neutral" theory will reflect to some extent the existing ideological or political sentiments of the day. At the very least, most criminological theories can be classified as conservative, radical, or liberal, or some analytical combination of these three political perspectives.

In theory, a scientific explanation of some phenomenon, including one of crime and criminals, is supposed to be value-free, uncontaminated by emotions and political circumstances. Yet funding decisions are often based on prevailing political concerns with public demands, and consequently the formulation of theory and the pursuits of research programs for scholars are affected. For instance, the disciplinary area of criminal justice administration, which has rapidly matured since the 1960s largely as a direct result of the massive infusion of federal funds, reflects concerns quite different from those of traditional criminology. Basically, criminal justice eschews any search for *causes* of criminal behavior. Instead, it tends to serve the needs of political funding agencies, which respond to the public's demand for solutions to the crime problem, and is therefore an atheoretical, applied academic discipline. The focus is on the development of strategies for administering more effectively the courts, the police, and the prisons.

Images of Society

A second dimension of any theory of crime causation, which also sometimes overlaps with ideological issues, is the image of society and of men and women contained within the theory. If criminals are seen as evil men and women contaminating an otherwise "pure" and "perfectable" society, then the explanation of crime that follows from this thinking will probably be a conservative one. That is, crime is a consequence of the individual offender's pathology.

By contrast, if crime is seen as a reaction against the inequities of the capitalist society or system, then the system, according to a crude variant of radical or Marxist criminology, is exclusively to blame. This theory's image of men and women is that they are inherently good but the system is bad and, through oppression, drives many to commit crimes.

The liberal image of men and women is that they are potentially good but that, through a combination of factors ranging from socialization to unfortunate circumstances, they can make mistakes. Reform of certain aspects of either society or individuals, or both, is suggested by this theoretical perspective.

Theory and Treatment
A third dimension of any theory of crime is an inherent treatment modality. The conservative explanation of crime would recommend punishment. As noted, the liberal perspective would recommend "treatment" or "rehabilitation" as well as possible economic reforms in society. A biological theory would have as part of its implicit treatment modality either sterilization, chemical therapy, or some kind of medical remedy directed at the individual offender.

Research Programs
A fourth dimension of criminological theories is that, in addition to having built-in ideological biases, however implicit, images of society and of men and women, and a concomitant treatment modality, they will have a specific research program. That is, each contains a particular methodological agenda. This, along with the other dimensions of a theory, is influenced by and influences the conceptualization of key theoretic concepts such as "crime" and "criminal." The exact scope of a theory is largely a result of how the element that the theory purports to explain is specifically defined. For instance, noted criminologist Edwin H. Sutherland's (1883–1950) classic definition of criminology is the study of the making of laws, the breaking of laws, and society's responses to these processes. This is a very comprehensive approach to criminology and technically includes both criminology and criminal justice. In actuality, criminologists have traditionally focused more heavily on studying the causes, rates, and distributions of crime. Criminal justice scholars have focused almost exclusively on society's responses to lawbreaking; that is, the criminal justice system. However, this historical distinction between the two has recently shown signs of collapse.

Other definitions and their theoretic frames of reference have been more narrow in scope. As a consequence, their research methodologies have also been more narrow than those working within Sutherland's tradition. For instance, a legalistic approach to criminology might emphasize simply the passage of laws. European criminologists, for example, for generations have emphasized the study of laws. American criminologists, by contrast, have studied criminals, crime, and prisons far more extensively.

A LOOK AT SOME THEORIES
Some criminologists develop novel definitions of crime. James Q. Wilson, for instance (see Issue 4), centers his theory of crime around predatory street crimes and ignores all other types. His work, to some extent, is reminiscent of the Italian jurist Garofalo, who in 1914 defined crimes as offenses against

society's ideas of "pity" and "probity." The offense also has to be injurious to society, Garofalo wrote.

The acts of defining and explaining some phenomenon, then, automatically set the boundaries for both the discipline itself and what is to be researched in that discipline (what kinds of crimes, who commits crime, etc.). For example, both formally and informally, rape was not considered a crime in many parts of the world. Informally, in the United States, it was often not treated as a crime, or at least not as a serious crime, although laws were always on the books against it. Until the past several years, it was not considered possible for a man to rape his wife. Indeed, in some states it was assumed that if a woman had invited a man to her home, then rape could not have occurred (only voluntary sexual intercourse). Thus, what your theory of crime consists of, how it defines crime, and what acts are included as crimes will all have a tremendous impact on your research and policy recommendations. That is why it is very important to inquire about a scholar's particular theoretic frame of reference.

Criminology in the United States grew up in the late 1800s basically as an applied study of the effects of prisons on criminals. It later received "academic respectability" through its inclusion within sociology departments at the turn of the century (for example, the University of Chicago). Almost from the very beginning, criminology as a subdiscipline of sociology emphasized a reformist, scientific orientation. It was assumed that, by scientifically understanding crime, criminals could be better controlled and helped. Thus, crime would be reduced. Most of the early theories, though, were a grab bag of different superstitions, Protestant reform sentiments, and pop biology and psychology, with some vague sociological or structural ideas thrown in. Generally, the sociological aspects of criminological theorizing were restricted to a focus upon the organization (or more typically, the perceived disorganization) of the family, the community, and the school. (See, for instance, Gillin's *Criminology and Penology*, 1926).

Throughout the 1940s and 1950s, the dominant theory within American criminology, by far, was that of Sutherland and later Sutherland and Donald R. Cressey. This perspective, though vast and complicated in many ways, is usually reduced to representing the symbolic interactionist sociological frame of reference. Within American sociology since the 1960s, there have been three dominant paradigms, or theories, explaining social behavior. These are the symbolic interactionist, the structural functional, and the conflict, or radical, perspectives.

As indicated, most criminological work was set within the symbolic interactionist frame of reference for several years. The emphasis was placed on how criminals were socialized into a world of crime through their interactions with criminal others. The importance of learning symbols, attitudes, and values conducive of crime commission from knowledgeable, experienced criminals was stressed. Later, the role (sometimes a fatal role) of labeling was incorporated into this perspective. The interaction between the police and alleged criminals, as well as between the courts and alleged criminals, was emphasized. However, economic factors as well as political ones were generally ignored by this perspective.

The structural functional perspective derives its thinking largely from the sociology of Emile Durkheim (see Issue 1). It has been elaborated on by a number of American sociologists. The most important bearer of Durkheim's tradition has been Robert Merton, whose elaborations upon Durkheim's work include his famous means-end scheme approach to explaining deviant behavior (first published in 1938). Later theorists writing in this tradition include Kingsley Davis and, more recently, Kai T. Erikson.

Structural functionalists attempt to determine what patterns of interaction or structures exist in various groups. They investigate what these patterns contribute to the maintenance of that group and of the society to which the group belongs. In the United States, for example, dating patterns and their relation to marriage are studied. Marriage patterns and their relation to the economy, to religion, and so on are traced. In addition, structural functionalists want to know about what consequences patterns of behavior have for groups, for members of groups, and for society as a whole. Such consequences can be both positive and negative, intentional and unintentional.

Radical or Marxist sociologists are similar to structural functionalists in that they frequently look at the entire society and try to determine how its various component parts interrelate. However, the radical or conflict theorist (these terms are often used interchangeably) generally sees as the core definers of society's interests those who dominate the economy. By contrast, structural functionalists seem to assume core values that are shared by members of society regardless of their position vis-à-vis the economy (whether they are workers, managers, or owners).

For the structural functionalist, crime results from people having their goals or values blocked. An example would be poor teenagers who share the American goal of material success but through lack of education, discrimination, and so on are not able to achieve success through the prescribed channels. Therefore, they commit crimes as a "short cut."

The Marxist would argue, by contrast, that often the system itself, through oppression, pressures the criminal to commit crimes. There are many variants of radical criminology. However, earlier variants insisted that criminals were often guilty only of political acts. The radical criminologists would also emphasize the unfair treatment society's disadvantaged are subjected to by agents of the criminal justice system, such as the police on the beat harassing the poor, the courts' unfair sentencing of them, and the prison's mistreatment of its inmates, usually poorer citizens. To the radical criminologist, the criminal justice system is little more than a handmaiden serving to protect the interests of the rich. The structural functionalists, then, obviously view crime in a very different way.

As a point of interest, an intellectual contradiction within criminology that parallels contradictions within broader institutional and cultural structures is the continued appeal of radical criminology. Logically, one might have predicted that, since the demise of the Soviet Union revealed the many sharp political and economic contradictions inherent in that former system's application of Marxian ideas, intellectuals in the West would have radically changed their perceptions of the relevancy of Marx. Within the social sciences, at least so far, this has not happened. Although many novel variants of criminological theory are rapidly emerging—including postmodernism, deconstructionism, feminist theory, and even applications of chaos theory— none of them can be seen as consistently Marxist. Yet a hard core of Marxist criminologists remains alive and well, threatened neither by the extremely punitive mood reflected by politicians and the public nor by the rapidly splintering groups developing within the social sciences.

SOME FINAL THOUGHTS

In the years between the publication of the first edition of this book in 1988 and now, there have been some noticeable changes on the crime scene, including the types of crime receiving public attention, the public perception of crime, how crime is depicted in the mass media, and, to some extent, changes within the criminal justice system itself. In the United States, a slightly more conservative cast has been evident in recent Supreme Court rulings due to the appointment of new justices. There have been sensational new trials, allegations of police brutality at the highest levels, the most lethal terrorist acts ever seen on U.S. soil, charges of corruption and cover-ups reaching as high as the White House, and overwhelming citizen support of a draconian punishment that was meted out to American teenager Michael Fay in Singapore. The 1995 O. J. Simpson murder trial and its media coverage dwarfed the 1992 Mike Tyson rape trial, the 1991 William Kennedy Smith rape trial, and the 1992 Jeffrey Dahmer murder trial combined. Ignoring the sensationalism and brutality of the double murders, the trial made "legal history" through its jurors' "going on strike." Many insist that regardless of the verdict of not guilty, and many more *because* of the verdict, the obvious inefficiency of the police and courts have further eroded Americans' faith in the criminal justice system (see Issue 11).

Both the 1993 bombing of the World Trade Center in New York City and that of a federal building in Oklahoma City in 1995 are feared to be an indication of things to come. In addition to the horror of the acts, one aspect of Oklahoma that caught many by surprise, including criminologists, is the revelation of powerful, well-armed militia groups reflecting deep disenchantment with what they see their country becoming. Prominent politicians and members of the public, though condemning the bombing, have openly defended militant groups who claim that federal agents' acts in areas in which shoot-outs have occurred are responsible for the unrest. The congressional investigations and criticisms that arose after a federal assault on the Branch Davidian religious cult in Waco, Texas, resulted in the deaths of 28 members, including many children, is possibly seen more as proof of government cover-ups and brutality than as a democratic system correcting itself.

Crime, the fear of it and the anxiety it provokes, seems to permeate all layers of American society and has assumed a permanent place on the cultural landscape. Even when the shared interpretations of crime and its dimensions are based upon inaccurate perceptions (as mentioned, women, children, and the elderly are generally far *less* likely to be homicide victims than young males), the public nonetheless "knows" that there is a serious crime problem eroding communities. Indeed, many measures have been implemented to fight this phenomenon, such as "three strikes" laws (see Issue 13), community notification laws (see Issue 8), and the movement of young offenders to adult courts and prisons (see Issue 6). Furthermore, in March 1998 the Oklahoma Senate approved legislation to castrate repeat sex offenders.

Whether or not criminologists, criminal justice practitioners, and other scholars and writers have anything meaningful to say about the current malaise, it is up to you and your generation to decide.

Meanwhile, it is interesting to note that the public, the police, and sometimes the courts often find scientific explanations threatening. Many police officers feel that criminologists, in searching for structural causes of crime, attempt to "excuse" delinquents, who the police may feel deserve a "good kick in the ass" along with jail time instead of "help" and "treatment." The public and the police are currently more comfortable with explanations of crime that assume individual responsibility for criminal acts. The courts, too, may object to studies that show racial patterns in sentencing and possibly expose prejudice. To judges and other officials, the "causes" of their sentencing and processing of criminals are a result of legal factors, not racial or economic ones.

Thus, as you begin your voyage into academic criminology and criminal justice, you should be aware of the fact that there are many scientific explanations of crime, some of which are politically and even morally threatening to various interest groups. At the same time, though, for you and your generation to have the capacity to help solve the crime problem, you will have to be able to sort out the competing explanations with their respective images of human beings and resulting crime treatment models. To ignore rationally assessing these controversial issues is to risk perpetuating the ignorance and myths that characterize many of the current crime theories and policies—the unanticipated and unintended consequence of which is frequently to magnify the crime problem instead of solving it.

On the Internet . . .

Critical Criminology Division of the ASC
This site of the American Society of Criminology links to basic criminology sources and to resources developed within a critical sociology framework.
http://sun.soci.niu.edu/~critcrim/

National Crime Victim's Research and Treatment Center
This site, sponsored by the National Crime Victim's Research and Treatment Center of the Medical University of South Carolina, describes the work of the center and provides an excellent list of related resources.
http://www.musc.edu/cvc/

Organized Crime Home Page
This page has been compiled by the Committee for a Safe Society (CSS) and is a jumping-off point for worldwide information about organized crime.
http://www.alternatives.com/crime/index.html

PART 1

Crime: Definitions and Causes

Exactly what is crime, who commits crime, and why, where, when, and how crimes are committed remain core questions for the public, criminal justice practitioners, and scholars alike. It would seem that defining crime, as well as explaining crime, is a straightforward matter. In reality, definitions, explanations, and even assessments of the harm that criminals do is problematic. Some experts, for instance, claim that crime is necessary and functional in all societies. Others say that society is concerned about the wrong kinds of crime. These questions are important for criminologists and policymakers.

■ Is Crime Always Functional?

■ Does Rap Music Contribute to Violent Crime?

■ Does IQ Significantly Contribute to Crime?

■ Is Street Crime More Serious Than White-Collar Crime?

■ Are General Theories of Crime Useful?

ISSUE 1

Is Crime Always Functional?

YES: Emile Durkheim, from *Rules of Sociological Method* (Free Press, 1938)

NO: Daniel Patrick Moynihan, from "Defining Deviancy Down," *The American Scholar* (Winter 1993)

ISSUE SUMMARY

YES: Classic sociologist Emile Durkheim (1858–1917) theorizes that crime exists in all societies because it reaffirms moral boundaries and at times assists needed social changes.

NO: U.S. senator (D-New York) and former Harvard professor Daniel Patrick Moynihan worries that Durkheim's thinking omits the possibility of "too much crime," especially violent crime, so that deviancy as a serious societal problem is not addressed.

What is crime? Who commits it? And why? The importance given to these questions, and their answers, varies among different categories of people, although there is little certainty that any one group's meanings and interpretations are superior to those of another.

For example, younger and older people have different perceptions of crime (older people are more likely to fear crime, even though younger people are far more likely to be victims of crime). Public officials also disagree about crime. During election years many politicians have inflated the number of crimes committed and have attributed crime to forces and influences that only the politicians, if elected, can combat.

Criminological and criminal justice scholars, although generally slightly less shrill and self-serving than politicians in their definitions and explanations of crime, are also very likely to disagree among themselves about what crime is and what its causes are. Unlike politicians, they do not follow four-year cycles in their crime conceptualizations, but they do reflect trends. For example, 20 years ago most criminologists probably reflected a liberal ideology in their crime explanations and suggested treatments. Today some are more likely to reflect an ideologically conservative scholarly bias. Radical or Marxist criminologists continue to have a marginal position within the discipline.

The seminal essay by Emile Durkheim, excerpted in the first selection, argues that deviancy, including crime, is functional and exists in all societies because it is needed to establish moral boundaries and to distinguish between those who obey and those who disobey society's rules. Although it was written almost 100 years ago, Durkheim's original structural or sociological approach continues to be relied on by criminological and criminal justice scholars.

There are, of course, many variants of the sociological approach to crime, its definitions, and its causes. However, Durkheim's approach is central for many criminologists and especially *structural functionalists*. Structural functionalists attempt to determine what patterns of interaction or structures exist in various groups. They investigate what these patterns contribute to the maintenance of a group and of the society to which the group belongs. In the United States, for example, dating patterns and their relation to marriage are studied. Marriage patterns and their relation to the economy, to religion, and so on are traced. In addition, structural functionalists want to know about the consequences of patterns of behavior for groups, for members of groups, and for society as a whole. Such consequences can be both positive and negative, intentional and unintentional.

Durkheim selects a pattern of behavior, in this case deviant acts, and attempts to determine what it contributes to the maintenance of society and what its consequences might be, including intended and unintended ones. Durkheim asserts that crime is functional (not necessarily good and certainly not to be encouraged) and helps to establish moral boundaries. Deviant acts also provide a sense of propriety and a feeling of righteousness for those who do not commit crimes, as they share sentiments of moral indignation about those who do violate society's norms. Durkheim says that crime also allows for a social change. It prevents a society from having too much rigidity and from becoming too slavish in its obedience to norms.

In the second selection, politician and sociologist Daniel Patrick Moynihan acknowledges his debt to Durkheim and to sociologist Kai T. Erikson, a follower of some of Durkheim's ideas. But he questions the soundness of Durkheim's contention that crime is functional for societies, especially in the context of violence-ridden 1990s America. Moynihan argues that on the one hand, certain classes of relatively harmless behavior are nowadays being defined as deviant, if not criminal (dysfunctional contraction of moral boundaries). On the other hand, and far more serious to Moynihan, moral boundaries are becoming too elastic as society expands its tolerance for serious crime. He asks, How can deviancy be said to be functional if citizens are no longer shocked by outrageous violence?

As you read the selections by Durkheim and Moynihan, consider examples from your life in which a type of deviancy might be functional, or an act that might have been viewed as criminal a generation ago but that is no longer viewed that way. In addition, what types of acts do you tolerate today that would have been morally outrageous to your grandparents? Have society's legal and ethical boundaries become "too elastic"?

YES

Emile Durkheim

THE NORMAL AND THE PATHOLOGICAL

Crime is present not only in the majority of societies of one particular species but in all societies of all types. There is no society that is not confronted with the problem of criminality. Its form changes; the acts thus characterized are not the same everywhere; but, everywhere and always, there have been men who have behaved in such a way as to draw upon themselves penal repression. If, in proportion as societies pass from the lower to the higher types, the rate of criminality, i.e., the relation between the yearly number of crimes and the population, tended to decline, it might be believed that crime, while still normal, is tending to lose this character of normality. But we have no reason to believe that such a regression is substantiated. Many facts would seem rather to indicate a movement in the opposite direction. From the beginning of the [nineteenth] century, statistics enable us to follow the course of criminality. It has everywhere increased. In France the increase is nearly 300 percent. There is, then, no phenomenon that presents more indisputably all the symptoms of normality, since it appears closely connected with the conditions of all collective life. To make of crime a form of social morbidity would be to admit that morbidity is not something accidental, but, on the contrary, that in certain cases it grows out of the fundamental constitution of the living organism; it would result in wiping out all distinction between the physiological and the pathological. No doubt it is possible that crime itself will have abnormal forms, as, for example, when its rate is unusually high. This excess is, indeed, undoubtedly morbid in nature. What is normal, simply, is the existence of criminality, provided that it attains and does not exceed, for each social type, a certain level, which it is perhaps not impossible to fix in conformity with the preceding rules.[1]

Here we are, then, in the presence of a conclusion in appearance quite paradoxical. Let us make no mistake. To classify crime among the phenomena of normal sociology is not to say merely that it is an inevitable, although regrettable phenomenon, due to the incorrigible wickedness of men; it is to affirm that it is a factor in public health, an integral part of all healthy societies. This result is, at first glance, surprising enough to have puzzled even ourselves for a long time. Once this first surprise has been overcome,

From Emile Durkheim, *Rules of Sociological Method* (Free Press, 1938). Translated by Sarah A. Solovay and John H. Mueller. Edited by George E. G. Catlin. Copyright © 1938 by George E. G. Catlin. Copyright renewed 1966 by Sarah A. Solovay, John H. Mueller, and George E. G. Catlin. Reprinted by permission of The Free Press, an imprint of Simon & Schuster, Inc.

however, it is not difficult to find reasons explaining this normality and at the same time confirming it.

In the first place crime is normal because a society exempt from it is utterly impossible. Crime, we have shown elsewhere, consists of an act that offends certain very strong collective sentiments. In a society in which criminal acts are no longer committed, the sentiments they offend would have to be found without exception in all individual consciousnesses, and they must be found to exist with the same degree as sentiments contrary to them. Assuming that this condition could actually be realized, crime would not thereby disappear; it would only change its form, for the very cause which would thus dry up the sources of criminality would immediately open up new ones.

Indeed, for the collective sentiments which are protected by the penal law of a people at a specified moment of its history to take possession of the public conscience or for them to acquire a stronger hold where they have an insufficient grip, they must acquire an intensity greater than that which they had hitherto had. The community as a whole must experience them more vividly, for it can acquire from no other source the greater force necessary to control these individuals who formerly were the most refractory. For murderers to disappear, the horror of bloodshed must become greater in those social strata from which murderers are recruited; but, first it must become greater throughout the entire society. Moreover, the very absence of crime would directly contribute to produce this horror; because any sentiment seems much more respectable when it is always and uniformly respected.

One easily overlooks the consideration that these strong states of the common consciousness cannot be thus reinforced without reinforcing at the same time the more feeble states, whose violation previously gave birth to mere infraction of convention—since the weaker ones are only the prolongation, the attenuated form, of the stronger. Thus robbery and simple bad taste injure the same single altruistic sentiment, the respect for that which is another's. However, this same sentiment is less grievously offended by bad taste than by robbery; and since, in addition, the average consciousness had not sufficient intensity to react keenly to the bad taste, it is treated with greater tolerance. That is why the person guilty of bad taste is merely blamed, whereas the thief is punished. But, if this sentiment grows stronger, to the point of silencing in all consciousnesses the inclination which disposes man to steal, he will become more sensitive to the offenses which, until then, touched him but lightly. He will react against them, then, with more energy; they will be the object of greater opprobrium, which will transform certain of them from the simple moral faults that they were and give them the quality of crimes. For example, improper contracts, or contracts improperly executed, which only incur public blame or civil damages, will become offenses in law.

Imagine a society of saints, a perfect cloister of exemplary individuals. Crimes, properly so called, will there be unknown; but faults which appear venial to the layman will create there the same scandal that the ordinary offense does in ordinary consciousnesses. If, then, this society has the power to judge and punish, it will define these acts as criminal and will treat them as such. For the same reason, the perfect and upright man judges his smallest failings with a severity that the majority reserve for acts more truly in the nature of an offense. Formerly, acts of violence against persons were more frequent than they are today, because respect for individual dignity was less strong. As this has increased, these crimes have become more rare; and also, many acts violating this sentiment have been introduced into the penal law which were not included there in primitive times.[2]

In order to exhaust all the hypotheses logically possible, it will perhaps be asked why this unanimity does not extend to all collective sentiments without exception. Why should not even the most feeble sentiment gather enough energy to prevent all dissent? The moral consciousness of the society would be present in its entirety in all the individuals, with a vitality sufficient to prevent all acts offending it—the purely conventional faults as well as the crimes. But a uniformity so universal and absolute is utterly impossible; for the immediate physical milieu in which each one of us is placed, the hereditary antecedents, and the social influences vary from one individual to the next, and consequently diversify consciousnesses. It is impossible for all to be alike, if only because each one has his own organism and that these organisms occupy different areas in space. That is why, even among the lower peoples, where individual originality is very little developed, it nevertheless does exist.

Thus, since there cannot be a society in which the individuals do not differ more or less from the collective type, it is also inevitable that, among these divergences, there are some with a criminal character. What confers this character upon them is not the intrinsic quality of a given act but that definition which the collective conscience lends them. If the collective conscience is stronger, if it has enough authority practically to suppress these divergences, it will also be more sensitive, more exacting; and, reacting against the slightest deviations with the energy it otherwise displays only against more considerable infractions, it will attribute to them the same gravity as formerly to crimes. In other words, it will designate them as criminal.

Crime is, then, necessary; it is bound up with fundamental conditions of all social life, and by that very fact it is useful, because these conditions of which it is a part are themselves indispensable to the normal evolution of morality and law.

Indeed, it is no longer possible today to dispute the fact that law and morality vary from one social type to the next, nor that they change within the same type if the conditions of life are modified. But, in order that these transformations may be possible, the collective sentiments at the basis of morality must not be hostile to change, and consequently must have but moderate energy. If they were too strong, they would no longer be plastic. Every pattern is an obstacle to new patterns, to the extent that the first pattern is inflexible. The better a structure is articulated, the more it offers a healthy resistance to all modification; and this is equally true of functional, as of anatomical, organization. If there were no crimes, this condition could not have been fulfilled; for such a hypothesis presupposes that collective sentiments have arrived at a degree of intensity unexampled in history. Nothing is good indefinitely and to an unlimited extent. The authority which the moral conscience enjoys must not be excessive;

otherwise no one would dare criticize it, and it would too easily congeal into an immutable form. To make progress, individual originality must be able to express itself. In order that the originality of the idealist whose dreams transcend this century may find expression, it is necessary that the originality of the criminal, who is below the level of his time, shall also be possible. One does not occur without the other.

Nor is this all. Aside from this indirect utility, it happens that crime itself plays a useful role in this evolution. Crime implies not only that the way remains open to necessary changes but that in certain cases it directly prepares these changes. Where crime exists, collective sentiments are sufficiently flexible to take on a new form, and crime sometimes helps to determine the form they will take. How many times, indeed, it is only an anticipation of future morality— a step toward what will be! According to Athenian law, Socrates was a criminal, and his condemnation was no more than just. However, his crime, namely, the independence of his thought, rendered a service not only to humanity but to his country. It served to prepare a new morality and faith which the Athenians needed, since the traditions by which they had lived until then were no longer in harmony with the current conditions of life. Nor is the case of Socrates unique; it is reproduced periodically in history. It would never have been possible to establish the freedom of thought we now enjoy if the regulations prohibiting it had not been violated before being solemnly abrogated. At that time, however, the violation was a crime, since it was an offense against sentiments still very keen in the average conscience. And yet this crime was useful as a prelude to reforms which daily become more necessary. Liberal philosophy had as its precursors the heretics of all kinds who were justly punished by secular authorities during the entire course of the Middle Ages and until the eve of modern times.

From this point of view the fundamental facts of criminality present themselves to us in an entirely new light. Contrary to current ideas, the criminal no longer seems a totally unsociable being, a sort of parasitic element, a strange and unassimilable body, introduced into the midst of society.[3] On the contrary, he plays a definite role in social life. Crime, for its part, must no longer be conceived as an evil that cannot be too much suppressed. There is no occasion for self-congratulation when the crime rate drops noticeably below the average level, for we may be certain that this apparent progress is associated with some social disorder. Thus, the number of assault cases never falls so low as in times of want.[4] With the drop in the crime rate, and as a reaction to it, comes a revision, or the need of a revision in the theory of punishment. If, indeed, crime is a disease, its punishment is its remedy and cannot be otherwise conceived; thus, all the discussions it arouses bear on the point of determining what the punishment must be in order to fulfil this role of remedy. If crime is not pathological at all, the object of punishment cannot be to cure it, and its true function must be sought elsewhere.

NOTES

1. From the fact that crime is a phenomenon of normal sociology, it does not follow that the criminal is an individual normally constituted from the biological and psychological points of view. The two questions are independent of each other. This independence will be better understood when

we have shown, later on, the difference between psychological and sociological facts.

2. Calumny, insults, slander, fraud, etc.

3. We have ourselves committed the error of speaking thus of the criminal, because of a failure to apply our rule (*Division du travail social*, pp. 395–96).

4. Although crime is a fact of normal sociology, it does not follow that we must not abhor it. Pain itself has nothing desirable about it; the individual dislikes it as society does crime, and yet it is a function of normal physiology. Not only is it necessarily derived from the very constitution of every living organism, but it plays a useful role in life, for which reason it cannot be replaced. It would, then, be a singular distortion of our thought to present it as an apology for crime. We would not even think of protesting against such an interpretation, did we not know to what strange accusations and misunderstandings one exposes oneself when one undertakes to study moral facts objectively and to speak of them in a different language from that of the layman.

NO   Daniel Patrick Moynihan

DEFINING DEVIANCY DOWN

In one of the founding texts of sociology, *The Rules of Sociological Method* (1895), Emile Durkheim set it down that "crime is normal." "It is," he wrote, "completely impossible for any society entirely free of it to exist." By defining what is deviant, we are enabled to know what is not, and hence to live by shared standards.... Durkheim writes:

> From this viewpoint the fundamental facts of criminology appear to us in an entirely new light.... [T]he criminal no longer appears as an utterly unsociable creature, a sort of parasitic element, a foreign, inassimilable body introduced into the bosom of society. He plays a normal role in social life. For its part, crime must no longer be conceived of as an evil which cannot be circumscribed closely enough. Far from there being cause for congratulation when it drops too noticeably below the normal level, this apparent progress assuredly coincides with and is linked to some social disturbance.

Durkheim suggests, for example, that "in times of scarcity" crimes of assault drop off. He does not imply that we ought to approve of crime—"[p]ain has likewise nothing desirable about it"—but we need to understand its function. He saw religion, in the sociologist Randall Collins's terms, as "fundamentally a set of ceremonial actions, assembling the group, heightening its emotions, and focusing its members on symbols of their common belongingness." In this context "a punishment ceremony creates social solidarity."

The matter was pretty much left at that until seventy years later when, in 1965, Kai T. Erikson published *Wayward Puritans*, a study of "crime rates" in the Massachusetts Bay Colony. The plan behind the book, as Erikson put it, was "to test [Durkheim's] notion that the number of deviant offenders a community can afford to recognize is likely to remain stable over time." The notion proved out very well indeed. Despite occasional crime waves, as when itinerant Quakers refused to take off their hats in the presence of magistrates, the amount of deviance in this corner of seventeenth-century New England fitted nicely with the supply of stocks and shipping posts. Erikson remarks:

> It is one of the arguments of the... study that the amount of deviation a community encounters is apt to remain fairly constant over time. To start at the beginning, it is a simple logistic fact that the number of deviancies which come

From Daniel Patrick Moynihan, "Defining Deviancy Down," *The American Scholar*, vol. 62, no. 1 (Winter 1993). Copyright © 1992 by Daniel Patrick Moynihan. Reprinted by permission of *The American Scholar*.

to a community's attention are limited by the kinds of equipment it uses to detect and handle them, and to that extent the rate of deviation found in a community is a least in part a function of the size and complexity of its social control apparatus. A community's capacity for handling deviance, let us say, can be roughly estimated by counting its prison cells and hospital beds, its policemen and psychiatrists, its courts and clinics. Most communities, it would seem, operate with the expectation that a relatively constant number of control agents is necessary to cope with a relatively constant number of offenders. The amount of men, money, and material assigned by society to "do something" about deviant behavior does not vary appreciably over time, and the implicit logic which governs the community's efforts to man a police force or maintain suitable facilities for the mentally ill seems to be that there is a fairly stable quota of trouble which should be anticipated.

In this sense, the agencies of control often seem to define their job as that of keeping deviance within bounds rather than that of obliterating it altogether. Many judges, for example, assume that severe punishments are a greater deterrent to crime than moderate ones, and so it is important to note that many of them are apt to impose harder penalties when crime seems to be on the increase and more lenient ones when it does not, almost as if the power of the bench were being used to keep the crime rate from getting out of hand.

Erikson was taking issue with what he described as "a dominant strain in sociological thinking" that took for granted that a well-structured society "is somehow designed to prevent deviant behavior from occurring." In both authors, Durkheim and Erikson, there is an undertone that suggests that, with deviancy, as with most social goods, there is the continuing problem of demand exceeding supply. Durkheim invites us to

imagine a society of saints, a perfect cloister of exemplary individuals. Crimes, properly so called, will there be unknown; but faults which appear venial to the layman will create there the same scandal that the ordinary offense does in ordinary consciousness. If, then, this society has the power to judge and punish, it will define these acts as criminal and will treat them as such.

Recall Durkheim's comment that there need be no cause for congratulations should the amount of crime drop "too noticeably below the normal level." It would not appear that Durkheim anywhere contemplates the possibility of too much crime. Clearly his theory would have required him to deplore such a development, but the possibility seems never to have occurred to him.

Erikson, writing much later in the twentieth century, contemplates both possibilities. "Deviant persons can be said to supply needed services to society." There is no doubt a tendency for the supply of any needed thing to run short. But he is consistent. There can, he believes, be *too much* of a good thing. Hence "the number of deviant offenders a community can *afford* to recognize is likely to remain stable over time." [My emphasis]

Social scientists are said to be on the lookout for poor fellows getting a bum rap. But here is a theory that clearly implies that there are circumstances in which society will choose *not* to notice behavior that would be otherwise controlled, or disapproved, or even punished.

It appears to me that this is in fact what we in the United States have been doing of late. I proffer the thesis that, over the past generation, since the time Erikson wrote, the amount of deviant behavior in American society has increased beyond the levels the community can "afford to recognize" and that, accordingly, we have been re-defining deviancy so as to exempt much conduct previously stigmatized, and also quietly raising the "normal" level in categories where behavior is now abnormal by any earlier standard. This redefining has evoked fierce resistance from defenders of "old" standards, and accounts for much of the present "cultural war" such as proclaimed by many at the 1992 Republican National Convention.

Let me, then, offer three categories of redefinition in these regards: the *altruistic*, the *opportunistic*, and the *normalizing*.

The first category, the *altruistic*, may be illustrated by the deinstitutionalization movement within the mental health profession that appeared in the 1950s. The second category, the *opportunistic*, seen in the interest group rewards derived from the acceptance of "alternative" family structures. The third category, the *normalizing*, is to be observed in the growing acceptance of unprecedented levels of violent crime....

Our *normalizing* category most directly corresponds to Erikson's proposition that "the number of deviant offenders a community can afford to recognize is likely to remain stable over time." Here we are dealing with the popular psychological notion of "denial." In 1965, having reached the conclusion that there

would be a dramatic increase in single-parent families, I reached the further conclusion that this would in turn lead to a dramatic increase in crime. In an article in *America*, I wrote:

From the wild Irish slums of the 19th century Eastern seaboard to the riot-torn suburbs of Los Angeles, there is one unmistakable lesson in American history: a community that allows a large number of young men to grow up in broken families, dominated by women, never acquiring any stable relationship to male authority, never acquiring any set of rational expectations about the future—that community asks for and gets chaos. Crime, violence, unrest, unrestrained lashing out at the whole social structure—that is not only to be expected; it is very near to inevitable.

The inevitable, as we now know, has come to pass, but here again our response is curiously passive. Crime is a more or less continuous subject of political pronouncement, and from time to time it will be at or near the top of opinion polls as a matter of public concern. But it never gets much further than that. In the words spoken from the bench, Judge Edwin Torres of the New York State Supreme Court, Twelfth Judicial District, described how "the slaughter of the innocent marches unabated: subway riders, bodega owners, cab drivers, babies; in laundromats, at cash machines, on elevators, in hallways." In personal communication, he writes: "This numbness, this near narcoleptic state can diminish the human condition to the level of combat infantrymen, who, in protracted campaigns, can eat their battlefield rations seated on the bodies of the fallen, friend and foe alike. A society that loses its sense of outrage is doomed to extinction." There is no expectation that this will change, nor any efficacious public insistence that it do so. The crime level has been *normalized*.

Consider the St. Valentine's Day Massacre. In 1929 in Chicago during Prohibition, four gangsters killed seven gangsters on February 14. The nation was shocked. The event became legend. It merits not one but two entries in the *World Book Encyclopedia*. I leave it to others to judge, but it would appear that the society in the 1920s was simply not willing to put up with this degree of deviancy. In the end, the Constitution was amended, and Prohibition, which lay behind so much gangster violence, ended.

In recent years, again in the context of illegal traffic in controlled substances, this form of murder has returned. But it has done so at a level that induces denial. James Q. Wilson comments that Los Angeles has the equivalent of a St. Valentine's Day Massacre every weekend. Even the most ghastly reenactments of such human slaughter produce only moderate responses. On the morning after the close of the Democratic National Convention in New York City in July, there was such an account in the second section of the *New York Times*. It was not a big story; bottom of the page, but with a headline that got your attention. "3 Slain in Bronx Apartment, but a Baby is Saved." A subhead continued: "A mother's last act was to hide her little girl under the bed." The article described a drug execution; the now-routine blindfolds made from duct tape; a man and a woman and a teenager involved. "Each had been shot once in the head." The police had found them a day later. They also found, under a bed, a three-month-old baby, dehydrated but alive. A lieutenant remarked of the mother, "In her last dying act she protected her baby. She probably knew she was going to die, so she stuffed the baby where she knew it would be safe." But the matter was left there. The police would do their best. But the event passed quickly; forgotten by the next day, it will never make *World Book*.

Nor is it likely that any great heed will be paid to an uncanny reenactment of the Prohibition drama a few months later, also in the Bronx. The *Times* story, page B3, reported:

9 Men Posing as Police

Are Indicted in 3 Murders

Drug Dealers Were Kidnapped for Ransom

The *Daily News* story, same day, page 17, made it *four* murders, adding nice details about torture techniques. The gang members posed as federal Drug Enforcement Administration agents, real badges and all. The victims were drug dealers, whose families were uneasy about calling the police. Ransom seems generally to have been set in the $650,000 range. Some paid. Some got it in the back of the head. So it goes.

Yet, violent killings, often random, go on unabated. Peaks continue to attract some notice. But these are peaks above "average" levels that thirty years ago would have been thought epidemic.

LOS ANGELES, AUG. 24. (Reuters) Twenty-two people were killed in Los Angeles over the weekend, the worst period of violence in the city since it was ravaged by riots earlier this year, the police said today.

Twenty-four others were wounded by gunfire or stabbings, including a 19-year old woman in a wheelchair who was shot in the back when she failed to respond to a motorist who asked for directions in south Los Angeles.

["The guy stuck a gun out of the window and just fired at her," said a police spokesman, Lieut. David Rock. The woman was later described as being in stable condition.

Among those who died was an off-duty officer, shot while investigating reports of a prowler in a neighbor's yard, and a Little League baseball coach who had argued with the father of a boy he was coaching.]

The police said at least nine of the deaths were gang-related, including that of a 14-year old girl killed in a fight between rival gangs.

Fifty-one people were killed in three days of rioting that started April 29 after the acquittal of four police officers in the beating of Rodney G. King.

Los Angeles usually has above-average violence during August, but the police were at a loss to explain the sudden rise. On an average weekend in August, 14 fatalities occur.

Not to be outdone, two days later the poor Bronx came up with a near record, as reported in *New York Newsday*:

Armed with 9-mm. pistols, shotguns and M-16 rifles, a group of masked men and women poured out of two vehicles in the South Bronx early yesterday and sprayed a stretch of Longwood Avenue with a fustillade of bullets, injuring 12 people.

A Kai Erikson of the future will surely need to know that the Department of Justice in 1990 found that Americans reported only about 38 percent of all crimes and 48 percent of violent crimes. This, too, can be seen as a means of *normalizing* crime. In much the same way, the vocabulary of crime reporting can be seen to move toward the normal-seeming. A teacher is shot on her way to class. The *Times* subhead reads: "Struck in

the Shoulder in the Year's First Shooting Inside a School." First of the season.

It is too early, however, to know how to regard the arrival of the doctors on the scene declaring crime a "public health emergency." The June 10, 1992, issue of the *Journal of the American Medical Association* was devoted entirely to papers on the subject of violence, principally violence associated with firearms. An editorial in the issue signed by former Surgeon General C. Everett Koop and Dr. George D. Lundberg is entitled: "Violence in America: A Public Health Emergency." Their proposition is admirably succinct.

Regarding violence in our society as purely a sociological matter, or one of law enforcement, has led to unmitigated failure. It is time to test further whether violence can be amenable to medical/public health interventions.

We believe violence in America to be a public health emergency, largely unresponsive to methods thus far used in its control. The solutions are very complex, but possible.

The authors cited the relative success of epidemiologists in gaining some jurisdiction in the area of motor vehicle casualties by re-defining what had been seen as a law enforcement issue into a public health issue. Again, this process began during the Harriman administration in New York in the 1950s. In the 1960s the morbidity and mortality associated with automobile crashes was, it could be argued, a major public health problem; the public health strategy, it could also be argued, brought the problem under a measure of control. Not in "the 1970s and 1980s," as the *Journal of the American Medical Association* would have us think: the federal legislation involved was signed in 1965. Such a strategy would surely produce insights into the control of violence that elude law enforcement professionals, but whether it would change anything is another question.

For some years now I have had legislation in the Senate that would prohibit the manufacture of .25 and .32 caliber bullets. These are the two calibers most typically used with the guns known as Saturday Night Specials. "Guns don't kill people," I argue, "bullets do."

Moreover, we have a two-century supply of handguns but only a four-year supply of ammunition. A public health official would immediately see the logic of trying to control the supply of bullets rather than of guns.

Even so, now that the doctor has come, it is important that criminal violence not be defined down by epidemiologists. Doctors Koop and Lundberg note that in 1990 in the state of Texas "deaths from firearms, for the first time in many decades, surpassed deaths from motor vehicles, by 3,443 to 3,309." A good comparison. And yet keep in mind that the number of motor vehicle deaths, having leveled off since the 1960s, is now pretty well accepted as normal at somewhat less then 50,000 a year, which is somewhat less than the level of the 1960s—the "carnage," as it once was thought to be, is now accepted as normal. This is the price we pay for high-speed transportation: there is a benefit associated with it. But there is no benefit associated with homicide, and no good in getting used to it. Epidemiologists have powerful insights that can contribute to lessening the medical trauma, but they must be wary of normalizing the social pathology that leads to such trauma.

The hope—if there be such—of this essay has been twofold. It is, first, to suggest that the Durkheim constant, as I put it, is maintained by a dynamic process which adjusts upwards and *downwards*. Liberals have traditionally been alert for upward redefining that does injustice to individuals. Conservatives have been correspondingly sensitive to downward redefining that weakens societal standards. Might it not help if we could all agree that there is a dynamic at work here? It is not revealed truth, nor yet a scientifically derived formula. It is simply a pattern we observe in ourselves. Nor is it rigid. There may once have been an unchanging supply of jail cells which more or less determined the number of prisoners. No longer. We are building new prisons at a prodigious rate. Similarly, the executioner is back. There is something of a competition in Congress to think up new offenses for which the death penalty is seemed the only available deterrent. Possibly also modes of execution, as in "fry the kingpins." Even so, we are getting used to a lot of behavior that is not good for us.

As noted earlier, Durkheim states that there is "nothing desirable" about pain. Surely what he meant was that there is nothing pleasurable. Pain, even so, is an indispensable warning signal. But societies under stress, much like individuals, will turn to pain killers of various kinds that end up concealing real damage. There is surely nothing desirable about *this*. If our analysis wins general acceptance, if, for example, more of us came to share Judge Torres's genuine alarm at "the trivialization of the lunatic crime rate" in his city (and mine), we might surprise ourselves how well we respond to the manifest decline of the American civic order. Might.

POSTSCRIPT

Is Crime Always Functional?

One of the first American sociologists to attempt to use the insights of Durkheim was Robert Merton in his classic article "Social Structure and Anomie," *American Sociological Review* (1938). Merton attempted to show the bearing that culturally established goals and legitimate means for achieving them or their absence has upon criminogenic behavior. For an excellent recent consideration of continuities between Merton and Durkheim, see N. Passas, "Continuities in the Anomie Tradition," in F. Adler and W. Laufer, eds., *The Legacy of Anomie Theory* (Transaction Publishers, 1995). In it, Passas briefly challenges Moynihan's contention that Durkheim neglected problems of "too much crime." A provocative interpretation of Durkheim's intellectual demise that is quite different from Moynihan's is C. Sumner's *The Sociology of Deviance: An Obituary* (Continuum, 1994).

Note that Moynihan argues roughly from the same theoretic tradition as Durkheim: structural functionalism. Their disagreement centers around when deviancy becomes dysfunctional. A third argument would be that of some Marxists who see crime, including violent crime, as *functional* but only for the *elite* because it deflects society's concerns away from their own corporate crimes. For an outstanding presentation of this view, see J. Reiman's *The Rich Get Richer and the Poor Get Prison: Ideology, Class, and Criminal Justice*, 5th ed. (Allyn & Bacon, 1998).

An excellent earlier work that clearly distinguishes between the Marxist perspective and the structural functional perspective is *Class and Class Conflict in Industrial Societies* by R. Dahrendorf (Stanford University Press, 1959). A recent work that partially parallels Moynihan's thinking is *Moral Judgment: Does the Abuse Excuse Threaten Our Legal System?* by J. Q. Wilson (Basic Books, 1997).

Two different conceptualizations are K. Beckett's *Making Crime Pay: Law and Order in Contemporary American Politics* (Oxford University Press, 1997) and G. Moss, "Explaining the Absence of Violent Crime Among the Semai of Malaysia: Is Criminological Theory Up to the Task?" *Journal of Criminal Justice* (vol. 25, no. 3, 1997). A good source for analyzing different approaches to crime is *Cross-National Crime: A Research Review and Sourcebook* by J. Neopolitan (Greenwood Press, 1997). The writings of Donald Black present a novel approach to order and law. See, for example, his "Epistemology of Pure Sociology," *Law and Social Inquiry* (vol. 20, no. 3, 1995). Two outstanding sources on feminism's contributions to the study of crime are *Feminism and Criminology* by N. Naffine (Polity Press, 1997) and N. Rafter and F. Heidensohn, eds., *International Feminist Perspectives in Criminology: Engendering a Discipline* (Open University Press, 1995).

ISSUE 2

Does Rap Music Contribute to Violent Crime?

YES: Dennis R. Martin, from "The Music of Murder," *ACJS Today* (November/December 1993)

NO: Mark S. Hamm and Jeff Ferrell, from "Rap, Cops, and Crime: Clarifying the 'Cop Killer' Controversy," *ACJS Today* (May/June 1994)

ISSUE SUMMARY

YES: Dennis R. Martin, president of the National Association of Chiefs of Police, theorizes that since "music has the power both to 'soothe the savage beast' and to stir violent emotions," then rising racial tensions and violence can be attributed to rock music's promotion of "vile, deviant, and sociopathic behaviors."

NO: Criminologists Mark S. Hamm and Jeff Ferrell reject Martin's analysis of the relationship between music and violence, charging that the theory is based on racism and ignorance of both music and broader cultural forces.

Traditionally, science has been about ascertaining causal relations between two or more variables. The producing, contributing, influencing, forcing, or cause variable is known as the *independent variable,* symbolized as X. The result, effect, outcome, produced, or caused variable is known as the *dependent variable,* or Y. In the social sciences, independent variables were generally traced to specific social factors (e.g., gender, wealth, education, neighborhood, family, race, religion, age, and so on). Such objective factors predicted or explained individuals' and groups' attitudes and behaviors.

Throughout the twentieth century, however, many philosophers of science have questioned the value and validity of causal analysis. This is especially true in the social sciences, including criminology. Drawing from the sixteenth-century philosopher David Hume, questions are asked about how we can ever "know" causes. Frequently, cause cannot be seen. In addition, in human behavior one must often take into account subjective attitudes, feelings, motivations, and such. There are no isomorphic relationships in criminology as there are in the physical sciences. That is, there are no one-to-one relationships, such as that at sea level, water will freeze at temperatures below 32 degrees or that what goes up on Earth must come down. Instead, there are only contingencies or probabilities, such as that living in an impoverished area and having a parent and several siblings in prison will probably result in a younger brother becoming a criminal as well. In such a situation there may be a *high probability*, but there is hardly a certain link between environment and behavior. Likewise, the child of a college professor will probably become a college student, but not necessarily.

Not only is there no inevitable relation between background factors and outcomes (such as crime), but usually the behavior of people has multiple causes: positive or negative parental role models, area of residency, types of and relations with peers, and so on. Sometimes influencing factors on subsequent behaviors lie dormant or gradually accumulate. Poverty, for instance, can demoralize individuals; coupled with racism, it can lead to low self-esteem and self-destructive behaviors such as alcoholism, partially resulting in medical problems, preventing working when jobs become available, which can lead to reinforcing prejudiced people's negative stereotyping that "poor people do not want to work anyway."

Due to these and other reasons, some social scientists eschew searching for causal relations. Instead, they search for correlations. For instance, when there is a poverty, racism, declining jobs, and so on, there is usually more crime. All of the identified variables would be examined to determine if they correlate with crime and, if so, what type.

Ascertaining the causes of most things, especially human behavior, is remarkably difficult, and many view such a search as a waste of time. When there are widespread perceptions that serious problems are upon us and that things are "out of control" (such as the current views toward violent crime), people demand immediate solutions. Often the entire scientific process and even reason itself are short-circuited because powerful figures—or those wanting to become powerful—formulate "self-evident" explanations of the problem.

Although scholars trained in scientific methodology can see the fallacies and dangers of glib explanations (and concomitant glib solutions), for others it makes sense to blame some misunderstood phenomenon or even categories of people for societal problems. In its extreme version, this is scapegoating.

In the following selections, Dennis R. Martin provides many examples through history of how music has been linked with violence. He also discusses the marketing of some gangsta rap albums, which he maintains generate hostilities toward police officers and others because of their lyrics and strident sounds. Mark S. Hamm and Jeff Ferrell dismiss Martin's linking of rap music and violence as bad sociology, bad history, and worse criminology. They attack Martin's historical analysis of current music as being racist because he does not mention the positive contributions of black musicians. They also maintain that rap musicians do little more than "tell it like it is" in inner cities.

What bearing do you think the recent murders of rappers Biggie Smalls (the Notorious B.I.G.) and Tupac Shakur will have on this debate?

YES
Dennis R. Martin

THE MUSIC OF MURDER

In my career in law enforcement I have weathered the rough seas of society, first as a patrol officer, then as a director of police training, shift commander, police chief, and now as the President of the National Association of Chiefs of Police. As tumultuous as contemporary society is, it could not exist without the foundation of law. We Americans are fortunate to live under a government of laws, not of men.

The United States Constitution is a remarkable and unique compact between the government and its people. The First Amendment, in particular, states a once revolutionary concept with great power and simplicity: "Congress shall make no law... abridging the freedom of speech". In our three-branched system of government, the will of the people is expressed through duly elected legislators in Congress and enforced by an elected executive; the Constitution finds its voice in the judicial branch. What are the people to do when the laws that are meant to ensure their freedom are abused in a manner that erodes the very foundation of law?

Early First Amendment cases sanctioned restrictions on speech where its free exercise created a clear, existing danger, or where a serious evil would result. In two centuries, First Amendment law has evolved to the point where practically the only prohibited speech involves the mention of God in public assemblies.

The misuse of the First Amendment is graphically illustrated in Time-Warner's attempt to insert into the mainstream culture the vile and dangerous lyrics of the Ice-T song entitled *Cop Killer*. The *Body Count* album containing *Cop Killer* was shipped throughout the United States in miniature body bags. Only days before distribution of the album was voluntarily suspended, Time-Warner flooded the record market with a half million copies. The *Cop Killer* song has been implicated in at least two shooting incidents and has inflamed racial tensions in cities across the country. Those who work closely with the families and friends of slain officers, as I do, volunteering for the American Police Hall of Fame and Museum, are outraged by the message of *Cop Killer*. It is an affront to the officers—144 in 1992 alone—who have been killed in

From Dennis R. Martin, "The Music of Murder," *ACJS Today* (November/December 1993). Copyright © 1993, 1996 by The National Association of Chiefs of Police, Inc. Reprinted by permission. All rights reserved.

the line of duty while upholding the laws of our society and protecting all its citizens.

Is it fair to blame a musical composition for the increase in racial tensions and the shooting incidents? Music has the power both to "soothe the savage beast" and to stir violent emotions in man. Music can create an ambiance for gentle romance, or unleash brutal sensuality. It can transcend the material world and make our hearts soar to a realm of spiritual beauty. Yet the trend in American rock music for the last decade has been to promote ever more vile, deviant, and sociopathic behaviors. Recognition, leading to fame and fortune far exceeding merit, propels performers and the industry to attack every shared value that has bound our society together for more than two centuries.

The power that music works on the human mind can be seen throughout history; it has existed in every known society. The Bible contains numerous references to music. Music is found in the ancient tales of China, as well as in the traditions of Native Americans. In the beginning of human history, music stood at the center of life, acting as an intermediary between the natural and supernatural. It was both handmaiden to religion and the cornerstone of education. While there may be music without culture, culture without music is unthinkable.

The earliest music consisted of a vocal melody with rhythmic, regular beats kept by the hands and feet. In time, the pattern of beats evolved into more complicated rhythms. Formal music found its roots in China, beginning around 2000 BC. Ritualistic music emerged around 1900 BC among the Israelites during the reign of the Canaanites. By setting stories and teachings to music, preliterate Hebrew leaders were able to memorize and recite

long passages, and to entertain and instruct their audience with greater impact than words alone could convey. One generation handed down to the next Hebrew laws, traditions, and important historic events in song, often accompanied by a simple harp.

Folk music is the basis for formal music. The march, for example, dates from the Roman Empire. Its insistent rhythm, powerful major chords, and strong simple melody were designed to ignite courage in the hearts of those preparing for battle (and, possibly, fear in the enemies' camp).

Led by St. Benedict, the early Christian Church developed the art of choral singing. Over the centuries, sacred choral music has provided us with a view of the world to come. A branch of choral music evolved into opera, a form of music more than once credited with inciting riots. In 1830, the Brussels premiere of *La Muette de Portici* by Daniel Esprit Auber ignited the Belgian independence movement against the Dutch. In 1842, Giuseppe Verdi achieved overnight fame after the debut of his third opera, *Nabucca*, which inspired rioting in Milan. One of the choruses, *Va Pensilero*, so touched the Italian soldiers that it was adopted as the Italian anthem.

Perhaps the greatest composition combining choral and symphonic modes is the *Ninth Symphony* of Beethoven. An utterly revolutionary work, both musically and politically, it proclaims that all men will be brothers when the power of joy resides in their hearts, binding together the fabric of society torn asunder by different cultural mores. This was not a popular sentiment to express in Vienna, the seat of power of the reactionary Austrian Empire.

The twentieth century brought new sounds to America: atonal classical music, the big band era, jazz, and country and western, among others. History recorded two world wars in which Germanic leaders preyed upon human society; the American musical response, spearheaded by George M. Cohan, was proudly defiant, full of valor and resolve. Across the Atlantic, German composer Paul Hindemith was charged with a war crime because his compositions reflected spiritual ideas and themes of renewal. He was barred from performing music.

The 1950s and '60s ushered in a new era for music in which elements of jazz, bluegrass, and country music combined to create early rock and roll. Bill Haley, of Bill Haley and the Comets, holds the distinction of being the country's first composer of rock and roll, in 1955. With the rise of "the King of Rock and Roll," Elvis Presley, rock and roll forever changed the world. For the first time, contemporary music did not reflect the values of society but glamorized rebelliousness and adolescent sexuality.

Later, lyrics of the 1960s and '70s espoused drug abuse. Heavy metal bands of the '70s, '80s, and even into the '90s with bands such as Guns 'N' Roses, promote a panoply of anti-social behaviors and attitudes. The common denominator of their music is that self-gratification and self-expression excuse aggressively violent and sexual behavior inflicted on others.

The new kid on the popular music scene has stretched the fabric of our First Amendment like none before. Rap music is a culmination of the course charted by Elvis Presley. Put his rebellion, swagger, and sexuality into the pressurized cauldron of a black ghetto and the resulting music explodes with rage. It is primi-tive music—stripped of melodic line and original chord progressions. The beat alone propels the street smart rhyming verse lyrics through topics of deprivation, rebellion, poverty, sex, guns, drug abuse, and AIDS.

Since the Rodney King incident* and the subsequent riots in Los Angeles, the media has contributed to a climate wherein police bashing is socially and politically correct. Ignored is the role police play in safe-guarding the lives and liberties of all law-abiding citizens. The ingrained hatred of police authority, already prevalent in poor urban "hoods" is easily mobilized by the suggestive lyrics of rap.

The framers of the Constitution lived in a world far different from our own. Could they have imagined a day when music would become a tool to destabilize a democratic society by provoking civil unrest, violence, and murder? Yet, the lyrics of rapper Ice-T's *Cop Killer* do precisely that by describing steps to kill a cop. Time-Warner's recording company not only defended the "instructional" song, but marketed the album by shipping it in miniature body bags, complete with a three by four foot poster graphically depicting a cop killer. The company flooded the United States market with an additional half-million copies just prior to Ice-T's announcement that distribution would be suspended voluntarily.

While on patrol in July 1992, two Las Vegas police officers were ambushed

*[This refers to the severe beating of black motorist Rodney King by four white Los Angeles police officers in 1991, which was captured on videotape by a bystander and broadcast on national television. The later acquittal of the officers sparked public outrage and touched off the 1992 Los Angeles riots. —Ed.]

and shot by four juvenile delinquents who boasted that Ice-T's *Cop Killer* gave them a sense of duty and purpose, to get even with "a f—king pig". The juveniles continued to sing its lyrics when apprehended.

Notwithstanding the predictability of police being ambushed after such a rousing call-to-arms, Time-Warner continues to defend the song. In a letter addressed to Chief Gerald S. Arenberg, Executive Director of the National Association of Chiefs of Police, Time-Warner Vice Chairman Martin D. Payson gave his rationale for Warner Bros recording and mass-marketing *Cop Killer*:

> Ice-T is attempting to express the rage and frustration a young black person feels in the face of official brutality and systematic racism. Though the incidents of brutality may be perpetrated by a small number of police, the impact on the black community is intense and widespread. The anger that exists is neither an invention of Ice-T's nor a figment of the creative imagination. It is real and growing. Our job as a society is to address the causes of this anger, not suppress its articulation.

This last sentence is disingenuous at best. Is Time-Warner addressing the causes of black anger, or is it magnifying isolated instances of anger into a fashionable popular sentiment and reaping handsome profits in the process?

Would Thomas Jefferson have advocated using the First Amendment as a shield to publish a step-by-step guide on how to ambush and murder the police? The *Body Count* album also contains *Smoked Pork*, a song describing how Ice-T murders two police officers, with dialogue so graphic the lyrics were not printed with the album. Freedom of speech ought to end short of advocat-ing violent physical harm to fellow members of society. If Ice-T had, instead, produced a song describing how to sexually abuse and torture young children, perhaps there would be an appropriate public outcry. A full measure of consideration ought to be given to the lives and welfare of our nation's police officers and their families.

Safety and order in any community requires a partnership of a type that can exist only in a functioning democracy. Public attitudes toward the police may play a part in the frightening rise in crime rates. Disrespect for the law enforcement officer breeds disrespect for the law. A child who is raised to laugh at cops is not likely to grow up with any great respect for the laws that the police enforce. Youthful experimenters, confused by adolescent anxiety, look up to Ice-T as a powerful role model who supports hatred, racism, sexual abuse, and vile crimes that he depicts through dialogue in his lyrics.

Decades of misrepresentation and abuse of law enforcement in entertainment and education have left their mark. Society is now finding that it cannot ridicule the enforcers of the law on one hand and build respect for the law on the other. You cannot separate the two, any more than you can separate education from teachers, justice from judges, and religion from the ministry.

It is a sad irony that, in our society, scandal breeds financial gain. Sales of *Cop Killer*, and the *Body Count* album on which it appears, have soared since law enforcement officers from around the country rallied behind police organizations like the National Association of Chiefs of Police, CLEAT (Combined Law Enforcement Officers of Texas), and the American Federation of Police.

Ice-T is but one rapper encouraging violent reaction to the presence of law enforcement. Rap group Almighty RSO defiantly sings *One in the Chamber*, referring to the bullet they would use to kill a cop. Kool G-Rap and DJ Polo's song *Live and Let Die* describes how G-Rap brutally murders two undercover police officers as he tries to complete a drug deal.

Tragically, this violent message is too often followed by its young audience. On April 11, 1992, Trooper Bill Davidson, formerly with the Texas Department of Public Safety, was killed in cold blood as he approached the driver of a vehicle he had stopped for a defective headlight. The trooper's widow, Linda Davidson, described to me an account of the events surrounding the killing and the impact of this tragedy on the Davidson family. The teen-age killer, Ronald Howard, explained to law enforcement authorities that he felt hypnotized by the lyrics of six songs by the rap group 2 Pac, from their album 2 *Pacalyypse Now,* which urge the killing of police officers. Howard claims that the lyrical instructions devoured him like an animal, taking control over his subconscious mind and compelling him to kill Trooper Davidson as he approached Howard's vehicle. The rap's influence, however, apparently continues to affect Howard's judgment. Two psy-chiatrists found that the music still affects his psycho-social behavior. In a meeting with Linda Davidson, Howard expressed his desire to completely carry out the rap's instruction by putting away a pig's wife and dusting his family. Howard's re-action has left Linda dumfounded, confused, bewildered, and most of all, angry.

The Davidsons' anger is aimed not solely at Howard, but has also expressed itself in a civil lawsuit against Time-Warner, the company that promotes 2 Pac. Again, Time-Warner claims the First Amendment protects its right to promote songs that advocate the killing of police. In preparation for trial, the corporation's lawyers are closely observing the criminal trial of Ron Howard. Given the current state of American law, one can only hope that Time-Warner will tire of the expense of defending state court actions prompted by such lyrics and attacks on police.

With growing lawlessness and violence in our society, every American is at risk of losing his property and his life to criminals. Police officers risk their lives daily to preserve peace and property rights for all Americans. The officers deserve protection from abusive speech when that abuse imperils not only their ability to protect citizens, but also their ability to protect their very lives.

NO

Mark S. Hamm and Jeff Ferrell

RAP, COPS, AND CRIME: CLARIFYING THE "COP KILLER" CONTROVERSY

Perhaps the most enduring feature of the ACJS [Academy of Criminal Justice Sciences] is that it routinely brings practitioners and researchers together in a public forum where they can debate the current state of criminal justice. In this spirit, we offer a counterpoint to the attacks made by Dennis R. Martin, President of the National Association of Chiefs of Police, on rapper Ice-T's song "Cop Killer" and its alleged relationship to violent acts ("The Music of Murder," *ACJS Today*, Nov/Dec 1993).

"COP KILLER" IN CULTURAL CONTEXT

As a starting point, Martin offers a truncated and distorted description of rap's gestation that largely misses the music's social and cultural meanings. To suggest, as does Martin, that rap is "a culmination of the course charted by Elvis Presley" is to commit a double fallacy. First, Martin's characterization of Elvis Presley as the founder of rock 'n' roll, and Bill Haley as "the country's first composer of rock and roll," constitutes a racist and revisionist rock history which curiously excludes Louis Jordan, Chuck Berry, Bo Diddley, and a host of other black musicians and musical traditions which established the essentials of rock 'n' roll. (This sort of myopic ethnic insensitivity echoes in Martin's subsequent claim that rap is "primitive" (!) music.)

Second, Martin compounds these sorts of mistakes by tracing rap's lineage to rock 'n' roll—or, apparently, white Southern rockabilly. Rap artists have in fact explicitly denied this lineage. Early rappers, for example, sang "no more rock 'n' roll," and rappers Public Enemy have attacked Elvis Presley, and his racist attitudes, specifically. To draw a parallel between white Southern rockabilly of the mid-1950's and today's black urban rap is therefore analogous to comparing Joshua's trumpets at the battle of Jericho with the Wagnerian operas of Nazi storm troopers, or to equating the horn-calls which led Caesar's troops into England with the thrash metal of Slaughter and Megadeth

From Mark S. Hamm and Jeff Ferrell, "Rap, Cops, and Crime: Clarifying the 'Cop Killer' Controversy," *ACJS Today* (May/June 1994). Copyright © 1994 by Mark S. Hamm. Reprinted by permission. References omitted.

absorbed by US Air Force pilots prior to bombing raids during the Persian Gulf War. Other than to say that militaries have routinely used music to lead soldiers into battle, the analogies have little heuristic value. What Martin's analysis lacks is the crucial historical specificity and sociological contextualization, the framework of conceptual clarity and appreciation necessary to explain the complex relationship between particular forms of music, popular culture dynamics, and incidents of violence.

Most commentators, in fact, locate the beginnings of rap (or, more broadly, hip-hop) in the funkadelic period of the mid–late 1970s, a la George Clinton, Parliament, P-Funk, Kurtis Blow, and Grandmaster Flash and the Furious Five. Evolving from this musical base, rap gained its popular appeal in the grim ghettos of New York City—first in the Bronx, and then in Harlem and Brooklyn. Rap caught the sounds of the city, capturing the aggressive boasts and stylized threats of street-tough black males. By the mid-1980s, rap was injected into the American mainstream via Run-D.M.C.'s version of Aerosmith's "Walk this Way" and other cross-over hits. MC Hammer, Tone Loc, Public Enemy, Ice-T, NWA (Niggers with Attitude), De La Soul, and a legion of others soon followed, infusing rap with R and B, jazz, and other influences, and introducing rap to world-wide audiences of all ethnicities.

In ignoring this rich history, Martin misunderstands both the aesthetics and the politics of rap. Martin, for example, leaps to the extraordinary conclusion that rap is a "vile and dangerous" form of cultural expression, a "primitive music" that attacks "every shared value that has bound our society together for more than two-hundred years." From within this sort of uncritical, consensus model of contemporary society, Martin then locates this portentous social threat in a wider cultural crisis. "[T]he trend in American rock music for the last decade," he argues, "has been to promote ever more vile, deviant, and sociopathic behaviors." And if this trend is not reversed, Martin concludes, "every American is at risk of losing his [sic] property and his life to criminals." A careful analysis of rock's lyrical diversity and social effects would, of course, undermine these sorts of hysterical generalizations. A careful analysis of rap music's lyrical content and cultural context likewise reveals a very different social dynamic.

"Message Rap" (or "Gangster Rap," the focus of the remainder of this essay) deals head-on with universal themes of injustice and oppression—themes which have both bound and divided US society from its inception. But at the same time, gangster rap is proudly localized as "ghetto music," thematizing its commitment to the black urban experience. (This is also, by the way, part of what constitutes rap's appeal for millions of middle-class white kids who have never been inside a black ghetto.) In fact, rap focuses on aspects of ghetto life that most adult whites, middle-class blacks, and self-protective police officers and politicians would rather ignore. Rappers record the everyday experiences of pimping, prostitution, child abandonment, AIDS, and drugs (as in Ice-T's *anti*-drug song, "I'm Your Pusher"). Other rappers deal with deeper institutionalized problems such as poverty, racial conflict, revisionist history books, the demand for trivial consumer goods, the exploitation of disenfranchised blacks through military service, and black dislocation from Africa. And still other rap songs lay bare the desperate and often violent nature of ghetto life, as played out in individual and collective fear, sadly misogynistic and homophobic fantasies, street killings, and, significantly, oppressive harassment by police patrols.

These themes are packed in the aesthetic of black ghetto life, an aesthetic which features verbal virtuosity as a powerful symbol in the negotiation of social status. Rap is developed from US and Jamaican verbal street games like "signifying," "the dozens," and "toasting." Rap in turn encases this verbal jousting in the funky beat of rhythms reworked through the formal musical devices which give birth to the rap sound: "sampling," "scratch mixing," and "punch phrasing" (hardly the "primitive" or "stripped" music which Martin describes). The result of this complex artistic process is a sensual, bad-assed gangster who "won't be happy till the dancers are wet, out of control" and wildly "possessed" by the rapper's divine right to rhyme the ironies, ambiguities, and fears of urban ghetto life (Ice-T, "Hit the Deck"). Musically, rap certainly emerges more from studio funk and street poetry than the blues; but like Sonny Boy Williamson, Muddy Waters, Willie Dixon and a host of other great postwar US bluesmen, Ice-T and other rappers twist and shout from within a world of crippling adversity.

"COP KILLER" ON TRIAL

Because he misses this cultural context, it is no surprise that Martin attempts to "kill the messenger" by attacking rap music as itself a social problem. His choicest blows are saved for Ice-T, whose album *Body Count* integrates rap and "metal" styling, and includes a trilogy of protest sirens on police brutality written "for every pig who ever beat a brother down": "Smoked Pork," "Out in the Parking Lot," and "Cop Killer." Martin argues that one of these, "Cop Killer," is a "misuse of the First Amendment" because it has been "implicated in at least two shooting incidents and has inflamed racial tensions in cities across the country."

Here, though, is the available evidence on "Cop Killer": Since its release in early 1992, an unknown number of persons have heard the song. Martin claims that Time-Warner shipped 500,000 copies of *Body Count* upon its *initial* release. This number is important because subsequent pressings of *Body Count* did not contain "Cop Killer." It was pulled by Time-Warner after US Vice-President Dan Quayle, Parents' Music Resource Center spokeswoman and future Vice-Presidential associate Tipper Gore, and a host of influential media personalities and "moral entrepreneurs" leveled a highly organized and well-publicized campaign of "moral panic" against the song (see Becker, 1963; Cohen, 1972).

But our repeated inquiries to Time-Warner revealed that no such sales figures are available. We were told that Ice-T has since left Time-Warner and is now under contract with Profile records. Yet Profile cannot document sales figures for the first *Body Count* album either, claiming that these figures are known only to Ice-T himself—who, despite our attempts to reach him, remains unavailable for comment. We simply don't know—and neither does Martin—how many young Americans have heard "Cop Killer."

Setting all this aside, let's assume that the President of the National Association of Chiefs of Police is correct: some 500,000 persons have heard "Cop Killer" via the music recording industry. Because popular music is a highly contagious commodity (especially among the young), we may cautiously estimate that three times that number have listened to this song (each buyer sharing the song with just two others). From this very conservative estimate, then, it is not unreasonable to conclude that at least 1.5 million young Americans have heard "Cop Killer."

According to Martin, 144 US police officers were killed in the line of duty during 1992. This is indeed a tragic fact, the seriousness of which we do not wish in any way to diminish. But the fact also remains that there is no evidence to show that the perpetrators of these 144 homicides were influenced by "Cop Killer." Martin bases his argument on a brief review of four juveniles arrested in Las Vegas (NV) for wounding two police officers with firearms, allegedly behind the emotional impetus of "Cop Killer." Put another way, while some 1.5 million persons may have listened to this song, only four may have acted on its message. Thankfully, none were successful.

In summary, Martin claims that "Ice-T's *Cop Killer* [sic] gave [the Las Vegas youths] a sense of duty and purpose, to get even with a f—king pig." If so, we should expect this same "sense of duty and purpose" to influence the behavior of some of the other 1.5 million listeners. Martin, in fact, describes popular music as "a tool to destabilize a democratic society by provoking civil unrest, violence, and murder," and argues that "the lyrics of rapper Ice-T's 'Cop Killer' do precisely that…". He further notes the "predictability of police being ambushed after such a rousing call-to-arms…". But we cannot, in fact, find another "predictable" case. The relationship between listening to "Cop Killer"

and committing subsequent acts of violence appears to more closely resemble a statistical accident than a causal equation. (The probability of attacking a police officer with a loaded firearm after listening to "Cop Killer" is, according to Martin's count, less than 1 in 375,000). Treating this relationship as one of cause and effect therefore not only misrepresents the issues; it intentionally engineers self-serving moral panic around rap music, and obstructs solutions to the sorts of problems which rap portrays.

"COP KILLER," CULTURE, AND CRIME

Ice-T is not the first artist to embed a "cop killer" theme in United States popular culture. This theme has been the subject of countless cinematic and literary works, and has appeared many times before in popular music. During the Great Depression, for example, musicians celebrated Pretty Boy Floyd and his exploits, which included the murder of law enforcement personnel. Similarly, the highly respected fiddler Tommy Jarrell wrote and sang "Policeman," which begins, "Policeman come and I didn't want to go this morning, so I shot him in the head with my 44." But perhaps the best-known case is Eric Clapton's cover version of Bob Marley and the Wailers' "I Shot the Sheriff," which reached the top of the US music charts in the mid-1970s (a feat not approached by Ice-T). "I Shot the Sheriff," though, never suffered the sort of moral and political condemnation leveled at "Cop Killer." How do we account for this difference?

First, "I Shot the Sheriff" was released by a white artist, and in an era when the availability and allure of firearms and ammunition had not reached the saturation point we see today. Clapton's white bread portrayal of an armed and heroic Jamaican "rudeboy" was therefore comfortably abstract and romantic. In contrast, Ice-T's shotgun-toting black US gangster is all too concrete, stripped of romantic pretense and lodged uncomfortably in everyday life. Firearms and ammunition are now prevalent in the black community, and are the leading cause of death among young black males. Within the context of gangster rap, artists like Ice-T portray, with chilling clarity, this tragic obsession with lethal weapons.

Second, the social aesthetic of rap music creates a key cultural and political difference. Because rap constitutes a strident form of cultural combat and critique, it generates in response organized censorship, blacklisting, arrests, and the police-enforced cancellation of concerts. Rap's cultural roots and primary audience are among the impoverished, minority residents of US inner cities. While many of these citizens are unable or unwilling to speak out—for lack of access to cultural channels, for fear of reprisal—rappers invoke a militant black pride, and portray and confront social injustice in ways that threaten the complacent status quo of mainstream society. And as part of this critique, rappers lay bare the daily reality of police violence against minority populations, and remind us how many Rodney Kings haven't made it onto videotape.

For these reasons, Dennis Martin and other defenders of the status quo are loath to acknowledge or appreciate rap on any level—as innovative music, verbal virtuosity, or cultural critique. In fact, their discomfort with rap's politics intertwines with their displeasure over its style and sound. Gangster rap is frequently raunchy, sometimes violent,

and often played loud, with a heavy emphasis on the staccato, thumping back beat. By artistic design, it is meant to be "in your face" and threatening. This, in combination with the evocative power of rap's imagery, generates loud and urgent condemnations of rap from those who benefit, directly and indirectly, from contemporary social arrangements. For them, personal offense becomes a measure of political superiority.

Finally, the remarkable attention given to "Cop Killer" reflects a growing concern, among both criminologists and the general public, over the intersections of popular culture and crime. Our own studies in this area have led us to conclude that contemporary music can in some cases be significantly linked to criminality—but only when particular forms of music take on meaning within the dynamics of specific subcultures like neo-Nazi skinheads (Hamm, 1993) or hip-hop graffiti artists (Ferrell, 1993). And in this regard, we end by commending Martin for an important discovery. The fact that four youths may have in fact used the cultural material of "Cop Killer" as an epistemic and aesthetic framework for attacking two police officers is cause for serious criminological concern. And to demonstrate *how* this song may have changed the social and political consciousness of these would-be cop killers, within the dynamics of their own subcultural arrangements, is of paramount importance for understanding the situated social meanings of gangster rap.

But this sort of research requires something more than Martin offers in his essay. It demands an attention to ethnographic particulars, in place of Martin's wide generalizations and blanket condemnations. It calls for a sort of criminological *verstehen*, a willingness to pay careful attention to the lyrics of gangster rap and to the lives of those who listen to it, in place of Martin's dismissive disregard. Ultimately, it requires that criminologists confront and critique the kinds of social injustices which rap exposes, rather than participating, as does Martin, in their perpetuation.

POSTSCRIPT

Does Rap Music Contribute to Violent Crime?

Neither Martin nor Hamm and Ferrell mention that in many ways the twentieth century is relatively unique in that much of the popular music sharply divides generations. In the past, it was rare to think about "old people's music," "teenagers' music," and so on. Today's popular music often functions to divide generations as well as regions, races, and ethnic groups (although within generations, popular music frequently unites younger listeners).

Both sides of this issue are highly selective in their sensitivities. Martin is offended because police are treated with contempt in some rap albums. Hamm and Ferrell are indignant that racism and poverty are facts of life. Neither side of the controversy considers the fact that rates of violence and homicide committed by young blacks against other blacks is skyrocketing. Might teenagers in inner cities listening to messages of violence turn heightened hostilities on each other instead of the police or whites? Note that the alleged criminal acts of performers such as Snoop Doggy Dogg, Dr. Dre, Marion "Suge" Knight (currently serving nine years for assault), and others involved black, not white, victims (see J. D. Considine, "Gangsta R.I.P.?" *Baltimore Sun*, March 10, 1998). Some are equally critical of the perceived degradation of women in rap songs.

Many black religious and political leaders, writers, and columnists would be amused by criminologists' characterizing rappers as Robin Hoods, romantic messengers, voices of the oppressed, and such. Hamm and Ferrell's discrediting of Martin for characterizing gansta rap as primitive might bring belly laughs to blacks who in their speeches and columns refer to such music as trash or worse. Some blacks resent what they see as whites' justifying rap lyrics because they allegedly speak for poor (or any) blacks.

For a follow-up of this debate, see L. Crzycki, "It's Not That Simple!" *ACJS Today* (September/October 1994) and W. Hall, "We Should Not Tolerate Lyrics That Insult Women," *Baltimore Sun* (May 18, 1995). For some balanced accounts of rap music, see F. Krohn, "Contemporary Urban Music: Controversial Messages in Rap Music and Hip Hop," *ETC* (Summer 1995) and T. Dodge, "From Spirituals to Gospel Rap," *Serials Review* (vol. 20, no. 4, 1994). Also see the technical discussion *Spectacular Vernaculars: Hip-Hop and the Politics of Postmodernism* by R. Porter (State University of New York Press, 1995).

ISSUE 3

Does IQ Significantly Contribute to Crime?

YES: Richard J. Herrnstein and Charles Murray, from *The Bell Curve: Intelligence and Class Structure in American Life* (Free Press, 1994)

NO: Francis T. Cullen et al., from "Crime and the Bell Curve: Lessons from Intelligent Criminology," *Crime and Delinquency* (October 1997)

ISSUE SUMMARY

YES: The late psychologist and criminologist Richard J. Herrnstein and Charles Murray, a fellow of the American Enterprise Institute, argue that a significant cause of crime is low IQ. Indeed, criminological theories and policies ignore this at great peril, they contend.

NO: Criminologists Francis T. Cullen, Paul Gendreau, G. Roger Jarjoura, and John Paul Wright concede that IQ at times may have a minor role in crime commission and that rational penal policies ought to take that into account. However, they assert that Herrnstein and Murray utilize faulty data, ignore the many significant environmental factors related to both crime and intelligence, and derive mean-spirited and repressive policy conclusions.

Two things should be noted about this controversy. First, while the issue goes directly to Richard J. Herrnstein and Charles Murray's theory of crime causation—low IQ, or being "cognitively disadvantaged"—the authors also work out an implicit treatment modality from their theory. All criminological and criminal justice theories contain concomitant treatment modalities that are logically derived from the theory. For example, if the theory is that crime results from poverty or blocked opportunities, then the implicit solution is to provide funds and jobs. If crime results from unfair, discriminatory laws or selective enforcement, then change the legal system. If crime results from a lack of proper adult role models or from delinquent peer pressure, then provide mentors or alternative friends for juveniles, or provide delinquent peers with socially acceptable activities, such as organized basketball games or job training.

Each theory's treatment modality can become the basis of policies to respond to and prevent crimes. As you read the following debate, you will notice that Francis T. Cullen et al. reject any theory of crime that gives low IQ centrality, especially the theory of Herrnstein and Murray. They also challenge the alleged benevolence of Herrnstein and Murray's policy conclusions, claiming that the scholars are simply bootlegging their conservative agenda.

Theories or explanations of crime based on race, genes, or biology have been shunned since the 1930s. From a sociology of knowledge perspective, the idea that traits (including IQ) are passed on through genes instead of through cultural transmission (learned behavior) is considered by most people to be empirically absurd and politically incorrect. Hence, the enormous amount of controversy generated by the publication of *The Bell Curve*, the book in which Herrnstein and Murray delineate their theory of crime as based on low IQ.

As various groups representing the knowledge industry square off against *The Bell Curve* because of political, social, and personal reasons (it *is* a genuine threat to traditional social scientific conceptions of reality), others' attacks reflect philosophy of science concerns. There is simply no such thing as "IQ," some claim. Moreover, it is argued, all IQ tests are biased in favor of middle-class students and against poor or ethnic test takers, who frequently have abilities drawn from their social class or ethnic groups that are utterly ignored in most tests. The idea that entire groups on the average have lower IQs smacks of racism, critics say.

Criminological critics point out that crime rates vary dramatically between and even within the same generation. Therefore, since IQs are not likely to increase or decrease in such a short span of time, what possible bearing could they have on crime? These critics insist that we must look elsewhere for explanations, such as to traditional theories linking environmental factors (culture, socioeconomic status, neighborhood, peers) with crime and delinquency. But Herrnstein and Murray maintain that, although traditional factors may be contributors, when explanatory models are reduced to the single most important variables, then IQ is often the best predictor. Indeed, they argue that IQ explains most structural or sociological variables, such as income of parents, neighborhoods, amount of education, and so on.

Cullen et al. (and others) argue that *The Bell Curve*'s test of IQ and crime and many of its own tables actually refute its argument. Intellectually disadvantaged people are not more likely to commit crimes, they say. Moreover, within criminological theory, efforts to link IQ, race, biology, or genes to crime functioned as what some philosophers of science refer to as a "negative heuristic." That is, explanations based on those variables were thought to have been discredited long ago, with most, if not all, "acceptable" criminological theories constituting a refutation of Herrnstein and Murray's theory.

As you read the following selections, note how crucial concepts are operationalized (measured) and defined. What is the structure of Herrnstein and Murray's theory? What is Cullen et al.'s theoretical perspective? What are the protagonists' policy solutions? What seems to be the scope of their respective theories (e. g., which crimes are included, excluded, or ignored in their explanations)? Is there any hope of a synthesis of the two positions?

YES

Richard J. Herrnstein and Charles Murray

CRIME

Among the most firmly established facts about criminal offenders is that their distribution of IQ scores differs from that of the population at large. Taking the scientific literature as a whole, criminal offenders have average IQs of about 92, eight points below the mean. More serious or chronic offenders generally have lower scores than more casual offenders. The relationship of IQ to criminality is especially pronounced in the small fraction of the population, primarily young men, who constitute the chronic criminals that account for a disproportionate amount of crime. Offenders who have been caught do not score much lower, if at all, than those who are getting away with their crimes. Holding socioeconomic status constant does little to explain away the relationship between crime and cognitive ability.

High intelligence also provides some protection against lapsing into criminality for people who otherwise are at risk. Those who have grown up in turbulent homes, have parents who were themselves criminal, or who have exhibited the childhood traits that presage crime are less likely to become criminals as adults if they have high IQ.

These findings from an extensive research literature are supported by the evidence from white males in the NLSY [National Longitudinal Survey of Youth]. Low IQ was a risk factor for criminal behavior, whether criminality was measured by incarceration or by self-acknowledged crimes. The socioeconomic background of the NLSY's white males was a negligible risk factor once their cognitive ability was taken into account.

Crime can tear a free society apart, because free societies depend so crucially on faith that the other person will behave decently. As one grows, society must substitute coercion for cooperation. The first penalty is not just freedom but the bonds that make community life attractive. Yes, it is always possible to buy better locks, stay off the streets after dark, regard every stranger suspiciously, post security guards everywhere, but these are poor substitutes for living in a peaceful and safe neighborhood.

Most Americans think that crime has gotten far too high. But in the ruminations about how the nation has reached this state and what might be done, too little attention has been given to one of the best-documented relationships in the study of crime: As a group, criminals are below average in intelligence.

... [T]hings were not always so bad. Good crime statistics do not go back very far in the United States, but we do not need statistics to remind Americans alive in the 1990s of times when they felt secure walking late at night, alone, even in poor neighborhoods and even in the nation's largest cities. In the mid-1960s, crime took a conspicuous turn for the worse....

[C]rime that worries most people most viscerally: violent crime, which consists of robbery, murder, aggravated assault, and rape. From 1950 through 1963, the rate for violent crime was almost flat, followed by an extremely rapid rise from 1964 to 1971, followed by continued increases until the 1980s. The early 1980s saw an interlude in which violent crime decreased noticeably. But the trend-line for 1985–1992 is even steeper than the one for 1963–1980, making it look as if the lull was just that—a brief respite from an increase in violent crime that is now thirty years old....

DEPRAVED OR DEPRIVED?

The juvenile delinquents in Leonard Bernstein's *West Side Story* tell Officer Krupke that they are "depraved on account of we're deprived," showing an astute grasp of the poles in criminological theory: the psychological and the sociological. Are criminals psychologically distinct? Or are they ordinary people responding to social and economic circumstances?

Theories of criminal behavior were mostly near the sociological pole from the 1950s through the 1970s. Its leading scholars saw criminals as much like the rest of us, except that society earmarks them for a life of criminality. Some of these scholars went further, seeing criminals as free of personal blame, evening up the score with a society that has victimized them. The most radical theorists from the sociological pole argued that the definition of crime was in itself ideological, creating "criminals" of people who were doing nothing more than behaving in ways that the power structure chose to define as deviant. In their more moderate forms, sociological explanations continue to dominate public discourse. Many people take it for granted, for example, that poverty and unemployment cause crime —classic sociological arguments that are distinguished more by their popularity than by evidence.

Theories nearer the psychological pole were more common earlier in the history of criminology and have lately regained acceptance among experts. Here, the emphasis shifts to the characteristics of the offender rather than to his circumstances. The idea is that criminals are distinctive in psychological (perhaps even biological) ways. They are deficient, depending on the particular theory, in conscience or in self-restraint. They lack normal attachment to the mores of their culture, or they are peculiarly indifferent to the feelings or the good opinion of others. They are overendowed with restless energy or with a hunger for adventure or danger....

We are at neither of these theoretical poles. Like almost all other students of crime, we expect to find explanations from both sociology and psychology. The reason for calling attention to the contrast between the theories is that public discussion has lagged; it remains more nearly stuck at the sociological pole in public discourse than it is among experts.... [W]e are interested in the role that cognitive ability plays in creating criminal offenders. This by no means requires us to deny that sociology, economics, and public policy might play an important part in sharing crime rates....

Among the arguments often made against the claim that criminals are psychologically distinctive, two are arguments in principle rather than in fact....

Argument 1: Crime rates have changed in recent times more than people's cognitive ability or personalities could have. We must therefore find the reason for the rising crime rates in people's changing circumstances.

... [P]ersonal characteristics need not change everywhere in society for crime's aggregate level in society to change. Consider age, for example, since crime is mainly the business of young people between 15 and 24. When the age distribution of the population shifts toward more people in their peak years for crime, the average level of crime may be expected to rise. Or crime may rise disproportionately if a large bulge in the youthful sector of the population fosters a youth culture that relishes unconventionality over traditional adult values. The exploding crime rate of the 1960s is, for example, partly explained by the baby boomers' reaching adolescence. Or suppose that a style of child rearing sweeps the country, and it turns out that this style of child rearing leads to less control over the behavior of rebellious adolescents. The change in style of child rearing may predictably be followed, fifteen or so years later, by a change in crime rates. If, in short, circumstances tip toward crime, the change will show up most among those with the strongest tendencies to break laws (or the weakest tendencies to obey them). Understanding those tendencies is the business of theories at the psychological pole.

Argument 2: Behavior is criminal only because society says so. There cannot be psychological tendencies to engage in behavior defined so arbitrarily.

This argument, made frequently during the 1960s and 1970s and always most popular among intellectuals than with the general public, is heard most often opposing any suggestion that criminal behavior has biological roots. How can something so arbitrary, say, as not paying one's taxes or driving above a 55 mph speed limit be inherited? the critics ask. Behavior regarding taxes and speed limits certainly cannot be coded in our DNA; perhaps even more elemental behaviors such as robbery and murder cannot either.

Our counterargument goes like this: Instead of crime, consider behavior that is less controversial and even more arbitrary, like playing the violin. A violin is a cultural artifact, no less arbitrary than any other man-made object, and so is the musical scale. Yet few people would argue that the first violinists in the nation's great orchestra are a random sample of the population. The interests, talents, self-discipline, and dedication that it takes to reach their level of accomplishment have roots in individual psychology—quite possibly even in biology. The variation across people in *any* behavior, however arbitrary, will have such roots....

But even if crime is admitted to be a psychological phenomenon, why should intelligence be important? What is the logic that might lead us to expect low intelligence to be more frequently linked with criminal tendencies than high intelligence is?

One chain of reasoning starts from the observation that low intelligence often translates into failure and frustration in school and in the job market. If, for example, people of intelligence have a hard time finding a job, they might have more reason to commit crimes as a way of making a living. If people of low intelligence have a hard time acquiring status through the ordinary ways, crime might seem like a good alternative route. At the least, their failures in school and at work may foster resentment toward society and its laws.

Perhaps the link between crime and low IQ is even more direct. A lack of foresight, which is often associated with low IQ, raises the attractions of the immediate gains from crime and lowers the strength of the deterrents, which come later (if they come at all). To a person of low intelligence, the threats of apprehension and prison may fade to meaninglessness. They are too abstract, too far in the future, too uncertain.

Low IQ may be part of a broader complex of factors. An appetite for danger, a stronger-than-average hunger for the things that you can get only by stealing if you cannot buy them, an antipathy toward conventionality, an insensitivity to pain or to social ostracism, and a host of derangements of various sorts, combined with low IQ, may set the stage for a criminal career.

Finally, there are moral considerations. Perhaps the ethical principles for not committing crimes are less accessible (or less persuasive) to people of low intelligence. They find it harder to understand why robbing someone is wrong, find it harder to appreciate the values of civil and cooperative social life, and are accordingly less inhibited from acting in ways that are hurtful to other people and to the community at large....

THE LINK BETWEEN COGNITIVE ABILITY AND CRIMINAL BEHAVIOR: AN OVERVIEW

The statistical association between crime and cognitive ability has been known since intelligence testing began in earnest. The British physician Charles Goring mentioned a lack of intelligence as one of the distinguishing traits of the prison population that he described in a landmark contribution to modern criminology early in the century. In 1914, H. H. Goddard, an early leader in both modern criminology and the use of intelligence tests, concluded that a large fraction of convicts were intellectually subnormal.

The subsequent history of the study of the link between IQ and crime replays the larger story of intelligence testing, with the main difference being that the attack on the IQ/crime link began earlier than the broader attempt to discredit IQ tests. Even in the 1920s, the link was called into question, for example, by psychologist Carl Murchison, who produced data showing that the prisoners of Leavenworth had a higher mean IQ than that of enlisted men in world War I. Then in 1931, Edwin Sutherland, America's most prominent criminologist, wrote "Mental Deficiency and Crime," an article that effectively put an end to the study of IQ and crime for half a century. Observing (accurately) that the ostensible IQ differences between criminals and the general population were diminishing as testing procedures improved, Sutherland leaped to the conclusion that the remaining differences would disappear altogether as the state of the art improved.

The difference, in fact, did not disappear, but that did not stop criminology from denying the importance of IQ as a predictor of criminal behavior. For decades, criminologists who followed Sutherland argued that the IQ numbers said nothing about a real difference in intelligence between offenders and nonoffenders. They were skeptical about whether the convicts in prisons were truly representative of offenders in general, and they disparaged the tests' validity. Weren't tests just measuring socioeconomic status by other means, and weren't they biased against the people from the lower socioeconomic classes or the minority groups who were most likely to break the law for other reasons? they asked. By the 1960s, the association between intelligence and crime was altogether dismissed in criminology textbooks, and so it remained until recently....

It took two of the leading criminologists of another generation, Travis Hirschi and Michael Hindelang, to resurrect the study of IQ and criminality that Sutherland had buried. In their 1977 article, "Intelligence and Delinquency: A Revisionist View," they reviewed many studies that included IQ measures, took into account the potential artifacts, and concluded that juvenile delinquents were in fact characterized by substantially below-average levels of tested intelligence. Hirschi and Hindelang's work took a while to percolate through the academy, ... but by the end of the 1980s, most criminologists accepted not just that an IQ gap separates offenders and nonoffenders, but that the gap is genuinely a difference in average intellectual level. ...

The Size of the IQ Gap

How big is the difference between criminals and the rest of us? Taking the literature as a whole, incarcerated offenders average an IQ of about 92, 8 points below the mean. The population of nonoffenders averages more than 100 points; an informed guess puts the gap between offenders and nonoffenders at about 10 points. More serious or more chronic offenders generally have lower scores than more casual offenders. The eventual relationship between IQ and repeat offending is already presaged in IQ scores taken when the children are 4 years old.

Not only is there a gap in IQ between offenders and nonoffenders, but a disproportionately large fraction of all crime is committed by people toward the low end of the scale of intelligence....

Do the Unintelligent Ones Commit More Crimes—or Just Get Caught More Often?

Some critics continue to argue that offenders whose IQs we know are unrepresentative of the true criminal population; the smart ones presumably slipped through the net. Surely this is correct to some degree.... Is there a population of uncaught offenders with high IQs committing large numbers of crimes? The answer seems to be no....

[T]he IQs of uncaught offenders are not measurably different from the ones who get caught. Among those who have criminal records, there is still a significant negative correlation between

IQ and frequency of offending. Both of these kinds of evidence imply that differential arrests of people with varying IQs, assuming they exist, are a minor factor in the aggregate data.

Intelligence as a Preventative
Looking at the opposite side of the picture, those who do not commit crimes, it appears that high cognitive ability protects a person from becoming a criminal even if the other precursors are present. One study followed a sample of almost 1,500 boys born in Copenhagen, Denmark, between 1936 and 1938. Sons whose fathers had a prison record were almost six times as likely to have a prison record themselves (by the age of 34–36) as the sons of men who had no police record of any sort. Among these high-risk sons, the ones who had no police record at all had IQ scores one standard deviation higher than the sons who had a police record.

The protective power of elevated intelligence also shows up in a New Zealand study....

Children growing up in troubled circumstances on Kauai in the Hawaiian chain confirm the pattern....

THE LINK BETWEEN COGNITIVE ABILITY AND CRIMINAL BEHAVIOR: WHITE MEN IN THE NLSY

In the United States, where crime and race have become so intertwined in the public mind, it is especially instructive to focus on just whites. To simplify matters, we also limit the NLSY sample to males. Crime is still overwhelmingly a man's vice. Among whites in the sample, 83 percent of all persons who admitted to a criminal conviction were male.

Interpreting Self-Report Data
In the 1980 interview wave, the members of the NLSY sample were asked detailed questions about their criminal activity and their involvement with the criminal justice system. These data are known as self-report data, meaning that we have to go on what the respondent says. One obvious advantage of self-reports is that they presumably include information about the crimes of offenders whether or not they have been caught. Another is that they circumvent any biases in the criminal justice system, which, some people argue, contaminate official criminal statistics.... [W]e will concentrate in this analysis on events that are on the public record (and the respondent knows are on the public record): being stopped by the police, formal charges, and convictions. In doing so, we are following a broad finding in crime research that official contacts with the law enforcement and criminal justice system are usefully accurate reflections of the underlying level of criminal activity....

IQ and Types of Criminal Involvement
The typical finding has been that between a third and a half of all juveniles are stopped by police at some time or another (a proportion that has grown over the last few decades) but that 5 to 7 percent of the population account for about half the total number of arrests....

Something similar applies as we move up the ladder of criminal severity. Only 18 percent of white males had ever formally been charged with an offense, and a little less than 3 percent of them accounted for half the charges. Only 13 percent of white males had ever been convicted of anything, and 2 percent accounted for half of the convictions....

Like studies using all races, the NLSY results for white males show a regular relationship between IQ and criminality.... Those who reported they had never even been stopped by the police (for anything other than a minor traffic violation) were above average in intelligence, with a mean IQ of 106, and things went downhill from there. Close to a standard deviation separated those who had never been stopped by the police from those who went to prison [IQ = 93]....

In addition to self-reports, the NLSY provides data on criminal behavior by noting where the person was interviewed. In all the interviews from 1979 to 1990, was the young man ever interviewed in a correctional facility? The odds... that a white male had ever been interviewed in jail were fourteen times greater for Class V [bottom five percent] than for white males anywhere in the top quartile of IQ.

... The NLSY sample of white males echoes the scientific literature in general in showing a sizable IQ gap between offenders and nonoffenders at each level of involvement with the criminal justice system.

The Role of Socioeconomic Background

We will use both self-reports and whether the interviewee was incarcerated at the time of the interview as measures of criminal behavior.... Our definition of criminality here is that the man's description of his own behavior put him in the top decile of frequency of self-reported criminal activity. The other measure is whether the man was ever interviewed while being confined in a correctional facility between 1979 and 1990....

For both measures, after controlling for IQ, the men's socioeconomic background had little or nothing to do with crime. In the case of the self-report data, higher socioeconomic status was associated with *higher* reported crime after controlling for IQ. In the case of incarceration, the role of socioeconomic background was close to nil after controlling for IQ, and statistically insignificant. By either measure of crime, a low IQ was a significant risk factor.

The Role of a Broken Home

When people think about the causes of crime, they usually think not only of the role of juvenile delinquent's age and socioeconomic background but also of what used to be called "broken homes." It is now an inadequate phrase, because many families do not even begin with a married husband and wife, and many broken homes are reconstituted (in some sense) through remarriage. But whatever the specific way in which a home is not intact, the children of such families are usually more likely to get in trouble with the law than children from intact families....

Although family setting had an impact on crime, it did not explain away the predictive power of IQ. For example, a young man from a broken family and an average IQ and socioeconomic background had a 4 percent chance of having been interviewed in jail. Switch his IQ to the 2d centile, and the odds rise to 22 percent....

The Role of Education

Scholars have been arguing about the relationship of education to crime and delinquency for many years without settling the issue. The case of the NLSY white males is a classic example. Of those who were ever interviewed in jail, 74 percent had not gotten a high school diploma. None had a college degree. Clearly something about getting seriously involved in crime competes with staying in school. Low IQ is part of that "something" in many cases, but the relationship is so strong that other factors are probably involved—for example, the same youngster who is willing to burglarize a house probably is not the most obedient of pupils; the youngster who commits assaults on the street probably gets in fights on the school grounds;... and so forth....

CRIME, COGNITIVE ABILITY, AND CONSCIENCE

By now, you will already be anticipating the usual caution: Despite the relationship of low IQ to criminality, the great majority of people with low cognitive ability are law abiding. We will also take this opportunity to reiterate that the increase in crime over the last thirty years (like the increases in illegitimacy and welfare) cannot be attributed to changes in intelligence but rather must be blamed on other factors, which may have put people of low cognitive ability at greater risk than before.

The caveats should not obscure the importance of the relationship of cognitive ability to crime, however. Many people tend to think of criminals as coming from the wrong side of the tracks. They are correct, insofar as that is where people of low cognitive ability disproportionately live. They are also correct insofar as people who live on the right side of the tracks—whether they are rich or just steadily employed working-class people —seldom show up in the nation's prisons. But the assumption that too glibly

follows from these observations is that the economic and social disadvantage is in itself the cause of criminal behavior. That is not what the data say, however. In trying to understand how to deal with the crime problem, much of the attention now given to problems of poverty and unemployment should be shifted to another question altogether: coping with cognitive disadvantage....

Making It Easier to Live a Virtuous Life
... Human beings in general are capable of deciding between right and wrong. This does not mean, however, that everyone is capable of deciding between right and wrong with the same sophistication and nuances. The difference between people of low cognitive ability and the rest of society may be put in terms of a metaphor: Everyone has a moral compass, but some of those compasses are more susceptible to magnetic storms than others....

Imagine living in a society where the rules about crime are simple and the consequences are equally simple. "Crime" consists of a few obviously wrong acts: assault, rape, murder, robbery, theft, trespass, destruction of another's property, fraud. Someone who commits a crime is probably caught—and almost certainly punished. The punishment almost certainly hurts (it is meaningful). Punishment follows arrest quickly....

Now imagine that all the rules are made more complicated. The number of acts defined as crimes has multiplied, so that many things that are crimes are not nearly as obviously "wrong" as something like robbery or assault. The link between moral transgression and committing crime is made harder to understand. Fewer crimes lead to an arrest. Fewer arrests lead to prosecution.... When people are convicted, the consequences have no apparent connection to how much harm they have done. These events are typically spread out over months and sometimes years. To top it all off, even the "wrongness" of the basic crimes is called into question. In the society at large (and translated onto the television and movie screens), it is commonly argued that robbery, for example, if not always wrong if it is in a good cause (stealing medicine to save a dying wife) or if it is in response to some external condition (exploitation, racism, etc.)....

The two worlds we have described are not far removed from the contrast between the criminal justice system in the United States as recently as the 1950s and that system as of the 1990s. We are arguing that a person with comparatively low intelligence, whose time horizon is short and ability to balance many competing and complex incentives is low, has much more difficulty following a moral compass in the 1990s than he would have in the 1950s.... People of limited intelligence can lead moral lives in a society that is run on the basis of "Thou shalt not steal." They find it much harder to lead moral lives in a society that is run on the basis of "Thou shalt not steal unless there is a really good reason to."

The policy prescription is that the criminal justice system should be made *simpler*. The meaning of criminal offenses used to be clear and objective, and so were the consequences. It is worthy trying to make them so again.

NO
Francis T. Cullen et al.

CRIME AND THE BELL CURVE

In their best-selling book, The Bell Curve, *[Richard J.] Herrnstein and [Charles] Murray argue that IQ is a powerful predictor of a range of social ills including crime. They use this "scientific reality" to oppose social welfare policies and, in particular, to justify the punishment of offenders. By reanalyzing the data used in* The Bell Curve *and by reviewing existing meta-analyses assessing the relative importance of criminogenic risk factors, the present authors show empirically that Herrnstein and Murray's claims regarding IQ and crime are misleading. The authors conclude that Herrnstein and Murray's crime control agenda is based on ideology, not on intelligent criminology.*

In the aftermath of the publication of the *The Bell Curve: Intelligence and Class Structure in American Life*, Charles Murray has remained remarkably calm amid a storm of criticism that has accused him of being stupid about intelligence and, still worse, of giving solace to racists.... Murray repeatedly informs interviewers that he simply is being a good social scientist who is conveying unpleasant truths that can be ignored only at the nation's long-term peril.

At least with regard to crime, we claim otherwise; Murray's social science is misleading, and his message is erroneous. He needs a boost in his criminological intelligence. The apparent persuasiveness of *The Bell Curve*, which Murray coauthored with the late Richard Herrnstein, is that it purports to show that IQ has *powerful* and largely *immutable* effects across a range of behaviors. If "cognitively disadvantaged," a person is going to commit crimes, fail at school, be unemployed, end up on welfare, produce illegitimate kids, and be a lousy citizen. But if these effects do not in fact exist, or if these effects are in fact amenable to reversal, then the foundation on which Herrnstein and Murray's thesis is built crumbles.

We evaluate *The Bell Curve* only with regard to claims made about crime and, in turn, about crime-related policies. If Herrnstein and Murray are wrong about crime, then their science elsewhere in the book may be equally suspect —a fact other social scientists have attempted to demonstrate....

From Francis T. Cullen et al., "Crime and the Bell Curve: Lessons from Intelligent Criminology," *Crime and Delinquency,* vol. 43, no. 4 (October 1997). Copyright © 1997 by Sage Publications, Inc. Reprinted by permission. Notes and some references omitted.

We also should note that the initial wave of reviews of *The Bell Curve* primarily criticized Herrnstein and Murray for employing a narrow, outdated conceptualization of "intelligence," for claiming that IQ is difficult to boost, and for implying that African Americans are intellectually inferior....

Toward this end, we reanalyze the data on crime reported in *The Bell Curve* and show that the effects of IQ on criminal involvement are, at best, modest. We then supplement this reanalysis by summarizing previous meta-analyses and studies of the predictors of crime. We show, again, that IQ is a weak to modest risk factor in offending and that its criminogenic effects are dwarfed by a range of factors, many of which are amenable to change.

... [W]e contend that Herrnstein and Murray's policies to control crime, especially among the cognitively disadvantaged, have virtually no empirical support and, on their face, are certainly preposterous.... We consider these policy proposals as dangerous not so much because they may be implemented but because they reinforce—persuasively, we must admit—a way of thinking about crime that is seductive, simplistic, and punitive.... We believe that it is important to use "intelligent criminology" to deconstruct [their] "science" and to unmask the ideology underlying *The Bell Curve*.

... [W]e contend that cognitive differences among offenders should not be ignored but rather taken into account when dispensing treatments—a far different perspective from that of Herrnstein and Murray, who dismiss a treatment agenda. We also suggest that criminologists should remain attentive to efforts within psychology to reconceptualize IQ, which in turn may lead to even more constructive methods of delivering effective services to offenders.

CRIME AND THE BELL CURVE: A REASSESSMENT

Analysis in The Bell Curve

In *The Bell Curve*, Herrnstein and Murray use data from the National Longitudinal Survey of Youth (NLSY). The NLSY, initiated in 1979, surveyed 12,686 respondents ages 14 to 22 years. The study oversampled minorities and low-income groups; however, with weighted scores, the data provide nationally representative estimates. In 1980, the NLSY added a measure of cognitive ability, the Armed Forces Qualification Test (AFQT). Herrnstein and Murray claim that the AFQT is a psychometrically valid and reliable test that correlates well with standard IQ tests and measures general intelligence (the so-called "g factor")....

The NLSY contains several measures of crime. In 1980, the respondents were asked to complete a standard 20-item self-report delinquency scale. The sample members also self-reported the extent of their "penetration" into the criminal justice system, that is, whether they had been "stopped by the police but not booked, booked but not convicted, convicted but not incarcerated, [or] sentenced to a correctional facility" (Herrnstein and Murray). The NLSY also can determine whether respondents ever were interviewed in jail when the annual NLSY survey was conducted between 1979 and 1990.

Herrnstein and Murray devote a full chapter of *The Bell Curve* to crime. Their general strategy is to show the salience of IQ in crime causation. In using the

NLSY data, they first establish that those with lower AFQT scores have higher odds of penetrating the criminal justice system. They then show that even with SES [socioeconomic status] controlled, the IQ-crime relationship holds both for self-reported crime and for being interviewed while in jail; in fact, SES effects are minimal and, if anything, are positive. They also report that being from a "broken home" increases the risk of crime, but it too does not eliminate IQ's criminogenic influence. They offer a convoluted discussion of the "role of education" in which they show that poor educational performance is associated with being interviewed in jail. Strangely, however, how IQ is implicated in the school-crime relationship is not pursued empirically or theoretically....

Reanalysis of the NLSY Data

We attempt to show below that Herrnstein and Murray's analysis of the NLSY data misleads about the relationship between IQ and crime. In investigating these data, we are prepared, for the sake of argument, to accept their much-contested assumption that general intelligence exists and can be measured through a single IQ score. Furthermore, we are prepared to ignore white-collar crime, a domain of lawlessness peculiarly suited to the cognitive elite. Instead, our goal is to demonstrated that even on their own terms, Herrnstein and Murray's claims about crime are based on questionable science and... furnish a "shaky bridge to policy."

Explained Variation

The existing research suggests that intelligence is *a* risk factor in juvenile and adult crime. The key issue, however, is whether the *magnitude* of IQ's effects on criminal behavior is small or large. Small effects would discourage making intelligence a major determinant of social policy, whereas large effects would suggest that crime control policies should be reformulated to focus directly on cognitive disadvantage—which, of course, is Herrnstein and Murray's position.

A common way in which to assess the importance of a theoretical variable (in this case, IQ) is to see how much variation the variable can explain in type dependent variable (in this case, crime). As readers familiar with statistics know, the term R^2 typically is used to measure the amount of explained variation. Herrnstein and Murray do not report the R^2s for their analyses in the text of *The Bell Curve* but instead confine them to an appendix. As several critics note, the amount of variance that IQ explains across many outcomes is weak to modest. Crime is no exception to this pattern.

... [T]he authors provide the logistic regression analyses for only two measures of crime: being in the top decile on the self-report crime scale and having been interviewed in a correctional facility between 1979 and 1990. With the AFQT score, age, and SES in the equation, the analysis explains 1.5% of the variation in self-reported crime and 9.6% of the variation in being interviewed in jail.

We are interested in assessing the amount of explained variation in the different measures of crime that could be attributed solely to the AFQT. Therefore, we reestimate the Herrnstein and Murray models after removing SES.... The results are reported based on both the 1980 and 1990 sample weights.

... [F]or the three measures of self-reported crime, less than 1% of the variation is explained. Regardless of whether the 1980 or 1990 sample weights are used, the R^2 climbs at most to 2.6% for ever interviewed in jail and to 3.4% for penetration into the criminal justice system (i.e., none to being sentenced to a correctional facility). Again, we would not dismiss these findings on IQ as being unimportant. We question, however, whether explaining less than 4% of the variation in crime warrants an 845-page book whose underlying goal ostensibly is to use science to justify dismantling social welfare approaches to crime and other societal problems.

Misspecified Models

As noted, Herrnstein and Murray seek to establish the causal significance of IQ by showing how AFQT scores are related more strongly to crime than to social class with age controlled in the analysis. Other factors—family structure and education—are considered haphazardly. This methodological approach, which characterizes much of *The Bell Curve*, obviously is flawed....

In a normal scientific approach, Herrnstein and Murray would have first identified the known predictors of crime and then sought to demonstrate that IQ could explain variation above and beyond these criminogenic risk factors.... By limiting their analysis primarily to three factors—IQ, SES, and age—they risk misspecifying their model and inflating the effects of IQ....

The NLSY data set is not ideal for studying crime causation because it was not designed to operationalize the major psychological or sociological theories of criminality. For illustrative purposes, however, we more fully specified Herrnstein and Murray's model by including urban-rural residence, family structure (living with mother and father at age 14), frequency of religious participa-

tion, internal locus of control (youth reports having little influence over things that happen to him), and a range of items that might be seen as indicators of conventional bonds and attitudes (youth would shoplift if unable to support family, would choose to work if he could live comfortably without working, and expects to be working in five years; highest grade youth would like to complete). Like Herrnstein and Murray, we use logistic analysis to assess two crime measures: being in the top decile of self-reported crime and being interviewed in a correctional facility at least once between 1979 and 1990.

... [T]he Herrnstein and Murray three-variable model suggests that IQ is significantly related to self-reported crime. In the more fully specified model, however, IQ no longer retains statistical significance. By contrast, a number of social variables have a significant impact on crime. Thus, being in the top decile on the 20-item self-report scale is positively related to urban residence and social class and is negatively related to living with one's father at age 14, frequency of religious participation, commitment to a work ethic, and academic aspirations.

... [I]n the fully specified model, IQ's effects on being interviewed in a correctional facility are reduced but not eliminated. Even so, the crime measure is related negatively to living with one's father at age 14, religious participation, expectations of being able to work, and academic aspirations.

These analyses are not simply an exercise in statistical gymnastics but rather make a telling point: The effects of the sociological variables are not eliminated by IQ and, in fact, outweigh the causal importance of intelligence.... [T]heir analysis pits IQ against a sociological variable,

SES, long known to be a weak predictor of crime. On this basis, they dismiss social welfare interventions and urge that social policy be driven by the overriding reality that people differ in their cognitive abilities.

In their own data, however, the potential importance of social factors could easily have been demonstrated. But to do so would have raised two disturbing—to Herrnstein and Murray—policy implications. First, IQ is merely one of many predictors of crime and, thus, is hardly in a position to dictate the future of crime control policy. Second, because factors such as religious participation, attitudes, conventional bonds, or even living at home with one's father are not immutable, the NLSY data provide a basis for designing programs that target criminogenic risk factors for change.

Crime or Detection?

In both Herrnstein and Murray's and our analysis of the NLSY data, IQ is weakly related or unrelated to self-reported crime but is more strongly related, albeit modestly, to measures of crime that depend on a respondent being processed by the criminal justice system such as being in jail or penetrating into the system (we refer to these as "system measures of crime"). Herrnstein and Murray's explanation for this finding, of course, is that the cognitively disadvantaged are more involved in crime. An alternative explanation, however, is that individuals' levels of intelligence affect not their criminality but rather the likelihood that, if they break the law, they will be caught and processed by the justice system; in short, smarter criminals are better at avoiding detection. The research on this topic is limited, but previous studies tend to suggest that such a detection

effect does not exist or that, if it does exist, it is not substantively meaningful. This conclusion usually is made on the grounds that IQ is related to both self-report and official measures of crime in roughly similar magnitudes.

We hasten to point out that this is *not* the case in the NLSY data, a fact that Herrnstein and Murray ignore. As seen in the more fully specified equations, IQ is not statistically related to self-reported crime but is related to being interviewed in a correctional facility. Furthermore, IQ explains different amounts of variation in self-report and system measures of crime....

THE RELATIVE IMPORTANCE OF IQ AS A CRIMINOGENIC RISK FACTOR

In addition to analyzing NLSY data, Herrnstein and Murray provide a selective review of previous empirical studies that illustrate the negative relationship of IQ to crime. Their review of this research is not so much wrong as it is misleading; although they discuss the IQ-crime link, they remain silent on how powerfully IQ is associated with criminal behavior versus other potential risk factors. Remember, the critical issue is not whether IQ is related to crime but rather whether it is, as Herrnstein and Murray claim, the *overriding* factor. Resolving this criminological question is critical because it is the basis for evaluating Herrnstein and Murray's policy claims. Only if IQ is a powerful risk factor in crime should cognitive differences be allowed to play a salient role in formulating crime control and related social policies.

Perhaps the best method to assess the relative importance of causal variables is through a quantitative research synthesis or meta-analysis, a technique that dates back more than 50 years and that has gained increasing use in medicine and in the social sciences, including criminology, over the past two decades. Meta-analytic techniques are especially useful in providing a relatively precise quantitative assessment of how strongly two variables are associated when their relationship is calculated across a number of studies in which the two variables appear.

Fortuitously, there recently have been four meta-analyses on the predictors of recidivism for various types of adult male offenders and one on male and female juvenile offenders. Taken together, these meta-analyses encompass almost 500 studies and 4,000 effect sizes or correlations between predictors and crime. From these, we abstracted 86 effect sizes or correlations between IQ and recidivism based on studies that assess a total of 42,831 offenders....

Two major conclusions can be drawn. First, the effect size or correlation between IQ and crime is weak to modest in magnitude with no effect size in the meta-analyses for adults exceeding .10. For juveniles, the correlation climbs upward but only to a high of .17. Second, in the relative ranking of predictors, IQ generally is among the weakest of the risk factors assessed in the meta-analyses. For example, across all the meta-analyses, IQ is in the top half of the predictors only once. On average, approximately 80% of the competing risk factors rank as more powerful predictors than intelligence when examining the unweighted effect sizes; the comparable mean score across the weighted effect sizes is about 70%. It appears, therefore, that IQ is hardly the preeminent determinant of crime that Herrnstein and Murray claim it to be.

... [A]mong the most powerful predictors is a class of risk factors that Andrews and Bonta call "criminogenic needs": attitudes, values, beliefs, and behaviors (e.g., having delinquent associates) that support an antisocial lifestyle. ... [C]riminogenic needs usually have larger effect sizes than even the best results in favor of IQ....

Criminogenic need factors not only are robust predictors of crime but also are "dynamic" in nature; that is, they can change and, thus, are amenable to correctional treatment. This reality contravenes the bell curve paradigm put forth by Herrnstein and Murray, which sees crime as rooted in the supposedly immutable trait of low IQ. An approach that stresses criminogenic needs leads to a progressive correctional agenda based on intervention and offender rehabilitation.... Herrnstein and Murray, by embracing the bell curve paradigm and ignoring the scientific evidence on criminogenic needs and rehabilitation, ultimately draw the "logical" but misguided conclusion that punishing the cognitively disadvantaged is the best means of achieving a safer society.

THE BELL CURVE AND CRIME CONTROL POLICY

By itself, Herrnstein and Murray's discussion of IQ and crime might be seen as provocative and as a useful, albeit exaggerated, corrective to those who dismiss out of hand the idea that criminal behavior could be linked to cognitive ability. In the end, however, the agenda of *The Bell Curve* is not science but rather social policy....

The Dangers of Bell Curve Thinking

... As supposed friends of the cognitively disadvantaged, Herrnstein and Murray warn that American society increasingly is being socially and physically segregated by intelligence. They offer the dire prediction that unless this trend is reversed, we will head toward a "custodial state" in which the cognitively advantaged will use their brains, affluence, and political power to have the state isolate, monitor, coercively punish, and generally neglect the well-being of stupid Americans. In Herrnstein and Murray's scenario, fed up with the dangerous and profligate behaviors of low-IQ citizens, the cognitive elite will use their influence to create "a high tech and more lavish version of the Indian reservation for some substantial minority of the nation's population, while the rest of America tries to go about its business."

How might we reverse "the way we are headed"? Herrnstein and Murray's solution is to recreate a society, much like small towns used to be in the 1950s, in which "everyone has a valued place" in local communities and in which life is governed by "simple rules" uncomplicated by unnecessary government interference. And how, then, might this approach solve America's enduring crime problem? In the kinder and gentler society that Herrnstein and Murray envision, steps would be taken to "make it easier to live a virtuous life." Thus, the rules about violating the law would be made "simpler" and highlighted with a bold magic marker so that even the cognitively disadvantaged would understand them....

[T]hese simple crime rules become clear and morally vivid only if violating them has consequences. Legal transgressions would have to trigger unambigu-ously administered *punishments* that give short shrift to personal excuses or social circumstances. This is the way it once was, Herrnstein and Murray claim, back in the 1950s when the United States was morally uncomplicated and crime was commensurately lower....

One might have expected that in advancing this policy proposal, Herrnstein and Murray would have made some attempt to show that it was based on scientific evidence rather than on pure speculation. For example, they might have tried to show that because the United States was "simpler" in the 1950s, the relationship of IQ to crime was much lower in that era than it is in today's complex society where victim ideology and the "abuse excuse" supposedly make moral messages weak and unclear. Or, they might have marshaled cross-cultural data showing that in "simpler" or more communal societies—say, New Zealand —IQ does not predict crime. If they had undertaken these comparative analyses, however, then they would have learned that the data do not support these suppositions.

They also might have tried to cite data showing that maximally effective punishment-based strategies work better with dull people or dull criminals than with smart ones. Again, there are no data to support this idea either in the experimental or the clinical punishment literature....

The danger is not that legislators will rush off to write simpler laws but rather that *The Bell Curve*—and other works like it—will help to legitimize a way of thinking about crime that will both be ineffective and contribute to what Clear (1994) calls the "penal harm movement." This mind-set typically combines three features. First, it reduces the complex phenomenon of crime and its control to a simple equation.... Second, offenders are seen to have some immutable trait, in this case low intelligence. Third, although this trait cannot be changed through the delivery of social services, offenders still can be induced to conform through punishment, that is, by seeing that bad acts have "consequences." Therefore, logic dictates that the solution to crime is to inflict pain on offenders. Indeed, whether in the "custodial state" or in the "virtuous society," Herrnstein and Murray see stupid people who break the law as ending up in jail.

The scientific poverty of this thinking is readily apparent. IQ is at best a modest predictor of crime; many other factors, which are amenable to change, are much stronger criminogenic risk factors; and deterrence-based interventions generally have been shown to be ineffective in reducing, if not positively related to, offender recidivism. In light of this scientific knowledge base, to propose formulating simple rules backed up by punishment as the main solution to crime control strains credulity. Such a proposal could come only from those who are criminologically challenged or intellectually duplicitous....

The Responsible Use of IQ

Although we are highly critical of Herrnstein and Murray's slanted analysis of IQ and crime, we believe that criminologists should not "throw the baby out with the bathwater" and ignore the role of intelligence in crime and corrections. Both the NLSY data and the meta-analyses reveal that IQ is a criminogenic risk factor and, thus, is an individual difference that must be included in theories of crime causation....

Herrnstein and Murray favor an approach to IQ that stresses the immutability of cognitive ability and the ineffectiveness of government-run interventions aimed at improving people's lives (other than, of course, building a "simpler" society). By contrast, we see IQ as information that can be used to design and deliver more effective treatment interventions. In the end, when people violate the law, Herrnstein and Murray's policy agenda offers punishment and incapacitation. Our agenda offers the hope, rooted in scientific criminology, that positive behavioral change is possible and can be made more likely when treatment interventions take into account people's individual differences including their intellectual competencies.

CONCLUSION: INTELLIGENT CRIMINOLOGY

Close scrutiny of *The Bell Curve* reveals both the lack of and the important role to be played by intelligent criminology. We argue that Herrnstein and Murray are "cognitively challenged" criminologists. Their analysis exaggerates the causal importance of intelligence in criminal behavior and ignores an enormous body of research on competing predictors of crime. Their failure to consider alternative criminogenic risk factors is inexcusable not only because the research documenting their salience is readily available but also because doing so leads them to justify ill-conceived, repressive crime policies. By portraying offenders as driven into crime predominantly by cognitive disadvantage, Herrnstein and Murray mask the reality that stronger risk factors not only exist but also are amenable to effective correctional intervention.

We hope, however, that we have illuminated how positivist criminology can be valuable in deconstructing bell curve "science" and in revealing its ideological base. In this instance, we tried to move beyond the type of broad, ideologically inspired condemnation found in many reviews of Herrnstein and Murray's work. Instead, our goal was to show that the best way in which to fashion an intelligent criminological response to *The Bell Curve* was to draw on the discipline's empirical knowledge base. To the extent that we have achieved this goal, we trust that we have provided a more general lesson in the power of a scientific approach to criminology to combat mean-spirited ideology and to justify confronting crime with a more progressive policy agenda.

REFERENCES

Glass, Gene V., Barry McGaw, and Mary Lee Smith. 1981. *Meta-Analysis in Social Research.* Beverly Hills, CA: Sage.

Harland, Alan T., ed. 1996. *Choosing Correctional Options That Work: Defining the Demand and Evaluating the Supply.* Thousand Oaks, CA: Sage.

Hauser, Robert M. 1995. "Symposium: *The Bell Curve.*" *Contemporary Sociology* 24: 149–153.

Hunt, Morton. 1997. *How Science Takes Stock: The Story of Meta-Analysis.* New York: Russell Sage.

Ward, David A. and Charles R. Tittle. 1994. "IQ and Delinquency: A Test of Two Competing Explanations." *Journal of Quantitative Criminology* 10: 189–212.

POSTSCRIPT

Does IQ Significantly Contribute to Crime?

In the parlance of philosophy of science, a "paradigmatic shift" may be occurring, at least if Herrnstein and Murray are to be believed (Cullen et al.'s acknowledgment of the limited role of IQ actually lends some support to this thesis). Since the time of criminologist Edwin Sutherland, biological factors as causes of crime were viewed as a negative heuristic. Following the horrors of the Nazi genocide program in the 1940s, genetic links to crime were even more vehemently rejected as terrible, dangerous criminology, if not evil.

Yet there have always been at least some distinguished scholars, including within criminology and psychology, who long for a reconsideration of biological influences. Today, unlike 20 or 30 years ago, virtually all standard texts dealing with causes of crime examine biological variants. These often are no longer treated exclusively as historical relics (e.g., discussions of highly selected aspects of pioneer criminologist Cesare Lombroso and other nineteenth-century writings). Does this mean that a paradigmatic shift is occurring within criminology and criminal justice? Will criminology students now be trained in biology, physiology, and genetics, instead of sociology, political science, and traditional psychology? Will structural theories of crime (environmental, sociocultural explanations) be abandoned?

Probably not. As Cullen et al. make clear, the task of sound theory is to explain variations in behavior. They argue that IQ explains relatively little about variations in crime, while traditional independent variables (causes) such as socioeconomic status, neighborhood, peers, and so on explain far more.

A related issue is that genetic explanations are only one variant of biological ones. For instance, diet, presence of lead in the home, neurological disorders, toxic poisoning, and many other biological factors could contribute to crime (and other forms of behavior). These generally have little direct relation to genetics (such correlations are unlikely to be passed on or be disproportionately in one group of people if these factors are removed). While these factors still explain a relatively small percentage of variations in crime rates, they are far more palpable empirically, theoretically, and ethically to most criminologists. From a sociology of knowledge perspective, it is intriguing to theorize about why genetic-biological theories are currently emerging in abundance (Cullen et al., like many others, simply link it with the conservative political mood America is currently in).

Part of the reason why *The Bell Curve* has been so vehemently attacked by traditional scholars may be that they perceive a hidden racist agenda in efforts to link IQ with negative behavior such as crime. Although the studies drawn from in the excerpt by Herrnstein and Murray deal with white subjects, much of the thrust of their book seems to be developing the argument that blacks, on average, have lower IQs and, hence, cannot compete as well in a rapidly changing technological society. For many, the political and moral implications of the *Bell Curve* theory are extremely harmful. For example, neither side considers the logical, if hideous, treatment modality implicit in the IQ-crime theory: sterilization or extermination of "biologically unfit" people. For the first third of the twentieth century, at least 16 states had sterilization laws. In *Buck v. Bell* (1927) Chief Justice Oliver Wendell Holmes proclaimed, "Three generations of imbeciles are enough," allowing Virginia to forceably sterilize a woman. And many sociology textbooks before World War II devoted several pages to favorable discussions of eugenics.

Another policy implication of the theory not considered fully has been posed by independent criminological scholar Horst Senger, who stated, "Those who claim they have found a gene for criminality must explain how a gene knows what is a crime.... They will also have to abolish the concept of guilt, for the born criminal can hardly be more responsible for his supposed criminality than for the color of his eye."

If IQ does influence criminal behavior, then there are many additional issues to address. Luckily, there is a growing literature dealing with this controversy. Among the best works looking at IQ testing from both the sociology of knowledge and the philosophy of science perspectives are S. Gould, *The Mismeasure of Man* (W. W. Norton, 1996); L. Kamin, *The Science and Politics of IQ* (Lawrence Erlbaum, 1974); L. Kamin, "Behind the Curve," *Scientific American* (February 1995); and C. Fischer et al., *Inequality by Design* (Princeton University Press, 1996). Special issues devoted to *The Bell Curve* include *Science and Society* (Summer 1996), *The Economist* (July 13, 1996), *Current Anthropology* (February 1996), *American Behavioral Scientist* (September/October 1995), and *The Black Scholar* (Winter 1995). Anthologies include R. Jacoby and N. Glauberman, eds., *The Bell Curve Debate: History, Documents, Opinions* (Times Books, 1995) and *Measured Lies: The Bell Curve Examined* edited by J. L. Kincheles, S. R. Steinberg, and A. D. Gresson III (St. Martin's Press, 1996).

Several excellent studies and texts utilizing biological theories include "Gene-Based Evolutionary Theories in Criminology," by L. Ellis and A. Walsh, *Criminology* (May 1997); "Criminologenic Traits," by R. Herrnstein, in J. Q. Wilson and J. Petersilia, eds., *Crime* (ICS Press, 1995); *Biosociology* by A. Walsh (Praeger, 1995), chapter 8; *Psychopathology of Crime* by A. Raine (Academic Press, 1993); G. Bock and J. Goode, eds., *Genetics of Criminal and Antisocial Behavior* (John Wiley, 1996); L. Ellis and H. Hoffman, eds., *Crime in Biological, Social, and Moral Contexts* (Praeger, 1990); and a work that is sympathetic toward the *Bell Curve* thesis, J. P. Rushton's *Race, Evolution and Behavior: A Life History Perspective* (Transaction, 1995). Also of interest is *Biology of Violence* by R. Wright (Vintage, 1995).

ISSUE 4

Is Street Crime More Serious Than White-Collar Crime?

YES: James Q. Wilson and Richard J. Herrnstein, from *Crime and Human Nature* (Simon & Schuster, 1985)

NO: Jeffrey Reiman, from *The Rich Get Richer and the Poor Get Prison: Ideology, Class, and Criminal Justice,* 5th ed. (Allyn & Bacon, 1998)

ISSUE SUMMARY

YES: Professor of management and public policy James Q. Wilson and the late psychologist Richard J. Herrnstein argue that the focus of crime study ought to be on people who "hit, rape, murder, steal, and threaten."

NO: Professor of philosophy Jeffrey Reiman contends that a focus on street crimes is little more than a cover-up for more serious crimes such as pollution, medical malpractice, and dangerous working conditions that go uncorrected.

Scholars and the general public differ intellectually, ideologically, and politically in their definitions of crime as well as with regard to why it exists. Liberal, conservative, and radical ideologies are likely to generate different definitions and explanations of crime.

One aspect of American society is its extremely heavy emphasis on economic success. Apparently, for many who desire the material benefits that "the haves" seem to take for granted but who are thwarted by lack of training or skills or by discrimination, one recourse is to engage in predatory street crimes. Others are able to succeed financially because they are taught how to and are fully allowed to participate: they can attend good schools, join a solid corporation, and work their way up the ladder. Probably very few business executive types would dream of holding up someone, breaking into a house, or attacking someone in a rage.

Yet in certain companies, the pressure to succeed, to keep corporate profits up, and to fulfill the expectations of managers and administrators drives many to commit white-collar crimes. No one knows for sure how many street crimes occur each day (many are not reported). Nor do we know how many white-collar crimes occur each day. The latter are much more likely to be carefully hidden and their consequences delayed for months or even years. Moreover, white-collar crimes are far more likely to be dismissed as "just another shrewd business practice by an ambitious executive in order to keep ahead of competitors." Most of us never directly see the results of white-collar crimes, nor do we know many people who are visibly harmed by them. By contrast, many of us have been victims of street crimes or know such victims. The results of a direct physical assault or the fear of discovering a burglarized home or a stolen car are relatively easy to observe in a victim of these crimes.

But how should we view those who shiver in the cold because their utility bills were hiked illegally, forcing them to keep their thermostats under 60 degrees? Or those robbed of health because of lung infections contracted while they worked in unsafe mines or around unsafe chemicals? Are they usually thought of as the victims of criminals? Are people who are killed in traffic accidents because their automobiles left the factory in unsafe condition —with the factory's full knowledge and approval—thought of as murder victims?

Frequently, both the general public and criminologists concentrate on street crimes, their perpetrators and victims, while ignoring white-collar crimes. But beginning with the seminal work of Edwin Sutherland, *White Collar Crime,* some criminologists have demonstrated concern with this form of violation.

In spite of the fact that, in general, white-collar crime receives less attention and less serious attention than street crime, several white-collar criminals have in recent years been the focus of extensive media coverage. Yet in almost each case, the criminals have been viewed as isolated deviants who just happened to engage in wrongdoing. Neither the organizations for which they worked nor the broader corporate system and the values it promotes came under much scrutiny by the public. Among the more widely known corporate criminals of the past few years are Ivan Boesky and Michael Milken (who served 22 months in prison for a variety of securities law violations).

White-collar crimes are currently being investigated at the top levels of government. For example, part of the investigation into the Whitewater Development Company, an Arkansas company linked to a failed savings and loan institution with which President Bill Clinton and Hillary Clinton were involved (when he was still governor of Arkansas), has resulted in the imprisonment of some close friends of the Clintons. A congressional committee was organized to look into possible wrongdoing on the part of Hillary Clinton herself, as well as the Arkansas law firm she was a part of. In spite of this and other sensational cases and allegations of corruption, corporate misdealings, and white-collar crime, the focus in the general public's perception and the media remains on street criminals. Is this fair?

As you study the position of James Q. Wilson and Richard J. Herrnstein and that of Jeffrey Reiman, notice that it remains problematic as to not only what crime is and what its most adequate scientific explanations are but also which crimes are the most harmful and dangerous to members of society.

YES

James Q. Wilson and Richard J. Herrnstein

CRIME AND HUMAN NATURE

CRIME AND ITS EXPLANATION

Predatory street crimes are most commonly committed by young males. Violent crimes are more common in big cities than in small ones. High rates of criminality tend to run in families. The persons who frequently commit the most serious crimes typically begin their criminal careers at a quite young age. Persons who turn out to be criminals usually do not do very well in school. Young men who drive recklessly and have many accidents tend to be similar to those who commit crimes. Programs designed to rehabilitate high-rate offenders have not been shown to have much success, and those programs that do manage to reduce criminality among certain kinds of offenders often increase it among others.

These facts about crime—some well known, some not so well known— are not merely statements about traits that happen occasionally, or in some places but not others, to describe criminals. They are statements that, insofar as we can tell, are pretty much true everywhere. They are statements, in short, about human nature as much as about crime.

All serious political and moral philosophy, and thus any serious social inquiry, must begin with an understanding of human nature. Though society and its institutions shape man, man's nature sets limits on the kinds of societies we can have. Cicero said that the nature of law must be founded on the nature of man (*a natura hominis discenda est natura juris*).... We could have chosen to understand human nature by studying work, or sexuality, or political activity; we chose instead to approach it through the study of crime, in part out of curiosity and in part because crime, more dramatically than other forms of behavior, exposes the connection between individual dispositions and the social order.

The problem of social order is fundamental: How can mankind live together in reasonable order? Every society has, by definition, solved that problem to some degree, but not all have done so with equal success or without paying a high cost in other things—such as liberty—that we also value. If we believe that man is naturally good, we will expect that the problem of order can be rather easily managed; if we believe him to be naturally wicked, we will expect the provision of order to require extraordinary measures; if we believe his nature to be infinitely plastic, we will think the problem of order can be solved entirely by plan and that we may pick and choose freely among all possible plans. Since every known society has experienced crime, no society has ever entirely solved the problem of order. The fact that crime is universal may suggest that man's nature is not infinitely malleable, though some people never cease searching for an anvil and hammer sufficient to bend it to their will.

Some societies seem better able than others to sustain order without making unacceptable sacrifices in personal freedom, and in every society the level of order is greater at some times than at others. These systematic and oft-remarked differences in the level of crime across time and place suggest that there is something worth explaining. But to find that explanation, one cannot begin with the society as a whole or its historical context, for what needs explanation is not the behavior of "society" but the behavior of individuals making up a society. Our intention is to offer as comprehensive an explanation as we can manage of why some individuals are more likely than others to commit crimes.

THE PROBLEM OF EXPLANATION

That intention is not easily realized, for at least three reasons. First, crime is neither easily observed nor readily measured. ... [T]here is no way of knowing the true crime rate of a society or even of a given individual. Any explanation of why in-

dividuals differ in their law-abidingness may well founder on measurement errors. If we show that Tom, who we think has committed a crime, differs in certain interesting ways from Dick, who we think has not, when in fact both Tom and Dick have committed a crime, then the "explanation" is meaningless.

Second, crime is very common, especially among males. Using interviews and questionnaires, scholars have discovered that the majority of all young males have broken the law at least once by a relatively early age. By examining the police records of boys of a given age living in one place, criminologists have learned that a surprisingly large fraction of all males will be arrested at least once in their lives for something more serious than a traffic infraction. Marvin Wolfgang found that 35 percent of all the males born in Philadelphia in 1945 and living there between the ages of ten and eighteen had been arrested at least once by their eighteenth birthday.[1] Nor is this a peculiarly American phenomenon. Various surveys have found that the proportion of British males who had been convicted in court before their twenty-first birthday ranged from 15 percent in the nation as a whole to 31 percent for a group of boys raised in London. David Farrington estimates that 44 percent of all the males in "law-abiding" Britain will be arrested sometime in their lives.[2] If committing a crime at least once is so commonplace, then it is quite likely that there will be few, if any, large differences between those who never break the law and those who break it at least once—even if we had certain knowledge of which was which. Chance events as much as or more than individual predispositions will determine who commits a crime.

Third, the word "crime" can be applied to such varied behavior that it is not clear that it is a meaningful category of analysis. Stealing a comic book, punching a friend, cheating on a tax return, murdering a wife, robbing a bank, bribing a politician, hijacking an airplane—these and countless other acts are all crimes. Crime is as broad a category as disease, and perhaps as useless. To explain why one person has ever committed a crime and another has not may be as pointless as explaining why one person has ever gotten sick and another has not. We are not convinced that "crime" is so broad a category as to be absolutely meaningless—surely it is not irrelevant that crime is that form of behavior that is against the law—but we do acknowledge that it is difficult to provide a true and interesting explanation for actions that differ so much in their legal and subjective meanings.

To deal with these three difficulties, we propose to confine ourselves, for the most part, to explaining why some persons commit serious crimes at a high rate and others do not. By looking mainly at serious crimes, we escape the problem of comparing persons who park by a fire hydrant to persons who rob banks. By focusing on high-rate offenders, we do not need to distinguish between those who never break the law and those who (for perhaps chance reasons) break it only once or twice. And if we assume (as we do) that our criminal statistics are usually good enough to identify persons who commit a lot of crimes even if these data are poor at identifying accurately those who commit only one or two, then we can be less concerned with measurement errors.

THE MEANING OF CRIME

A crime is any act committed in violation of a law that prohibits it and authorizes punishment for its commission. If we propose to confine our attention chiefly to persons who commit serious crimes at high rates, then we must specify what we mean by "serious." The arguments we shall make and the evidence we shall cite... will chiefly refer to aggressive, violent, or larcenous behavior; they will be, for the most part, about persons who hit, rape, murder, steal, and threaten.

In part, this limited focus is an unfortunate accident: We report only what others have studied, and by and large they have studied the causes of what we call predatory street crime. We would like to draw on research into a wider variety of law-violating behavior—embezzlement, sexual deviance, bribery, extortion, fraud—but very little such research exists.

But there is an advantage to this emphasis on predatory crime. Such behavior, except when justified by particular, well-understood circumstances (such as war), is condemned, in all societies and in all historical periods, by ancient tradition, moral sentiments, and formal law. Graeme Newman... interviewed people in six nations (India, Indonesia, Iran, Italy, the United States, and Yugoslavia) about their attitudes toward a variety of behaviors and concluded that there is a high—indeed, virtually universal—agreement that certain of these behaviors were wrong and should be prohibited by law.[3] Robbery, stealing, incest, and factory pollution were condemned by overwhelming majorities in every society; by contrast, abortion and homosexuality, among other acts, were thought to be crimes in some places but not in others. Interestingly, the characteristics of the individual respondents in these countries —their age, sex, education, social class— did not make much difference in what they thought should be treated as crimes. Newman's finding merely reinforces a fact long understood by anthropologists: Certain acts are regarded as wrong by every society, preliterate as well as literate; that among these "universal crimes" are murder, theft, robbery, and incest.[4]

Moreover, people in different societies rate the seriousness of offenses, especially the universal crimes, in about the same way. Thorsten Sellin and Marvin E. Wolfgang developed a scale to measure the relative gravity of 141 separate offenses. This scale has been found to be remarkably stable, producing similar rankings among both American citizens and prison inmates,[5] as well as among Canadians,[6] Puerto Ricans,[7] Taiwanese,[8] and Belgian Congolese.[9]

By drawing on empirical studies of behaviors that are universally regarded as wrong and similarly ranked as to gravity, we can be confident that we are in fact theorizing about *crime* and human nature and not about actions that people may or may not think are wrong. If the studies to which we refer were to include commercial price-fixing, political corruption, or industrial monopolization, we would have to deal with the fact that in many countries these actions are not regarded as criminal at all. If an American business executive were to bring all of the nation's chemical industries under his control, he would be indicted for having formed a monopoly; a British business executive who did the same thing might be elevated to the peerage for having created a valuable industrial empire. Similarly, by omitting studies of sexual deviance (except forcible rape), we avoid modifying our theory to take into account changing social standards as to the wrongness of these acts and the legal culpability of their perpetrators. In short, we seek ... to explain why some persons are more likely than others to do things that all societies condemn and punish.

To state the same thing a bit differently, we will be concerned more with criminality than with crime. Travis Hirschi and Michael Gottfredson have explained this important distinction as follows. *Crimes* are short-term, circumscribed events that result from the (perhaps fortuitous) coming together of an individual having certain characteristics and an opportunity having certain (immediate and deferred) costs and benefits.... *Criminality* refers to "stable differences across individuals in the propensity to commit criminal (or equivalent) acts."[10] The "equivalent" acts will be those that satisfy, perhaps in entirely legal ways, the same traits and predispositions that lead, in other circumstances, to crime. For example, a male who is very impulsive and so cannot resist temptation may, depending on circumstances, take toys from his playmates, money from his mother, billfolds from strangers, stamps from the office, liquor in the morning, extra chocolate cake at dinner time, and a nap whenever he feels like it. Some of these actions break the law, some do not.

THE CATEGORIES OF EXPLANATION

Because we state that we intend to emphasize individual differences in behavior or predisposition, some readers may feel that we are shaping the argument in an improper manner. These critics believe that one can explain crime only by beginning with the society in which it is found. Emile Durkheim wrote: "We must, then, seek the explanation of social life in the nature of society itself."[11] Or, put another way, the whole is more than the sum of its parts. We do not deny that social arrangements and institutions, and the ancient customs that result from living and working together, affect behavior, often profoundly. But no explanation of social life explains anything until it explains individual behavior. Whatever significance we attach to ethnicity, social class, national character, the opinions of peers, or the messages of the mass media, the only test of their explanatory power is their ability to account for differences in how individuals, or groups of individuals, behave.

Explaining individual differences is an enterprise much resisted by some scholars. To them, this activity implies reducing everything to psychology, often referred to as "mere psychology." David J. Bordua, a sociologist, has pointed out the bias that can result from an excessive preference for social explanations over psychological ones.[12] Many criminologists, he comments, will observe a boy who becomes delinquent after being humiliated by his teacher or fired by his employer, and will conclude that his delinquency is explained by his "social class." But if the boy becomes delinquent after having been humiliated by his father or spurned by his girl friend, these scholars will deny that these events are explanations because they are "psychological." Teachers and employers are agents of the class structure, fathers and girl friends are not; therefore, the behavior of teachers and employers must be more important.

We believe that one can supply an explanation of criminality—and more important, of law-abidingness—that begins with the individual in, or even before, infancy and that takes into account the impact on him of subsequent experiences in the family, the school, the neighborhood, the labor market, the criminal justice system, and society at large. Yet even readers who accept this plan of inquiry as reasonable may still doubt its importance. To some, explaining crime is unnecessary because they think the explanation is already known; to others, it is impossible, since they think it unknowable.

Having taught a course on the causes of crime, and having spoken to many friends about our research, we have become acutely aware that there is scarcely any topic—except, perhaps, what is wrong with the Boston Red Sox or the Chicago Cubs—on which people have more confident opinions. Crime is caused, we are told, by the baby boom, permissive parents, brutal parents, incompetent schools, racial discrimination, lenient judges, the decline of organized religion, televised violence, drug addiction, ghetto unemployment, or the capitalist system. We note certain patterns in the proffered explanations. Our tough-minded friends blame crime on the failings of the criminal justice system; our tender-minded ones blame it on the failings of society.

We have no *a priori* quarrel with any of these explanations, but we wonder whether all can be true, or true to the same degree. The baby boom may help explain why crime rose in the 1960s and 1970s, but it cannot explain why some members of that boom became criminals and others did not. It is hard to imagine that both permissive and brutal parents produce the same kind of criminals, though it is conceivable that each may contribute to a different kind of criminality. Many children may attend bad schools, but only a small minority become serious criminals. And in any case, there is no agreement as to what constitutes an incompetent school. Is it an overly strict one that "labels" mischievous children as delinquents, or is it an overly lax one that allows normal mischief to degenerate into true delinquency? Does broadcast violence include a football or hockey game, or only a detective story in which somebody shoots somebody else? Economic conditions may affect crime, but since crime rates were lower in the Great Depression than during the prosperous years of the 1960s, the effect is, at best, not obvious or simple. The sentences given by judges may affect the crime rate, but we are struck by the fact that the most serious criminals begin offending at a very early age, long before they encounter, or probably even hear of, judges, whereas those who do not commit their first crime until they are adults (when, presumably, they have some knowledge of law and the courts) are the least likely to have a long or active criminal career. Racism and capitalism may contribute to crime, but the connection must be rather complicated, since crime has risen in the United States (and other nations) most rapidly during recent times, when we have surely become less racist and (given the growth of governmental controls on business) less capitalist. In any event, high crime rates can be found in socialist as well as capitalist nations, and some capitalist nations, such as Japan and Switzerland, have very little crime. In view of all this, some sorting out of these explanations might be useful.

But when we discuss our aims with scholars who study crime, we hear something quite different. There is no well-accepted theory of the causes of crime, we are told, and it is unlikely that one can be constructed. Many

explanations have been advanced, but all have been criticized. What is most needed is more research, not better theories. Any theory specific enough to be testable will not explain very much, whereas any theory broad enough to explain a great deal will not be testable. It is only because they are friends that some of our colleagues refrain from muttering about fools rushing in where wise men, if not angels, fear to tread....

But there is one version of the claim that explaining crime is impossible to which we wish to take immediate exception. That is the view, heard most frequently from those involved with criminals on a case-by-case basis (probation officers and therapists, for example), that the causes of crime are unique to the individual criminal. Thus, one cannot generalize about crime because each criminal is different. Now, in one sense that argument is true—no two offenders are exactly alike. But we are struck by the fact that there are certain obvious patterns to criminality, suggesting that something more than random individual differences is at work. We think these obvious patterns, if nothing else, can be explained.

PATTERNS IN CRIMINALITY

Crime is an activity disproportionately carried out by young men living in large cities. There are old criminals, and female ones, and rural and small-town ones, but, to a much greater degree than would be expected by chance, criminals are young urban males. This is true, insofar as we can tell, in every society that keeps any reasonable criminal statistics.[13] These facts are obvious to all, but sometimes their significance is overlooked. Much time and effort may be expended in trying to discover whether children from broken homes are more likely to be criminals than those from intact ones, or whether children who watch television a lot are more likely to be aggressive than those who watch it less. These are interesting questions, and we shall have something to say about them, but even if they are answered satisfactorily, we will have explained rather little about the major differences in criminality. Most children raised in broken homes do not become serious offenders; roughly half of such children are girls, and... females are often only one-tenth as likely as males to commit crimes. Crime existed abundantly long before the advent of television and would continue long after any hint of violence was expunged from TV programs. Any worthwhile explanation of crime must account for the major, persistent differences in criminality.

The fact that these regularities exist suggests that it is not impossible, in principle, to provide a coherent explanation of crime. It is not like trying to explain why some people prefer vanilla ice cream and others chocolate. And as we shall see... there are other regularities in criminality beyond those associated with age, sex, and place. There is mounting evidence that, on the average, offenders differ from nonoffenders in physique, intelligence, and personality. Some of these differences may not themselves be a cause of crime but only a visible indicator of some other factor that does contribute to crime.... [W]e shall suggest that a certain physique is related to criminality, not because it causes people to break the law, but because a particular body type is associated with temperamental traits that predispose people to offending. Other individual differences, such as in personality, may directly contribute to criminality.

There are two apparent patterns in criminality that we have yet to mention, though they are no doubt uppermost in the minds of many readers—class and race. To many people, it is obvious that differences in social class, however defined, are strongly associated with law-breaking. The poor, the unemployed, or the "underclass" are more likely than the well-to-do, the employed, or the "respectable poor" to commit certain kinds of crimes. We are reluctant, however, at least at the outset, to use class as a major category of explanations of differences in criminality for two reasons.

First, scholars who readily agree on the importance of age, sex, and place as factors related to crime disagree vigorously as to whether social class, however defined, is associated with crime. Their dispute may strike readers who have worked hard to move out of slums and into middle-class suburbs as rather bizarre; can anyone seriously doubt that better-off neighborhoods are safer than poorer ones? As John Braithwaite has remarked, "It is hardly plausible that one can totally explain away the higher risks of being mugged and raped in lower class areas as a consequence of the activities of middle class people who come into the area to perpetrate such acts."[14]

We have much sympathy with his view, but we must recognize that there are arguments against it. When Charles R. Tittle, Wayne J. Villemez, and Douglas A. Smith reviewed thirty-five studies of the relationship between crime rates and social class, they found only a slight association between the two variables.[15] When crime was measured using official (e.g., police) reports, the connection with social class was stronger than when it was measured using self-reports (the crimes admitted to by individuals filling out a questionnaire or responding to an interview). This conclusion has been challenged by other scholars who find, on the basis of more extensive self-report data than any previously used, that crime, especially serious crime, is much more prevalent among lower-class youth.[16] Michael J. Hindelang, Travis Hirschi, and Joseph G. Weis have shown that self-report studies tend to measure the prevalence of trivial offenses, including many things that would not be considered a crime at all (e.g., skipping school, defying parents, or having unmarried sex).[17] Even when true crimes are reported, they are often so minor (e.g., shoplifting a pack of gum) that it is a mistake—but, alas, a frequently made mistake—to lump such behavior together with burglary and robbery as measures of criminality. We agree with Hindelang et al., as well as with many others,[18] who argue that when crime is properly measured, the relationship between it and social class is strong—lower-class persons are much more likely to have committed a serious "street" crime than upper-status ones. But we recognize that this argument continues to be controversial, and so it seems inappropriate to begin an explanation of criminality by assuming that it is based on class.

Our second reason for not starting with class as a major social factor is, to us, more important. Unlike sex, age, and place, class is an ambiguous concept. A "lower-class" person can be one who has a low income, but that definition lumps together graduate students, old-age pensioners, welfare mothers, and unemployed steelworkers—individuals who would appear to have, as far as

crime is concerned, little in common. Many self-report studies of crime use class categories so broad as to obscure whatever connection may exist between class and criminality.[19] And studies of delinquency typically describe a boy as belonging to the class of his father, even if the boy in his own right, in school or in the labor force, is doing much better or much worse than his father.[20] By lower class one could also mean having a low-prestige occupation, but it is not clear to us why the prestige ranking of one's occupation should have any influence on one's criminality.

Class may, of course, be defined in terms of wealth or income, but using the concept in this way to explain crime, without further clarification, is ambiguous as to cause and effect. One's wealth, income, status, or relationship to the means of production could cause certain behavior (e.g., "poor people must steal to eat"), or they could themselves be caused by other factors (impulsive persons with low verbal skills tend to be poor and to steal). By contrast, one's criminality cannot be the cause of, say, one's age or sex....

Race is also a controversial and ambiguous concept in criminological research. Every study of crime using official data shows that blacks are heavily over-represented among persons arrested, convicted, and imprisoned.[21] Some people, however, suspect that official reports are contaminated by the racial bias of those who compile them. Self-report studies, by contrast, tend to show fewer racial differences in criminality, but these studies have the same defect with respect to race as they do with regard to class—they overcount trivial offenses, in which the races do not differ, and undercount the more serious offenses, in which they do differ.[22] Moreover, surveys of the victims of crimes reveal that of the offenders whose racial identity could be discerned by their victims, about half were black; for the most serious offenses, two-thirds were black.[23] Though there may well be some racial bias in arrests, prosecutions, and sentences, there is no evidence . . . that it is so great as to account for the disproportionate involvement of blacks in serious crime, as revealed by both police and victimization data and by interviews with prison inmates.[24]

Our reason for not regarding, at least at the outset, race as a source of individual differences in criminality is not that we doubt that blacks are overrepresented in crime. Rather, there are two other considerations. First, racial differences exist in some societies and not others, yet all societies have crime. Though racial factors may affect the crime rate, the fundamental explanation for individual differences in criminality ought to be based—indeed, must be based, if it is to be a general explanation—on factors that are common to all societies.

Second, we find the concept of race to be ambiguous, but in a different way from the ambiguity of class. There is no reason to believe that the genes determining one's skin pigmentation also affect criminality. At one time in this nation's history, persons of Irish descent were heavily overrepresented among those who had committed some crime, but it would have been foolish then to postulate a trait called "Irishness" as an explanation. If racial or ethnic identity affects the likelihood of committing a crime, it must be because that identity co-varies with other characteristics and experiences that affect criminality. The proper line of inquiry, then, is first to examine those other characteristics and experiences to see how

and to what extent they predispose an individual toward crime, and then to consider what, if anything, is left unexplained in the observed connection between crime and racial identity. After examining constitutional, familial, educational, economic, neighborhood, and historical factors, there may or may not be anything left to say on the subject of race. . . .

ARE THERE TYPES OF CRIMINALS?

We are concerned mainly with explaining criminality—why some people are more likely than others to commit, at a high rate, one or more of the universal crimes. But even if the behaviors with which we are concerned are alike in being universally regarded as serious crimes, are not the *motives* for these crimes so various that they cannot all be explained by one theory? Possibly. But this objection assumes that what we want to know are the motives of lawbreakers. It is by no means clear that the most interesting or useful way to look at crime is by trying to discover the motives of individual criminals—why some offenders like to steal cash, others like stolen cash plus a chance to beat up on its owner, and still others like violent sex—any more than it is obvious that the best way to understand the economy is by discovering why some persons keep their money in the bank, others use it to buy tickets to boxing matches, and still others use it to buy the favors of a prostitute. The motives of criminal (and of human) behavior are as varied as the behavior itself; we come to an understanding of the general processes shaping crime only when we abstract from particular motives and circumstances to examine the factors that lead people to run greater or lesser risks in choosing a course of action.

To us, offenders differ not so much in what kind of crimes they commit, but in the rate as which they commit them. In this sense, the one-time wife murderer is different from the persistent burglar or the organized drug trafficker—the first man breaks the law but once, the latter two do it every week or every day.... [T]he evidence suggests that persons who frequently break universal laws do not, in fact, specialize very much. A high-rate offender is likely to commit a burglary today and a robbery tomorrow, and sell drugs in between.

Explaining why some persons have a very high rate and others a low one is preferable, we think, to the major alternative to this approach: trying to sort offenders and offenses into certain categories or types. Creating—and arguing about—typologies is a major preoccupation of many students of crime because, having decided that motives are what count and having discovered that there are almost as many motives as there are people, the only way to bring any order to this variety is by reducing all the motives to a few categories, often described as personality types.

For example, a common distinction in criminology is between the "subcultural" offender and the "unsocialized" or "psychopathic" one. The first is a normal person who finds crime rewarding (perhaps because he has learned to commit crimes from friends he admires) and who discounts heavily the risks of being punished. The second is abnormal: He commits crimes because he has a weak conscience and cares little about the opinions of friends. Now, as even the authors of such distinctions acknowledge, these categories overlap (some sub-

cultural thieves, for example, may also take pleasure in beating up on their victims), and not all offenders fit into either category. But to us, the chief difficulty with such typologies is that they direct attention away from individual differences and toward idealized—and abstract—categories.

Crime is correlated, as we have seen, with age, sex, and place of residence, and it is associated... with other stable characteristics of individuals. Understanding those associations is the first task of criminological theory. Our approach is not to ask which persons belong to what category of delinquents but rather to ask whether differences in the frequency with which persons break the law are associated with differences in the rewards of crime, the risks of being punished for a crime, the strength of internalized inhibitions against crime, and the willingness to defer gratifications, and then to ask what biological, developmental, situational, and adaptive processes give rise to these individual characteristics.

NOTES

1. Wolfgang, 1973.
2. Farrington, 1979c, 9$_{25}$, 1981.
3. Newman, G., 1976.
4. Hoebel, 1954.
5. Sellin and Wolfgang, 1964; Figlio, 1972.
6. Akman and Normandeau, 1968.
7. Valez-Diaz and Megargee, 1971.
8. Hsu, cited in Wellford, 1975.
9. DeBoeck and Houschou, cited in Wellford, 1975.
10. Hirschi and Gottfredson, 1984.
11. Durkheim, 1964, p. 102.
12. Bordua, 1962.
13. Radzinowicz and King, 1977; Archer, Gartner, Akert, and Lockwood, 1978.
14. Braithwaite, 1981.
15. Tittle, Villemez, and Smith, 1978.
16. Elliott and Ageton, 1980; Elliott and Huizinga, 1983.

17. Hindelang, Hirschi, and Weis, 1979, 1981.

18. For example, Kleck, 1982.

19. Johnson, R. E., 1979.

20. Braithwaite, 1981.

21. For example, Wolfgang, Figlio, and Sellin, 1972.

22. Hindelang, Hirschi, and Weis, 1979, 1981; Berger and Simon, 1982.

23. Hindelang, Hirschi, and Weis, 1979, p. 1002; Hindelang, 1978.

24. Blumstein, 1982; Petersilia, 1983.

NO

Jeffrey Reiman

A CRIME BY ANY OTHER NAME...

If one individual inflicts a bodily injury upon another which leads to the death of the person attacked we call it manslaughter; on the other hand, if the attacker knows beforehand that the blow will be fatal we call it murder. Murder has also been committed if society places hundreds of workers in such a position that they inevitably come to premature and unnatural ends. Their death is as violent as if they had been stabbed or shot.... Murder has been committed if society knows perfectly well that thousands of workers cannot avoid being sacrificed so long as these conditions are allowed to continue. Murder of this sort is just as culpable as the murder committed by an individual.

—Frederick Engels
The Condition of the Working Class in England

WHAT'S IN A NAME?

If it takes you an hour to read this chapter, by the time you reach the last page, three of your fellow citizens will have been murdered. *During that same time, at least four Americans will die as a result of unhealthy or unsafe conditions in the workplace!* Although these work-related deaths could have been prevented, they are not called murders. Why not? Doesn't a crime by any other name still cause misery and suffering? What's in a name?

The fact is that the label "crime" is not used in America to name all or the worst of the actions that cause misery and suffering to Americans. It is primarily reserved for the dangerous actions of the poor.

In the February 21, 1993, edition of the *New York Times*, an article appears with the headline: "Company in Mine Deaths Set to Pay Big Fine." It describes an agreement by the owners of a Kentucky mine to pay a fine for safety misconduct that may have led to "the worst American mining accident in nearly a decade." Ten workers died in a methane explosion, and the company pleaded guilty to "a pattern of safety misconduct" that included falsifying reports of methane levels and requiring miners to work under unsupported roofs. The company was fined $3.75 million. The acting foreman at the mine was the only individual charged by the federal government, and for his

From Jeffrey Reiman, *The Rich Get Richer and the Poor Get Prison: Ideology, Class, and Criminal Justice,* 5th ed. (Allyn & Bacon, 1998). Copyright © 1979, 1984, 1990, 1995, 1998 by Jeffrey Reiman. Reprinted by permission of Allyn & Bacon. Notes omitted.

cooperation with the investigation, prosecutors were recommending that he receive the minimum sentence: probation to six months in prison. The company's president expressed regret for the tragedy that occurred. And the U.S. attorney said he hoped the case "sent a clear message that violations of Federal safety and health regulations that endanger the lives of our citizens will not be tolerated."

Compare this with the story of Colin Ferguson, who prompted an editorial in the *New York Times* of December 10, 1993, with the headline: "Mass Murder on the 5:33." A few days earlier, Colin had boarded a commuter train in Garden City, Long Island, and methodically shot passengers with a 9-millimeter pistol, killing 5 and wounding 18. Colin Ferguson was surely a murderer, maybe a mass murderer. My question is, Why wasn't the death of the miners also murder? Why weren't those responsible for subjecting ten miners to deadly conditions also "mass murderers"?

Why do ten dead miners amount to an "accident," a "tragedy," and five dead commuters a "mass murder"? "Murder" suggests a murderer, whereas "accident" and "tragedy" suggest the work of impersonal forces. But the charge against the company that owned the mine said that they "repeatedly exposed the mine's work crews to danger and that such conditions were frequently concealed from Federal inspectors responsible for enforcing the mine safety act." And the acting foreman admitted to falsifying records of methane levels only two months before the fatal blast. Someone was responsible for the conditions that led to the death of ten miners. Is that person not a murderer, perhaps even a *mass murderer?*

These questions are at this point rhetorical. My aim is not to discuss this case but rather to point to the blinders we wear when we look at such an "accident." There was an investigation. One person, the acting foreman, was held responsible for falsifying records. He is to be sentenced to six months in prison (at most). The company was fined. But no one will be tried for *murder.* No one will be thought of as a murderer. *Why not? ...*

Didn't those miners have a right to protection from the violence that took their lives? *And if not, why not?*

Once we are ready to ask this question seriously, we are in a position to see that the reality of crime—that is, the acts we label crime, the acts we think of as crime, the actors and actions we treat as criminal—is *created:* It is an image shaped by decisions as to *what* will be called crime and *who* will be treated as a criminal.

THE CARNIVAL MIRROR

It is sometimes coyly observed that the quickest and cheapest way to eliminate crime would be to throw out all the criminal laws. There is a sliver of truth to this view. Without criminal laws, there would indeed be no "crimes." There would, however, still be dangerous acts. This is why we cannot really solve our crime problem quite so simply. The criminal law *labels* some acts "crimes." In doing this, it identifies those acts as so dangerous that we must use the extreme methods of criminal justice to protect ourselves against them. This does not mean the criminal law *creates* crime—it simply "mirrors" real dangers that threaten us. What is true of the criminal law is true of the whole justice system. If police did not arrest or prosecutors charge or juries convict, there would be no "criminals." This does not mean that police or prosecutors or juries create criminals any more than legislators do. They *react* to real dangers in society. The criminal justice system—from lawmakers to law enforcers—is just a mirror of the real dangers that lurk in our midst. *Or so we are told.*

How accurate is this mirror? We need to answer this in order to know whether or how well the criminal justice system is protecting us against the real threats to our well-being. The more accurate a mirror is, the more the image it shows is created by the reality it reflects. The more misshapen a mirror is, the more the distorted image it shows is created by the mirror, not by the reality reflected. It is in this sense that I will argue that the image of crime is created: The American criminal justice system is a mirror that shows a distorted image of the dangers that threaten us—an image created more by the shape of the mirror than by the reality reflected. What do we see when we look in the criminal justice mirror?

On the morning of September 16, 1975, the *Washington Post* carried an article in its local news section headlined "Arrest Data Reveal Profile of a Suspect." The article reported the results of a study of crime in Prince George's County, a suburb of Washington, D.C. It read in part as follows:

The typical suspect in serious crime in Prince George's County is a black male, aged 14 to 19....

This report is hardly a surprise. The portrait it paints of "the typical suspect in serious crime" is probably a pretty good rendering of the image lurking in the back of the minds of most people who fear crime.... [T]he portrait generally fits the national picture presented in the FBI's *Uniform Crime Reports* for the same year, 1974. In Prince George's County, "youths between the ages of 15 and 19 were accused of committing nearly half [45.5 percent] of all 1974 crimes."...

That was 1974. But little has changed since. In his 1993 book, *How to Stop Crime,* retired police chief Anthony Bouza writes: "Street crime is mostly a black and poor young man's game." And listen to the sad words of the Reverend Jesse Jackson: "There is nothing more painful to me at this stage of my life than to walk down the street and hear footsteps and start thinking about robbery—and then look around and see someone white and feel relieved."

This, then, is the Typical Criminal, the one whose portrait President Reagan described as "that of a stark, staring face, a face that belongs to a frightening reality of our time—the face of a human predator, the face of the habitual criminal. Nothing in nature is more cruel and more dangerous." This is the face that Ronald Reagan saw in the criminal justice mirror, more than a decade ago. Let us look more closely at the face in today's criminal justice mirror, and we shall see much the same Typical Criminal:

He is, first of all, a *he.* Out of 2,012,906 persons arrested for FBI Index crimes [which are criminal homicide, forcible rape, robbery, aggravated assault, burglary, larceny, and motor vehicle theft] in 1991, 1,572,591, or 78 percent, were males. Second, he is a *youth.*... Third, he is predominantly *urban.*... Fourth, he is disproportionately *black*—blacks are arrested for Index crimes at a rate three times that of their percentage in the national population.... Finally, he is *poor:* Among state prisoners in 1991, 33 percent were unemployed prior to being arrested

—a rate nearly four times that of males in the general population....

This is the Typical Criminal feared by most law-abiding Americans. Poor, young, urban, (disproportionately) black males make up the core of the enemy forces in the war against crime. They are the heart of a vicious, unorganized guerrilla army, threatening the lives, limbs, and possessions of the law-abiding members of society—necessitating recourse to the ultimate weapons of force and detention in our common defense.

But how do we know who the criminals are who so seriously endanger us that we must stop them with force and lock them in prisons?

... "Arrest records" reflect decisions about which crimes to investigate and which suspects to take into custody. All these decisions rest on the most fundamental of all *decisions:* the decisions of legislators as to which acts shall be labeled "crimes" in the first place.

The reality of crime as the target of our criminal justice system and as perceived by the general populace is not a simple objective threat to which the system reacts: *It is a reality that takes shape as it is filtered through a series of human decisions running the full gamut of the criminal justice system*—from the lawmakers who determine what behavior shall be in the province of criminal justice to the law enforcers who decide which individuals will be brought within that province.

Note that by emphasizing the role of "human decisions," I do not mean to suggest that the reality of crime is voluntarily and intentionally "created" by individual "decision makers." Their decisions are themselves shaped by the social system, much as a child's decision to become an engineer rather than a samurai warrior is shaped by the social system in which he or she grows up. Thus, to have a full explanation of how the reality of crime is created, we have to understand how our society is structured in a way that leads people to make the decisions they do. In other words, these decisions are part of the social phenomena to be explained—they are not the explanation.

... Where the reality of crime does not correspond to the real dangers, we can say that it is a reality *created* by those decisions. And then we can investigate the role played by the social system in encouraging, reinforcing, and otherwise shaping those decisions.

It is to capture this way of looking at the relation between the reality of crime and the real dangers "out there" in society that I refer to the criminal justice system as a "mirror." Whom and what we see in this mirror is a function of the decisions about who and what are criminal, and so on. Our poor, young, urban, black male, who is so well represented in arrest records and prison populations, appears not simply because of the undeniable threat he poses to the rest of society. As dangerous as he may be, he would not appear in the criminal justice mirror *if* it had not been decided that the acts he performs should be labeled "crimes," *if* it had not been decided that he should be arrested for those crimes, *if* he had access to a lawyer who could persuade a jury to acquit him and perhaps a judge to expunge his arrest record, and *if* it had not been decided that he is the type of individual and his the type of crime that warrants imprisonment. *The shape of the reality we see in the criminal justice mirror is created by all these decisions.* We want to know how accurately the reality we see in this mirror reflects the real dangers that threaten us in society.

... The acts of the Typical Criminal are not the only acts that endanger us, nor are they the acts that endanger us the most. As I shall show..., we have as great or sometimes even a greater chance of being killed or disabled by an occupational injury or disease, by unnecessary surgery, or by shoddy emergency medical services than by aggravated assault or even homicide! Yet even though these threats to our well-being are graver than those posed by our poor young criminals, they do not show up in the FBI's Index of serious crimes. The individuals responsible for them do not turn up in arrest records or prison statistics. *They never become part of the reality reflected in the criminal justice mirror, although the danger they pose is at least as great and often greater than the danger posed by those who do!*

Similarly, the general public loses more money *by far*... from price-fixing and monopolistic practices and from consumer deception and embezzlement than from all the property crimes in the FBI's Index combined. Yet these far more costly acts are either not criminal, or if technically criminal, not prosecuted, or if prosecuted, not punished, or if punished, only mildly.... *Their faces rarely appear in the criminal justice mirror, although the danger they pose is at least as great and often greater than that of those who do....*

The criminal justice system is like a mirror in which society can see the face of the evil in its midst. Because the system deals with some evil and not with others, because it treats some evils as the gravest and treats some of the gravest evils as minor, the image it throws back is distorted like the image in a carnival mirror. Thus, the image cast back is false not because it is invented out of thin air but because the proportions of the real are distorted....

If criminal justice really gives us a carnival-mirror of "crime," we are doubly deceived. First, we are led to believe that the criminal justice system is protecting us against the gravest threats to our well-being when, in fact, the system is protecting us against only some threats and not necessarily the gravest ones. We are deceived about how much protection we are receiving and thus left vulnerable. The second deception is just the other side of this one. If people believe that the carnival mirror is a true mirror—that is, if they believe the criminal justice system simply *reacts* to the gravest threats to their well-being—they come to believe that whatever is the target of the criminal justice system must be the greatest threat to their well-being....

A CRIME BY ANY OTHER NAME...

Think of a crime, any crime. Picture the first "crime" that comes into your mind. What do you see? The odds are you are not imagining a mining company executive sitting at his desk, calculating the costs of proper safety precautions and deciding not to invest in them. Probably what you do see with your mind's eye is one person physically attacking another or robbing something from another via the threat of physical attack. Look more closely. What does the attacker look like? It's a safe bet he (and it is a *he*, of course) is not wearing a suit and tie. In fact, my hunch is that you—like me, like almost anyone else in America—picture a young, tough lower-class male when the thought of crime first pops into your head. You (we) picture someone like the Typical Criminal described above. The crime itself is one in which the Typical Criminal sets out to attack or rob some specific person.

This last point is important. It indicates that we have a mental image not only of the Typical Criminal but also of the Typical Crime. If the Typical Criminal is a young, lower-class male, the Typical Crime is *one-on-one harm*—where harm means either physical injury or loss of something valuable or both. If you have any doubts that this is the Typical Crime, look at any random sample of police or private eye shows on television. How often do you see the cops on "NYPD Blue" investigate consumer fraud or failure to remove occupational hazards? And when Jessica Fletcher (on "Murder, She Wrote") tracks down well-heeled criminals, it is almost always for garden-variety violent crimes like murder.... [C]riminals portrayed on television are on the average both older and wealthier than the real criminals who figure in the FBI *Uniform Crime Reports*, "TV crimes are almost 12 times as likely to be violent as crimes committed in the real world." TV crime shows broadcast the double-edged message that the one-on-one crimes of the poor are the typical crimes of all and thus not uniquely caused by the pressures of poverty; *and* that the criminal justice system pursues rich and poor alike—thus, when the criminal justice system happens mainly to pounce on the poor in real life, it is not out of any class bias.

In addition to the steady diet of fictionalized TV violence and crime, there has been an increase in the graphic display of crime on many TV news programs. Crimes reported on TV news are also far more frequently violent than real crimes are.... [A] new breed of nonfictional "tabloid" TV show has appeared in which viewers are shown films of actual violent crimes—blood, screams, and all—or reenactments of actual violent crimes, sometimes using the actual victims playing themselves! Among these are "COPS," "Real Stories of the Highway Patrol," "America's Most Wanted," and "Unsolved Mysteries." Here, too, the focus is on crimes of one-on-one violence, rather than, say, corporate pollution. The *Wall Street Journal*, reporting on the phenomenon of tabloid TV, informs us that "Television has gone tabloid. The seamy underside of life is being bared in a new rash of true-crime series and contrived-confrontation talk shows." Is there any surprise that a survey by *McCall's* indicates that its readers have grown more afraid of crime in the mid-1980s—even though victimization studies show a stable level of crime for most of this period?

It is important to identify this model of the Typical Crime because it functions like a set of blinders. It keeps us from calling a mine disaster a mass murder even if ten men are killed, even if someone is responsible for the unsafe conditions in which they worked and died. I contend that this particular piece of mental furniture so blocks our view that it keeps us from using the criminal justice system to protect ourselves from the greatest threats to our persons and possessions.

What keeps a mine disaster from being a mass murder in our eyes is that it is not a one-on-one harm. What is important in one-on-one harm is not the numbers but the *desire of someone (or ones) to harm someone (or ones) else*. An attack by a gang on one or more persons or an attack by one individual on several fits the model of one-on-one harm; that is, for each person harmed there is at least one individual who wanted to harm that person. Once he selects his victim, the rapist, the mugger, the murderer all want this person they have selected to suffer. A mine executive, on the other hand, does not want his employees to be harmed. He would truly prefer that there be no accident, no injured or dead miners. What he does want is something legitimate. It is what he has been hired to get: maximum profits at minimum costs. If he cuts corners to save a buck, he is just doing his job. If ten men die because he cut corners on safety, we may think him crude or callous but not a murderer. He is, at most, responsible for an *indirect harm*, not a one-on-one harm. For this, he may even be criminally indictable for violating safety regulations —but not for murder. The ten men are dead as an unwanted consequence of his (perhaps overzealous or undercautious) pursuit of a legitimate goal. So, unlike the Typical Criminal, he has not committed the Typical Crime—or so we generally believe. As a result, ten men are dead who might be alive now if cutting corners of the kind that leads to loss of life, whether suffering is specifically aimed at or not, were treated as murder.

This is my point. Because we accept the belief... that the model for crime is one person specifically trying to harm another, we accept a legal system that leaves us unprotected against much greater dangers to our lives and well-being than those threatened by the Typical Criminal....

According to the FBI's *Uniform Crime Reports,* in 1991, there were 24,703 murders and nonnegligent manslaughters, and 1,092,739 aggravated assaults. In 1992, there were 23,760 murders and non-negligent manslaughters, and 1,126,970 aggravated assaults.... Thus, as a measure of the physical harm done by crime in the beginning of the 1990s, we can say that reported crimes lead to roughly 24,000 deaths and 1,000,000 instances of serious bodily injury short of death a year. As a measure of monetary loss due to

property crime, we can use $15.1 billion —the total estimated dollar losses due to property crime in 1992 according to the UCR. Whatever the shortcomings of these reported crime statistics, they are the statistics upon which public policy has traditionally been based. Thus, I will consider any actions that lead to loss of life, physical harm, and property loss comparable to the figures in the UCR as actions that pose grave dangers to the community comparable to the threats posed by crimes....

Work May Be Dangerous to Your Health
Since the publication of *The President's Report on Occupational Safety and Health* in 1972, numerous studies have documented the astounding incidence of disease, injury, and death due to hazards in the workplace *and* the fact that much or most of this carnage is the consequence of the refusal of management to pay for safety measures and of government to enforce safety standards—and sometimes of willful defiance of existing law.

In that 1972 report, the government estimated the number of job-related illnesses at 390,000 per year and the number of annual deaths from industrial disease at 100,000. For 1990, the Bureau of Labor Statistics (BLS) of the U.S. Department of Labor estimates 330,800 job-related illnesses and 2,900 work-related deaths. Note that the latter figure applies only to private-sector work environments with 11 or more employees. And it is not limited to death from occupational disease but includes all work-related deaths, including those resulting from accidents on the job.

Before we celebrate what appears to be a dramatic drop in work-related mortality, we should point out that the BLS itself "believes that the annual survey significantly understates the number of work-related fatalities." And there is wide agreement that occupational diseases are seriously underreported. ...

For these reasons, plus the fact that BLS's figures on work-related deaths are only for private workplaces with 11 or more employees, we must supplement the BLS figures with other estimates. In 1982, then U.S. Secretary of Health and Human Services Richard Schweiker stated that "current estimates for overall workplace-associated cancer mortality vary within a range of five to fifteen percent. With annual cancer deaths currently running at about 500,000, that translates into about 25,000 to 75,000 job-related cancer deaths per year. More recently, Edward Sondik, of the National Cancer Institute, states that the best estimate of cancer deaths attributable to occupational exposure is 4 percent of the total, with the range of acceptable estimates running between 2 and 8 percent. That translates into a best estimate of 20,000 job-related cancer deaths a year, within a range of acceptable estimates between 10,000 and 40,000.

Death from cancer is only part of the picture of death-dealing occupational disease. In testimony before the Senate Committee on Labor and Human Resources, Dr. Philip Landrigan, director of the Division of Environmental and Occupational Medicine at the Mount Sinai School of Medicine in New York City, stated that

> Recent data indicate that occupationally related exposures are responsible each year in New York State for 5,000 to 7,000 deaths and for 35,000 new cases of illness (not including work-related injuries). These deaths due to occupational disease include 3,700 deaths from cancer....

> [I]t may be calculated that occupational disease is responsible each year in the United States for 50,000 to 70,000 deaths, and for approximately 350,000 new cases of illness.

... The BLS estimate of 330,000 job-related illnesses for 1990 roughly matches Dr. Landrigan's estimates. For 1991, BLS estimates 368,000 job-related illnesses. These illnesses are of varying severity. ... Because I want to compare these occupational harms with those resulting from aggravated assault, I shall stay on the conservative side here too, as with deaths from occupational diseases, and say that there are annually in the United States approximately 150,000 job-related serious illnesses. Taken together with 25,000 deaths from occupational diseases, how does this compare with the threat posed by crime?

Before jumping to any conclusions, note that the risk of occupational disease and death falls only on members of the labor force, whereas the risk of crime falls on the whole population, from infants to the elderly. Because the labor force is about half the total population (124,810,000 in 1990, out of a total population of 249,900,000), to get a true picture of the *relative* threat posed by occupational diseases compared with that posed by crimes, we should *halve* the crime statistics when comparing them with the figures for industrial disease and death. Using the crime figures for the first years of the 1990s,... we note that the *comparable* figures would be

	Occupational Disease	Crime (halved)
Death	25,000	12,000
Other physical harm	150,000	500,000

... Note... that the estimates in the last chart are *only* for occupational *diseases* and deaths from those diseases. They do not include death and disability from work-related injuries. Here, too, the statistics are gruesome. The National Safety Council reported that in 1991, work-related accidents caused 9,600 deaths and 1.7 million disabling work injuries, a total cost to the economy of $63.3 billion. This brings the number of occupation-related deaths to 34,600 a year and other physical harms to 1,850,000. If, on the basis of these additional figures, we recalculated our chart comparing occupational harms from both disease and accident with criminal harms, it would look like this:

	Occupational Hazard	Crime (halved)
Death	34,600	12,000
Other physical harm	1,850,000	500,000

Can there be any doubt that workers are more likely to stay alive and healthy in the face of the danger from the underworld than in the work-world? If any doubt lingers, consider this: Lest we falter in the struggle against crime, the FBI includes in its annual *Uniform Crime Reports* a table of "crime clocks," which graphically illustrates the extent of the criminal menace. For 1992, the crime clock shows a murder occurring every 22 minutes. If a similar clock were constructed for occupational deaths— using the conservative estimate of 34,600 cited above and remembering that this clock ticks only for that half of the population that is in the labor force—this clock would show an occupational death about every 15 minutes! In other words, in the time it takes for three murders on the crime clock, four workers have died *just from trying to make a living.*

To say that some of these workers died from accidents due to their own carelessness is about as helpful as saying that some of those who died at the hands of murderers asked for it. It overlooks the fact that where workers are careless, it is not because they love to live dangerously. They have production quotas to meet, quotas that they themselves do not set. If quotas were set with an eye to keeping work at a safe pace rather than to keeping the production-to-wages ratio as high as possible, it might be more reasonable to expect workers to take the time to be careful. Beyond this, we should bear in mind that the vast majority of occupational deaths result from disease, not accident, and disease is generally a function of conditions outside a worker's control. Examples of such conditions are the level of coal dust in the air ("260,000 miners receive benefits for [black lung] disease, and perhaps as many as 4,000 retired miners die from the illness or its complications each year"; about 10,000 currently working miners "have X-ray evidence of the beginnings of the crippling and often fatal disease") or textile dust... or asbestos fibers... or coal tars...; (coke oven workers develop cancer of the scrotum at a rate five times that of the general population). Also, some 800,000 people suffer from occupationally related skin disease each year....

To blame the workers for occupational disease and deaths is to ignore the history of governmental attempts to compel industrial firms to meet safety standards that would keep dangers (such as chemicals or fibers or dust particles in the air) that are outside the worker's control down to a safe level. This has been a continual struggle, with firms using everything from their own "independent" research institutes to more direct and often questionable forms of political pressure to influence government in the direction of loose standards and lax enforcement. So far, industry has been winning because OSHA [Occupational Safety and Health Administration] has been given neither the personnel nor the mandate to fulfill its purpose. It is so understaffed that, in 1973, when 1,500 federal sky marshals guarded the nation's airplanes from hijackers, only 500 OSHA inspectors toured the nation's workplaces. By 1980, OSHA employed 1,581 compliance safety and health officers, but this still enabled inspection of only roughly 2 percent of the 2.5 million establishments covered by OSHA. The *New York Times* reports that in 1987 the number of OSHA inspectors was down to 1,044. As might be expected, the agency performs fewer inspections that it did a dozen years ago....

According to a report issued by the AFL-CIO [American Federation of Labor and Congress of Industrial Organizations] in 1992, "The median penalty paid by an employer during the years 1972–1990 following an incident resulting in death or serious injury of a worker was just $480." The same report claims that the federal government spends $1.1 billion a year to protect fish and wildlife and only $300 million a year to protect workers from health and safety hazards on the job....

Is a person who kills another in a bar brawl a greater threat to society than a business executive who refuses to cut into his profits to make his plant a safe place to work? By any measure of death and suffering the latter is by far a greater danger than the former.

Because he wishes his workers no harm, because he is only indirectly responsible for death and disability while pursuing legitimate economic goals, his acts are not called "crimes." Once we free our imagination from the blinders of the one-on-one model of crime, can there be any doubt that the criminal justice system does *not* protect us from the gravest threats to life and limb? It seeks to protect us when danger comes from a young, lower-class male in the inner city. When a threat comes from an upper-class business executive in an office, the criminal justice system looks the other way. This is in the face of growing evidence that for every three American citizens murdered by thugs, at least four American workers are killed by the recklessness of their bosses and the indifference of their government.

Health Care May Be Dangerous to Your Health

... On July 15, 1975, Dr. Sidney Wolfe of Ralph Nader's Public Interest Health Research Group testified before the House Commerce Oversight and Investigations Subcommittee that there "were 3.2 million cases of unnecessary surgery performed each year in the United States." These unneeded operations, Wolfe added, "cost close to $5 billion a year and kill as many as 16,000 Americans." ...

In an article on an experimental program by Blue Cross and Blue Shield aimed at curbing unnecessary surgery, *Newsweek* reports that

a Congressional committee earlier this year [1976] estimated that more than 2 million of the elective operations performed in 1974 were not only unnecessary—but also killed about 12,000 patients and cost nearly $4 billion.

Because the number of surgical operations performed in the United States rose from 16.7 million in 1975 to 22.4 million in 1991, there is reason to believe that at least somewhere between... 12,000 and... 16,000 people a year still die from unnecessary surgery. In 1991, the FBI reported that 3,405 murders were committed by a "cutting or stabbing instrument." Obviously, the FBI does not include the scalpel as a cutting or stabbing instrument. If they did, they would have had to report that between 15,405 and 19,405 persons were killed by "cutting or stabbing" in 1991.... No matter how you slice it, the scalpel may be more dangerous than the switchblade....

Waging Chemical Warfare Against America

One in 4 Americans can expect to contract cancer during their lifetimes. The American Cancer Society estimated that 420,000 Americans would die of cancer in 1981. The National Cancer Institute's estimate for 1993 is 526,000 deaths from cancer. "A 1978 report issued by the President's Council on Environmental Quality (CEQ) unequivocally states that 'most researchers agree that 70 to 90 percent of cancers are caused by environmental influences and are hence theoretically preventable.'" This means that a concerted national effort could result in saving 350,000 or more lives a year and reducing each individual's chances of getting cancer in his or her lifetime from 1 in 4 to 1 in 12 or fewer. If you think this would require a massive effort in terms of money and personnel, you are right. How much of an effort, though, would the nation make to stop a foreign invader who was killing a thousand people and bent on capturing one-quarter of the present population?

In face of this "invasion" that is already under way, the U.S. government has allocated $1.9 billion to the National Cancer Institute (NCI) for fiscal year 1992, and NCI has allocated $219 million to the study of the physical and chemical (i.e., environmental) causes of cancer. Compare this with the (at least) $45 billion spent to fight the Persian Gulf War. The simple truth is that the government that strove so mightily to protect the borders of a small, undemocratic nation 7,000 miles away is doing next to nothing to protect us against the chemical war in our midst. This war is being waged against us on three fronts:

- Pollution
- Cigarette smoking
- Food additives

... The evidence linking *air pollution* and cancer, as well as other serious and often fatal diseases, has been rapidly accumulating in recent years. In 1993, the *Journal of the American Medical Association* reported on research that found "'robust' associations between premature mortality and air pollution levels." They estimate that pollutants cause about 2 percent of all cancer deaths (at least 10,000 a year)....

A... recent study... concluded that air pollution at 1988 levels was responsible for 60,000 deaths a year. The Natural Resources Defense Council sued the EPA [Environmental Protection Agency] for its foot-dragging in implementation of the Clean Air Act, charging that "One hundred million people live in areas of unhealthy air."

This chemical war is not limited to the air. The National Cancer Institute has identified as carcinogens or suspected carcinogens 23 of the chemicals commonly found in our drinking water.

Moreover, according to one observer, we are now facing a "new plague—toxic exposure." ...

The evidence linking *cigarette smoking* and cancer is overwhelming and need not be repeated here. The Centers for Disease Control estimates that cigarettes cause 87 percent of lung cancers—approximately 146,000 in 1992. Tobacco continues to kill an estimated 400,000 Americans a year. Cigarettes are widely estimated to cause 30 percent of all cancer deaths. ...

This is enough to expose the hypocrisy of running a full-scale war against heroin (which produces no degenerative disease) while allowing cigarette sales and advertising to flourish. It also should be enough to underscore the point that once again there are threats to our lives much greater than criminal homicide. The legal order does not protect us against them. Indeed, not only does our government fail to protect us against this threat, it promotes it! ...

If you think that tobacco harms only people who knowingly decide to take the risk, consider the following: Documents recently made public suggest that, by the mid-1950's, Liggett & Myers, the makers of Chesterfield and L&M cigarettes, had evidence that smoking is addictive and cancer-causing, and that they were virtually certain of it by 1963—but they never told the public and "actively misled" the U.S. surgeon general. Moreover, the cigarette industry intentionally targets young people—who are not always capable of assessing the consequences of their choices—with its ads, and it is successful. Some 2.6 million youngsters between the ages of 12 and 18 are smokers.

In addition, the Environmental Protection Agency has released data on the dangers of "secondhand" tobacco smoke (which nonsmokers breathe when smoking is going on around them). They report that each year secondhand smoke causes 3,000 lung-cancer deaths, contributes to 150,000 to 300,000 respiratory infections in babies, exacerbates the asthmatic symptoms of 400,000 to 1,000,000 children with the disease, and triggers 8,000 to 26,000 new cases of asthma in children who don't yet have the disease. A 1993 issue of the *Journal of the American Medical Association* reports that tobacco contributes to 10 percent of infant deaths.

The average American consumes *one pound* of chemical *food additives* per year. ... A hard look at the chemicals we eat and at the federal agency empowered to protect us against eating dangerous chemicals reveals the recklessness with which we are being "medicated against our will." ...

Based on the knowledge we have, there can be no doubt that air pollution, tobacco, and food additives amount to a chemical war that makes the crime wave look like a football scrimmage. Even with the most conservative estimates, it is clear that *the death toll in this war is far higher than the number of people killed by criminal homicide!*

Poverty Kills

... We are prone to think that the consequences of poverty are fairly straightfoward: less money means fewer things. So poor people have fewer clothes or cars or appliances, go to the theater less often, and live in smaller homes with less or cheaper furniture. This is true and sad, but perhaps not intolerable. However, in addition, one of the things poor people have less of is *good health*. Less money means less nutritious food, less heat in winter, less fresh air in summer, less distance from other sick people or from unhealthy work or dumping sites, less knowledge about illness or medicine, fewer doctor visits, fewer dental visits, less preventive health care, and (in the United States at least) less first-quality medical attention when all these other deprivations take their toll and a poor person finds himself or herself seriously ill. The result is that the poor suffer more from poor health and die earlier than do those who are well off. Poverty robs them of their days while they are alive and kills them before their time. A prosperous society that allows poverty in its midst is a party to murder.

A review of more than 30 historical and contemporary studies of the relationship of economic class and life expectancy affirms the obvious conclusion that "class influences one's chances of staying alive. Almost without exception, the evidence shows that classes differ on mortality rates." An article in the November 10, 1993 issue of the *Journal of the American Medical Association* confirms the continued existence of this cost of poverty:

> People who are poor have higher mortality rates for heart disease, diabetes mellitus, high blood pressure, lung cancer, neural tube defects, injuries, and low birth weight, as well as lower survival rates from breast cancer and heart attacks.
>
> ... In short, *poverty hurts, injures, and kills—just like crime.* A society that could remedy its poverty but does not is an accomplice in crime.

SUMMARY

Once again, our investigations lead to the same result. The criminal justice system does not protect us against the gravest threats to life, limb, or possessions. Its definitions of crime are not simply a reflection of the objective dangers that threaten us. The workplace, the medical profession, the air we breathe, and the poverty we refuse to rectify lead to far more human suffering, far more death and disability, and take far more dollars from our pockets than the murders, aggravated assaults, and thefts reported annually by the FBI. What is more, this human suffering is preventable. A government really intent on protecting our well-being could enforce work safety regulations, police the medical profession, require that clean air standards be met, and funnel sufficient money to the poor to alleviate the major disabilities of poverty—but it does not. Instead we hear a lot of cant about law and order and a lot of rant about crime in the streets. It is as if our leaders were not only refusing to protect us from the major threats to our well-being but trying to cover up this refusal by diverting our attention to crime—as if this were the only real threat.

As we have seen, the criminal justice system is a carnival mirror that presents a distorted image of what threatens us. The distortions do not end with the definitions of crime.... All the mechanisms by which the criminal justice system comes down more frequently and more harshly on the poor criminal than on the well-off criminal take place *after* most of the dangerous acts of the well-to-do have been excluded from the definition of crime itself. The bias against the poor within the criminal justice system is all the more striking when we recognize that the door to that system is shaped in a way that excludes in advance the most dangerous acts of the well-to-do.

POSTSCRIPT

Is Street Crime More Serious Than White-Collar Crime?

American society is currently in the throes of disdain, if not out-and-out hatred, for street crimes and the people who commit them. Yet according to Reiman and others, street thugs are not nearly as dangerous or harmful to life and limb as corporate criminals are. Ironically, many political candidates have made a partial career out of attacking street criminals while at the same time generously borrowing some of their verbal mannerisms. For instance, on more than one occasion, President Ronald Reagan challenged drug dealers and the like to give him the opportunity to "stomp them" or, in his inimitable vernacular, to "make my day."

Among the more recent works by Wilson is *Moral Judgment: Does the Abuse Excuse Threaten Our Legal System?* (Basic Books, 1997). A current book by Reiman is *Critical Moral Liberalism: Theory and Practice* (Rowman & Littlefield, 1997).

Similarly to Wilson and Herrnstein, Paul Tappan, in "Who Is the Criminal?" *American Sociological Review* (February 1947), insists that white-collar criminals and the like are not really the concerns of criminologists—at least not until laws are passed prohibiting certain acts. Otherwise, to attack corporations simply because we may disagree with their standards or efforts to make a profit is to dilute our definition of crime. Mainstream criminology probably rejects this perspective. See J. Albanese, ed., *Contemporary Issues in Organized Crime* (Criminal Justice Press, 1995); K. Jamieson, *Organization of Corporate Crime* (Sage Publications, 1994); *White-Collar Crime* edited by D. Nelken (Dartmouth, 1995); and M. Tonry and A. Reiss, eds., *Beyond the Law: Crime in Complex Organizations* (University of Chicago Press, 1993).

For a provocative view of crimes of criminal justice agencies, see J. Henderson and D. Simon's *Crimes of the Criminal Justice System* (Andersen, 1994). For four outstanding articles looking at organized crime in Europe and the United States, see *Journal of Contemporary Criminal Justice* (December 1994). A good introduction to the issue that parallels Reiman's views is *Corporate Crime, Corporate Violence: A Primer* by M. Lynch and N. Frank (Harrow & Heston, 1994).

ISSUE 5

Are General Theories of Crime Useful?

YES: Charles R. Tittle, from "The Assumption That General Theories Are Not Possible," in Robert F. Meier, ed., *Theoretical Methods in Criminology* (Sage Publications, 1985)

NO: Michael J. Lynch and W. Byron Groves, from "In Defense of Comparative Criminology: A Critique of General Theory and the Rational Man," in Freda Adler and W. S. Laufer, eds., *The Legacy of Anomie Theory* (Transaction, 1993)

ISSUE SUMMARY

YES: Criminologist Charles R. Tittle links the advancement of science with general theory building and insists that criminology will remain stagnant if it continues to neglect general theory.

NO: Professors Michael J. Lynch and W. Byron Groves argue that building general theories is unproductive. They insist that it is better to develop specific, grounded theories and to engage in careful comparative criminology.

For several years within the social sciences, including criminology but especially in sociology, students and professors debated furiously over what was more important: theory or research methods. Others argued over what was "better" theory: microstructural or macrostructural theory. That is, should criminologists attempt to explain and study only small slices of reality, such as child molestation or burglary, or should they develop large, comprehensive theories? In the debate that follows, Charles R. Tittle links scientific advancement with the development of a comprehensive, or general, theory of criminology. Tittle says that we need a good general theory of crime, however difficult formulating such a theory might be.

Michael J. Lynch and W. Byron Groves reject this ambitious call to arms. To begin with, they assert, no theory can explain *all* types of crime, even within the same society or historical period. They attack Tittle's idea and argue that if such a general theory were developed, it would force different kinds of crime into one false mold.

As a point of interest, the debate over what is more important, theory or research methods, has largely been resolved. Criminologists now realize that both are equally important: one is blind without good theory to guide research, and theory that does not generate hypotheses for testing is scientifically worthless. Moreover, many of the pioneering American criminological theorists, such as Sellin, Sutherland, and Cressey, as well as distinguished current criminologists, such as Hagan, Hirschi, Gottfredson, and Wilson, are also well known as researchers. They are theoreticians who also do important criminological research.

But the debate over theory continues, and, to a certain extent, it boils down to a debate between a "nomothetic" position and an "idiographic" one. During the early development of the various social science disciplines, most social scientists maintained that their work was involved with abstract, general, or universal statements. They were *not* interested in simply describing a single event or thing, such as a revolution, a crime (or even a type of crime), or a specific government. Instead, as scientists, they were interested in searching for uniform patterns and in coming up with explanations in terms of laws or principles or generalized statements. Their work was *nomothetic*. Instead of discussing Revolution-1, R-2, R-3, and so on, or Crime-1, C-2, C-3, etc., their task would be to develop a *theory* of revolutions or crime and then to study each revolution or crime as a particular empirical case.

In contrast to early efforts by some social scientists to develop general explanations, others (for example, some historians and anthropologists) tended to emphasize the unique or particular nature of social events. This is referred to as an *idiographic* approach. Historians often attempted to gather as much data or facts as possible on some unique historical event, such as a particular revolution or a particular president. The goal was to *describe* as fully as possible the unique event, not to try to form abstract theories or generalizations. Many anthropologists also tended to zero in on one culture or society, or even to select elements within specific societies (for example, dating customs, technology, or religious rites), at specific historical periods.

As you read the selection by Tittle, think about his many interesting ideas in terms of whether or not they apply to criminological realities as you understand them. Could you consider creating a general theory of crime that would enable us to better understand crime?

As you read the selection by Lynch and Groves, determine whether or not you agree with their understanding of theory. In what ways are they highly selective in their criticisms of Tittle? Whose *style of understanding* of crime (and other types of behavior) are you most comfortable with as a student of criminology: the particularistic approach of Lynch and Groves or the abstract theorizing called for by Tittle?

YES

Charles R. Tittle

THE ASSUMPTION THAT GENERAL
THEORIES ARE NOT POSSIBLE

THE PROBLEM

There is evidence that the majority of criminologists at least pay lip service
to the goal of developing general theory. Yet considerable ambivalence is obvious. There are strong and influential undercurrents declaring that theory is
impossible, undesirable, or of only ancillary import. Some of these dyspeptic
views stem from conviction that science is inappropriate for studying social
phenomena, others flow from faulty perceptions of the scientific process, and
a few reflect frustration at slow progress toward general theory. Yet they
all share a common assumption: Pursuit of general theory is a fool's errand
because of inherent features of criminological phenomena.

I contend that this is an erroneous assumption and that general theory is
quite possible....

Complexity

To most criminologists, the best known and probably most discouraging
barrier to general theory is the supposed fact that social phenomena are too
complex, involving a multitude of causes, to permit one explanatory scheme.
This belief rests on two assumptions: (1) Any theory can conceivably explain
only those phenomena that are essentially alike, and (2) a single theory implies
a single cause or process....

This pessimistic axiom, however, seriously underestimates the potentiali-
ties of theory, and its assumptions are mistaken. First, it is incorrect to assume
that all phenomena to be explained by a single theory must be empirically
alike. Phenomena have only to be subsumable within a similar causative
process. The object of theory building is to rise above the confines of everyday categorization and causal assumptions to grasp the ways in which
phenomena are abstractly connected. The first step in that process is conceptualization that captures theoretical commonality in the fact of empirical
dissimilarity. For example, theft, burglary, rape, homicide, and voyeurism
seem quite unalike, each a product of different causal factors, when viewed

with the cognitive tools provided by the cultures in which they occur. But on an abstract level all may be perceived as instances of the same act—intrusion into private domains. In most Western societies, at least, individuals are entrusted with control of the properties they use every day, their residential domains, and their lives, and with decisions as to who may observe their performance of bodily functions. Burglary, rape, and other crimes intrude into one of these private domains and are therefore theoretically alike, although not essentially alike in an empirical, culturally defined sense.

Second, all of these intrusions may be encompassed within a similar causal theory that provides explanation for intrusive as well as other behaviors. Such a theory necessarily also rests upon integration of divergent causative variables within unifying conceptual categories. For instance, broken homes, personality disorders, and peer pressures have all been implicated as relevant but desultory and fundamentally different causes, or factors, in various empirically distinct behaviors that are here regarded as conceptually similar instances of intrusion. But they may all reflect a single underlying construct that might be theoretically labeled as *interpersonal insecurity*. This generic concept varies independently of whether a child resides with both parents, although it might have some general association with family intactness; it subsumes many psychological variables often thought to express personality disorders; and it reflects an antecedent condition allowing peer influences to prevail. Thus what appear to be different causes may really be expressions of a common causal dimension.

Further, a general theory spelling out the causal intricacies of interpersonal insecurity and intrusive behavior as well as other causal dimensions and other abstract patterns of behavior, all of which would be included in the same domain of individual conduct, is logically conceivable. At the risk of being accused of setting forth yet another incomplete and faulty theory, I will continue with a hypothetical example to illustrate the form such a theory might take. Suppose a theorist begins with a general statement that all behavior (deviant or otherwise) involves five variables: (1) motivation (impulse, instigation, utility, desire, drive), (2) competing motivations, (3) constraint (cost, inhibition, restraint, control), (4) opportunity to commit the act, and (5) ability to perform the behavior. The theory then postulates that *any specific behavior* will result whenever there is X amount of opportunity to commit that behavior, the actor has Y degrees of ability to act, the strength of motivation to do it exceeds, by Z degrees, the motivation to do something else, and, by Q degrees, the strength of restraint. Borrowing from others, the theorist contends that one variable in the equation—the degree of *motivation* to do anything—is a product of (1) past differential association with social definitions favorable to doing it, (2) the relationship between culturally defined goals and means, (3) various biological conditions, (4) previous reinforcements for similar behavior, and (5) interpersonal insecurity. Under various conditions, these factors are postulated to contribute different amounts to motivation. For one condition, intrusive behavior, the theory suggests that interpersonal insecurity will account for 60 percent of the motivation to intrude, past association will account for 25 percent and so on. Continuing, the theorist maintains that another variable in the equation—the degree of *constraint* for any individual contemplating intrusive behavior—is a product of (1) social bonds to conforming other, (2) perceived chances of being sanctioned by the law, (3) level of moral feelings against particular types of acts, (4) certain biological conditions, and (5) a particular kind of bodily chemical imbalance. The theory postulates that these factors contribute variously to constraint under different conditions and that in the case of intrusive behavior, social bonds contribute 50 percent to the level of constraint, perceived chances of being sanctioned by the law, 30 percent and so on. Similarly, the processes and variables affecting the other variables in the equation—*competing motives, opportunity, and ability*—are spelled out.

Furthermore, the theory provides an intellectual rationale for all its internal linkages and postulates, continually attempting to answer the question of why at all steps along the way. For instance, in this hypothetical example interpersonal insecurity is theorized to be the primary determinant of motivation to intrude into the private domains of others. The theorist might maintain that this is because interpersonal insecurity causes anxiety about personal autonomy in regulating one's own privacy, making the individual feel relatively disadvantaged in the social arena, where others are perceived as having more complete control of their domains. Since feelings of disadvantage are discomforting, the individual attempts to reduce them by intruding into the privacy of others to equalize autonomy.

In like manner, and calling often upon other theory fragments, the scheme provides explanatory rationales for every proposed interconnection that will in the aggregate specify the conditions under which each element of the main causal statement takes various values. Moreover, the theory goes on to show how the inputs to that main causal process are themselves influenced by other causal processes. Thus the degrees of interpersonal insecurity, differential association, social bonds, and so on must themselves be explained by designation of the variables or processes influencing them to various degrees under given conditions and by provision of theoretical rationales for these effects.

The result of all this would be a pyramidlike edifice of general theory. The most abstract statement would be at the apex because it applies to all instances. Other abstract statements would be at a lower level in the pyramid because each applies only to specific parts of the more abstract statement at the top and each is expressed in conditional terms. And still less abstract, more conditional, statements will fit at a still lower level toward the base of the pyramid. In this way all supposed causal variables and processes having a systematic influence are part of one theory, linked together in a hierarchical network to feed one causal process at the top. Any degree of complexity and any number of causal factors could thereby be accommodated, and the explanatory process could extend as far down as anybody wanted to take it.

Failure

... A sense of theoretical failure has also been fostered by a malfunctioning interplay between theory and research. Theory grows as initial formulations are modified in light of empirical evidence. But criminologists rarely modify their theories through research reciprocation.

Like all social scientists, they repeatedly test original statements, conclude they are wrong, and let it go at that. For instance, anomie theory is much the same today as it was when first formulated, despite decades of empirical research, and it is regarded as just one of many failed general theories. Had anomie theory been expanded, altered, conditionalized, refined, and restructured by various scholars as the results of research and logical critique were fed back into it, it would now be quite different, having a cosmopolitan texture, and producing better explanations that would be more congruent with empirical facts. And had this same process been followed for each of the various theories in the criminological repertoire at the same time that they were being merged into one general theory along the lines suggested before, judgments about the failure of general theory would probably now be muted.

The tendency to preserve theories in their original infantile state while condemning them as failures is also the result of misapplied criteria of success. If A causes B, it does so under particular conditions, including specific degrees of A and other variables such as C, D, ... Z, and it produces specific degrees of B. The ultimate job of theory is to detail those conditions, tell why the process works as it does, and portray the circumstances under which A, C, D, ... Z will assume particular values. But this full conditional specification cannot emerge full blown from the minds of individual thinkers. To achieve it, one must continuously pump research information back into the theoretical structure and elaborate the theory to accommodate that information. This means that scholars must treat universal-appearing assertions, such as "A causes B," that might be derived from infan-

tile theories as actually only tentative, incomplete starting points. When such hypotheses are regarded as actual truth claims to be accepted or refuted whole, theories are killed before they can grow. Rigid testing of hypotheses strictly for judging the merits of a theory is appropriate only for the ad vanced stages of theoretical development, when mature schemes are comprehensively structured and deductively organized. Judging infant theories by adult standards is self-defeating and leads to unwarranted pessimism.

In light of all this, it cannot be said that efforts to construct general theories in criminology have failed or must necessarily fail; it is more appropriate to say that such efforts have never really been put forth. We have no idea what might be accomplished because criminologists have never seriously engaged in a collective movement to *build* general theory.

DISCIPLINARY OBSTRUCTIONS

Characteristics of the subject matter of criminology such as ambiguity, uniqueness, apparent indeterminacy, and complexity do not preclude general theory, nor does the relative weakness of the current product. They do, however, mandate careful attention to strategy. The tactics necessary for building general theory include (1) abstractive categorization and generalization; (2) integrative, hierarchical, conditional structuring of diverse causal processes; and (3) flexible reciprocation between theory and research. Yet it is precisely these strategic tactics that have been suppressed by academic subcultural and organizational norms and processes.

The first of these obstructions is the inability of the criminological community to mobilize enough scientifically oriented scholars to do the job. Theory building is a collective endeavor that requires a lot of people to add their contributions within a similar framework. But, despite ostensible commitment to science, criminology is actually so fragmented in its work philosophy that concerted efforts are difficult. Many criminologists literally have no consistent sense of what they are doing or how to do it. Scientific scholarship oriented from beginning to end toward theory is not a clear enough priority, and even those who claim to appreciate the theoretical task often misunderstand what it is....

Second, employment of the necessary tactics for building general theory has been impeded by a collective adversarial approach to theoretical work. It seems that the social scientific community is more united in trying to prove the impossibility of general theory than it is in trying to construct one. New ideas or attempts to advance the theoretical enterprise are typically greeted with a barrage of attacks designed to refute those ideas rather than evaluate and use them. Innovators feel compelled to defend their offerings as if they were the whole truth, resisting modifications; and the collectivity refuses to rest until it has convinced itself of the utter worthlessness of a given theoretical effort. Thus the academic community polarizes itself into opposing camps, with critics bent on making would-be theorists admit they are wrong (as well as naive for ever having thought they might make a contribution to theory), while innovators and their defenders feel forced to prove they are right. The result is little cooperative movement toward achieving a common goal and, in addition, thinkers are made reluctant to

introduce bold, clear statements for fear of being mauled....

Third, scholarly training has failed to convey the crucial difference between empirical variables and theoretical constructs, thereby hampering abstract formulation and research-theory reciprocation. Inability to understand and act on this fundamental duality has caused much grief. Among other things, it allows some to think they can measure aspects of empirical reality without theoretical guidance; that is, that important features inhere in phenomena themselves. And it leads others into despair because empirical observations per se refuse to yield to theoretical expression.... This two-way street mandates imagination on one hand and empirical discipline on the other. Unfortunately, students are sometimes persuaded that imagination is enough, although this is a rare fault. More often they are misled into believing that empirical discipline will suffice, particularly as this is embodied in routinized methodological procedures. Learning standard methods for data collection and analysis often diverts students from the ultimate goal, encouraging the belief that data contain within themselves knowledge that can be ferreted out mechanically. Tools in the hands of a skilled carpenter with a plan can lead to wonderful things, but their use without a plan will rarely produce anything worthwhile....

Fourth, the criminological community has rendered theoretical progress difficult by promoting status criteria that emphasize individualized achievement rather than collective benefit. Social scientists are taught to be loners, self-possessed and defensive. Theories are assumed to belong to individuals and are not be to tampered with except by the inventors. This means that they cannot easily be adjusted to empirical results or merged into a larger scheme. But it is totally unrealistic to imagine that any one person can invent an adequate general theory. Such a theory must grow through the cooperative efforts of many scholars, as they add their small contributions. Criminology will be on the right track when its practitioners stop talking about so-and-so's theory and begin to speak of the theory of socially disapproved behavior, the theory of law (or social disapproval), or the theory of managerial organization (as it bears on management of socially disapproved behavior), signifying by these designations integrated products with many subparts. Then theory will rightfully be regarded as every scholar's responsibility.

Finally, criminologists have handicapped theoretical work by tolerating confusing, tautological, amphibolic writing. Theories must contain clear, unequivocal ideas, propositions, and implications, so that they can be understood and manipulated, and made to yield genuine predictions for empirical test. Otherwise there can be no meaningful feedback and no progress... Since communication is never completely successful, even under the best of conditions, it is mandatory that any scholarly endeavor strive for clarity, particularly in its theoretical work. But the criminological community has been so tolerant of meaningless language that many empty, disappointing schemes have provoked serious attention because it took so long to figure out what they were saying.

CONCLUSION

Although general theory is the preeminent goal of scientific criminology, not all agree that it is possible or desirable. Examination of aspects of criminological phenomena that have been alleged to prevent general theory suggests that critics are mistaken. Cultural and organizational features of the community of scholars have, however, thwarted the theoretical enterprise, and will continue to do so unless corrected. Nevertheless, there are hopeful signs that the theoretical enterprise is healthier than many realize.

NO

Michael J. Lynch and W. Byron Groves

IN DEFENSE OF COMPARATIVE CRIMINOLOGY: A CRITIQUE OF GENERAL THEORY AND THE RATIONAL MAN

This [essay] offers a defense of criminological research and theory that is both historically and culturally grounded, in light of a growing literature arguing in favor of general theory (e.g., Hirschi and Gottfredson 1986, 1987a, b, 1988, 1989; Gottfredson and Hirschi 1989, 1990; Tittle 1985). We offer this defense because we believe that general theory speaks against comparative theory; that it does so without providing an adequate critique of a comparative perspective; that it fails to pay heed to comparative research findings, especially those that demonstrate that "irregularities" require explanation (Kohn 1987); and because general theory fails to pay adequate attention to history and culture as important explanatory variables (Mills 1959/1977). Further, general theories are thought to be the end process of "science"; they result when enough particular problems have been solved, and enough evidence is amassed to allow the construction of general explanations from existing evidence (see Turner 1976; Aubert 1952: 263). We do not believe that criminology has reached such a stage.

We offer no specific comparative theory of crime . . . , since to do so would be at odds with our stated goal: criticizing general theory. Our goal is to defend historically informed comparative approaches by pointing out how and why general theories fail as explanations of crime.

. . . In our opinion, historically specific, culturally informed, and empirically valid theory is needed if criminology is to free itself from universal claims that exhibit ethnocentric biases and a retreat to the realm of metaphysical explanation. . . .

GENERAL THEORY AND COMPARATIVE CRIMINOLOGY

My purpose in all this is to help grand theorists get down from their useless heights.

—C. Wright Mills,
The Sociological Imagination

The claim that comparative criminology should seek out universal causes of crime can be found in numerous works (e.g., Glueck 1964; Rokkan 1964; Cavan and Cavan 1968; Newman 1976; Clinard and Abbot 1973; Slomczynski, Miller, and Kohn 1981; Shelley 1981; Tittle 1985; Hirschi and Gottfredson 1987a, 1987b; Kohn 1987). As the name implies, advocates of universal (general) theory wish to ensure that causal regularities are not "mere particularities, the product of some limited set of historical or cultural or political circumstances" (Kohn 1987: 13). Thus, whatever the cause, the general theorist's concern is that it apply to all persons, cultures, and historical periods without exception.

In attempting to accomplish this goal, general theories differ with regard to the universal cause(s) of crime they specify. Sometimes the cause is found in human nature (e.g., crime is caused by the unbridled pursuit of pleasure), sometimes in drawn-out historical processes (e.g., crime is caused by modernization or industrialization) that are decontextualized or made abstract by the claim that the same process occurs everywhere, and sometimes in abstract principles (e.g., crime is behavior that promotes interpersonal insecurity). Regardless of the specific assumptions concerning crime, general theories favor interpretations that are "quintessentially transhistorical" (Kohn 1987: 729), lacking culturally grounded or historically specific qualifiers.

In addition to this transhistorical preference, general theory is ambitious in another regard. The flavor of that ambition is captured by Hirschi and Gottfredson's (1987a: 958) claim that their theory "is designed to account for the distribution of *all forms* of criminal behavior" (emphasis ours). This ambition is also evident in the work of Charles Tittle (1985: 101), who believes that all crime—acts as diverse as homicide and failure to stop at a traffic light—can be subsumed under one general theory. But, general theories of crime go much further than this when they claim that there is no need to explain different forms of crime with different forms of explanation (Hirschi and Gottfredson 1987a: 950), or even to address whether the same form of crime committed in different cultures or historical eras is caused by a different set of factors. The assumption has been made that the causes are the same, everywhere and always—seemingly without respect to the empirical evidence (e.g., see Katz 1988)....

Logical Style of General Theories

... Advocates of general theory tend to employ a similar logical style in constructing cross-cultural theories of crime. This style is drawn from a deductive model (Fay 1980: 30–36) which assumes that particular events (e.g., a crime) can be deduced from general assertions concerning those events (e.g., a general theory). Sutherland's theory of differential association, long thought to have cross-cultural applicability, is one example of this type of deductive reasoning (Friday 1974). In Sutherland's theory, the general assertion is that criminal behavior is learned, while the deductions entailed specification of the conditions and content of learned behavior (e.g., criminal behavior is learned from other persons in intimate groups, while the content of this learned behavior includes definitions favorable to law violation, techniques for committing crime, etc.; see Vold and Bernard 1985: 211). Tittle (1985: 112) highlights the top-to-bottom flavor of the deductive style as follows:

> The results of all this would be a pyramid-like edifice of general theory. The most abstract statement would be at the apex because it applies to all instances. Other abstract statements would be at a lower level in the pyramid.... And still less abstract, more conditional statements will fit at a still lower level toward the base of the pyramid. In this way all the supposed causal variables and processes having systematic influences are part of one theory..., and the explanatory process could extend as far down as anybody wanted to take it.

The problem with this approach, in our view, is not only with how far down this process is taken, but how far up (how general or universal) the argument is extended—or with how abstract the general theory becomes. The deductive style, in short, not only leads to reductionist arguments that can be extended down to the smallest unit (e.g., molecules, atoms, etc.; see Turner 1976: 253–57 and discussion below), but to abstractions that become meaningless because they lack a tangible connection to the lives of real individuals living in real, concrete social circumstances (Mills 1959/1977)....

Levels of Abstraction

... The following discussion provides a brief summation of [C. Wright] Mills' objections to general theory.

First, Grand Theorists tend to work with Concepts, thus excluding an examination of structural arrangements basic to an understanding of social life (Mills 1959/1977: 35). In short, the theorists who construct grand theory play a "conceptual game" devoted to defining concepts they believe necessary to an understanding of social order. In reality, these concepts fail to be meaningful since, in the construction of these concepts, the theorist omits a critical examination of how real-life structures, not theoretical concepts, affect life processes. In short, contextual theoretical development is sacrificed to conceptual development and clarification.

Second, Grand Theorists tend to begin with a priori assumptions (e.g., concerning human nature, the nature of social interactions, the nature of social order, etc.) that serve as nonempirical anchoring points for subsequent arguments (Mills 1959/1977: 39–42). Thus, the Grand Theorist's arguments are not only abstract because the discussion is confined to conceptual definitions, but also because theoretical assumptions and concepts are not grounded in the empirical realities generated by social structure.

Third, because Grand Theorists believe that their conceptions are of general or universal import, they are inclined to ignore historically specific empirical problems (Mills 1959/1977: 49; see also Kohn 1987). In effect, certain types of empirical evidence are ignored in general theory construction and concept building. As a result, historically specific instances that contradict the logic of the theory are ignored and treated as deviations from the norm that require no special explanation (see Kohn 1987 for further criticisms of this approach).

Finally, the fetishized concepts of grand theorists serve ideological and legitimation purposes (Mills 1959/1977: 48–49). General theory is not, as is commonly assumed, a neutral or objective framework through which social processes can be examined. Rather, general theory supports a particular (usually unstated) value position (see Myrdal 1969 for discussion of the problem of objectivity). Thus, the theory's structure mirrors and incorporates values that reflect idealistic versions of social processes. The purpose of such theory is to reinforce and legitimize values and interests that support the theory— values and interests that cannot be empirically grounded....

HIRSCHI AND GOTTFREDSON: A GENERAL THEORY OF CRIME

Under the heading "A General Theory of Crime," Hirschi and Gottfredson (1987b: 15; see also 1990, 1989, 1987a for similar arguments) propose the following program for comparative research:

> We ... *assume* ... that *cultural variability is not important* in the causation of crime, that we should look for constancy rather than variability in the definition and causes of crime, and that a single theory of crime can encompass the reality of cross-cultural differences in crime rates. From all this it follows that a general theory of crime is possible. (Emphasis ours)

Consistent with their view that partisans of universal theory should look for constancy in the definition and causes of crime, Hirschi and Gottfredson (1987b: 15–16) argue that the concept of crime must not build culture into its definition, and must not be defined in a strictly legalistic manner. Were crime defined in a legalistic way (as it has in fact been defined in a variety of cultures), then the general theorist would have to contend with the slew of objections concerning cultural (as well as historical) variations in the definitions of illegal behaviors (see Beirne 1983a: 383, 1983b for review of objections to this position). To avoid this problem, the authors sidestep empirical referents (cultural and historical variation in the definition of crime) and derive their definition of crime from a transhistorical conception of human nature. According to Hirschi and Gottfredson, "the conception of human nature that satisfies these requirements is found in the classical assumption that human behavior is motivated by pleasure and the avoidance of pain. Crimes, then, are events in which force or fraud are used to satisfy self-interest...." (1987b: 16, see also 1987a: 959, 1989: 360, 362). Grafting an individualistic emphasis onto this assumption, these authors argue that criminals are people who pursue short-term personal gratification without regard to long-term social interests (1987a: 959–60; 1989: 360). And finally, with reference to the issue of why persons might be inclined to seek immediate gratification, the authors state that "individual differences in the tendency to commit criminal acts are established early in life (in preadolescence) and are relatively stable thereafter" (Hirschi and Gottfredson 1987b: 19).

In the following sections we outline several objections to this style of theorizing. Some of these objections are external to the theory (i.e., they concern issues or assumptions not directly addressed by the authors but which nevertheless underlie the general assertion); while others concern internal components of the theory (i.e., the use of terms, assumptions, and deductions specified in the model).

External Objections

First, there is no reference to the considerable literature rejecting or sharply qualifying Hirschi and Gottfredson's assumptions concerning human nature; they do not attempt to account for the widely held view that human nature is historically variable or socially constructed (e.g., Allport 1955; Rogers 1961; Becker 1971; Henry 1963; Mills 1959/1977; Maslow 1982; Grose and Groves 1988)....

Second, there is no attempt to account for the sociological premise that motives are social rather than personal (Mills 1974; Becker 1964; Goffman 1959); nor is there reference to concrete historical circumstances and structures that guide motivations and intentions (Gerth and Mills 1964; Mills 1974); nor is there reference to the historically contingent relationship between opportunities and crime (Cohen and Felson 1979; Cohen, Felson, and Land 1980; Groves and Frank 1987). To give a brief example of an argument that links motivations to historically and culturally specific structures, we refer to the work of Jules Henry. Henry (1963: 20) notes that industrialized cultures have a market-driven mandate to create desire and stimulate consumption that required a mass psychological reorientation of society. Part of the psychic reorganization required in industrial cultures was the unleashing of impulse controls prevalent in Hebrew, Indo-European, and Islamic societies. Our point: There are clear and major theoretical differences between Henry's and Hirschi and Gottfredson's attempts to understand behavior. Henry, using a broad historically and culturally informed approach, situates drives for immediate gratification in an empirical, historical, and cultural context, while Hirschi and Gottfredson root drives in ahistorical/universal drives (for similar criticism of Homans' exchange theory see Turner 1976: 258–60). Henry's approach allows us to understand the behavior in different cultures on their own terms; Hirschi and Gottfredson's model forces the behavior of diverse cultures into an a priori theoretical framework, destroying any variation that existed in the object of study.

Third, there is no reference to literature in developmental psychology, or the existential tradition that challenges the claim that personality is fixed in preadolescence. Speaking directly to the claim that criminal predispositions are set in childhood, Harry Stack Sullivan (1953: 252) argued that "the notion that preadolescence readily constitutes a criminal, antisocial career is the most shocking kind of nonsense...." (see also Erikson 1959; Allport 1955; and Sartre 1962).

Fourth, there is no reference to literature linking personality to social relationships, social relationships to productive relationships, and productive relationships to specific historical context (Colvin and Pauly 1983; Turner 1976: 259)....

Fifth, there is no reference to literature in the philosophy of science that questions the applicability of this logical (deductive) style to the study of human behavior (Habermas 1971; Von Wright 1971; Bernstein 1971; Fay 1980; MacIntyre 1984; Otto-Apel 1984)....

Sixth, the deductive style of logic employed in Hirschi and Gottfredson's argument is reductionist....

And finally, there is no attempt to treat history as a variable of sociological relevance. History, in other words, is viewed as a description of factual relationships rather than a social record of processes reflecting cultural power relations....

Internal Objections

First, Hirschi and Gottfredson's use of the term *fraud* threatens their argument with circularity. On one hand, fraud is a legal category, and hence it is tautological to argue that criminals fraudulently pursue self-interest. On the other hand, if fraud is meant to be used in a broader, nonlegalistic sense, as these authors argue, then a variety of legally acceptable behaviors could be classified as fraud (i.e., criminal). The use of the term *force* poses similar problems. If force includes rapes, assaults, and robberies, we again face the tautological issue. If force is used in a broader sense, then a vast range of noncriminal behaviors might fall under this definition of criminality.

Second, Hirschi and Gottfredson's use of the terms *force* and *fraud* are not clearly defined. For example, we are instructed that "crimes are events in which force or fraud are used to satisfy self-interest" (1987a: 959), yet many noncriminal events involve the use of "force" and "fraud" to achieve the individual's desired goal. For instance, university professors often compel (force) their students to perform reading assignments by threatening to administer nonexistent quizzes (fraud) or in order to insure that classroom discussions run smoothly (the professor's self-interest). Here we have Hirschi and Gottfredson's three components of crime, yet no crime, as legally recognized, has occurred.

Third, the use of pleasure and pain and the relationship between pleasure and pain is caricatured.... Motivations, in other words, are far more complex than a simple pleasure/pain dichotomy suggests....

Fourth, there is no discussion of ways in which social structural arrangements central to any sociologically sound explanation define the contents of pleasure and pain, or determine those behaviors that will be responded to as force or fraud within a given cultural or historical era. In market economies, for example, the acquisition of commodities is "pleasurable."... In short, what counts as pleasure cannot be discussed apart from cultural definitions of the "good life."

Fifth, there is no discussion of ways in which social-structural arrangements condition the relative availability of, as well as access to, culturally defined pleasures and pains (Cloward and Ohlin 1960; Merton 1938)....

THE ROLE OF HISTORY AND CULTURE IN CRIMINOLOGICAL THEORY

... First and foremost, history is important insofar as it allows us to explain cross-cultural *differences* in rates of crime or the meaning of crime within a particular culture (Kohn 1987). For example, in order to make sense of the discrepant crime rates and approaches to crime in the United States and Japan, an extended analysis would have be performed that would incorporate the following historical materials: (1) A review of geographic and demographic differences, including relative population density, ethnic homogeneity/heterogeneity; (2) the relatively short history of the United States compared with the 1400-year written history of Japan, which has considerable impact on the importance of tradition in each culture; (3) the difference between Japan's historically situated aristocratic hierarchy and the United States's short history of nominal democracy and equality and how these traditions affect attitudes toward and respect for authority; (4) the differences between a recently emergent industrial/technological society in the United States, and a slowly evolving "rice economy" that requires cooperative efforts and centralized leadership for survival in Japan; and (5) the ways in which all of the above culminate in different cultural emphasis (i.e., on group relatedness, respect for authority, and work in Japan, and on individualism and competition in the United States; see Westerman and Burfeind 1986; Fishman and Dinitz 1989).... [B]y neglecting history and culture and their impact, general theory may well be producing claims that depend upon spurious relationships, and certainly upon relations and explanations abstracted from their social, historical, and cultural context....

THE RATIONAL "MAN"

The construct of the rational man is part of all theoretical structures that owe a dept to the utilitarian tradition. Hirschi and Gottfredson's approach is no exception.

The idea behind this approach can be boiled down to the claim that rational or calculating individuals assess the costs and rewards of their behavior before acting, pursuing self-interest and pleasure while avoiding pain. There is an undeniable link between this position and the approach adopted by economists who defended capitalist social relations as an outgrowth of human nature (cf. Smith 1776/1982; Turner 1976: 2ll). This construct, rather than being a description of real, human behavior, is a description of what "ought" to be, at least under a capitalist system of production (Smith 1776/1982). In short, the premises of the utilitarian approach are historically specific constructs that fit societies, like capitalism, in which self-interest and the pursuit of pleasure are paramount concerns. Thus, such principles cannot apply to all situations, nor can they explain behaviors that are undertaken outside the context of market economies (Henry 1963)....

The Limits of Rational Man Models as Explanations for Crime

It is now well accepted within criminology that a theory of crime must explain at least three things in order to be complete and efficient: (1) motivation/cause; (2) opportunity structure; and (3) law enforcement activity and the structure of laws to be enforced, or reactive variables (Cohen, Felson, and Land 1980; Cohen and Felson 1979; Gibbs 1987: 831–33). A general theory that relies upon a rational man or pleasure/pain argument may successfully (though we do not believe it does) explain motivation, but it fails to address the other major elements that make up crime (e.g., opportunity structure, enforcement/reactions). Thus, even if we grant, for the moment, that Hirschi and Gottfredson are correct and that all people in all cultures and historical time periods act according to pleasure/pain determinations, it is still impossible to say anything of importance about crime, given that (1) rationality is a constant, meaning that it cannot explain cross-cultural or interpersonal variations in crime rates, and (2) that both opportunity and enforcement must be considered in order to explain variations in crime (Cohen and Felson 1979; Cohen, Felson, and Land 1980). For example, before there were laws expressly forbidding theft (see

Hall 1952), an individual who took something that did not belong to him or her was not committing a crime, since in that culture and at that time, taking was not a crime. Likewise, hijacking of planes was impossible before the advent of the plane; the invention of the plane and its uses in modern society, coupled with political goals and motivations, create the opportunity for this type of behavior. . . .

CONCLUSIONS

In sum, we have argued that a general theory of crime—a theory that attempts to explain crime in all cultural and historical milieus without reference to history or culture, but with reference to static, immutable forces—is impossible. There is too much variation in human behavior, criminal motives, cultures, economic conditions and circumstances, and historical contexts to expect *one* theory to be applicable in all cultures and eras, or even in the majority of circumstances. General theory, in other words, is too broad to provide enough specific detail to explain crime.

What we argue in favor of is theory that is culturally and historically specific (see also Laufer and Adler 1989), and speaks directly to the context in which crime is committed, reacted to and constructed (e.g., Quinney 1970). According to this view, an adequate theory of crime must (1) address multiple levels of causation; (2) demonstrate a connection between structural and subjective factors (Groves and Lynch 1990); (3) include a discussion of opportunity structure as an important (but not the only) dimension of understanding crime; (4) discuss the effects of enforcement policy, the content and construction of law as these elements bear upon the social construction of crime; (5) build theory from the bottom up (from the concrete), keeping in mind the cultural and historical limits of explanation (Mills 1959/1977; Kohn 1987); and (6) construct explanations for crime that are grounded in empirical realities while avoiding the pitfalls of brute empiricism (Groves 1985; Lynch 1987; Beirne 1979). . . .

In conclusion, we would also like to note that the history of criminology is replete with attempts to construct and apply general or universal theories of crime. Such an approach has yielded few answers to the problem of crime. Thus, it may be time to tear down the walls built by general theory and reconstruct a criminology that is sensitive to culture and history.

POSTSCRIPT

Are General Theories of Crime Useful?

Lynch and Groves reject the goal of eventually developing general theory. They contend that such a theory of crime would be no theory at all because a general theory is both an empirical and logical impossibility. In this sense, it would seem that Lynch and Groves part company with many social scientists.

Tittle provides several reasons why he feels criminologists are so defeatist about general theory. He suggests that general theory has not failed, it simply has not yet been tried!

Within his discussion, Tittle advances a "mini-theory" of the forces, or the organizational constraints, that have worked against the development of a general theory. However, he omits discussion of several additional cultural factors equally inhibiting of general theory. These include the many research-funding organizations that are interested in financing fairly narrow crime control studies, not broad, abstract theory building.

The current political situation is also one in which both politicians and the public tend to desire studies of how to more efficiently arrest, process, manage, and punish criminals. Theories, general or otherwise, about why people commit crimes are not particularly in vogue among policymakers. Moreover, a criminal justice administration mentality is far more appealing even to many criminologists. Traditionally, criminal justice has been an athe-oretical, applied science interested in policy solutions to managing criminals. Although more progressive criminal justice programs are changing so that theory is being discussed more frequently, the political and financial situation seeks a very different kind of scholarly agenda than theory building.

Yet it can be argued that as rates of incarceration rapidly increase, and as the fear of crime and the perception of violent crime escalate, perhaps we are more in need of scientific explanations of crime than ever before. Many scholars would agree with Tittle's argument that general theory is a requirement for science. Efforts to incarcerate ever more citizens as a response to political and/or public hysteria border on the absurd, if not the dangerous. If crime is truly a problem, then what is needed is good theory to explain what is happening and to provide knowledgeable, logical, empirically based social responses. Tittle insists that general criminological theory can provide that knowledge.

Unfortunately, it is possible that this issue is so completely removed from the arena of academic organizations and discussions that the Tittle and Lynch-Groves debate matters little. Ironically, it seems that some people want the perception of a "quick fix" crime solution, such as increasing incarceration and/or executions, not theory (general or otherwise).

A recent work by Tittle that expands his thinking is *Control Balance: Toward a General Theory of Deviance* (Westview Press, 1996). Among Lynch's recent studies is *Justice With Prejudice: Race and Criminal Justice in America,* coedited with E. Patterson (Harrow & Heston, 1996).

A mere 15 years ago there were almost no books on theoretical criminology or criminal justice as such. Now there are dozens of articles and texts. Among the more accessible undergraduate works are G. B. Vold, T. J. Bernard, and J. B. Snipes, eds., *Theoretical Criminology* (Oxford University Press, 1998); S. Walklate, *Understanding Criminology: Current Theoretical Debates* (Open University Press, 1998); and D. Milovanovic, ed., *Chaos, Criminology, and Social Justice: The New Orderly (Dis)order* (Praeger, 1997). For several studies involving the building of general theories, see T. Hirschi and M. Gottfredson, eds., *The Generality of Deviance* (Transaction Publishers, 1994). J. Holman and J. Quinn's *Criminology: Applying Theory* (West, 1992) is one of the clearest statements of applied criminological theory. Also see J. R. Lilly et al., *Criminological Theory: Context and Consequences,* 2d ed. (Sage Publications, 1995). Two excellent criminological theory primers are R. Acker's *Criminological Theories,* 2d ed. (Roxbury, 1997) and D. Gibbons's *Talking About Crime and Criminals* (Prentice Hall, 1994). Two good philosophy of science of criminology primers are B. DiCristina's *Methods in Criminology* (Harrow & Heston, 1995) and W. Einstadter and S. Henry's *Criminological Theory* (Harcourt Brace, 1995). Among the few books dealing with theory within criminal justice are M. Davis's *To Make the Punishment Fit the Crime: Essays in the Theory of Criminal Justice* (Westview, 1992) and R. D. Ellis and C. S. Ellis's *Theories of Criminal Justice: A Critical Reappraisal* (Hollowbrook, 1989).

Articles that examine criminological and/or criminal justice theories include T. Bernard and R. Ritti, "The Role of Theory in Scientific Research," in *Measurement Issues in Criminology* edited by K. L. Kempft (Springer-Verlag, 1990) and D. Garland, "Criminological Knowledge and Its Relation to Power," *British Journal of Criminology* (Autumn 1992).

One of the clearest statements as to what theory is that is still useful is R. Merton's *Social Theory and Social Structure* (Free Press, 1968). For a discussion of comparative criminology, see D. Nelken, "Whom Can You Trust? The Future of Comparative Criminology," in D. Nelken, ed., *The Futures of Criminology* (Sage Publications, 1994). An interesting analysis of feminist orientations within criminology that parallels Lynch and Groves's selection is S. Caulfield and N. Wonders, "Gender and Justice: Feminist Contributions to Criminology," in G. Barak, ed., *Varieties of Criminology* (Praeger, 1994). Other feminist theory discussions are M. Schwartz and D. Milovanovic, eds., *Race, Gender, and Class in Criminology* (Garland Publishing, 1996) and the special issue of *Social Pathology* (Summer 1997) on women, crime, and criminology. Finally, for a seminal delineation of the development of general theories within the social sciences, see E. Tiryakian's "Hegemonic Schools and the Development of Sociology," in R. Monk, ed., *Structures of Knowing* (University Press of America, 1986).

On the Internet . . .

American Society of Criminology
An excellent starting point for a study of all aspects of criminology and criminal justice, this page provides links to sites on criminal justice in general, international criminal justice, juvenile justice, courts, the police, and the government. *http://www.bsos.umd.edu/asc/four.html*

Basics of Juvenile Justice
A list of similarities and differences between juvenile and adult justice systems is available at this site. Also listed are changes in the philosophy of juvenile justice by time periods.
http://www.uaa.alaska.edu/just/just110/intro2.html

Juvenile Delinquency
Click on "Juvenile Justice" for an extensive site sponsored by the Department of Justice that includes more than 30 documents, newsletter articles, and fact sheets on a wide variety of juvenile delinquency issues.
http://www.soc.american.edu/justice/corrjuv.htm

National Institute of Justice
The National Institute of Justice (NIJ) sponsors projects and conveys research to practitioners in the field. At its home page you can access the four initiatives of the 1994 Violent Crime Control and Law Enforcement Act, apply for NIJ grants, monitor international criminal activity, and link to the National Criminal Justice Reference Service home page, the Partnerships Against Violence Network (PAVNET), and the National Archive of Criminal Justice Data.
http://www.ncjrs.org/nijhome.htm

Office for Victims of Crime
The Office for Victims of Crime (OVC) was established by the 1984 Victims of Crime Act to oversee diverse programs that benefit victims of crime. From this Web site of the OVC, you can download a great deal of pertinent information. *http://www.ojp.usdoj.gov/ovc/*

Partnerships Against Violence Network
The Partnerships Against Violence Network is a virtual library of information about violence and at-risk youth, representing data from seven different federal agencies.
http://www.pavnet.org/

PART 2

Race, Gender, Youth, and the Criminal Justice System

Understanding society's reactions to crime—such as investigating, arresting, and incarcerating criminals, as well as providing alternatives to incarceration—is often complicated. Scholars and practitioners also have to reckon with the unanticipated negative outcomes of that system. The criminal justice system has been accused of ignoring crimes and injustices committed against women, racial and ethnic minorities, and children. Some say that policies and procedures adopted in fighting the war on crime may very well be more harmful than helpful. In addition, people have questioned efforts to protect children against predators, both on the streets and on the Internet; the effects of the war on drugs on the black, inner-city community; and the rationality of juries' acquitting guilty defendants to protest racial inequities in the criminal justice system. These issues are explored in this section.

- Should the Federal Government Have a Major Role in Reducing Juvenile Crime?

- Are the Dangers of Internet Child Pornography Exaggerated?

- Are the New Sex Offender Laws Rational?

- Does Arresting Batterers Do More Harm Than Good?

- Are Blacks Helped by the Drug War?

- Should Jury Nullification Be Used to Reduce Ethnic and Racial Inequities?

ISSUE 6

Should the Federal Government Have a Major Role in Reducing Juvenile Crime?

YES: Office of Juvenile Justice and Delinquency Prevention, from "Should the Federal Government Have a Major Role in Reducing Juvenile Crime? Pro," *Congressional Digest* (August–September 1996)

NO: Patrick Fagan, from "Should the Federal Government Have a Major Role in Reducing Juvenile Crime? Con," *Congressional Digest* (August–September 1996)

ISSUE SUMMARY

YES: The U.S. Department of Justice's Office of Juvenile Justice and Delinquency Prevention (OJJDP) contends that since its founding in 1974, it has immensely helped the states. Furthermore, with rising juvenile violent crime rates, federal help is needed even more to identify the best strategies for dealing with juveniles, coordinating states' efforts to reduce crime, and providing technical assistance and training.

NO: Patrick Fagan, a William H. G. FitzGerald Senior Fellow in Family and Cultural Issues at the Heritage Foundation, synthesizes strands from several theories of delinquency to argue that the government has made matters far worse by promoting false explanations of crime and by ignoring the vital role of the local trinity of family, school, and church in reducing crime.

In 1996, according to Office of Juvenile Justice and Delinquency Prevention (OJJDP) statistics, 37 percent of all burglary arrests, 32 percent of robbery arrests, 24 percent of weapons arrests, and 15 percent of homicide and aggravated assault arrests were juveniles. The number of eighth graders experimenting with heroin doubled between 1991 and 1996. Of the 19,645 homicides in 1997, 5,285 of the victims were juveniles.

Some criminologists, apparently influenced by the media, refer to many of America's kids as "superpredators." Assuming a metaphysical and theological stance, these scholars describe teenagers as having a hollow, vacant look, eyes devoid of humanity, and experiencing no remorse. Conservative politicians also hold negative views of America's youth. A Florida congressman, for example, recently declared America's teenagers to be the "most violent criminals on the face of the earth." Among other things, he calls for waiving juveniles as young as 13 to adult courts and expelling school children for six months if they are caught smoking cigarettes. President Bill Clinton's 1994 crime bill allows 13-year-olds to be prosecuted by the federal government for violent crimes. Currently, two states are in the process of handing over to federal authorities for prosecution teenage offenders accused of serious violent crimes. In early 1998 all U.S. states except Hawaii had transferred some youths to adult courts; approximately 12,300 youngsters were prosecuted as adults in 1997.

Critics of these reactions are quick to point out that since 1899, when the first juvenile court was begun in Chicago, there has been a steady movement toward viewing children as needing special protections. The idea of *parens patriae*—literally, "the state as the parent"—evolved as a doctrine. It was embraced by most progressive scholars and citizens. As noted by the OJJDP in the following selection, one of the most vital tasks mandated by the Juvenile Justice and Delinquency Prevention Act in 1974 was utilizing federal clout to get states to separate juveniles from adults and to deinstitutionalize status offenders. These status offenders were truants and runaways who were often incarcerated with hardcore delinquents and even adult felons. Although the latter aim was achieved, it appears that the thrust is now toward reintegrating juveniles and adults in America's prisons. Critics of this trend note that states that have higher percentages of juveniles transferred to adult courts and/or have lower ages for juvenile offenders (e.g., 16 years) have rates of juvenile crime, including homicides, that are as high as or higher than other states. They also mention that out of 1,200 cases of parricide (the killing of a parent) committed in 1990–1993, about 1 in 10 (118) were in Texas. This state has one of the highest rates of executions in the recent history of the world.

Another irony is that in spite of the doom and gloom statistics regarding juvenile crime, crime in America in every major category has shown significant decreases since 1995. While more eighth graders are trying heroin, drug use among the young is probably declining. According to FBI statistics for 10–17-year-olds, in 1994 there were 527 violent crimes for every 100,000; in 1995 the figure was 512, and an even more dramatic decline of 465 was seen in 1996. Only approximately 0.5 percent of all 10–17-year-olds were arrested for a violent crime in 1996. Moreover, recent statistics analyzed by Vincent Schiraldi and Eric Lotke in 1996 show that nearly one-third of juvenile murder arrests are in four cities and one-half in six states. As terrible as such acts may be, the indication is that there may not be a national epidemic.

As you read the following selections, notice the radically different explanations of the role of government in solving America's problems. What are the various criminological theories that Patrick Fagan draws from in accounting for juvenile crime? What respective treatment modalities does he emphasize? Which of the two authors sees a more important role for juvenile incarceration or waiver to adult courts and facilities?

YES

Office of Juvenile Justice and Delinquency Prevention

SHOULD THE FEDERAL GOVERNMENT HAVE A MAJOR ROLE IN REDUCING JUVENILE CRIME?

The problem of juvenile crime and violence is serious—in terms of both personal and social costs—and, based upon population trends, it will be getting worse in the coming years as the youth population grows, unless we prevent it and effectively intervene when it occurs. In response to this problem, there is a flurry of activity taking place across this country—new laws being passed, facilities being built, programs being added to State and local systems. To enhance our chances for success, we must ensure that these activities are not being undertaken in a piecemeal fashion, but instead as part of a comprehensive plan.

What the Office of Juvenile Justice and Delinquency Prevention (OJJDP) offers is a coordinated response to the crisis of youth violence and concrete support to State and local jurisdictions for accomplishing the necessary reform to the juvenile justice system so that it can effectively and comprehensively intervene with youth violence.

A Comprehensive Plan: Basing What We Do on What Works
Our success is contingent on using the knowledge we have about the nature and extent of juvenile delinquency and violence and what works and what doesn't work to prevent and reduce the problem.

OJJDP has made great progress in identifying effective and promising prevention, intervention, and treatment programs and practices. Because OJJDP works with all of the States, we keep our finger on the pulse of new and emerging issues and effective approaches to prevent delinquency and control violent crime. For example, OJJDP's *National Report on Juvenile Violence and Victimization* provides the most comprehensive compilation of data on juvenile crime and victimization from more than 50 sources. This report is a useful tool for understanding national dimensions and patterns of juvenile crime and victimization and for guiding prevention and intervention efforts....

Based upon this research on the causes of delinquency and input from the States, OJJDP has produced a *Comprehensive Strategy for Serious, Violent, and Chronic Juvenile Offenders* and *The Guide for Implementing the Comprehensive Strategy for Serious, Violent, and Chronic Juvenile Offenders.* The *Comprehensive Strategy* takes the lessons learned and wisdom from experts in the field—statistics, research, and program evaluations—to put together a model that people can understand, support, and advocate. The *Comprehensive Strategy* encourages all of us to take part in the continuum of activity —from the earliest of preventive activities to strengthen families, communities, and social institutions and provide opportunities for the healthy development of young people, to the deepest of interventions for the repeat juvenile offender, including the development of a system of graduated sanctions and the possible transfer of the most serious, violent, and chronic offenders for criminal prosecution. Through broad dissemination of the *Comprehensive Strategy*—and information on the 209 effective programs described with the *Guide*—OJJDP has served as a conduit to begin implementing the best programs and practices in the country to address juvenile violence and delinquency.

Since its release in 1993, the *Comprehensive Strategy* has already served as a basis for statutory reform efforts in several States, including Connecticut and New Jersey. We are devoting extensive training and technical assistance resources to assisting local jurisdictions to implement risk-focused prevention under OJJDP's Formula Grants and Title V Prevention Grants Programs....

Here are a few examples of what OJJDP is doing to implement the *Action Plan* and to provide leadership and support for reducing youth violence in this country.

Supports Strengthening the Juvenile Justice System. Over the last 20 years of its existence, OJJDP has established a sturdy infrastructure to support State and local implementation of a juvenile justice system that provides for public safety and serves the children that look to it for protection and treatment.

Since the Juvenile Justice and Delinquency Prevention Act was enacted in 1974, State activities have resulted in dramatic changes in the processing of juvenile offenders. States have substantially removed status and nonoffender juveniles from secure facilities; separated juveniles from incarcerated adults in secure institutions; sought to remove juveniles from adult jails and lockups; and worked to reduce disproportionate minority confinement in secure facilities. The core requirements of the Act have provided important protections for juvenile offenders. Setting these standards, providing assistance to the States in meeting these standards, and monitoring compliance has assured better treatment interventions for juvenile offenders nationwide.

Through Formula Grants, Local Delinquency Prevention Incentive Grants (Title V), and State Challenge Grants Programs, OJJDP has provided funds to States to plan and implement comprehensive State and local programs to prevent and control delinquency, and seeded innovative programs to address State and local needs. States have implemented a variety of sanctions from secure juvenile corrections to nonsecure alternatives such as bootcamps, electronic monitoring, intensive supervision, and community-based programs....

Targets Youth Gun, Gang, and Drug Violence. The number of homicides juveniles commit with guns more than doubled between 1985 and 1992. When the President signed the Violent Crime Control and Law Enforcement Act of 1994, he also signed into law the Youth Handgun Safety Act. To assist State and local jurisdictions in implementing the Act, the Administration, through OJJDP, is developing a model juvenile handgun law and, working with governors, attorneys general, and State legislators, will encourage the adoption of such legislation in all 50 States and U.S. territories. It is this type of Federal, State, and local partnership that is critical to winning the battle against the violence that is killing our children and endangering our communities.

Similarly, youth gangs today are found in almost all 50 States. Experts estimate that more than 3,875 youth gangs with a total of more than 200,000 members are established in the 79 largest U.S. cities. To address this problem, OJJDP has researched and developed a model, comprehensive, community-wide approach to the suppression, intervention, and prevention of gangs. This model is being implemented and tested in five jurisdictions....

Finally, through its Community Anti-Drug Abuse Technical Assistance Voucher project and support of the Congress of National Black Churches' National Anti-Drug/Violence Campaign, OJJDP assists grassroots organizations that are working to solve the problem of juvenile drug abuse. OJJDP is also working with the American Probation and Parole Association to train and assist juvenile justice practitioners to identify and intervene with drug-involved youth....

Provides Opportunities for Young People. A 1992 study conducted by the Carnegie Foundation determined that only 60 percent of an adolescent's non-sleeping time is taken up by school, homework, chores, meals, or employment. Many adolescents spend the remaining 40 percent of their nonsleeping time alone, with peers without adult supervision, or with adults who might negatively influence their behavior. A recent study found that 27 percent of eighth graders spent two or more hours alone after school and that low-income youth were more likely than others to be home alone for three or more hours. It is not surprising, therefore, that most violent crimes committed by juveniles take place at the close of the school day, when fewer opportunities for constructive activities are available. Therefore, OJJDP is supporting a number of efforts to provide constructive alternatives and positive skills to young people at risk of becoming delinquent....

In addition to our professional development training for youth workers, our Law-Related Education program, and Teens, Crime, and the Community, which encourages young people to get involved in community safety efforts, OJJDP has also provided programmatic support, technical assistance, and training to 41 mentoring programs funded under the Juvenile Mentoring Program (JUMP) and SafeFutures. Mentoring programs like these have made juveniles less likely to start using drugs and alcohol, and less likely to hit someone; have improved school attendance and performance; and have improved peer and family relationships.

Children at Risk (CAR), jointly funded by the Bureau of Justice Assistance, the National Institute of Justice, OJJDP, and a consortium of private sources, has provided case management, family services, education services, after-school and summer activities, mentoring, community policing and enhanced enforcement, and criminal/juvenile justice interventions for young people.... Youth in the Children at Risk program have had fewer contacts with police than youth in a randomly assigned control group....

Just this month, OJJDP sponsored a national satellite teleconference on Conflict Resolution Programming in School, Community, and Juvenile Justice Settings. This satellite teleconference provided information to over 485 downlink sites and approximately 10,000 participants on conflict resolution programs that have reduced the number of violent juvenile acts in schools, homes, and neighborhoods; decreased the number of chronic school absences; reduced the number of disciplinary referrals and suspensions; and increased academic instruction during the school day.

Funded by OJJDP in collaboration with the Departments of Health and Human Services, Commerce, and Defense, the Cities in Schools dropout prevention program reaches over 97,000 youths and their families and has increased students' likelihood of staying enrolled in school, and academic performance....

Strengthens Families and Breaks the Cycle of Violence. In 1994, there were 3.1 million reports of child abuse in America. Nearly 300,000 of these children received no therapy or support. Based upon OJJDP research, as well as other studies, we know that children who experience multiple forms of violence

in their homes have double the chance of engaging in violent or delinquent behavior as a juvenile. Therefore, an effective reduction in youth violence will require breaking the cycle of violence in children's homes.

OJJDP has funded four regional children's advocacy centers... to coordinate the judicial and social service systems' response to victims of child abuse.... [N]early 300 communities have children's advocacy centers to improve management of abuse and neglect cases, increase the rate of prosecutions, and ensure that victims and their families receive coordinated treatment services.

In addition, due in part to OJJDP support, about 700 communities across the Nation operate Court Appointed Special Advocate (CASA) Programs to advocate for victimized children in court proceedings and recommend plans that best serve children.

Mobilizes Communities. OJJDP is also helping communities implement comprehensive plans to prevent juvenile delinquency. In 1994, OJJDP provided $13 million through the Title V Delinquency Prevention Incentive Grants and in 1995 provided an additional $20 million. Title V funds have now been distributed to 52 States and territories, and nearly 4,000 local participants, representing a cross-section of communities nationwide, attended Title V delinquency prevention training sessions....

Conclusion
In order to effectively reduce delinquency and later criminality, there must be a substantial, sustained investment—both public and private, and in terms of both financial and human resources—in families, communities, and the systems

that support and protect them. To obtain and keep public support for the juvenile justice system, we are going to have to provide both effective, immediate responses that ensure the public safety and long-term, preventive solutions to the problem of juvenile delinquency and violence. And, most important, we are going to have to use our resources wisely.

The activities I have described illustrate the critical role OJJDP plays. They demonstrate not only how we support national efforts to reduce youth violence and delinquency, but how we collect, coordinate, and disseminate information; support targeted replication; and provide seed money to implement the most effective practices known to address this critical problem.

This is an appropriate Federal role; one that OJJDP is fulfilling. With our State and local partners, we are addressing juvenile delinquency and violence in a coordinated and cost-effective manner and working to reverse the statistical projections and stem the tide of youth violence that has engulfed the Nation.

NO

Patrick Fagan

SHOULD THE FEDERAL GOVERNMENT HAVE A MAJOR ROLE IN REDUCING JUVENILE CRIME?

Policymakers at last are coming to recognize the connection between the breakdown of American families and various social problems. The unfolding debate over welfare reform, for instance, has been shaped by the wide acceptance in recent years that children born into single-parent families are much more likely than children of intact families to fall into poverty and welfare dependency themselves in later years. These children, in fact, face a daunting array of problems.

While this link between illegitimacy and chronic welfare dependency now is better understood, policymakers also need to appreciate another strong and disturbing pattern evident in scholarly studies: the link between illegitimacy and violent crime and between the lack of parental attachment and violent crime. Without an understanding of the root causes of criminal behavior—how criminals are formed—Members of Congress and State legislators cannot understand why whole sectors of society, particularly in urban areas, are being torn apart by crime. And without that knowledge, sound policymaking is impossible.

A review of the empirical evidence in the professional literature of the social sciences gives policymakers an insight into the root causes of crime. Consider, for instance:

Over the past 30 years, the rise in violent crime parallels the rise in families abandoned by fathers.

From Patrick Fagan, "Should the Federal Government Have a Major Role in Reducing Juvenile Crime? Con," *Congressional Digest: The Pro and Con Monthly*, vol. 75, no. 8–9 (August–September 1996). Copyright © 1996 by The Congressional Digest Corp., Washington, DC (202) 333-7332, http://www.congressionaldigest.com. Reprinted by permission.

High-crime neighborhoods are characterized by high concentrations of families abandoned by fathers.

State-by-State analysis by Heritage scholars indicates that a 10 percent increase in the percentage of children living in single-parent homes leads typically to a 17 percent increase in juvenile crime.

The rate of violent teenage crime corresponds with the number of families abandoned by fathers.

The type of aggression and hostility demonstrated by a future criminal often is foreshadowed in unusual aggressiveness as early as age five or six.

The future criminal tends to be an individual rejected by other children as early as the first grade who goes on to form his own group of friends, often the future delinquent gang.

On the other hand:

Neighborhoods with a high degree of religious practice are not high-crime neighborhoods.

Even in high-crime inner-city neighborhoods, well over 90 percent of children from safe, stable homes do not become delinquents. By contrast, only 10 percent of children from unsafe, unstable homes in these neighborhoods avoid crime.

Criminals capable of sustaining marriage gradually move away from a life of crime after they get married.

The mother's strong affectionate attachment to her child is the child's best buffer against a life of crime.

The father's authority and involvement in raising his children are also a great buffer against a life of crime.

The scholarly evidence, in short, suggests that at the heart of the explosion of crime in America is the loss of the capacity of fathers and mothers to be responsible in caring for the children they bring into the world. This loss of love and guidance at the intimate levels of marriage and family has broad social consequences for children and for the wider community. The empirical evidence shows that too many young men and women from broken families tend to have a much weaker sense of connection with their neighborhood and are prone to exploit its members to satisfy their unmet needs or desires. This contributes to a loss of a sense of community and to the disintegration of neighborhoods into social chaos and violent crime. If policymakers are to deal with the root causes of crime, therefore, they must deal with the rapid rise of illegitimacy.

OFFICIAL WASHINGTON'S VIEW OF CRIME

The professional literature on criminology is quite at odds with orthodox thinking in official Washington. Many lawmakers in Congress assume that the high level of crime in America must have its roots in material conditions, such as poor employment opportunities and a shortage of adequately funded social programs. But Members of Congress and other policymakers cannot understand the root causes of crime if they insist on viewing it purely in material terms.

This view blinds policymakers to the personal aspects of crime, including moral failure, the refusal to exercise personal responsibility, and the ability or refusal to enter into family and community relationships based on love, respect, and attachment both to the broader community and to a common code of conduct.

The central proposition in official Washington's thinking about crime is that poverty is the primary cause of crime. In its simplest form, this contention is absurd; if it were true, there would have been more crime in the past, when more people were poorer. And in poorer nations, the crime rates would be higher than in the United States. More significantly, history defies the assumption that deteriorating economic circumstances breed crime (and improving conditions reduce it). Instead, America's crime rate gradually rose during the long period of real economic growth: 1905 to 1933. As the Great Depression set in and incomes dropped, the crime rate also dropped. It rose again between 1965 and 1974 when incomes rose steadily. Most recently, during the recession of 1982, there was a slight dip in crime, not an increase.

There is a widespread belief that race is a major explanatory cause of crime. This belief is anchored in the large disparity in crime rates between whites and blacks. However, a closer look at the data shows that the real variable is not race but family structure and all that it implies in commitment and love between adults. Illegitimacy is the key factor. It is the absence of marriage, and the failure to form and maintain intact families, that explains the incidence of high crime in a neighborhood among whites as well as blacks. This contradicts conventional wisdom.

FIVE STEPS TO VIOLENT CRIME

Propensity to crime develops in stages associated with major psychological and sociological factors. The factors are not caused by race or poverty, and the stages are the normal tasks of growing up that every child confronts as he gets older. In the case of future violent criminals, these tasks—in the absence of love, affection, and dedication of both his parents—become perverse exercises, frustrating his needs and stunting his ability to belong. The stages are:

- **Step One:** Parental neglect and abandonment in early home life....
- **Step Two:** The embryonic gang becomes a place to belong....
- **Step Three:** The emergence of the gang....
- **Step Four:** Serious crime begins....
- **Step Five:** A new child, and a new generation of criminals, begins....

In all of these stages, the lack of dedication and the atmosphere of rejection or contact within the family diminish the child's experience of his personal life as one of love, dedication, and a place to belong. Instead, it is characterized increasingly by rejection, abandonment, conflict, isolation, and even abuse....

THE SOCIAL CONDITIONS OF A SAFE SOCIETY

Most ordinary Americans do not need to survey the social science literature to know that a family life of affection, cohesion, and parental involvement prevents delinquency. In particular, they know almost instinctively that maternal affection, maternal self-confidence, and the father's esteem for the mother are among the critical elements in raising well-balanced children. The literature bears out these common assumptions. Most Americans, too, know that in a law-abiding family, the parents encourage the moral development of their children and promote an understanding and acceptance of traditional moral norms.

Moreover, most Americans know that this moral development of children usually is accomplished within the context of religious belief and practice. The government's own surveys of the literature confirm this view.

The root cause of violent crime thus is found in failed intimate relationships of love in marriage and in the family. The breakdown of stable communities into crime-infested neighborhoods flows directly from this failure. In contrast, addressing the root causes of crime requires an understanding of the crucial elements of supportive family and community life....

It is no coincidence that one of the central rules in the traditional moral codes of all communities at all times, in all places, and in all cultures is the prohibition against giving birth to children outside of marriage. Societies all over the world have recognized that this prohibition is essential to social stability and to raising members of each new generation with the proper respect for their community and their peers. Unfortunately, and with disastrous consequences, this prohibition is ignored today in American society at all levels, but most especially in central-city neighborhoods. Having a child outside of marriage virtually guarantees a teenage woman and her children a life of poverty, low education, low expectations, and low achievement. It gradually puts in place the conditions which foster rejection and, ultimately, crime.

Whenever there is too high a concentration of such broken families in any community, that community will disintegrate. Only so many dysfunctional families can be sustained before the moral and social fabric of the community itself breaks down. Re-establishment of the basic community code of children within marriage is necessary both for the future happiness of American families and for a reduction in violent crime.

It follows, then, that the real work of reducing violent crime is the work of rebuilding the family. Institutions in the community, such as the church and the school, have demonstrated their importance in helping restore stability. Government agencies, on the other hand, are powerless to increase marital and parental love; they are powerless to increase or guarantee care and attention in a family; they are powerless to increase the ability of adults to make and keep commitments and agreements. Instead, thanks to policies that do little to preserve the traditional family and much to undermine it, government continues to misdiagnose the root cause of social collapse as an absence of goods and services. This misdiagnosis is government's own contribution to the growth of crime. Having misdiagnosed, it misleads.

There is a role for political leadership in the current crisis. It is not to take the place of family and community, however, but to articulate a compelling, positive vision of the Nation in terms of family and community life. As President John F. Kennedy inspired thousands of young people to serve others overseas, another must inspire today's youth to rebuild America's families and community. This is the work not of government, but of the Nation's primary nurturing institutions: family, church, and school. The missions of these institutions are missions of love and the moral and the spiritual formation of a people.

The alternative is continued social disintegration.

WHAT GOVERNMENT CAN DO

Hold hearings on the real causes of crime. Given the disconnect between the assumptions behind the social spending in the Omnibus Crime Bill of 1994 and the real root causes of crime, a major correction in thinking is needed. The Judiciary Committees of Congress should conduct a series of hearings on the root causes—the long-term causes—of crime. These should focus on the relationship of family structure, and particularly of marriage and religious practice, to the prevention of violent crime. The literature, the scholarship, and particularly the experience are wide and deep.

Conduct a serious review of all national social programs....

Commission geographical mapping of social problems and their related conditions. Congress should require the Departments of Health and Human Services, Labor, and Commerce to provide it with geographical mapping of the conditions known to be related to crime and other social problems. Among the problem indices that should be mapped:

- the different types of crime;
- drug use;
- long-term welfare dependency (over two years);
- school performance;
- out-of-wedlock births;
- domestic violence, by types;
- child abuse;
- sexually transmitted disease, including AIDS.

Congress should also require information to examine the relationships between other social indicators and the lack of crime....

Request research on the effects on children of the intergenerational transmission of the single-parent family structure....

Reform the welfare system. Welfare today is a destructive Faustian bargain between all potential mothers and the government. As the condition for receiving cash—as opposed to real community support—the system requires that women and girls abandon the traditional moral code. Explains Heritage Foundation Senior Policy Analyst Robert Rector: "The woman has a contract with the government: She will continue to receive her 'paycheck' as long as she fulfills two conditions: 1) she must not work; and 2) she must not marry an employed male."

Whatever good intentions were served by the welfare system, the evidence shows that its perverse financial incentives discourage the formation of intact families and the pursuit of work. These are the outcomes of the current "community code" on which high-crime neighborhoods are built. Thus, current government policy is a powerful facilitator of the long-term rise in the crime rate....

Promote—through leadership in ideas, not national funding—volunteer community efforts, including the efforts of religious institutions. Amid the social collapse of so many neighborhoods, there are stunning examples of successful efforts to turn around the lives of young people previously immersed in crime.

These efforts invariably possess two features. One is a strong system of rules within an organization characterized by the love and firm guidance seen in a supportive family. The other is a strong spiritual dimension, most commonly a profound religious commitment.

... These relationships do not take money, but they do take a generous commitment of personal time, as in Big Brothers and Sisters. Government cannot purchase these efforts. If it tries, it will vitiate them by turning moral relationships into monetary ones.

Promote, through leadership in ideas, the benefits to the Nation of regular worship at religious institutions. The importance of codes of conduct and religious practice can hardly be overstated. According to the professional literature, active participation in a church significantly correlates with decreased incidence of crime. Expansion of active church membership and religious worship in a community contributes to the reduction of crime.

Government cannot re-empower religious institutions, for their essential nature is moral and spiritual. But it can be less hostile to their traditional areas of competence and mission. The potential for good among many religiously inspired schools, especially in America's inner cities, is well-known. But Congress and the courts insist that the price of government cooperation in education is noncooperation among the three nurturing institutions of family, church, and school. This strategy weakens communities.

Conduct inner-city experiments with school vouchers. Schools that maintain discipline and strong moral values can help support families that value these virtues and may make a difference in communities that have broken down. Parents need to be able to select such schools when their children are at risk. ...

Recent poll data in California and New Jersey confirm the general pattern of support for vouchers; not surprisingly, it is the poor who most want vouchers for private schools for their children. The poor well understand the importance of good schools in giving young people in crime-ridden neighborhoods the chance for a productive life.... Such schools can be crucial allies for parents. Vouchers provide the constitutional and financial means for this close and effective cooperation between school and family in the moral formation of children.

Remove barriers to adoption. Many children would have the benefit of a stable, two-parent family—reducing the probability that they would descend into crime—if adoption were made easier. Unfortunately, there are many frustrating barriers to adoption....

Reduce taxes on marriage and children. The Federal tax code discriminates against the institution of marriage and the raising of children. Since the early 1950s, the tax system each year has increased the tax burden at a much faster rate on families raising children than on any other form of household. Talk of "family" values is largely meaningless if it does not address this central economic relationship between government and family....

One such egregious feature is the "marriage penalty" on fathers and mothers who move from cohabitation to married family status. Another step Congress can take is to enact tax credits or other tax relief for parents with children. Adjusting the tax system to benefit the intact family silently but powerfully upholds marriage and the family.

CONCLUSION

... Government can staff and manage the criminal justice system efficiently and prevent crime in the short term by locking up violent teenage criminals so that they are no longer a danger to others. But it lacks both the capacity and competence to tackle the root causes of crime. That is the mission of three other basic institutions of society: the family, the church, and the school. For close to five decades, government has increasingly burdened these institutions —has even become hostile to them. It is now time to help these institutions fulfill their missions by reversing course and removing these burdens.

POSTSCRIPT

Should the Federal Government Have a Major Role in Reducing Juvenile Crime?

Tom Gitchoff, a professor of criminal justice at San Diego State University, insists that America's most precious asset is its youth. Both the OJJDP and Fagan would likely agree with Gitchoff. Yet their disagreements on how to mine this resource are profound. The OJJDP's position is that only efforts closely coordinated by the federal government through its research, training, evaluation, funding, policy recommendations, and monitoring can make any difference in reducing juvenile crime. The many achievements of the federal government in addressing this problem are pointed out in the office's selection, including vital publications with an agenda for solving local crime problems, providing seed money for states to implement innovative programs, and so on.

Fagan is not convinced. He seems to suggest that although the federal agencies pay lip service to the role of the family and communities, they actually have contributed to the destruction of many families through welfare requirements. Churches, he also insists, have been utterly ignored. Whatever crime reductions have been experienced in the recent past Fagan attributes to better police work and longer jail sentences, not the role of the OJJDP or other federal departments.

Neither author seems to address what many feel is a significant problem engulfing the United States: the extreme conservative backlash that may be leading to a dismantling of the juvenile justice system at both the state and federal levels. Independent of Fagan's comments, for example, both the 1994 Crime Prevention Act and current state and federal legislation seem oriented to reversing the stated goals of the OJJDP regardless of how successful that and other agencies were in achieving them.

What would your solutions be for the problem of juvenile crime? What roles might local, state, and federal governments have, if any, in this regard? What about the family, colleges, or religious institutions? How would you research possible innovative programs? Who would initiate them?

For an update on the OJJDP's thinking, see "Making a Difference: On the Front Lines With OJJDP Administrator Shay Bilchik," by E. Appleby, Jr., *Juvenile Justice* (December 1997). For useful statistics on delinquency, see the OJJDP's *Juvenile Offenders and Victims: 1997 Update on Violence* (August 1997); *State Responses to Serious and Violent Juvenile Crime*, published by the U.S. Department of Justice (July 1996); and the OJJDP's *Juvenile Arrests in 1996* (November 1997). An excellent exposé of the media/politician/conservative criminologists' hype of juvenile crime is V. Schiraldi and E. Lotke's "An

Analysis of Juvenile Homicides: Where They Occur and the Effectiveness of Adult Court Intervention," *Journal of Juvenile Justice and Detention Services* (July 1996). A useful report from the Center on Juvenile and Criminal Justice is *Out of Sight, Out of Mind: The Plight of Adolescent Girls in the San Francisco Juvenile Justice System* (July 1996). The January/April 1996 edition of *Law and Policy* has eight excellent articles on the issues of juvenile and criminal justice and placing juveniles into the adult system. A discussion of efforts at changing attitudes of juveniles is, "Is This a Camp or Jail?" by A. Cohen, *Time* (January 16, 1998). An outstanding collection of essays dealing with theories of crime and delinquency is *Developmental Theories of Crime and Delinquency* edited by T. Thornberry (Transaction Publishers, 1997). A recent work that addresses the debate from a broader historical perspective is *Balancing Juvenile Justice* by S. Guarino-Ghezzi and E. Loughran (Transaction Publishers, 1996). A seminal work on the unanticipated consequences of reform movements and their hidden agendas is T. Platt's *The Child Savers* (University of Chicago Press, 1969).

ISSUE 7

Are the Dangers of Internet Child Pornography Exaggerated?

YES: Julia Wilkins, from "Protecting Our Children from Internet Smut," *The Humanist* (September/October 1997)

NO: Bob Trebilcock, from "Child Molesters on the Internet: Are They in Your Home?" *Redbook* (April 1997)

ISSUE SUMMARY

YES: Julia Wilkins, a writer of books and articles on educating children, argues that claims of Internet dangers are simply an example of "moral panic" causing otherwise sensible people to overreact.

NO: Magazine writer Bob Trebilcock contends that the Internet is a real danger to children because it provides easy access to pornography, encourages the creation and dissemination of child pornography, and provides pedophiles with a new crop of children to prey upon.

I have sworn upon the altar of God, eternal hostility against every form of tyranny over the mind of man.

—Thomas Jefferson

Congress shall make no law respecting an establishment of religion, or prohibiting the free exercise thereof; or abridging the freedom of speech, or of the press.

—First Amendment of the U.S. Constitution

In spite of these valiant declarations, there have always been restraints on speech and writing with both practical and legal supports. Not that the issue of freedom of expression (including speaking, writing, publishing, painting, photography, and, more recently, Internet communications) has ever been close to a settled one. To the literate and the cultural elite, the very idea of outside constraints on expression is unacceptable. To the religious right and a variety of special interest groups, society simply could not function if there were no regulations on communication that might threaten decency.

Chief Justice Oliver Wendell Holmes ruled over 70 years ago that the First Amendment does not allow someone the right to shout "Fire!" in a crowded theater because of the harm that such an act could cause. This ruling, though frequently ignored in current debates, supports advocates of Internet control.

It also reflects the thinking of a growing number of scholars and activists who insist that words and images can be psychologically or even physically harmful and hence should be illegal.

What are the dangers of the Internet with regard to child pornography? Do we need special safeguards? In 1997 the U.S. Supreme Court ruled that the Communications Decency Act (CDA) passed by Congress violated the First Amendment. The Court did *not* say that existing laws prohibiting obscenity, child pornography, libel, copyright infringements, and the like do not apply to the Internet. The Court simply decided that the CDA was far more restrictive of free speech than was constitutional.

Hundreds of concerned citizens, especially parents, are forming coalitions. They are demanding legal actions to close down Web sites that are perceived as dangerous and to control computer use and programs in all public arenas, especially public libraries and schools. As of July 1997, according to the National Center for Missing and Exploited Children, only 25 children or so have been entrapped in exploitative situations as a consequence of online encounters. However, since July there have been at least six more serious encounters, including the killing of a child lured by an online chat-room pervert. Other examples cited by proponents of Internet control include a February 1998 arrest of police officers in four states who held sexual conversations with a 17-year-old girl in chat rooms.

Any technological innovations will generate strains. Since its creation in 1969 by the Department of Defense, initially with only four computers, the Internet has gone through several generations. Yet it is still remarkably new. Its influence, however, could be as pervasive as any invention of the past 100 years.

As you read the following selections by Julia Wilkins and Bob Trebilcock, reflect on your own experiences with computers and the Internet. Is access to pornography as difficult to block as Trebilcock implies? Will Wilkins's ideas for parental control work? How does the issue relate to broader conceptual arguments over technology? In what ways are the problems identified in this issue related to problems in other media, such as pornographic books and magazines? In what ways do they differ? Is the revolution resulting from Internet communication creating more serious crime problems?

YES
Julia Wilkins

PROTECTING OUR CHILDREN FROM INTERNET SMUT

The term *moral panic* is one of the more useful concepts to have emerged from sociology in recent years. A moral panic is characterized by a wave of public concern, anxiety, and fervor about something, usually perceived as a threat to society. The distinguishing factors are a level of interest totally out of proportion to the real importance of the subject, some individuals building personal careers from the pursuit and magnification of the issue, and the replacement of reasoned debate with witchhunts and hysteria.

Moral panics of recent memory include the Joseph McCarthy anti-communist witchhunts of the 1950s and the satanic ritual abuse allegations of the 1980s. And, more recently, we have witnessed a full-blown moral panic about pornography on the Internet. Sparked by the July 3, 1995, *Time* cover article "On a Screen Near You: Cyberporn," this moral panic has been perpetuated and intensified by a raft of subsequent media reports. As a result, there is now a widely held belief that pornography is easily accessible to all children using the Internet. This was also the judgment of Congress, which, proclaiming to be "protecting the children," voted overwhelmingly in 1996 for legislation to make it a criminal offense to send "indecent" material over the Internet into people's computers.

The original *Time* article was based on its exclusive access to Marty Rimm's *Georgetown University Law Journal* paper, "Marketing Pornography on the Information Superhighway." Although published, the article had not received peer review and was based on an undergraduate research project concerning descriptions of images on adult bulletin board systems in the United States. Using the information in this paper, *Time* discussed the type of pornography available online, such as "pedophilia (nude pictures of children), hebephelia (youths) and . . . images of bondage, sadomasochism, urination, defecation, and sex acts with a barnyard full of animals." The article proposed that pornography of this nature is readily available to anyone who is even remotely computer literate and raised the stakes by offering quotes from worried parents who feared for their children's safety. It also presented the possibility that pornographic material could be mailed to children without their

From Julia Wilkins, "Protecting Our Children from Internet Smut," *The Humanist* (September/October 1997). Copyright © 1997 by Julia Wilkins. Reprinted by permission.

parents' knowledge. *Time*'s example was of a ten-year-old boy who supposedly received pornographic images in his e-mail showing "10 thumbnail size pictures showing couples engaged in various acts of sodomy, heterosexual intercourse and lesbian sex." Naturally, the boy's mother was shocked and concerned, saying, "Children should not be subject to these images." *Time* also quoted another mother who said that she wanted her children to benefit from the vast amount of knowledge available on the Internet but was inclined not to allow access, fearing that her children could be "bombarded with X-rated pornography and [she] would know nothing about it."

From the outset, Rimm's report generated a lot of excitement—not only because it was reportedly the first published study of online pornography but also because of the secrecy involved in the research and publication of the article. In fact, the *New York Times* reported on July 24, 1995, that Marty Rimm was being investigated by his university, Carnegie Mellon, for unethical research and, as a result, would not be giving testimony to a Senate hearing on Internet pornography. Two experts from *Time* reportedly discovered serious flaws in Rimm's study involving gross misrepresentation and erroneous methodology. His work was soon deemed flawed and inaccurate, and *Time* recanted in public. With Rimm's claims now apologetically retracted, his original suggestion that 83.5 percent of Internet graphics are pornographic was quietly withdrawn in favor of a figure less than 1 percent.

Time admitted that grievous errors had slipped past their editorial staff, as their normally thorough research succumbed to a combination of deadline pressure and exclusivity agreements that barred them from showing the unpublished study to possible critics. But, by then, the damage had been done: the study had found its way to the Senate.

GOVERNMENT INTERVENTION

Senator Charles Grassley (Republican–Iowa) jumped on the pornography bandwagon by proposing a bill that would make it a criminal offense to supply or permit the supply of "indecent" material to minors over the Internet. Grassley introduced the entire *Time* article into the congressional record, despite the fact that the conceptual, logical, and methodological flaws in the report had already been acknowledged by the magazine.

On the Senate floor, Grassley referred to Marty Rimm's undergraduate research as "a remarkable study conducted by researchers at Carnegie Mellon University" and went on to say:

> The university surveyed 900,000 computer images. Of these 900,000 images, 83.5 percent of all computerized photographs available on the Internet are pornographic.... With so many graphic images available on computer networks, I believe Congress must act and do so in a constitutional manner to help parents who are under assault in this day and age.

Under the Grassley bill, later known as the Protection of Children from Pornography Act of 1995, it would have been illegal for anyone to knowingly or recklessly transmit indecent material to minors. This bill marked the beginning of a stream of Internet censorship legislation at various levels of government in the United States and abroad.

The most extreme and fiercely opposed of these was the Communications Decency Act, sponsored by former Senator James Exon (Democrat–Nebraska) and Senator Dan Coats (Republican–Indiana). The CDA labeled the transmission of "obscene, lewd, lascivious, filthy, indecent, or patently offensive" pornography over the Internet a crime. It was attached to the Telecommunications Reform Act of 1996, which was then passed by Congress on February 1, 1996. One week later, it was signed into law by President Clinton. On the same day, the American Civil Liberties Union filed suit in Philadelphia against the U.S. Department of Justice and Attorney General Janet Reno, arguing that the statute would ban free speech protected by the First Amendment and subject Internet users to far greater restrictions than exist in any other medium. Later that month, the Citizens Internet Empowerment Coalition initiated a second legal challenge to the CDA, which formally consolidated with *ACLU v. Reno*. Government lawyers agreed not to prosecute "indecent" or "patently offensive" material until the three-judge court in Philadelphia ruled on the case.

Although the purpose of the CDA was to protect young children from accessing and viewing material of sexually explicit content on the Internet, the wording of the act was so broad and poorly defined that it could have deprived many adults of information they needed in the areas of health, art, news, and literature —information that is legal in print form. Specifically, certain medical information available on the Internet includes descriptions of sexual organs and activities which might have been considered "indecent" or "patently offensive" under the act—for example, information on breastfeeding, birth control, AIDS, and gynecological and urinological information. Also, many museums and art galleries

now have websites. Under the act, displaying art like the Sistine Chapel nudes could be cause for criminal prosecution. Online newspapers would not be permitted to report the same information as is available in the print media. Reports on combatants in war, at the scenes of crime, in the political arena, and outside abortion clinics often provoke images or language that could be constituted "offensive" and therefore illegal on the net. Furthermore, the CDA provided a legal basis for banning books which had been ruled unconstitutional to ban from school libraries. These include many of the classics as well as modern literature containing words that may be considered "indecent."

The act also expanded potential liability for employers, service providers, and carriers that transmit or otherwise make available restricted communications. According to the CDA, "knowingly" allowing obscene material to pass through one's computer system was a criminal offense. Given the nature of the Internet, however, making service providers responsible for the content of the traffic they pass on to other Internet nodes is equivalent to holding a telephone carrier responsible for the content of the conversations going over that carrier's lines. So, under the terms of the act, if someone sent an indecent electronic comment from a workstation, the employer, the e-mail service provider, and the carrier all could be potentially held liable and subject to up to $100,000 in fines or two years in prison.

On June 12, 1996, after experiencing live tours of the Internet and hearing arguments about the technical and economical infeasibility of complying with the censorship law, the three federal judges in Philadelphia granted the request for a preliminary injunction against the CDA.

The court determined that "there is no evidence that sexually oriented material is the primary type of content on this new medium" and proposed that "communications over the Internet do not 'invade' an individual's home or appear on one's computer screen unbidden. Users seldom encounter content 'by accident.'" In a unanimous decision, the judges ruled that the Communications Decency Act would unconstitutionally restrict free speech on the Internet.

The government appealed the judges' decision and, on March 19, 1997, the U.S. Supreme Court heard oral arguments in the legal challenge to the CDA, now known as *Reno v. ACLU*. Finally, on June 26, the decision came down. The Court voted unanimously that the act violated the First Amendment guarantee of freedom of speech and would have threatened "to torch a large segment of the Internet community."

Is the panic therefore over? Far from it. The July 7, 1997, *Newsweek*, picking up the frenzy where *Time* left off, reported the Supreme Court decision in a provocatively illustrated article featuring a color photo of a woman licking her lips and a warning message taken from the website of the House of Sin. Entitled "On the Net, Anything Goes," the opening words by Steven Levy read, "Born of a hysteria triggered by a genuine problem—the ease with which wired-up teenagers can get hold of nasty pictures on the Internet—the Communications Decency Act (CDA) was never really destined to be a companion piece to the Bill of Rights." At the announcement of the Court's decision, anti-porn protesters were on the street outside brandishing signs which read, "Child Molesters Are Looking for Victims on the Internet."

Meanwhile, government talk has shifted to the development of a universal Internet rating system and widespread hardware and software filtering. Referring to the latter, White House Senior Adviser Rahm Emanuel declared, "We're going to get the V-chip for the Internet. Same goal, different means."

But it is important to bear in mind that children are still a minority of Internet users. A contract with an Internet service provider typically needs to be paid for by credit card or direct debit, therefore requiring the intervention of an adult. Children are also unlikely to be able to view any kind of porn online without a credit card.

In addition to this, there have been a variety of measures developed to protect children on the Internet. The National Center for Missing and Exploited Children has outlined protective guidelines for parents and children in its pamphlet, *Child Safety on the Information Superhighway*. A number of companies now sell Internet newsfeeds and web proxy accesses that are vetted in accordance with a list of forbidden topics. And, of course, there remain those blunt software instruments that block access to sexually oriented sites by looking for keywords such as *sex, erotic,* and *X-rated*. But one of the easiest solutions is to keep the family computer in a well-traveled space, like a living room, so that parents can monitor what their children download.

FACT OR MEDIA FICTION?

In her 1995 *CMC* magazine article, "Journey to the Centre of Cybersmut," Lisa Schmeiser discusses her research into online pornography. After an exhaustive search, she was unable to find any pornography, apart from the occasional commercial site (requiring a credit card for access), and concluded that one would have to undertake extensive searching to find quantities of explicit pornography. She suggested that, if children were accessing pornography online, they would not have been doing it by accident. Schmeiser writes: "There will be children who circumvent passwords, Surfwatch software, and seemingly innocuous links to find the 'adult' material. But these are the same kids who would visit every convenience store in a five-mile radius to find the one stocking *Playboy*." Her argument is simply that, while there is a certain amount of pornography online, it is not freely and readily available. Contrary to what the media often report, pornography is not that easy to find.

There *is* pornography in cyberspace (including images, pictures, movies, sounds, and sex discussions) and several ways of receiving pornographic material on the Internet (such as through private bulletin board systems, the World Wide Web, newsgroups, and e-mail). However, many sites just contain reproduced images from hardcore magazines and videos available from other outlets, and registration fee restrictions make them inaccessible to children. And for the more contentious issue of pedophilia, a recent investigation by the *Guardian* newspaper in Britain revealed that the majority of pedophilic images distributed on the Internet are simply electronic reproductions of the small output of legitimate pedophile magazines, such as *Lolita*, published in the 1970s.

Clearly the issue of pornography on the Internet is a moral panic—an issue perpetuated by a sensationalistic style of reporting and misleading content in newspaper and magazine articles. And

probably the text from which to base any examination of the possible link between media reporting and moral panics is Stanley Cohen's 1972 book, *Folk Devils and Moral Panic*, in which he proposes that the mass media are ultimately responsible for the creation of such panics. Cohen describes a moral panic as occurring when "a condition, episode, person or group of persons emerges to become a threat to societal values and interests;... the moral barricades are manned by editors... politicians and other 'right thinking' people." He feels that, while problematical elements of society can pose a threat to others, this threat is realistically far less than the perceived image generated by mass media reporting.

Cohen describes how the news we read is not necessarily the truth; editors have papers to sell, targets to meet, and competition from other publishers. It is in their interest to make the story "a good read"—the sensationalist approach sells newspapers. The average person is likely to be drawn in with the promise of scandal and intrigue. This can be seen in the reporting of the *National Enquirer* and *People*, with their splashy pictures and sensationalistic headlines, helping them become two of the largest circulation magazines in the United States.

Cohen discusses the "inventory" as the set of criteria inherent in any reporting that may be deemed as fueling a moral panic. This inventory consists of the following:

Exaggeration in reporting. Facts are often overblown to give the story a greater edge. Figures that are not necessarily incorrect but have been quoted out of context, or have been used incorrectly to shock, are two forms of this exaggeration.

Looking back at the original *Time* cover article, "On a Screen Near You: Cyberporn, "this type of exaggeration is apparent. Headlines such as "The Carnegie Mellon researches found 917,410 sexually explicit pictures, short stories and film clips online" make the reader think that there really is a problem with the quantity of pornography in cyberspace. It takes the reader a great deal of further exploration to find out how this figure was calculated. Also, standing alone and out of context, the oft-quoted figure that 83.5 percent of images found on Usenet Newsgroups are pornographic could be seen as cause for concern. However, if one looks at the math associated with this figure, one would find that this is a sampled percentage with a research leaning toward known areas of pornography.

The repetition of fallacies. This occurs when a writer reports information that seems perfectly believable to the general public, even though those who know the subject are aware it is wildly incorrect. In the case of pornography, the common fallacy is that the Internet is awash with nothing but pornography and that all you need to obtain it is a computer and a modem. Such misinformation is integral to the fueling of moral panics.

Take, for example, the October 18, 1995, *Scotland on Sunday*, which reports that, to obtain pornographic material, "all you need is a personal computer, a phone line with a modem attached and a connection via a specialist provider to the Internet." What the article fails to mention is that the majority of pornography is found on specific Usenet sites not readily available from the major Internet providers, such as America Online and Compuserve. It also fails to mention that this pornography needs to be downloaded and converted into a viewable form, which requires certain skills and can take considerable time.

Misleading pictures and snappy titles. Media representation often exaggerates a story through provocative titles and flashy pictorials—all in the name of drawing in the reader. The titles set the tone for the rest of the article; the headline is the most noticeable and important part of any news item, attracting the reader's initial attention. The recent *Newsweek* article is a perfect example. Even if the headline has little relevance to the article, it sways the reader's perception of the topic. The symbolization of images further increases the impact of the story. *Time*'s own images in its original coverage—showing a shocked little boy on the cover and, inside, a naked man hunched over a computer monitor—added to the article's ability to shock and to draw the reader into the story.

Through sensationalized reporting, certain forms of behavior become classified as *deviant*. Specifically, those who put pornography online or those who download it are seen as being deviant in nature. This style of reporting benefits the publication or broadcast by giving it the aura of "moral guardian" to the rest of society. It also increases revenue.

In exposing deviant behavior, newspapers and magazines have the ability to push for reform. So, by classifying a subject and its relevant activities as deviant, they can stand as crusaders for moral decency, championing the cause of "normal" people. They can report the subject and call for something to be done about it, but this power is easily abused. The *Time* cyberporn article called for reform on the basis of Rimm's findings, proclaiming, "A new study shows us how pervasive and wild [pornography on the Internet] really is. Can we protect our kids—and free speech?" These cries to protect our children affected the likes of Senators James Exon and Robert Dole, who took the *Time* article with its "shocking" revelations (as well as a sample of pornographic images) to the Senate floor, appealing for changes to the law. From this response it is clear how powerful a magazine article can be, regardless of the integrity and accuracy of its reporting.

The *Time* article had all of Cohen's elements relating to the fueling of a moral panic: exaggeration, fallacies, and misleading pictures and titles. Because certain publications are highly regarded and enjoy an important role in society, anything printed in their pages is consumed and believed by a large audience. People accept what they read because, to the best of their knowledge, it is the truth. So, even though the *Time* article was based on a report by an undergraduate student passing as "a research team from Carnegie Mellon," the status of the magazine was great enough to launch a panic that continues unabated—from the halls of Congress to the pulpits of churches, from public schools to the offices of software developers, from local communities to the global village.

NO

Bob Trebilcock

CHILD MOLESTERS ON THE INTERNET

Like many parents of young children, I'd read the headlines about pedophiles trying to seduce kids and swapping pornography on the Internet. This sort of deviant behavior, I assumed, must lurk in deep, all-but-impenetrable recesses of cyberspace. But when I got this assignment to report on the 'Net's red-light district, I decided to see what an on-line novice like myself could find.

Armed with a hint or two from a computer consultant, I turned on the standard-issue computer in my family room and clicked on Usenet, a section of the World Wide Web, where anyone can post or access messages and photographs related to a specific topic, and typed in the words "alt.sex.incest." In less than a minute, I was scrolling through hundreds of brief text messages from guys who offered to swap photographs or described their sexual fantasies with children. One message was repeated four times: "subject: Re: z9 × 7 I lookin' 4 cindys series...." I clicked my mouse.

The text came up quickly, a request for a series of photos. "I only have cindy 1, 2, 8, 15, 17 ... if someone can repost 'em all ... thanx."

Underneath was a reply from another user: "Here's 3, 4, and 5. Enjoy! Rick." Below the text, a color image appeared on my screen, slowly unrolling from top to bottom like a window blind. As the first image formed, I took a sharp, deep breath. At the top of the photo, a pair of chubby, dimpled knees was spread apart. Naked from the waist down, Cindy was lying on her back, legs apart. It was a typical centerfold pose, but Cindy was no typical centerfold model. She was not much older than 6.

Eleven more shots formed on my screen, the same little girl performing oral sex on an adult male. As I exited the file, my hands were shaking and my stomach was churning.

I looked at my watch. In less than 15 minutes, without any special software or expert knowledge, I'd found a deviant world without sexual boundaries, one that could be located by curious teenagers and potential child molesters alike. Though I called the police to report what I'd seen, I still didn't sleep well that night. Who was Cindy? Who was forcing her to do those things? And, given the rash of recent headlines about computer-related sex crimes, is any child safe from sexual exploitation in the age of the mouse and the modem?

Make no mistake about it: The Internet is a powerful tool that levels the information playing field. On-line in your home, you can view the Louvre's art collection, chat with David Bowie on his fiftieth birthday, and access research from top academic institutions across the country. No wonder the 'Net is growing so explosively. In just three years, America Online, the largest commercial service provider, has expanded from 1 million to 8 million households, and, globally, 30 million people are estimated to be logging on-line.

Granted, the vast majority of what's on the Internet is entertaining, informative, if not educational. But the 'Net does have a dark side. "I call the Internet the playground of the nineties for pedophiles," says Donna Rice Hughes, director of marketing and communications for Enough Is Enough, a Fairfax, Virginia, nonprofit group that campaigns to make the Internet safe for children.

Hughes may have a point. In addition to housing pictures of dozens of children, like the ones of Cindy, the Internet has spawned sites featuring snapshots of children—unwittingly photographed while at play in parks and at the beach—who serve as pedophiles' love objects; kids-only chat rooms where child molesters prowl; and electronic support groups in which "boy-lovers" validate each other's most disturbed impulses.

Could these pedophiles be reaching right into your home via the family PC? What are authorities doing to regulate this booming and, at times, unsettling new forum? And what can you, as a parent, do to protect your children?

CAN WE TALK? THE DANGER OF CHAT ROOMS

"How old are u?"

The words appeared simultaneously on screens in New Hampshire and California.

"I am 14," the user in California replied.

"love to do u then," the man in New Hampshire typed.

"I would like that," the boy replied.

The man's name was Alan Hicks. A 46-year-old mechanical engineer and one-time Big Brother, Hicks was also a convicted pedophile who had served time for molesting young boys. After his release on parole, Hicks joined a treatment group and agreed to make a training film about his life for the benefit of law enforcement officials.

He also discovered the Internet. During one year on-line, he befriended numerous boys in chat rooms. When the boys were willing, Hicks took the conversations private, where he talked graphically about sex and E-mailed pornographic photos. In return, he asked for favors—a pair of underwear, even samples of boys' urine and semen.

Hicks would probably still be on-line today if he hadn't sent a nude photo of himself to a police informant who turned it over to James McLaughlin, a Keene, New Hampshire, police detective currently working with federal authorities on a nationwide probe of child exploitation on the Internet. By coincidence, Detective McLaughlin recognized Hicks from that training film he made, and helped return him to jail last November.

The Hicks case illustrates the most palpable danger to children on-line: child molesters lurking in chat rooms devoted to innocent subjects like sports and

"WHY PEDOPHILES GO ON-LINE": ONE CONVICT'S STORY

"Child pornography is the pedophile's rock cocaine. It's a quick fix. It's cheap, and thanks to the Internet, it's everywhere."

The speaker's name is "Bob," and he's a computer expert in his forties. He's also a recovering pedophile who has spent 20 years on the wrong side of the law. Talking to me by phone from a southern state he will not identify, Bob says he's watched the explosive growth of pedophiles on the Internet from both sides of the fence.

Why is the Internet so enticing for pedophiles? "It's created easily accessible stimulation for child molesters," says Bob. "You can download pictures in complete anonymity. You do not have to make any kind of human contact."

Anonymity is so crucial, says Bob, because your average pedophile "is not the dirty old man in a trench coat, but a teacher at your local elementary school. The Internet becomes his outlet."

Bob acknowledges that chat rooms pose the greatest physical danger to your child on-line. However, he notes, "On the computer, the search for a victim is an arduous task that's fraught with danger due to the intensity of law enforcement."

"Besides," he adds, "victims are too easy to find in other places." Successful pedophiles, he explains, "are better with your children than you are. They give them more attention. They are your swim coach, your Sunday school teacher—people you trust to come into contact with your child every single day."

Which children, I ask, were safe from these predators? Kids who got a lot of love, attention, and time from their parents, Bob said, were least likely to be curious about what another adult might offer.

music. "Ultimately," McLaughlin says, "pedophiles will try to get the kids to agree to phone or mail contact, and then arrange for a meeting."

The scary truth is, some succeed. Last November, Cary Bodenheimer, a 30-year-old engineer for a major aircraft manufacturer in the Philadelphia area, pled guilty to having had sex in an Illinois motel room with a 13-year-old girl he had met over the Internet. A year earlier, James Heigh, 29, of Keizer, Oregon, was convicted of third-degree rape after he met a 14-year-old girl on-line, engaged her in lengthy phone calls, and then had sex with her.

Granted, the number of cases is relatively small, and only 23 incidents involving chat rooms were reported between 1994 and 1996, according to the National Center for Missing and Exploited Children. But warns J. Robert Flores, senior trial attorney with the Department of Justice Child Exploitation and Obscenity Section, "This is a new crime that's just three or four years old.

Not all law enforcement agencies are reporting their numbers."

Insidiously, these overtures by pedophiles are often made while mom and dad are in the next room, pleased that their child is learning to use the computer rather than watching mindless TV. Teens, for their part, are often bolder on-line than they would be in the real world. "Sex is on the minds of a lot of 12- and 13-year-olds," says Gary Hewitt, a psychotherapist in Rochester, New York, who has worked with children who were abducted and exploited by strangers. "They'll go on-line and open up. A pedophile will then tell that child whatever he or she wants to hear to bond with them."

To safeguard children from these anonymous predators, America Online has added guards to monitor the kids-only chat rooms for suspicious dialogue. A good first step, but private messages —invisible to the rest of the chat room —cannot be screened, and that's where a pedophile is likely to begin forging a relationship with a child.

Experts agree that the best way to keep your child safe in cyberspace is the same as keeping your child safe in the real world: parental involvement. Says Sergeant Nick Battaglia, former supervisor of the child exploitation unit of the San Jose Police Department, and an expert on computer-related sex crimes, "Just like you wouldn't let your child play alone in an urban park for three hours, you shouldn't let them play alone on the Internet."

Battaglia urges parents to keep the computer in a central location, limit how much time your child spends on-line, and educate yourself about the technology so you can monitor what your child is doing. Most critically, go on-line with your child as often as possible to help her identify inappropriate requests, and emphasize that people encountered in chat rooms are strangers, just like the ones you've warned them about in the real world. Finally, insist that your child never give out personal information— home address, phone number, school name—on-line without first asking your permission, and never agree to meet someone in person without a parent being present.

KIDDIE PORN'S NEW LIFE ON-LINE

While on-line chat rooms pose a new threat to our children, authorities also credit the Internet with reviving an old foe: child pornography. The problem is pressing enough that the FBI formed the "Innocent Images" task force, a three-year undercover investigation focusing on the use of on-line computer services to distribute kiddie porn which has led to about 70 felony convictions. But to be candid, FBI spokesperson Larry Foust admits, they have only scratched the surface.

Indeed, it's never been a better time to be a pedophile: The Internet has opened up a new, anonymous way for pedophiles to exchange and expand their collections of porn, says Don Huycke, program manager of the Child Pornography Enforcement Program for the U.S. Customs Service, the long-standing experts in kiddie porn, since so much of it has been produced overseas. "They'll say: I want two little girls age 6 to 9 having sex. We find guys making 40 to 50 downloads per night of child pornography."

The resurgence of kiddie porn marks an end to one of law enforcement's success stories. In 1982, a Supreme

Court decision approved the ban on the distribution of material depicting children engaged in sexual conduct, virtually shutting down the U.S. kiddie porn industry by the end of the decade. By 1993, all that had changed with the mushrooming popularity of the Internet: In the last fiscal year, the number of search warrants issued by Customs involving child pornography increased by 220 percent, with the majority of those cases involving the use of computers. Though most child pornography on-line has been culled from magazines produced in the seventies and early eighties, some experts hint that the Internet encourages new images to be created. Thanks to new technology, like digital cameras, porn can be produced directly on-line, without leaving the literal paper trail that photos do when developed and published.

Child porn is dangerous, the experts say, not just because kids are molested during the production but because pedophiles use the images to convince children that sex with adults is enjoyable and natural. What's more, mental health professionals worry about the long-term impact of child pornography on the Internet. Says David N. Greenfield, Ph.D., a Hartford, Connecticut, psychologist who has studied the phenomenon of Internet addiction, "I'm concerned about kids being exposed to this material when they are too young to realize it's an unrealistic portrayal of sexual behavior. Seeing child pornography on the 'Net legitimizes it, which is dangerous."

Can anything be done to wipe this sort of material off the Internet? Authorities hope so. Last year, Congress passed the Communications Decency Act, which prohibits the knowing distribution of indecent material to minors by computer. A bill introduced by Senator Orrin G. Hatch, which passed in September 1996, makes it illegal to produce "morphed" child pornography, in which perfectly innocent pictures of children are altered by computer to show them engaged in sex acts, say, by grafting the head of a child onto the body of a nude, slender adult.

Enforcing the law, however, is the real challenge. Given the millions of web sites—and the ability of pedophiles to encrypt photos, or put them in a code that can only be translated with special software—most police departments are ill-equipped to find such pornography. Until the police catch up with the child pornographers, parents can rely on "net nanny" software programs (similar to the V-chip for your television set) to control the sites a child can browse on the web. Some service providers, such as America Online, perform the same function.

COULD MY CHILD'S PHOTO BE ON THE 'NET?

More alarmingly, authorities are finding that even children with absolutely no connection to child pornography are turning up on-line as love objects for pedophiles. Consider the case of George Chamberlain, a 56-year-old pedophile serving a 35-year sentence in Minnesota for child sexual assault. In 1995, authorities seized a prison computer used by Chamberlain as part of a computer programming and telemarketing business run by prison inmates. Connected to the information superhighway, he also swapped child pornography and E-mail message with other pedophiles on the Internet.

Worse still, investigators discovered a list stored on computer with the names, ages, and addresses of 3,000 children, culled from seemingly harmless listings in local newspapers. Though Chamberlain denied compiling the names, to investigators, they looked like a virtual catalog of potential abuse victims. The list's mere existence raises the question: Could my child be on the Internet without my knowledge?

Though unlikely, the answer is yes. Circulating in Usenet groups are photos of fully clothed cheerleaders, gymnasts, and little girls at play, snapped by pedophiles' cameras and posted in files labeled "erotica"—clearly, someone's fantasy material. On the World Wide Web, some sites created by self-described "boy-lovers"—men infatuated with young or teenage boys—receive almost a quarter-million visitors in a given four-month period. Visit the "Boys in the Real World" site to see photos of prepubescent boys at play taken at Disneyland, Sea World, and the San Diego Zoo. At ComQuest Boys, a message by the web page's producer describes how he took his photos of boys frolicking on a Santa Monica beach: "I had to get within about 12 feet of my unsuspecting subjects in order to fill the frame, which is a challenge to say the least. If I... visit a beach... again, I hope to get beautiful boys to volunteer to be photographed and show their smiling faces and newly forming muscles."

Authorities stress that these photos serve solely as fantasy material for pedophiles who are unlikely to try to find or make contact with the children depicted. Yet, as a cop and a parent, Nick Battaglia admits, "Those sites are very upsetting, because someone's taking your privacy and exploiting your child." Unfortunately, he adds, "there's nothing illegal about it." And there's very little you can do to protect your family, beyond confronting anyone who seems to be taking inappropriate photos of your—or anyone else's—child.

HOW CHILD MOLESTERS NETWORK IN CYBERSPACE

Beyond trading fantasy material, pedophiles have even formed on-line support groups, in which they bolster one another's egos and share tips. "Boy-lovers with integrity and courage can use the resources of the Internet... to break through the boundaries that others would impose in this culture," asserts the NAMBLA Bulletin, the voice of the North American Man/Boy Love Association. In the past, pedophiles were fundamentally an isolated group. Thanks to the Internet, that's changing—and fast—as pedophile support groups spring up on-line. One site, alt.support.boy-lovers, provides answers to frequently asked questions like "What do boy-lovers feel?" and recommends literary works with a boy-lover theme, such as Thomas Mann's *Death in Venice.* The site's mission: to provide acceptance "for boy-lovers who do not consider themselves in need of conversion to an orientation other than their natural one."

The quest for acceptance is precisely what concerns law enforcement officers and mental health professionals. Chris Hatcher, Ph.D., a clinical professor of psychology at the University of California in San Francisco who studies pedophiles and child abductors, has coined the phrase "virtual validation" to describe the burgeoning network of pedophiles on-line. "They're able to be in contact with sometimes hundreds of other people with similar beliefs," explains Dr. Hatcher. "That is a level of validation they were never able to obtain before."

Coupled with the availability of child pornography on the 'Net, Dr. Hatcher argues that the virtual validation pedophiles find on-line may encourage someone who has not yet molested a child to do so. "Pedophiles who make contact with children have a developmental pattern," says Dr. Hatcher. It begins with fantasy, moves to gratification through pornography, then voyeurism, and finally to contact. "The 'Net accelerates that pattern. It gives them a level of virtual validation that would have otherwise taken years to obtain." Adds Gary Hewitt, "The support group sites give pedophiles a real sense of power, and the impetus to go out and molest someone." Protected by First Amendment rights, these cyberspace support-group sites are difficult to restrict.

WHAT'S NEXT?

Last April, a 10-year-old girl was invited to a slumber party at the home of another little girl in Greenfield, California. What her parents didn't know: The friend's father, Ronald Riva, was a member of the Orchid Club, an on-line group of men who met in pedophile chat rooms and used the Internet to swap pornography and true-life stories of child molestation.

That night, Riva and another club member, who was visiting, awoke the girl, then fondled her in front of a digital camera attached to a computer. The images of her molestation were broadcast to other members of the group, who watched the live event on their computers and responded interactively,

typing in what they'd like to see happen next.

This shocking crime led to an investigation by U.S. Customs and other agencies, ending in the indictments of 16 members of the Orchid Club. The first known example of pedophiles using the Internet for real-life abuse of a child, the Orchid club might be a barometer of where we are headed on the Internet.

Most experts agree that the Internet phenomenon is still too new to predict the future danger to children. As more people become familiar with the 'Net, and the potential dangers of this otherwise positive medium, kids may be safer than ever. Or the threat could snowball. Technology like digital cameras and video conferencing that download images directly into the computer may create more home-grown child pornography, as in the Orchid Club case.

Despite the high-tech wizardry employed by the Orchid Club members, the case serves as a cautionary reminder about how pedophiles always have—and probably always will—operate. The 10-year-old victim met her molesters in the neighborhood. Observes Burt G. Hollenbeck Jr., Ph.D., a New Hampshire psychologist who has treated around 400 pedophiles, "The focus on computers as a threat to our children obscures the fact that the real danger is in our backyards. As a society, we'd rather think the molester is some faceless guy at a computer terminal. But, every guy at a PC has another identity. He's also grandpa, the teacher, or our next-door neighbor."

POSTSCRIPT

Are the Dangers of Internet Child Pornography Exaggerated?

Wilkins identifies notable exaggerations of Internet smut dangers, including the 1995 *Time* story alleging that "83.5 percent of Internet graphics are pornographic." Some suggest that an unfortunate result of living in a highly moralized and politicized age is that people who should know better will resort to lies to make their points. Yet Trebilcock is correct that serious cases of child cyberporn and other sex problems are surfacing on the Internet. These include virtually all of the traditional kiddie porn practices as well as Internet innovations such as "morphed" pornography and chat-room conversations that become private and obscene.

Are parent-level practices such as keeping the home computer in plain view, utilizing "nanny nets" to block objectionable material on the Internet, and explaining to youngsters potential dangers and trusting them not to take risks (e.g., giving out their names or phone numbers) enough? Many insist that they are, especially with vigorous enforcement. Some, such as *Wired* magazine editor Jon Katz, say that we do our children a disservice by not trusting them, after proper training, to use the Internet wisely.

What about Internet users and the producers of Web material in general? Not considered by either protagonist is these pioneers' well-known free spirit and pride in bringing in a new information order. They vehemently oppose more controls. An additional array of related issues include "flaming" (attacking others, often viciously, on the Internet) and Web spite (e. g., "rogue" sites that start with "I hate" followed by horrendous denunciations ranging from advocating raping Barney the dinosaur to decapitating Donald Duck). Moreover, the number of hate groups reflecting Nazi, Ku Klux Klan, and other such sentiments as well as right-wing sites with manuals on how to make a bomb has doubled to 600 in the past year, according to the Simon Wiesenthal Center.

Are Internet dangers, including pornography, exaggerated? Alternatively, are the dangers of proposed solutions (e.g., censorship and erosion of freedom) exaggerated?

Other interrelated Internet issues are also important. Helpful overviews include "Cyber Phobia: Are You Afraid of the Internet?" by R. Walker, *University Faculty Voice* (February 1998); *Virtual Reality* by J. Katz (Random House, 1997); and J. Katz, "The Trouble With Giving a Safety Net," *The Washington Post* (July 6, 1997). An optimistic view of Internet changes is *Release 2.0: A Design for Living in the Digital Age* by E. Dyson (Broadway Books, 1997). A profile of Dyson, one of three women participating in the CEO 100-person summit led by Bill Gates, is "Philosopher in the Digital Age," by J. Mathews, *The Baltimore Sun* (March 3, 1998).

Articles supportive of Trebilcock include "Did the Net Kill Eddie?" by S. Levi, *Newsweek* (October 13, 1997) and "Is the Fairfax Library Board Ready to Face the 'P' Word?" by Karen Jo Gounaud, *Arlington Journal* (September 12, 1997). Concern with false information and hatred on the Internet is evident in "Web Spite," by T. Ikenberg, *The Baltimore Sun* (October 22, 1997) and *Deeper: My Two-Year Odyssey in Cyberspace* by J. Seabrook (Simon & Schuster, 1997). A different concern is expressed in "Internet Addiction Can Be as Debilitating and Expensive as Any Addiction," by P. Cassels, *Baltimore Gay Paper* (February 13, 1998).

For a discussion of the potential legal problems facing students and professors who misuse the Internet, see "The Laws of Cyberspace: What Colleges Need to Know," by S. McDonald, *Chronicle of Higher Education* (October 31, 1997). An interesting discussion of the Internet from a female perspective is "A Feminist Scholar Questions How Women Fare in Distance Education," by G. Blumenstyk, *Chronicle of Higher Education* (October 31, 1997).

ISSUE 8

Are the New Sex Offender Laws Rational?

YES: Bruce Fein, from "Community Self-Defense Laws Are Constitutionally Sound," *ABA Journal* (March 1995)

NO: Edward Martone, from "Mere Illusion of Safety Creates Climate of Vigilante Justice," *ABA Journal* (March 1995)

ISSUE SUMMARY

YES: Journalist Bruce Fein contends that community notification laws of convicted sex offenders is necessary in lieu of increasing rage at violent child sex offenders, which could result in demands for excessive prison sentences if something is not done.

NO: Edward Martone, an American Civil Liberties Union activist, acknowledges community rage but maintains that the new laws create vigilantism, unfairly punish offenders, and contribute little to solving the problem of compulsive sex offenders.

The branding of deviants as a control mechanism can be seen throughout history. Nathaniel Hawthorne's classic novel *The Scarlet Letter,* for example, centers around a young mother who is forced to wear the letter *A* on her chest, signifying "adultress." In some countries, in earlier times, it was standard practice to cut off the hand of a thief (this is still done in Saudi Arabia). Similarly, concentration camp prisoners were identified in Nazi Germany by numbers tattooed on their wrists. Nowadays, in the United States, 44 states have laws requiring or encouraging community notification when convicted sex offenders are released from prison. New Jersey's version, "Megan's Law," has become a model for the rest of the nation.

There are many components to New Jersey's law, which was passed within 30 days of the July 1994 murder of seven-year-old Megan Kanka, who was lured into the home of twice-convicted violent sex offender Jesse Timmendequas. Apparently no one in the community knew of the predator's criminal history (or the fact that his two roommates were also convicted sex offenders). The most controversial aspect of Megan's Law pertains to the community notification part, which classifies sex offenders into three tiers. The first tier is relatively unproblematic, with no notification requirements. The second tier considers the offender risky but requires minimal notification (e.g., of the local police). The third tier, comprising serious offenders with a high probability of repeating offenses, is the source of controversy. Under this category, neighbors have to be informed of the released criminal coming to their community, schools have to be informed, and so on. In other states postcards have to be sent by the offender to his new neighbors, and his picture must be distributed to local organizations. In California, fairs were held recently to encourage concerned citizens to call a hot line to get information on convicted sex criminals throughout the state.

Critics assail Megan's Law as an invasion of privacy, as repeat punishment for people who have already served their sentences, as generating vigilante acts, as unfairly stigmatizing former convicts in need of support to get their lives back in order, and as ignoring the causes of these terrible acts (the vast majority of violent sexual offenders and child molesters had been victims of sexual predators as children themselves).

Defenders reject these arguments. "I have a dead little girl. How can they sit there and worry about if it's punishment?" Megan's mother recently said. While there have been hostilities against announced offenders, these have been controlled. Some suicides have resulted, but these generate little sympathy.

Recent federal law requiring all states to register convicted offenders and recent court decisions on the constitutionality of Megan's Law function to legitimize the many variants of community notification. While some worry that we are in the throes of an epidemic or a panic, others counter that at least *registering* sexual offenders has long been a standard policy. For instance, California has been registering sex offenders since 1947; now all states do.

Related sex laws include Washington's civil commitment statute (1990) and Kansas's 1994 Sexually Violent Predator Law. A key provision of these laws mandates holding a criminal who is judged highly likely to repeat violent sex offenses after he has served his time. Generally, the prisoner would be placed in a mental institution, ostensibly for treatment. This "civil commitment," done for the offender's and society's protection, would be for an indefinite period.

Although the Supreme Court's recent refusal to hear challenges to Megan's Law allows the law and others like it to remain in force, the controversy remains. As you read the following selections by Bruce Fein and Edward Martone, consider which sexual offenders, if any, should be affected by the community notification requirements. Colorado is one state that considers it a crime if someone 18 or over has sex with someone who is under 18. Should an 18-year-old who commits statutory rape with his 17-year-old girlfriend be held to community notification requirements? Should first-time, nonviolent molesters be subject to the new laws? What about a violent offender who has been clean for eight years and has fully cooperated with treatment programs?

YES

Bruce Fein

COMMUNITY SELF-DEFENSE LAWS ARE CONSTITUTIONALLY SOUND

Last July 29, 7-year-old Megan Kanka was sexually assaulted and murdered in a New Jersey township. Her neighbor, a twice-convicted sex offender, has been charged with the crime. More in sorrow than in anger, the New Jersey Legislature enacted Megan's Law to memorialize the girl's death and to reduce the likelihood of a tragic reprise.

Megan's Law requires government notice to communities of resident sex offenders believed by prosecutors to possess a high risk of recidivism. The offenses that require notice include sexual assault, engaging in conduct that would impair or debauch the morals of a child, and luring or enticing a minor. Risk factors include criminal history, victimizing a minor outside the offender's family circle, and using physical force or violence in the crime.

The community receives the offender's name, address, offense, place of employment or schooling, and license plate number, along with a recent photo and a physical description. The community is also admonished against vigilantism and is warned that crimes against the offender, the offender's family, employer or school will be unfailingly prosecuted. Indeed, New Jersey authorities recently arrested two men accused of vigilantism, pledged aggressive prosecutions and publicly condemned the barbarism.

The laudatory objective of Megan's Law is community self-defense, and the law is constitutionally irreproachable. Critics of such laws ignore the warning of Supreme Court Justice Robert Jackson in *Terminiello v. Chicago*, 337 U.S. 1 (1949), that doctrinaire logic must be tempered with a little practical wisdom to avoid converting "the constitutional Bill of Rights into a suicide pact."

Notice does not inflict "punishment" in the constitutional sense. The offender may be stigmatized within the community, but loss of reputation does not impair constitutionally protected liberty.

The Court explained this in *Paul v. Davis*, 424 U.S. 693 (1976), in which it found unobjectionable police distribution of fliers to merchants providing names and photos of recent arrestees believed to be "active shoplifters." Similarly, the FBI's "10 Most Wanted" list of criminal suspects is constitutionally unworrisome despite the stigma attached.

Neither does community notice violate a constitutional right of privacy. The Court in *Paul* lectured that government may publicize records of official acts, including convictions, so long as the person's freedom of action remains unrestricted. And the more comprehensive notice under Megan's Law responds to the wider opportunities for sex offenders to repeat their crimes.

Community notice imposes no government disability on the sex offender. If community members ostracize the criminal, that reflects a private choice uncoerced by government action. Government, of course, has no business exposing a private life for the sole sake of exposure, a hard-learned lesson of Sen. Joseph Mc-carthy's communist witchhunts. But government interest in arming communities with information that might curtail sexual offenses is compelling both because the crimes are especially heinous and because of concern about rates of recidivism.

Megan's Law is no panacea: its impact on the incidence of crime may prove marginal. But marginal improvement is welcome when little else is working. And critics should pause before unleashing their constitutional attacks. If community notice is scuttled, the political backlash will probably lengthen prison terms for sex offenders with no possibility of parole, thus deflating any litigation success to a Pyrrhic victory.

NO

Edward Martone

MERE ILLUSION OF SAFETY CREATES CLIMATE OF VIGILANTE JUSTICE

How can society protect itself from some of its most dangerous predators? That is the question posed by the debate over laws requiring community notification of the presence of convicted sex offenders released from prison.

This debate flared up last summer after a horrible crime shocked the entire country. New Jerseyans responded by calling for a community notification law, reasoning that if the public knew about the presence of sex offenders in their midst, they could take measures to protect themselves from being victimized.

The New Jersey Civil Liberties Union was almost alone in opposing the community notification bill. We argued that the law would merely create an illusion of safety, and that it would beget even more violence. Recent events have borne out our concerns.

In the early morning of Jan. 8, two men forced their way into a house in Phillipsburg, N.J., looking for 25-year-old Michael Groff, a paroled sex offender. They knew he was staying there because the police had notified the community of his whereabouts under the new law. The intruders announced they were looking for "the child molester" and then began beating the wrong man.

Fortunately, police arrived before anyone was seriously injured. Law enforcement officials quickly condemned the attack as unacceptable vigilantism. The local prosecutor insisted that the law "was never intended to permit or condone harassment or intimidation of individuals who have paid their debt to society." But unfortunately, such unintended consequences are inevitable and unavoidable.

The Phillipsburg assault was not the first. In Washington state, arson, death threats, slashed tires and loss of employment have been attributed to a similar community notification law enacted last year.

The public's rage against sex offenders is more than understandable. Their crimes, especially when visited upon children, leave life-long scars and offend the community's deepest sensibilities. But in our zeal to protect ourselves and our children, we should not enact measures that do more harm than good.

Besides creating a climate of ugly vigilantism, notification laws cause compulsive sex offenders to run from family, avoid treatment and seek the safety of anonymity by hiding out, thus subjecting the public to even greater risk.

So far, state and federal courts in California, Illinois, Arizona, New Hampshire and Alaska have struck down community notification provisions as unconstitutional.

In New Jersey, the law is being challenged by the ACLU. And in January, the federal district court in Newark issued a preliminary injunction against community notification in one released rapist's case.

The courts are concerned about the violation of ex post facto laws, although they have been less hospitable to privacy claims. The litigation will go on.

In New Jersey, about 4,000 sex offenders are convicted every year and are sent to prisons that offer little or no treatment. Eventually, they are released into a state in which there are no residential programs that accept sex offenders with criminal records. Many of these are juvenile offenders who, if untreated, will commit an average of 360 sex offenses in a lifetime.

Community notification laws offer little protection against this compulsive behavioral disorder. It is time we recognized that their sole function is political —to placate an angry public.

POSTSCRIPT

Are the New Sex Offender Laws Rational?

The New Jersey legislatures concocted the multifaceted Megan's Law within 30 days of Megan Kanka's death with no hearings or debates on the empirical, ethical, or legal merits of the laws. They were forged, some insist, for revenge. Yet there are some 234,000 rapists or criminals in or out of prison, convicted of sexual assault under the auspices of the criminal justice system. Since 1980 the rate of prisoners convicted of sexual assault has increased 15 percent per year, higher than any other violent crime category. However, does this reflect real increases in child abuse, incest, and molestation or simply that victims are more likely to report violence and sexual offenses than they used to be?

There is a tremendous unevenness in the new sex laws—their scope, penalties, implementation, and so on. Only 56 offenders registered in New Jersey have been classified as tier 3, which requires full community notification. The 1994 Kansas Act has resulted thus far in only 14 civil commitments. By contrast, in other states information on registered sex offenders has been made much more readily available. In California, for example, one can simply dial a hot line to obtain such information. Megan's Law in New Jersey largely excludes victims of incest, although in probably 75–85 percent of all child molestation cases, the perpetrator is a member of the family or a family friend. In Louisiana such a distinction is not made. Hence, many worry that victims of incest will be reluctant to press charges because their neighbors could then, through community notification, find out. The victims' rights in these cases are ignored. Is that good policy?

What treatments for sex offenders should accompany being registered, having one's community notified, or being civilly committed? In the past, sex offenders were considered among the worst candidates for cure. The "new view" argues that with relapse treatment (i.e., programs similar to those used to treat alcoholism) significant modifications in sexually deviant behavior are possible. This treatment assumes that the offender is never really "cured" but must always be on guard against relapses. Certainly, though, to succeed, offenders in these programs must be highly motivated, able to show empathy for their victims, and remorseful. Among drugs that may be helpful in rehabilitating sexual offenders are Depo-Provera, which reduces the sexual drive, and triptorelin, which blocks the male sex hormone, testosterone.

Meanwhile, some states are mandating chemical castration in extreme cases. Yet studies show that offenders surgically or chemically castrated are still quite capable of molestation. If castration always worked, would that justify it?

140

Megan's murderer had been adjudicated for a second offense and should have been sentenced to 30 years, but he received only 7 years. He was released from an overcrowded New Jersey prison against the advice of all relevant staff members. There was no follow-up, let alone treatment. Either a correct sentence or treatment might have prevented Megan's death. Sex offenders often receive less than two hours of treatment per week. These facts were not considered by the legislatures that passed the new sex offender laws. Most states have either made no effort to evaluate the results of the new laws or show contradictory findings. Implementation remains inconsistent and possibly unfair. Retroactive application of the new laws sometimes harm those long since successfully integrated in their community. Many first-time offenders are teenagers, not "dirty old men." Hence, the treatment and labelling issues are most relevant. Are the new laws rational?

Two relevant U.S. Department of Justice publications that are helpful are *Sex Offenses and Offenders* (January 1997) and *Sex Offender Community Notification* by P. Finn (February 1997). For a current overview with lists of contact sources, see "Sex Offender Community Notification: Policy Report," *National Criminal Justice Association* (October 1997). From a law enforcement view, see "Put on Notice: Police Agencies Wrestle With Sex-Offender Notification Issue," *Lens* (June 15, 1997). A description of one state's novel approach can be found in "At the Los Angeles County Fair: 'Outing' Sex Offenders," by W. Claiborne, *The Washington Post* (September 20, 1997).

A pointed attack on Kansas's 1994 Sexually Violent Predator Act is made by psychologist S. Lally in "Steel Beds v. Iron Bars: New Laws Muddle How to Handle Sex Offenders," *The Washington Post* (July 27, 1997). For a philosophical overview of some of the new laws, see "Megan's Law: Constitutionality and Policy," by A. Brooks, *Criminal Justice Ethics* (Winter/Spring 1996). For discussions of the more draconian aspects of the present movement, see "California Child Molesters Face 'Chemical Castration,'" by B. Ayres, Jr., *The New York Times* (August 27, 1997) and "The Many Myths About Sex Offenders," by G. Kolata, *The New York Times* (September 1, 1996). Among the many legal discussions are "Megan's Law: Can it Stop Sexual Predators—and at What Cost to Constitutional Rights?" by J. Rudin, *Criminal Justice* (Fall 1996) and the special issue of the *New York Law School Journal of Human Rights* entitled "Critical Perspectives on Megan's Law" (1996). For a moving account of pedophilia among priests, see C. Connors, "The Moment After Suffering: Lessons from the Pedophilia Scandal," *Commonweal* (October 21, 1996). A classic article by E. Sutherland is "Sexual Psychopath Laws," in *The Sutherland Papers*, edited by A. Cohen et al. (Indiana University Press, 1956).

ISSUE 9

Does Arresting Batterers Do More Harm Than Good?

YES: Janell D. Schmidt and Lawrence W. Sherman, from "Does Arrest Deter Domestic Violence?" in Eve S. Buzawa and Carl G. Buzawa, *Do Arrests and Restraining Orders Work?* (Sage Publications, 1996)

NO: Evan Stark, from "Mandatory Arrest for Batterers: A Reply to Its Critics," in Eve S. Buzawa and Carl G. Buzawa, *Do Arrests and Restraining Orders Work?* (Sage Publications, 1996)

ISSUE SUMMARY

YES: Janell D. Schmidt, supervisor of the Milwaukee County Child Protective Services, and professor of criminology Lawrence W. Sherman argue that arresting batterers in many cases does more harm than good, and they advocate alternatives to mandatory arrest.

NO: Associate professor of public administration and social work Evan Stark contends that those who argue against arresting batterers completely misunderstand the depth of women's exploitation by the legal system. He contends that arresting batterers is a vital step for female empowerment and for women's achieving full citizenship status.

Domestic violence. We do not know if spouse, lover, wife, or child abuse has actually increased significantly in the past several years or if such abuse has simply been discovered because the current political and social climate validates worrying about it, researching it, and demanding that something be done about it.

While there is little doubt that sexual, psychological, and physical assaults occur within all domestic arrangements regardless of race, socioeconomic status, religion, ethnic origin, and so on, solid information on the rate, intensity, and types of assault is not available. In the past, the received wisdom among police agencies was that cops should avoid intervening in domestic abuse cases. If intervention could not be avoided, however, then couples were to be counseled, but no arrests were to be made. But ways of thinking about and studying domestic violence changed dramatically in 1984 when Lawrence W. Sherman and Richard Berk published the results of their research on domestic violence in Minneapolis, Minnesota. They found that when the police arrested males involved in misdemeanor domestic assaults, the males the police arrested were less likely to assault in the future than those who were not arrested.

Sherman and Berk pointed out that their findings were tentative and that policies should *not* be based on a single study. Yet four months later the U.S. attorney general recommended that arrests be made in domestic assault cases. Within five years approximately 84 percent of urban police agencies had preferred or mandatory arrest policies for misdemeanor domestic assault cases. Sherman has insisted that the reversal of policy was largely a function of the presence of powerful vested interest groups, in addition to the fact that the time was ripe for a "get tough" approach toward men who assault their wives or girlfriends.

Shortly after the political and legal fallout from Sherman and Berk's 1984 study resulted in policies advocating arresting assaulters, a number of studies were done. Several of them, summarized in the following selection by Sherman and Janell D. Schmidt, found that arrest did *not* deter domestic assault in many cases. In fact, the charge was made that for poor, black, female victims, arresting the male only aggravated the situation.

Surprisingly, Sherman encouraged scholarly competitors to present alternative findings. From a philosophy of science perspective, one of the sharpest criticisms of the social sciences, including criminology, is that little room is allowed for scientific advances via rejection of one's own initial conclusions.

Then, as Evan Stark points out in the second selection, Sherman publicly recants, stating that the new studies indicate that his original theory that arresting batterers is probably helpful in most cases is simply wrong. Policies that call for mandatory arrests, Sherman seems to say, are clearly wrong. This is indeed a rare about-face.

Stark argues that Sherman should have stuck with his original interpretation: that arrest is helpful. However, Stark claims, even though his initial analysis is correct in terms of its policy implications, Sherman's work has been clouded by an overdependence on a narrow variant of positivistic science. That is, Sherman et al. never really looked at the big picture. Instead, they concentrated on the narrow, relatively easy-to-research issue of arrest and the subsequent behavior of batterers. Stark insists that Sherman et al. neglect the cultural-historical fact that women are far less powerful than men. For example, even when documentable physical abuse occurs, when male police show up, the female victim is under enormous pressure to not press charges, and the general lack of options available to women, especially those with children, prevent anything close to a fair legal or moral playing field. Mandatory arrests change this, at least somewhat, Stark contends.

As you read the following selections, notice the differences in how the issue itself is framed by each side. What bearing does that have on the authors' conclusions? Which side seems to have a better understanding of the problem? Which side offers more rational policy recommendations?

YES

Janell D. Schmidt and
Lawrence W. Sherman

DOES ARREST DETER
DOMESTIC VIOLENCE?

During the mid-1980s, widespread concern about the incidence and prevalence of domestic violence led many big-city police departments to change
radically the way they policed a crime that affects millions of women each
year. The often-maligned "arrest as a last resort" tradition was replaced with
written policies and state laws requiring arrest as the sole police recourse. Nationally, this enthusiastic shift generated, from 1984 to 1989, a 70% increase
in arrests for minor assaults, including domestic. Yet, the movement to arrest
batterers may be doing more harm than good. Research in six cities testing the
"arrest works best" premise in deterring future assaults has produced complex and conflicting results. Police and policymakers are now faced with the
dilemma that arrest may help some victims at the expense of others and that
arrest may assist the victim in the short term but facilitate further violence in
the long term.

The revolution in policing misdemeanor cases of domestic violence can
be attributed, in part, to the 1984 publication of the Minneapolis Domestic
Violence Experiment, the first controlled, randomized test of the effectiveness of arrest for any offense. Results from this endeavor were that arresting
abusers cut in half the risk of future assaults against the same victim during
a 6-month follow-up period. Alternative police responses tested were the
traditional "send the suspect away for 8 hours" and "advise the couple to
get help for their problems." The efficacy of each treatment was measured
by interviews with victims and official records tracking the offense and arrest history of each suspect. Because arrest worked better than separating
or advising couples, the authors recommended that states change laws prohibiting police from making warrantless arrests in misdemeanor domestic
violence cases. They also advocated that replication studies be conducted to
test the generalizability of the results in other cities with varying economic
conditions and demographic complexions. But absent further research results, their recommendation to law enforcement was "to adopt arrest as the

From Janell D. Schmidt and Lawrence W. Sherman, "Does Arrest Deter Domestic Violence?" in
Eve S. Buzawa and Carl G. Buzawa, *Do Arrests and Restraining Orders Work?* (Sage Publications,
1996). Copyright © 1996 by Sage Publications, Inc. Reprinted by permission.

preferred policy for dealing with such cases, unless there were clearly stated reasons to do something else" (Sherman, Schmidt, & Rogan, 1992, p. 3).

Although the study authors opposed mandating arrest until further studies were completed, within 8 years legislatures in 15 states (including 1 in which a replication was being conducted) and the District of Columbia moved to enact laws requiring police to arrest in all probable cause incidents of domestic violence. This dramatic expansion of arrest practices has also been attributed to successful litigation against police departments who failed to arrest, to the recommendations of the 1984 Attorney General's Task Force on Domestic Violence, and to political pressure applied by women's advocacy groups.

It is not clear, however, how well these policies and laws have been followed or whether they have controlled repetitive acts of domestic assault. Observations of compliance of the Phoenix, Minneapolis, and Milwaukee police departments found that only Milwaukee officers consistently adhered to the policy. More important, the lack of labeling cases as domestic prior to policy changes renders attempts at before/after measures difficult. Further complicating evaluation or comparison efforts is the variable threshold for probable cause to arrest in incidents of domestic assault. In Wisconsin, only a complaint of pain is needed for police to effect an arrest; in Nebraska, visible injuries are required. Until 4 years ago, Florida law required the parties to be married or formerly married in order for the incident to be considered domestic.

What is known about the impact of police arrest policies relative to domestic assault is that the vast bulk of cases brought to police attention involve lower-income and minority-group households. One reason may be a higher rate of domestic disputes among these groups; another reason may be a lack of alternatives short of police intervention that offer immediate relief. Although arresting thousands of unemployed minority males each year may assist the goals of victim advocates and provide a brief respite for the victims, the skepticism of many police and criminologists relative to the deterrent power of arrest still remains. The key question of whether other police alternatives could prove more powerful or whether the police could be effective at all led the National Institute of Justice (NIJ) to fund replication studies in six major urban cities.

Beginning in 1986 and early 1987, police in Omaha (Nebraska), Milwaukee (Wisconsin), Charlotte (North Carolina), Metro-Dade County (Miami, Florida), Colorado Springs (Colorado), and Atlanta (Georgia) began controlled experiments to replicate the Minneapolis findings. Each site was afforded leeway to improve the methodology of the Minneapolis study and to design alternative nonarrest treatments to build on its theoretical foundation. Researchers in all the cities sought to obtain a sample size larger than the 314 cases analyzed in Minneapolis in order to test for interaction effects among the various treatments. In Metro-Dade, for example, a sample of 907 cases was obtained so that researchers could compare arrest to no arrest, both with and without follow-up counseling by a specially trained police unit. In Colorado Springs, more than 1,600 cases were used to contrast arrest and nonarrest with immediate professional counseling at police headquarters or the issuance of an emergency protection order. In Milwaukee, police provided 1,200 cases for the researchers to test the length of time in custody—a short 2-hour arrest versus arrest with an overnight stay in jail, compared to no arrest. The experimental team in Charlotte included a citation response along with arrest, mediation, or separation treatments in its 686-case sample. Only Omaha followed the Minneapolis design with 330 cases but added an offender-absent window of cases to test the effect of having police pursue an arrest warrant.

The results from five of these six later studies (results from Atlanta are not forthcoming) have clouded the issue for police and policymakers, although some victim advocates remain strident in their view that arrest works best. Perhaps most striking is that none of the innovative treatments—namely, counseling or protective orders—produced any improvement over arrest versus no arrest. The citation used to notify offenders to appear at a future court date in Charlotte caused more violence than an arrest. Only Omaha broke ground and found an effective innovation in its offender-absent experiment. Offenders who left the scene before police arrived and whose cases were randomly assigned to the warrant group produced less repeat violence than did similarly absent offenders assigned to the nonwarrant group. The issuance of a warrant may have acted as a "sword of Damocles" hanging over an offender's head.

In short, the new experiments reported both deterrent and backfiring effects of arrest. Arrest cured some abusers but made others worse; arrest eased the pain for victims of employed abusers but increased it for those intimate with unemployed partners; arrest assisted white and Hispanic victims but fell short of deterring further violence among black victims. To understand these diverse findings and move toward a policy resolution, it is necessary first to focus on the effects of arrest compared to nonarrest, because that is the central issue for police and policymakers concerned with determining the most effective or appropriate police response (see Table 1).

One central finding is that arrest increased domestic violence recidivism among suspects in Omaha, Charlotte, and Milwaukee. Although these three cities produced some evidence of a deterrent effect of arrest within the first 30 days, victims found that this protective shield quickly evaporated and that they suffered an escalation of violence over a longer period of time. None of the follow-up measures produced the 6-month deterrent effect reported in Minneapolis. Some measures showed no difference in the recidivism of offenders arrested, compared with those whom police did not arrest.

Researchers in Colorado Springs and Metro-Dade found some support for the Minneapolis findings but only with limited measures. A narrow window of victim interview data (a 58% response rate in Colorado and 42% in Metro-Dade) confirms the deterrent power of arrest. But the less than ideal response rate might mean that victims who were interviewed were different from those who were not interviewed. Official records tracking recidivism in Colorado Springs did not uncover a deterrent effect of arrest, as some records did in Metro-Dade. Confounding the interpretation of the Colorado results was the fact that the vast majority of experimental cases (58%) were based on the offender's nonviolent harassing or menacing behavior toward the victim, perhaps distinct from the

Table 1

Summary of Results of Six Arrest Experiments for Repeat Violence Against the Same Victim

Finding	Minneapolis	Omaha	Charlotte	Milwaukee	Colorado Springs	Miami
6-month deterrence, official measures	Yes	No	No	No	No	1 of 2
6-month deterrence, victim interviews	Yes	Border	No	No	Yes	Yes
6- to 12-month escalation, official measures	No	Yes	Yes	Yes	No	No
6- 12-month escalation, victim interviews	*	No	No	No	No	No
30- to 60-day deterrence, official measures (any or same victim)	Yes	No	Border	Yes	No	1 of 2
Escalation effect for unemployed	*	Yes	*	Yes	Yes	*
Deterrence for employed	*	Yes	*	Yes	Yes	*

Note: * = relationship not reported.
Source: From Sherman, Schmidt, and Rogan, 1992, p. 129.

physical attack required to arrest for battery in the other cities.

The different results from different measures in these cities suggests, then, that arrest has a different effect on suspects from different kinds of households. This finding is best summarized by the following statement:

> Evidence that the effects of arrest vary by suspect comes from Milwaukee, Colorado Springs, and Omaha. In each of those cities, nonexperimental analyses of the official records data suggest that unemployed suspects become more violent if arrested, but that employed suspects do not. This consistent pattern supports a hypothesis that the effects of criminal punishment depend upon the suspect's "stakes in conformity," or how much he has to lose from the social consequences of arrest. Similar effects were found in Milwaukee for unmarried versus married suspects; unemployed, unmarried suspects experienced the greatest escalation of violence after arrest. The unemployment result is the single most consistent finding from the domestic violence experiments, and has not been contradicted in any of the analyses reported to date. (Sherman et al., 1992, p. 17)

Could other factors explain this varying effect of arrest on different suspects in different cities? A comparison of the data on prosecution rates, level of victim injury, number of married couples, unemployment rate, and ages of the suspects across all studies showed no consistent variation between the two groups of cities finding a deterrent or escalating effect of arrest. The only major difference was that a larger proportion of black suspects was found in the "arrest backfires" cities (Omaha, Charlotte, and Milwaukee), compared to the "arrest deters" cities (Colorado Springs, Minneapolis, and Metro-Dade). But this pattern is not consistent: One deterrent city (Metro-Dade) shared a similar rate of black suspects with a backfiring city (Omaha)—42% and 43%, respectively,

How carefully should policymakers and advocates tread through this maze of diverse findings? Applying these results to crime control strategies is complicated by the dilemmas and choices they present. Urban legislators and police chiefs in at least 35 states can choose between continuing the status quo and not mandating arrest, a choice that will continue to harm some victims. They can also legislate arrest, a choice that may harm victims currently served by a lack of policy. Choosing between the lesser of two evils is best guided by the following summary of the facts and dilemmas gleaned from the domestic violence research published to date (see Sherman et al., 1992, pp. 19–20):

1. *Arrest reduces domestic violence in some cities but increases it in others.* It is not clear from current research how officials in any city can know which effect arrest is likely to have in their city. Cities that do not adopt an arrest policy may pass up an opportunity to help victims of domestic violence. But cities that do adopt arrest policies—or have them imposed by state law—may catalyze more domestic violence than would otherwise occur. Either choice entails a possible moral wrong.

2. *Arrest reduces domestic violence among employed people but increases it among unemployed people.* Mandatory arrest policies may thus protect working-class women but cause greater harm to those who are poor. Conversely, not making arrests may hurt working women but reduce violence against economically poor women. Similar trade-offs may exist on the basis of race, marriage, education, and neighborhood. Thus, even in cities where arrest reduces domestic violence overall, as an unintended side effect it may increase violence against the poorest victims.

3. *Arrest reduces domestic violence in the short run but may increase it in the long run.* Three-hour arrests in Milwaukee reduced the 7% chance that a victim would be battered as soon as the police left to a 2% chance of being battered when the spouse returned from jail. But over the course of 1 year, those arrests doubled the rate of violence by the same suspects. No arrest means more danger to the victim now, whereas making an arrest may mean more danger of violence later for the same victim or for someone else.

4. *Police can predict which couples are most likely to suffer future violence, but our society values privacy too highly to encourage preventive action.* Largely because of the value our society attaches to privacy, especially marital and sexual privacy, no one has developed a recognized method, or even advice, for police to use in preventing domes-

tic violence. A small group of chronically violent couples and incidents reported in apartment buildings produce most of the cases of domestic violence that police learn about, but the only policies now available react to the *incidents*, rather than to the *patterns*. Ignoring those patterns allows violence to continue; addressing them requires methods that many Americans would call invasions of family privacy.

Concomitant with these dilemmas is an even tougher question for officials charged with implementing effective policing strategies: Just how much research is enough to inform policy? The authors of the Minneapolis results were the target of much second-guessing and criticism from their colleagues over the reported findings and influence that the study enjoyed. Criminologists sought a more rigorous testing of the initial conclusions, perhaps foreseeing the risk of policy changes later proving to be unwise. Advocates, whose beliefs were validated by the results, and police policymakers, at least in Milwaukee, used the study to adopt arrest as the mandatory police response. In 1988, the Wisconsin legislature, perhaps less cautious than criminologists and motivated by ideological or politically pragmatic grounds, passed a law mandating arrest as the statewide response. This action occurred despite their awareness of the ongoing replication in Milwaukee testing the specific deterrent power of arrest. If a little medicine was good, a lot was even better.

The dilemma between limited research results and the need to do something about today's problems is also clearly illustrated by the Omaha offender-absent experiment. These findings may be far

more compelling and relevant than the Minneapolis results because the offender is gone by the time police arrive in about half the cases brought to police attention. Yet, the study has had no observable influence on policy since its publication in an obscure journal. Modestly presented as a pilot study, no replications are being planned. Thus, there is little risk that the findings will inform policy and later be contradicted. In the meantime, assaults on thousands of victims could conceivably be thwarted if prosecutors heeded the policy implications.

Sherman et al. (1992) posited that

the replication dilemma thus also poses a choice between two wrongs. Both using and burying research results entail risks of harm. But as Americans become more sophisticated about the scientific process, they may come to expect revisions of policy based on new scientific evidence in this realm of knowledge as in others. Americans are accustomed to constant revisions of findings about diet and disease. Cholesterol, sugar, caffeine, alcohol, jogging... the "latest" evidence about their relations to health and longevity has changed significantly and repeatedly over the last twenty years, and many people and businesses have changed their behavior in response. (p. 21)

To some the choice between two wrongs invokes despair and inaction. Yet, policing domestic violence may not be hopeless. Careful review of the policy implications, combined with the freedom to test alternative policies, can lead to more effective solutions. Use of the best information that Sherman et al. (1992, pp. 23–24) have to date guides the following five policy recommendations:

1. *Repeal mandatory arrest laws.* The most compelling implication of these find-

ings is to challenge the wisdom of mandatory arrest. States and cities that have enacted such laws should repeal them, especially if they have substantial ghetto poverty populations with high unemployment rates. These are the settings in which mandatory arrest policies are most likely to backfire. It remains possible but unlikely that mandatory arrest creates a general deterrent effect among the wider public not arrested. Even if it does, however, increased violence among unemployed persons who are arrested is a serious moral stain on the benefits of general deterrence. The argument that arrest expresses the moral outrage of the state also appears weak if the price of that outrage is increased violence against some victims.

2. *Substitute structured police discretion.* Instead of mandating arrest in cases of misdemeanor domestic violence, state legislatures should mandate that each police agency develop its own list of approved options to be exercised at the discretion of the officer. Legislatures might also mandate 1 day of training each year to ensure that discretion is fully informed by the latest research available. The options could include allowing victims to decide whether their assailants should be arrested, transporting victims to shelters, or taking the suspects to an alcohol detoxification center.

3. *Allow warrantless arrests.* Whereas mandatory arrest has become the major issue in some states, warrantless arrest remains an issue in others. Sixteen jurisdictions have adopted mandatory arrest laws, but at last report 9 others have still not given officers full arrest powers in misde-

meanor domestic violence cases that they did not witness: Alabama, California, Michigan, Mississippi, Montana, Nebraska, New York, Vermont, and West Virginia. The success of arrest in some cities suggests that every state should add this option to the police tool kit. Deciding when to use it can then become a matter of police policy based on continuing research and clinical experience, rather than on the massive effort required to change state law.

4. *Encourage issuance of arrest warrants for absent offenders.* The landmark Omaha experiment suggests that more domestic violence could be prevented by this policy than by any offender-present policy. The kinds of people who flee the scene might be more deterrable than those who stay. A prosecutor willing to issue warrants and a police agency willing to serve them can capitalize on that greater deterrability. If the Omaha warrant experiment can be replicated in other cities —a very big if—then the warrant policy might actually deter more violence than do arrests of suspects who are still present. Because it will likely be years before more research on the question is done, such policies should be adopted now. They can easily be discarded later if they are found to be harmful or ineffective.

5. *Special units and policies should focus on chronically violent couples.* Because a limited number of couples produce most of the domestic violence incidents in any city, it makes little sense for police to treat all violent couples

alike. It makes even less sense to frame the whole policy debate around responses to *incidents* when most of the problem is those chronic *couples*. The challenge is to develop procedures for violent couples that do not invade family privacy. Trial and error through research and development is required for any major breakthroughs. But an effective policy for dealing with chronic couples would have more impact than any other breakthrough. It deserves the highest priority in policing domestic violence.

The opposition to mandatory arrest laws presented here may frustrate or even anger many tireless advocates who have relentlessly grasped arrest as the preferred police response to incidents of domestic violence. To them, the suggestion that other institutions, such as shelters for battered women, treatment programs

for victims and offenders, schools, and welfare agencies, may better serve victims is perhaps blasphemy. But they need not become too alarmed. However sensible that approach may be, the climate in many communities today is for law enforcement officials to get tough on crime. Regardless of the results of any scientific studies, the police will remain the primary institution coping with domestic violence among the poor and unemployed. This country's current fiscal crisis dooms any substantial investment in developing new programs in both the law enforcement and social services fields. The troublesome fact remains, however, that the punishment sought by advocates and community policymakers may encourage more crime.

REFERENCES

Sherman, L. W., Schmidt, J. D., & Rogan, D. P. (1992). *Policing domestic violence: Experiments and dilemmas.* New York: Free Press.

NO

Evan Stark

MANDATORY ARREST FOR BATTERERS: A REPLY TO ITS CRITICS

THE CONTEXT AND THE PLAYERS

As a long-time activist in the battered women's movement, I welcome the debate about mandatory arrest.

There is a certain irony in defending the police powers of the state against critics who helped lay the basis for the proarrest policy in the first place. Larry Sherman's conversion is the most remarkable. Relying on recent evidence that certain men become more violent after arrest, Sherman has replaced his erstwhile ardor for arrest with an equally passionate belief that mandatory arrest laws should be immediately repealed, especially in cities "with substantial ghetto poverty populations with high unemployment rates." ... [T]here are profound methodological flaws in both [Larry] Sherman and [Richard] Berk's original Minneapolis Domestic Violence Experiment and the replication studies that are the basis for Sherman's current position....

Sherman's picture is constructed from a bygone devotion to positivist criminology. His is a world defined by the technological optimism of the pre-1960s, yet to be polluted by culture, politics, gender, and history.... In Sherman's [world], causality is singular, universal, and undirectional, and social science research guides professional/government intervention to right injustice. In the post-Law Enforcement Assistance Administration (LEAA) era, this neo-Keynesian belief in state intervention appears as naive as an early Doris Day film. Still, there is something seductive about a "preventive conceit" ... that envisions modifying such complex behaviors as violence with minor adjustments in the criminal justice response (arrest vs. no arrest). Would it were so.

... Sherman's faith in the instrumentality of professional intervention—including the instrumentality of his own research—supports his belief that arrest increases violence. Hence, [the idea that] eliminating mandatory arrest will reduce the violent response [is] almost certainly wrong... because the paradigms from which they arise... discredit the role of social initiative—in this case, the role of the community-based women's movement—in shaping the outcome of policy change.

... I suspect that most people view policing as a body of available resources, like schooling or health care, say—a sort of lottery that circumstances periodically force us to enter. Given the complex political realities that shape crime (as well as, e.g., health, welfare, learning) and mediate how police and the public interact, it is hard to predict whether one's welfare will be helped or hindered in any given encounter or, more globally, what determines how a given set of actors (offenders, patients, students, police) will respond to a specific class of interventions (e.g., mandatory arrest). If people "play" nonetheless (call police, attend school, go to the emergency room), it is not because they believe they *will* win, but because this is one of the few shows in town at which they *can* win and because winning—in this case, having police resources at your disposal—is a highly desirable outcome in the long run.

... [O]ne can think of the proarrest strategy as a "basket of goods" that may include everything from a mere warning, handcuffing, or an arrest warrant through a weekend in jail, mandated treatment, a stalker's law, the community intervention programs,... real prison time, the provision of court-based advocates, and so forth.... Sherman... [is] recommending that this keystone to reform be removed from the basket because it fails to fulfill an important policy objective—the reduction of violence. Sherman's implication... [is] that the criminal justice system should no longer be the focal point of society's response to woman battering.

Even before we can ask whether the replication experiments are sufficiently robust to justify abandoning mandatory arrest, we need to question their fundamental premise: that the wisdom of arrest should be assessed solely in terms of its effects on violent behavior, *whatever they are*. To do this, we need to conceptualize the presumed object of the arrest policy—woman battering—and unpack the "demand" that arrest is designed to satisfy....

BATTERING: THE SOCIAL PHENOMENON

Feminists have hardly been unambivalent about the wisdom of a proarrest strategy. Who is more aware that depending on protective intervention by a male institution is a two-edged sword? As the concern with "wife torture" emerged from the movements in the 1870s to protect animals and children, British feminist Frances Power Cobbe addressed the same questions we are debating today, and she did so, incidentally, with the same sort of evidence.

Cobbe (1878) believed that battering was rooted in women's status as men's property and that the only effective response was full economic and political independence. Women's subordinate position in the public sphere and their private vulnerability were inextricable, each a precondition for the other. Cobbe supported the arrest and prosecution of batterers as means to reduce women's political isolation.... Noninterference when women were assaulted constituted active support for male dominance....

[A]fter studying arrest and court statistics, she concluded that the courts were focusing only on the most extreme cases of violence. As a result, she believed, criminal justice was effectively establishing a permissible level of harm: By punishing only "severe" injury, the court response actually caused the minimum levels of domestic violence to rise....

I share Cobbe's fundamental conviction that violence against women is a political fact. This means that everything about it—when, how, why, and where it is used, whom it affects, the nature of intervention, and most important, the consequences of intervention for all involved—reflects the relative power of men over women and the struggles by particular men to assert and women to escape this power. Whether this violence is expressed through child sexual abuse, harassment, rape, or battering, the key is the selection of females as victims on the basis of their gender. Because of its roots in sexual inequality, whatever occasions violence in a given encounter, the ultimate cause of "battering" (as well as its consequence) is the denial of women's *civil rights*....

In trying to conceptualize battering, we need to picture ongoing forms of control that are at once both personal and social, including economic exploitation, isolation from family and friends, intimidation, and a host of rules governing everyday activities. Ann Jones and Susan Schecter use the term *coercive control* to describe the systemic fusion of social and individual dominance that undermines the physical, psychological, or political autonomy of even the strongest, most aggressive and capable women....

The term *entrapment* describes the cumulative effects of having one's political, social, and psychological identity subordinated to the will of a more powerful other who controls resources that are vital to one's survival.

BATTERING: THE CRIME

... [A]lthough safety and the reduction of fear remain important goals, their realization depends on making women's "empowerment" the ultimate standard against which the efficacy of various interventions is judged.

... [B]attering, *the social phenomenon*, occurs at three levels simultaneously: the political level of female subordination, the level of interpersonal assault, and the level of coercive control at which women's social vulnerability is exploited for personal gain. *Battering, the experience*, arises from the particular ways in which these three levels interrelate in a given relationship over time. The challenge is for criminal justice to recontextualize the sorts of disembodied acts of assault recorded by medicine, such as "punched with fist."... [I]n terms of entrapment and control, Sherman recognizes that this episodic focus also governs police work. The same could be said of the calculus of harms that guides criminal proceedings in the courts. Lacking a conceptual frame to understand the historical nature of battering, police, judges, physicians, and other professionals fall back on kitsch psychology or on cultural stereotypes to explain the patterns they observe among individuals, families, or entire groups who appear "violence prone." Absent a theory of coercive control, the traumatic effects of battering seem to be derived from victim psychology....

Because the element of control is what links the assaultive dimensions of abuse to the political fact of female inequality, there can be no hope of preventing battering simply by regulating the degree of violence. This is why we call for "zero tolerance" of force in interpersonal relationships and oppose basing police intervention on a calculus of physical harm....

Reframing *battering, the crime,* in terms of inequality, coercive control, and entrapment allows us to think in new ways about mandatory arrest. The critics make three powerful points:

1. *Mandatory arrest does not work.* Although arrest might reduce violence in some instances, it may actually increase it in others. Only in allowing police to exercise informed discretion —what Sherman termed *structured discretion*—can we meet the objectives of deterrence....
2. *Mandatory arrest is inhumane.* Arrest does little for the victim and less for the offender. Worse, it jeopardizes the fundamental integrity of family life. It is far better to limit arrest to the most dangerous cases, use treatment for batterers, and offer a range of compassionate family supports....
3. *The very people we are trying to protect do not want it.* It appears contradictory for us to value a woman's claim to liberty as a fully endowed citizen and then to devalue her assessment of a policy carried out in her name, such as mandatory arrest. Allowing women —and police—the discretion to decide whether arrests should occur satisfies the consumer interest of the former and sustains the morale of the latter.

DOES MANDATORY ARREST WORK?

In one of the more dramatic self-critiques in the history of criminal justice research, Larry Sherman, an architect of the Minneapolis Domestic Violence Experiment, now argues that mandatory arrest does not deter domestic violence, ex-

cept among very select groups (e.g., married, employed men). If the replication experiments failed to show the deterrent value of arrest, they did show, Sherman claims, that arrest actually *increases* violence in the long run, particularly among unemployed, unmarried, and minority males. Although Sherman bemoans the rush to implement the earlier research findings, on the basis of current findings he argues that as a general practice mandatory arrest should be ended immediately, particularly in cities with large ghetto populations. In place of mandatory arrest, he favors "structured police discretion," presumably so that alternatives can be used in cases in which arrest has been shown to increase risk. Because one logical outcome of this position is clearly absurd—namely, to arrest only white, married, employed batterers—in effect, Sherman's argument would virtually end arrest in domestic violence cases, at least in all major urban centers, except in the most severe cases.

No mea culpas are required from Sherman because the results of his Minneapolis Domestic Violence Experiment were misinterpreted....

[T]he major importance of the Minneapolis Domestic Violence Experiment was to give women's advocates (who already favored arrest) a powerful weapon to use with lawmakers who viewed domestic violence, like child abuse, as a social welfare rather than a criminal justice problem.... [T]he Minneapolis results were accepted so uncritically because, as a management strategy, police discretion in domestic violence cases had already become *politically* untenable.

But what did the battered women's movement hope to accomplish through arrest? After all, having established an unprecedented woman-run, community-based alternative service movement, why risk losing our identity by placing so much emphasis on a male-run system that... we located on the far right of the political spectrum in terms of community participation, access to influence, attitudes toward women, and bureaucratic isolation?

The first reason for mandating arrest was to control police behavior.... The fact is that, in disregarding battering, minimizing its consequences, and blaming the victims of abuse, police were no different from other professional groups.... [T]here can be little question that police behavior has changed significantly with mandatory arrest. Whereas street-level resistance by police remains widespread, arrests for assault had risen 70% between 1984 and 1989, largely because of domestic violence laws.

However individual officers responded to calls for help, the absence of a standard for police practice increased women's sense of powerlessness and thus posed a major obstacle to their empowerment....

The interest in controlling the police response had as much to do with accountability to shelters as to women generally. The legal mandate that expands the package of services that shelters can offer, including services to police, increases the safe mobility of shelter residents and advocates, provides a rationale for a regular shelter presence in the courts, and lays an empirical basis that shelters can exploit for custodial orders, orders of protection, and expanded services. These functions, in turn, provide the substantive basis for ongoing negotiations among shelters, the criminal justice system, and family and children's services, negotiations that have been formalized in many cities through coordinating councils, networks, or other forums that assume quasi-official

oversight responsibility for the law. Because shelters often secure temporary restraining orders (TROs), their power has been greatly enhanced in places where police liability for failing to arrest has been extended to failure to enforce orders of restraint and protection. Liability is a particularly important source of redress....

The second reason for mandatory arrest involved immediate protection from current violence. Arrest provides a meaningful opportunity for battered women to consider their options and gives those women ready to end the relationship time to go elsewhere or to obtain a protective order. The amount of time the batterer is physically out of the picture is crucial. In Milwaukee, for example, a woman was three times as likely to be assaulted if police left without an arrest than if the batterer was arrested and then released....

Third in importance was the desire to reduce the overall incidence of domestic violence both directly, because arrest might deter recidivism, and by sending a clear message that battering was unacceptable. Whereas the replication studies clearly do not support the Minneapolis findings, other studies do. In Lincoln, Nebraska, for example, implementing a mandatory arrest law reduced recidivism dramatically—from 83% to 53%....

According to deterrence theory, the function of mandatory arrest is to convey the criminal nature of battering. Although arrests have risen for domestic violence, because prosecution and sentencing patterns in domestic assault cases have changed very little since battering was criminalized, it is unclear what the NIJ [National Institute of Justice] experiments were actually measuring. The results could just as readily be interpreted to mean that arrest is ineffective in isolation from other sanctions. Indeed, just as violence may increase where orders of protection are unenforced, so too is it likely that arrest without serious follow-up is interpreted by some as a license to abuse.... The policy of mandatory arrest also has the indirect function of setting a standard of zero tolerance for battering that other institutions can emulate.

Fourth, making battering the only crime in which police discretion is removed acknowledges a special social interest in redressing the legacy of discriminatory treatment of women by law enforcement. It also forces the law to juxtapose the subjective experience of women and its traditional accommodation to the interests of propertied (male) strata. Setting the crime of battering apart in this way also helps distinguish battering from the two sets of crimes with which it is commonly confused: *familial* abuse, in which the victim is a minor or a frail elderly dependent, and assaults or muggings by strangers. Mandating arrest communicates how seriously we take the crime of battering and may have an effect on subsequent violence that is independent of arrest as such.... Mandating equal protection in this way also helps counter the general reluctance of courts to extend to women the civil rights protection granted to racial minorities.

A final reason for supporting mandatory arrest was what might be termed its "redistributive" function: the perception that police service is a resource that had heretofore been hoarded by others and now should be made available to women on a more egalitarian basis....

The same historical and political context in which the proarrest strategy originated explains its uneven implementation. Differences in community response to mandated arrest reflect differences in this context.... Pennsylvania provides an interesting test case for the political hypothesis: There, despite the absence of a mandatory arrest law and the relative backwardness of the state's judiciary, powerful oversight of police practice by the battered women's coalition has made arrest of batterers routine.

The Minneapolis Domestic Violence Experiment also reflected this;... no area more supportive of battered women could have been chosen to prove the efficacy of arrest. But... the fact remains that the researchers, the Police Foundation, the NIJ, and those who supported and attacked the findings from Minneapolis failed to set their evidence in a historical, structural, or political context that could have made the contingent nature of deterrence intelligible to local policymakers. Whatever the replication experiments may or may not say about arrest, they speak eloquently to our failure to learn from our mistakes because they, like the original experiment, do not consider the political chain that might help us understand why arrest works in one setting but not in another. At a time when community support for police efforts is widely recognized as the single most important factor in police effectiveness, it is surprising that the NIJ gave no consideration to the political context that set the tone for enforcement either in selecting the research sites to replicate Minneapolis or in evaluating the findings. Shifting the blame to policymakers for implementing arrest prematurely simply makes it easier to curtail arrest now—a right hard-won by the battered women's movement —amid broad cuts in other services to women.

What are we to make of Sherman's conclusion that arrest works mainly with men who are employed and married and that recidivist violence after arrest in certain cities appears highest among minorities and the unemployed? Obvious structural factors are at work here. The correlation between crimes of violence (including assault) and the business cycle has been well known in criminology for some time. Because the replication experiments were conducted when the economy was entering the worst recession in three decades, with the most dramatic effects on minorities and the working poor, the most appropriate baseline is not prearrest levels of violence, but rather rates of violence in similar cities where no change was made in police policy....

[A]lthough the employed, white, middle-class husband may be less violent following arrest, he is also more able than his unemployed, black counterpart to leverage resources other than physical force to continue subjugating his wife. Open warfare may be temporarily over in his household, but the control and coercion go on undisturbed. Has arrest worked in this situation?

This point raises the larger issue of what the replication experiments mean *even if we accept the evidence as Sherman presents it.* Our assumptions about the three levels of battering give us no hint what a change in postarrest violence signifies in terms of coercive control, entrapment, and/or inequality.... [V]iolence may cease because, following arrest, threats of repeat violence may be sufficient to maintain a power advantage over a spouse, as in the case of the employed middle-class husband described above. Conversely, violence may increase because women are empowered by arrest and/or threaten to leave or to have the man arrested again. On the basis of evidence that abuse escalates

when males perceive their control threatened, as during separation and divorce, we would predict that postarrest violence would be greatest—as Sherman's data show it is—among those who are least integrated into the job market or other structures from which men garner their authority—namely, the poor, black, or unemployed. Again, violence may increase in this group because arrest works to empower women and undermine male control....

Evidence suggests that even men who become angry following arrest may be no more violent as a result and that men who are violent after arrest are not necessarily angrier than others about arrest itself. Even if we assume that arrest provokes greater violence among a substantial number of men, Sherman's proposal that we respond by eliminating mandatory arrest appears perverse (to say the least). A far more humane and rational response would be to expand protection for the most vulnerable female populations—namely, single, minority, and low-income women—as well as to better integrate batterers into opportunity structures *without diminishing women's access to resources.* The bottom line, however, is that assault is merely one among many means available to men in battering relationships and that its absence, even for some extended period, may signify greater equality or greater dominance.

Let's assume that violence increases following arrest among certain groups and that little can be done to inhibit it. Even this worst case scenario barely affects the most important rationales for mandatory arrest—namely, controlling police behavior, setting a public standard for police response, offering immediate protection, embodying women's civil rights claims, and affording women access to a new "package of resources."...

[O]ther data sets... indicate that mandatory arrest may meet a number of our more important objectives. With respect to protection and control, for instance, recent Supreme Court and appellate court decisions suggest that battered women in states with mandatory arrest laws have far stronger claims to police protection than do battered women in states without such statutes. Furthermore, states with broad mandatory arrest laws are far more likely to allow liability of police officers than might states without such laws, such as New York.

Minority women deserve particular attention because they are most likely to use the service system (including police) and to suffer powerlessness as a result of institutional discrimination. ... [T]he replication experiments indicate that minority women bear the major brunt of postarrest violence. As a result, argues Sherman, minority women would be the major beneficiaries if mandatory arrest is eliminated.

That arrest poses a series of unique dilemmas to minority women goes without question. But if police were reluctant to intervene generally in domestic violence cases prior to legal reform, they provided virtually no protection to blacks. ... [M]any police conceive of blacks as what sociologist Darnel Hawkins terms "normal primitives" and only intervene in "domestics" when violence overflows into the public arena. This is one reason why violence—almost always by a spouse or a lover—is the major cause of death among black women under 44 years of age. That such attitudes are self-fulfilling is suggested by Sherman's observation that police can "predict" which couples (and which apartment build-

ings!) are chronically violent. Eliminating mandatory arrest, then, would do little more than reestablish a brutal status quo....

CRIMINALIZATION AS SOCIAL CONTROL

[Here is] a final argument against mandatory arrest: that it reflects a trend to criminalize behaviors and, as such, is a conservative effort to extend "social control."... Echoes of the social control argument can... be found in Sherman's... warnings against interference in "family privacy."

... That such intervention may... become a vehicle for imposing other systemic biases (e.g., race or class prejudice) highlights the problems with enforcement but is not an inevitable consequence of society's legitimate interest in limiting unacceptable behavior. Nor is the control function of the law a reason to abandon women's larger justice claims for the equitable distribution of criminal sanctions.

Like legal control, criminalization may or may not advance personal liberty and social justice....

With respect to both control and criminalization,... there is simply no way to avoid the difficult process of making political decisions about where scarce resources will be distributed and on whose behalf. If we think of justice as a good in itself, not merely as a means to an end, we can ask whether the mandatory arrest of batterers represents a more or less equitable distribution of this good.

There is little question in my view that the mandatory arrest of batterers represents a progressive redistribution of justice on behalf of women. One measure of this is a growing suspicion among social scientists and policymakers that, in intervening to counteract the illegitimate coercive power of particular men, the law is being used "politically" to further the larger goals of sexual equality. Would it were so.

REFERENCES

Cobbe, F. P. (1878). Wife torture in England. *Contemporary Review, 32,* 55–87.

POSTSCRIPT

Does Arresting Batterers Do More Harm Than Good?

Domestic violence is a multifaceted issue. It includes violence of parents against their children, of husband against wife, of wife against husband, and of adult child against an elderly parent. The causes are usually obscure and complex. In short, as in many areas of human behavior, *why* anyone assaults another is problematic, as are the "cures" for such assaults. There likely is no single panacea.

Moreover, as Stark argues, attempting to isolate a single factor, such as arrests, then making policy recommendations based on some quasi-experimental design comparing that factor with others is dubious. However, even if it is conceded that arrest is *not* a deterrent in many cases, can we say that its symbolic function justifies making arrests mandatory anyway? If careful research shows, as Schmidt and Sherman contend, that arrests have limited value and often make matters worse, should such research be ignored in order to send the signal that society will no longer tolerate this form of brutality? In addition to more counseling programs and shelters for women, other proposals are being formulated for battered women (e.g., quick and easy divorce for battered victims). Should such steps be carefully researched before we embrace a policy like mandatory arrest that may have serious unanticipated negative consequences for many victims?

For an analysis of some chilling effects of "warrantless arrest," "pro-arrest," or "mandatory arrest" for domestic violence in Virginia, see "Fault Line," by L. Mundy, *The Washington Post Magazine* (October 26, 1997). Also see "Breaking Down the Myths of Domestic Violence," by A. O'Dell, *Community Policing Exchange* (November/December 1997); "Domestic Abuse Programming in the Dane County Jail," by J. Norwick and P. Seger, *American Jails* (July/August 1996); and "Message to Batterers: If You Hit, We'll Arrest," *Lens* (September 15, 1997).

Two outstanding books on the subject are *Domestic Violence: The Criminal Justice Response*, 2d ed., by E. Buzawa and C. Buzawa (Sage Publications, 1996) and C. Renzetti and K. Hamberger, *Domestic Partner Abuse* (Springer Publishing, 1996). For a discussion of black family violence, see *Violence in the Black Family* edited by R. L. Hampton (Lexington Books, 1987). Among the growing literature on gay domestic violence is *Men Who Beat the Men Who Love Them: Battered Gay Men and Domestic Violence* by D. Island and P. Letellier (Haworth Press, 1991).

ISSUE 10

Are Blacks Helped by the Drug War?

YES: James A. Inciardi, from "Against Legalization of Drugs," in Arnold S. Trebach and James A. Inciardi, *Legalize It? Debating American Drug Policy* (American University Press, 1993)

NO: Thomas Szasz, from *Our Right to Drugs: The Case for a Free Market* (Syracuse University Press, 1996)

ISSUE SUMMARY

YES: James A. Inciardi, director of the Center for Drug and Alcohol Studies at the University of Delaware, surveys several arguments supporting the legalization of drugs and rejects them all, insisting that blacks and others would be hurt by legalization.

NO: Psychiatrist and psychoanalyst Thomas Szasz maintains that the current drug war harms almost all people, especially blacks, and that its main function is to increase the power of the medical and criminal justice establishments.

Throughout the twentieth century, America's problems have often been traced to dubious origins that have served primarily as scapegoats. The shifting nature of the American family, the changing behavioral patterns of the young, the broadening of opportunities for blacks, women, and other minority groups, and increasing political disenchantment—which were all partially the result of increasing modernization, an unpopular war, and other specific structural precipitants—were variously blamed on the movie industry, comic books, bolshevism, gambling, alcohol, organized crime, and, now and then, the devil himself. Currently, the continued concern with the changing nature of the American family, the increasing fear of crime, and the widening generation gap are linked with drug use. If only we could get the dealers off the streets or at least get the kids to say no to drugs, then we could restore our family system. If only we could arrest everyone who takes drugs, then we could eliminate crime, since it is drugs that cause most people to commit crimes. If only the students in our junior high schools, high schools, and colleges were not taking drugs, then they would not only do better on their academic achievement scores but once again love and obey their parents.

The entire criminal justice system, it seems, has been marshalled to fight in the war on drugs. A 1998 report by the National Center on Addiction and Substance Abuse indicates that the tripling of the prison population from 500,000 in 1980 to 1.7 million in 1997 is largely attributable to drug dealing, abuse, and drug- and alcohol-related felonies. One of every 14 black males is behind bars (compared with one of every 144 U.S. citizens). In some urban areas, one of every four black males is under the auspices of the criminal justice system, many because of drug crimes. A young black male has a higher chance of being incarcerated than being in college.

The costs of fighting the drug war are enormous, and greater expenditures for police, prisons, and drug control continue with no end in sight. The drug war is seen by critics as demoralizing entire communities, especially the poor. Paradoxically, far more whites use drugs than blacks, but the war is clearly pitched at inner-city dwellers.

Opinions on this issue are divided. On the one hand, politicians frequently attack anyone who is seen as "soft" on drugs. On the other hand, many visible problems related to drug control grow. These include sharp criticisms by scholars that crime is not decreasing, minorities are becoming increasingly estranged from the police, and the costs are escalating. In addition, cases of police abuse are often uncovered, ranging from harassment of minorities to police themselves being arrested for trafficking in drugs (44 such arrests were made in early 1998 in Ohio).

Defenders of current drug policies counter that without the drug war (i.e., if drugs were decriminalized), crime, poverty, hopelessness, demoralization, and loss of direction, especially among the young and minorities, would be far worse than it is now. If we let up on fighting drugs, they assert, crime would skyrocket. For many, even the idea of providing clean needles to heroin addicts is offensive.

This debate is crucial for criminal justice. As you read the following selections, you will notice that it differs from most standard discussions of the issue: it puts up front the effects of the drug war on those who are most directly and frequently affected. James A. Inciardi itemizes specific types of drugs and their respective harms. As you read his ideas, consider how he debates and rejects legalizers' perspectives.

Thomas Szasz, emphasizing individual liberty, chides both the medical establishment, for usurping American's right to select drugs, and the criminal justice system, for defining drug use (and sales) as a crime. Szasz insists that adults should have the right to grow what they want, distribute what they want, and use what they want without being labeled "ill" or "criminal." Szasz also ridicules many black leaders for waging the drug war, claiming genocide and enslavement, and bootlegging victimhood as rational talk.

As you wrestle with this debate, consider what is meant by "harm." Think about who, if anyone, is currently being harmed the most, and how, by the war. Who might be harmed if drugs are allowed to be sold openly and legally?

YES
James A. Inciardi

AGAINST LEGALIZATION OF DRUGS

THE PRO-LEGALIZATION ISSUES AND CONTENDERS

The drug legalization debate emerged in both generic and specific configurations. In its most generic adaptation, it went something like this. First, the drug laws have created evils far worse than the drugs themselves—corruption, violence, street crime, and disrespect for the law. Second, legislation passed to control drugs has failed to reduce demand. Third, you should not prohibit that which a major segment of the population is committed to doing; that is, you simply cannot arrest, prosecute, and punish such large numbers of people, particularly in a democracy. And specifically in this behalf, in a liberal democracy the government must not interfere with personal behavior if liberty is to be maintained....

Thomas S. Szasz and the Control of Conduct   Thomas S. Szasz is a Hungarian-born psychiatrist who emigrated to the United States in 1938 and studied medicine at the University of Cincinnati. Trained in psychiatry at the University of Chicago, he became a well-known critic of his profession. Szasz has written that "mental illness" is a mythological concept used by the state to control deviants and thereby limit freedom in American society. In his view, the conditions comprising mental illness are social and moral problems, not medical ones. He repeatedly warns against replacing a theological worldview with a therapeutic one. Moreover, he is an uncompromising libertarian and humanist who has argued against involuntary psychiatric examination and hospitalization, and who believes that the psychoanalytic relationship should be free of coercion and control....

During the 1970s, relying on the postulates and assertions that he had applied to mental illness, Szasz became the most outspoken critic of the medical or "disease" model of addiction. His primary concern with the disease model is that it diminishes an individual's responsibility for his or her dysfunctional or antisocial behavior. He also argues that the concept of addiction as a disease places undue emphasis on medical authority in determining how society should manage what is actually an individual violation of legal and social norms.

On the matter of whether society should attempt to control, and hence "prohibit" the use of certain substances, he offers the following:

> The plain historical facts are that before 1914 there was no "drug problem" in the United States; nor did we have a name for it. Today there is an immense drug problem in the United States, and we have lots of names for it. Which came first: "the problem of drug abuse" or its name?... My point is simply that our drug abuse experts, legislators, psychiatrists, and other professional guardians of our medical morals have been operating chicken hatcheries; they continue—partly by means of certain characteristic tactical abuses of our language—to manufacture and maintain the "drug problem" they ostensibly try to solve (Szasz 1974).

What he was suggesting is something that nominalists have been saying for centuries: that a thing does not exist until it is imagined and given a name. For Szasz, a hopeless believer in this position, the "drug problem" in the United States did not exist before the passage of the Harrison Act in 1914, but became a reality when the behavior under consideration was *labeled* as a problem. Stated differently, he argues that the drug problem in America was created in great part by the very policies designed to control it.

For Szasz, the solution to the drug problem is simple. Ignore it, and it will no longer be a problem. After all, he maintained, there is precedent for it:

> ... Our present attitudes toward the whole subject of drug use, drug abuse, and drug control are nothing but the re-

flections, in the mirror of "social reality," of our own expectations toward drugs and toward those who use them; and that our ideas about and interventions in drug-taking behavior have only the most tenuous connection with the actual pharmacological properties of "dangerous drugs." The "danger" of masturbation disappeared when we ceased to believe in it: when we ceased to attribute danger to the practice and to its practitioners; and ceased to call it "self-abuse" (Szasz 1974).

What Szasz seems to be suggesting is that heroin, cocaine, and other "dangerous drugs" be legalized; hence, the problems associated with their use would disappear. And this is where he runs into difficulty, for his argument is so riddled with faulty scholarship and flagrant errors of fact that he lost credibility with those familiar with the history of the American drug scene.

Szasz's libertarian-laissez-faire position has continued into the 1990s. He perseveres in his argument that people should be allowed to ingest, inhale, or inject whatever substances they wish. And it would appear from his comments that he is opposed to drug regulation of any type, even by prescription....

Arnold S. Trebach and Harm Reduction
Perhaps most respected in the field of drug-policy reform is Arnold S. Trebach....

Briefly, his proposals for drug-policy are the following:

1. Reverse drug-policy funding priorities....

2. Curtail AIDS: Make clean needles available to intravenous drug addicts....

3. Develop a plan for drug treatment on demand, allow Medicaid to pay for the

poor, and expand the variety of treatment options available....

4. Stop prosecutions of pregnant drug users....

5. Make medical marijuana available to the seriously ill....

6. Appoint a commission to seriously examine alternatives to prohibition....

Although my objections and alternatives are discussed later, let me just say that Trebach has experienced a "conversion" of sorts in recent years. There was a time when he denied endorsing the legalization of drugs....

The Debate's Supporting Cast and Bit Players

An aspect of the drug-policy debates of the second half of the 1980s was a forum awash with self-defined experts from many walks of life.

The Bit Players The "bit players" were the many who had a lot to say on the debate, but from what I feel were not particularly informed positions. They wrote books, or they published papers, but they remained on the sidelines because either no one took them seriously, their work was carelessly done, or their arguments were just not persuasive....

A rather pathetically hatched entry to the debate was Richard Lawrence Miller's book, *The Case for Legalizing Drugs* (1991).... Perhaps most misleading in the book is the list of "benefits" of using illicit drugs. I'll cite but one example to provide a glimpse of the author's approach:

> Heroin can calm rowdy teenagers—reducing aggression, sexual drive, fertility, and teen pregnancy—helping ado-

lescents through that time of life (Miller 1991, 153).

I have a teenage daughter, so I guess I'll have to remember that if she ever gets rowdy. Enough!

Cameos and Comic Relief ... Such well-known personages as conservative pundit William F. Buckley, Jr., Nobel laureate economist Milton Friedman, former Secretary of State George P. Shultz, journalist Anthony Lewis, *Harper's* editor Lewis H. Lapham, and even Washington, D. C., Mayor Marion Barry came forward to endorse legalization. The "legalizers" viewed the support of these notables as a legitimation of their argument, but all had entered the debate from disturbingly uninformed positions. With the exception of Marion Barry, and I say this facetiously, none had any first-hand experience with the issues....

ARGUING AGAINST LEGALIZATION

... While there are numerous arguments *for* legalization, there are likely an equal or greater number *against*.

Some Public Health Considerations

Tomorrow, like every other average day in the United States, about 11,449.3 babies will be born, 90 acres of pizza will be ordered, almost 600,000 M&M candies will be eaten, and some 95 holes-in-one will be claimed. At the same time, 171 million bottles of beer will be consumed, and almost 1.5 billion cigarettes will be smoked (Ruth 1992). In 1965, the annual death toll from smoking-related diseases was estimated at 188,000. By the close of the 1980s that figure had more than doubled, to 434,000, and it is expected to increase throughout the 1990s (Centers for Disease Control 1990, 1991b). And these figures do not include the almost 40,000 nonsmokers who die each year from ailments associated with the inhalation of passive smoke.

... [I]t is estimated that there are 10.5 million alcoholics in the United States, and that a total of 73 million adults have been touched by alcoholism (*Alcoholism and Drug Abuse Weekly*, 9 October 1991, 1). Each year there are some 45,000 alcohol-related traffic fatalities in the United States (Centers for Disease Control 1991a), and thousands of women who drink during pregnancy bear children with irreversible alcohol-related defects (Steinmetz 1992). Alcohol use in the past year was reported by 54 percent of the nation's eighth graders, 72 percent of tenth graders, and 78 percent of twelfth graders, and almost a third of high school seniors in 1991 reported "binge drinking." ... [T]he cost of alcohol abuse in the United States for 1990 has been estimated at $136.31 billion (*Substance Abuse Report*, 15 June 1991, 3).

Sophism, Legalization, and Illicit Drug Use   Keep the above data in mind, and consider that they relate to only two of the *legal* drugs. Now for some reason, numerous members of the prolegalization lobby argue that if drugs were to be legalized, usage would likely not increase very much, if at all. The reasons, they state, are that "drugs are everywhere," and that everyone who wants to use them already does. But the data beg to differ. For example,... 56 percent of high school seniors in 1991 had never used an illicit drug in their lifetimes, and 73 percent had never used an illicit drug other than marijuana in their lifetimes.... [T]he absolute numbers

in these age cohorts who have never even *tried* any illicit drugs are in the tens of millions. And most significantly for the argument that "drugs are everywhere," half of all high school students do not feel that drugs are easy to obtain.

Going further,... most people in the general population do not use drugs. Granted, these data are limited to the "general population," which excludes such hard-to-reach populations as members of deviant and exotic subcultures, the homeless, and others living "on the streets," and particularly those in which drug use rates are highest. However, the data do document that the overwhelming majority of Americans do not use illicit drugs. This suggests two things: that the drug prohibitions may be working quite well; and that there is a large population who might, and I emphasize might, use drugs if they were legal and readily available....

An interesting variety of sophist reasoning pervades segments of the prolegalization thesis. It is argued over and over that drugs should be legalized because they don't really do that much harm.... The legalizers use... data to demonstrate that not too many people actually have adverse encounters with heroin, cocaine, and other illicit drugs, as compared with the hundreds of thousands of deaths each year linked to alcohol and tobacco use.... But interestingly, it is never stated that proportionately few people actually use illicit drugs, and that the segment of the population "at risk" for overdose or other physical complications from illegal drug use is but an insignificant fraction of that at risk for disease and death from alcohol and tobacco use.

The Problems With Illegal Drugs Considerable evidence exists to suggest that the legalization of drugs could create behavioral and public health problems that would far outweigh the current consequences of drug prohibition. There are some excellent reasons why marijuana, cocaine, heroin, and other drugs are now controlled, and why they ought to remain so....

Marijuana. There is considerable misinformation about marijuana. To the millions of adolescents and young adults who were introduced to the drug during the social revolution of the 1960s and early 1970s, marijuana was a harmless herb of ecstasy. As the "new social drug" and a "natural organic product," it was deemed to be far less harmful than either alcohol or tobacco (see Grinspoon 1971; Smith 1970; Sloman 1979). More recent research suggests, however, that marijuana smoking is a practice that combines the hazardous features of both tobacco and alcohol with a number of pitfalls of its own. Moreover, there are many disturbing questions about marijuana's effect on the vital systems of the body, on the brain and mind, on immunity and resistance, and on sex and reproduction (Jones and Lovinger 1985).

One of the more serious difficulties with marijuana use relates to lung damage.... Researchers at the University of California at Los Angeles reported... in 1988 that the respiratory burden in smoke particulates and absorption of carbon monoxide from smoking just one marijuana "joint" is some *four times greater* than from smoking a single tobacco cigarette.... [M]arijuana deposits four times more tar in the throat and lungs and increases carbon monoxide levels in the blood fourfold to fivefold.

... [A]side from the health consequences of marijuana use, recent research on the behavioral aspects of the drug suggests that it severely affects the social perceptions of heavy users. Findings from the Center for Psychological Studies in New York City, for example, report that adults who smoked marijuana daily believed the drug helped them to function better—improving their self- awareness and relationships with others (Hendin et al. 1987). In reality, however, marijuana had acted as a "buffer," enabling users to tolerate problems rather than face them and make changes that might increase the quality of their social functioning and satisfaction with life. The study found that the research subjects used marijuana to avoid dealing with their difficulties, and the avoidance inevitably made their problems worse, on the job, at home, and in family and sexual relationships.

... [W]hat has been said about cocaine also applies to crack, and perhaps more so. Crack's low price (as little as $2 per rock in some locales) has made it an attractive drug of abuse for those with limited funds. Its rapid absorption brings on a faster onset of dependence than is typical with other forms of cocaine, resulting in higher rates of addiction, binge use, and psychoses. The consequences include higher levels of cocaine-related violence and all the same manifestations of personal, familial, and occupational neglect that are associated with other forms of drug dependence....

Heroin. A derivative of morphine, heroin is a highly addictive narcotic, and is the drug historically associated with addiction and street crime. Although heroin overdose is not uncommon, unlike alcohol, cocaine, tobacco, and many prescription drugs, the direct physiological damage caused by heroin use tends to be minimal. And it is for this reason that the protagonists of drug legalization include heroin in their arguments. By making heroin readily available to users, they argue, many problems could be sharply reduced if not totally eliminated, including: the crime associated with supporting a heroin habit; the overdoses resulting from unknown levels of heroin purity and potency; the HIV and hepatitis infections brought about by needle-sharing; and the personal, social, and occupational dislocations resulting from the drug-induced criminal lifestyle.

The belief that the legalization of heroin would eliminate crime, overdose, infections, and life dislocations for its users is for the most part delusional. Instead, it is likely that the heroin-use lifestyle would change little for most addicts regardless of the legal status of the drug, an argument supported by ample evidence in the biographies and autobiographies of narcotics addicts, the clinical assessments of heroin addiction, and the drug abuse treatment literature. And to this can be added the many thousands of conversations I have had over the past 30 years with heroin users and members of their families.

The point is this. Heroin is a highly addicting drug. For the addict, it becomes life-consuming: it becomes mother, father, spouse, lover, counselor, and confessor. Because heroin is a short-acting drug, with its effects lasting at best four to six hours, it must be taken regularly and repeatedly. Because there is a more rapid onset when taken intravenously, most heroin users inject the drug. Because heroin has depressant effects, a portion of the user's day is spent in a semi-stupefied state. Collectively, these attributes result in a user more concerned with drug-taking and drug-seeking than health, family, work, relationships, responsibility, or anything else.

The Pursuit of Pleasure and Escape
... [R]esearch by professors Michael D. Newcomb and Peter M. Bentler of the University of California at Los Angeles has documented the long-term behavioral effects of drug use on teenagers (Newcomb and Bentler 1988). Beginning in 1976, a total of 654 Los Angeles County youths were tracked for a period of eight years. Most of these youths were only occasional users of drugs, using drugs and alcohol moderately at social gatherings, whereas upwards of 10 percent were frequent, committed users. The impact of drugs on these frequent users was considerable. As teenagers, drug use tended to intensify the typical adolescent problems with family and school. In addition, drugs contributed to such psychological difficulties as loneliness, bizarre and disorganized thinking, and suicidal thoughts. Moreover, frequent drug users left school earlier, started jobs earlier, and formed families earlier, and as such, they moved into adult roles with the maturity levels of adolescents. The consequences of this pattern included rapid family break-ups, job instability, serious crime, and ineffective personal relationships. In short, frequent drug use prevented the acquisition of the coping mechanisms that are part of maturing; it blocked teenagers' learning of interpersonal skills and general emotional development.

... [A]lthough we have no explicit data on whether the numbers of addicts and associated problems would increase if drugs were legalized, there are reasons to believe that they would, and rather dramatically. First, the number of people who actually use drugs is proportionately small. Second, the great majority of people in the United States have never used illicit drugs, and hence, have never been "at risk" for addiction. Third, because of the drug prohibition, illicit drugs are *not* "everywhere," and as a result, most people have not had the opportunity to even experiment with them. Fourth, alcohol *is* readily available, and the numbers of people who have been touched by alcoholism are in the dozens of millions.

Given this, let's take the argument one step further. There is extensive physiological, neurological, and anthropological evidence to suggest that we are members of a species that has been honed for pleasure. Nearly all people want and enjoy pleasure, and the pursuit of drugs—whether caffeine, nicotine, alcohol, opium, heroin, marijuana, or cocaine —seems to be universal and inescapable. It is found across time and across cultures (and species). The process of evolution has for whatever reasons resulted in a human neurophysiology that responds both vividly and avidly to a variety of common substances. The brain has pleasure centers—receptor sites and cortical cells—that react to "rewarding" dosages of many substances....

If the legalization model were of value, then ... the narcotic would just be there— attracting little attention. There would be minimal use, addiction, and the attendant social and public health problems—as long as the drug's availability was not restricted and legislated against.

... [C]onsider Poland. For generations, Poles have cultivated home-grown poppies for the use of their seeds as flavoring in breads, stews, pretzel sticks, cookies, cakes, and chocolates. During the early 1970s, many Polish farmers began transforming their poppy straw into what has become known as *jam, compote,* or "Polish heroin." Then, many Poles began using heroin, but the practice was for the most part ignored. By the end of the 1970s heroin use in Poland had escalated significantly, but still the situation was ignored. By late 1985, at a time when the number of heroin users was estimated at 600,000 and the number of heroin-dependent persons was fixed at 200,000, the Polish government could no longer ignore what was happening. The number of overdose deaths was mounting, and the range of psychosocial and public health problems associated with heroin use was beginning to affect the structure of the already troubled country. By 1986, feeling that heroin use had gotten out of hand, the Communist government in Poland placed controls on the cultivation of poppy seeds, and the transformation of poppy straw into heroin was outlawed....

Although the events in Poland have not been systematically studied, what is known of the experience suggests that introducing potent intoxicants to a population can have problematic consequences. Moreover, the notion that "availability creates demand" has been found in numerous other parts of the world, particularly with cocaine in the Andean regions of South America (see Inciardi 1992, 222).

The Legacy of Crack Cocaine
The great drug wars in the United States have endured now for generations, although the drug legalization debates have less of a history—on again, off again since the 1930s, with a sudden burst of energy at the close of the 1980s. But as the wars linger on and the debates abide, a coda must be added to both of these politically charged topics. It concerns crack cocaine, a drug that

has brought about a level of human suffering heretofore unknown in the American drug scene. The problem with crack is not that it is prohibited, but rather, the fact that it exists at all.... The chemistry and psychopharmacology of crack, combined with the tangle of socioeconomic and psychocultural strains that exist in those communities where the drug is concentrated, warrant some consideration of whether further discussion of its legality or illegality serves any purpose. Focusing on crack as an example, my intent here is to argue that both the "drug wars" and "harm reduction effort" are better served by a shifting away from the drug legalization debate.

Crack Cocaine in the United States
... For the inner cities across America, the introduction of crack couldn't have happened at a worse time. The economic base of the working poor had been shrinking for years, the result of a number of factors, including the loss of many skilled and unskilled jobs to cheaper labor markets, the movement of many businesses to the suburbs and the Sun Belt, and competition from foreign manufacturers. Standards of living, health, and overall quality of life were also in a downward direction, as consequences of suburbanization and the shrinking tax bases of central cities, combined with changing economic policies at the federal level that shifted the responsibility for many social supports to the local and private sectors. Without question, by the early to mid–1980s there was a growing and pervasive climate of hopelessness in ghetto America. And at the same time, as HIV and AIDS began to spread through inner-city populations of injectable drug users and their sex partners and as funding for drug abuse treat-

ment declined, the production of coca and cocaine in South America reached an all-time high, resulting in high-purity cocaine at a low price on the streets of urban America. As I said, crack couldn't have come to the inner city at a worse time....

I've been doing street studies in Miami, Florida, for more years than I care to remember, and during that time I've had many an experience in the shooting galleries, base houses, and open-air drug and prostitution markets that populate the local drug scene. None of these prepared me, however, with what I was to encounter in the crack houses. As part of a federally funded street survey and ethnography of cocaine and crack use, my first trip to a crack house came in 1988. I had gained entrée through a local drug dealer who had been a key informant of mine for almost a decade. He introduced me to the crack house "door man" as someone "straight but OK." After the door man checked us for weapons, my guide proceeded to show me around.

Upon entering a room in the rear of the crack house (what I later learned was called a "freak room"), I observed what appeared to be the forcible gang-rape of an unconscious child. Emaciated, seemingly comatose, and likely no older than 14 years of age, she was lying spread-eagled on a filthy mattress while four men in succession had vaginal intercourse with her. Despite what was happening, I was urged not to interfere. After they had finished and left the room, another man came in, and they engaged in oral sex.

Upon leaving the crack house sometime later, the dealer/informant explained that she was a "house girl"—a person in the employ of the crack house owner. He gave her food, a place to sleep, some cigarettes and cheap wine, and all the crack she wanted in return for her providing sex—any type and amount of sex—to his crack house customers.

That was my first trip to a crack house. During subsequent trips to this and other crack houses, there were other scenes: a woman purchasing crack, with an infant tucked under her arm—so neglected that she had maggots crawling out of her diaper; a man "skin-popping" his toddler with a small dose of heroin, so the child would remain quietly sedated and not interrupt a crack-smoking session; people in various states of excitement and paranoia, crouching in the corners of smoking rooms inhaling from "the devil's dick" (the stem of the crack pipe); arguments, fist fights, stabbings, and shootings over crack, the price of crack, the quantity and quality of crack, and the use and sharing of crack; any manner and variety of sexual activity—by individuals and/or groups, with members of the opposite sex, the same sex, or both, or with animals, in private or public, in exchange for crack. I also saw "drug hounds" and "rock monsters" (some of the "regulars" in a crack house) crawling on their hands and knees, inspecting the floors for slivers of crack that may have dropped; beatings and gang rapes of small-time drug couriers—women, men, girls, and boys—as punishment for "messing up the money"; people in convulsions and seizures, brought on by crack use, cocaine use, the use of some other drug, or whatever; users of both sexes, so dependent on crack, so desperate for more crack, that they would do anything for another hit, eagerly risking the full array of sexually transmitted diseases, including AIDS; imprisonment and sexual slavery, one of the ultimate results of crack addiction. ...

Many crack users engage in sexual behaviors with extremely high frequency. However, to suggest that crack turns men into "sex-crazed fiends" and women into "sex-crazed whores," as sensationalized media stories imply, is anything but precise. The situation is far more complex than that.

… Medical authorities generally concede that because of the disinhibiting effects of cocaine, its use among new users does indeed enhance sexual enjoyment and improve sexual functioning, including more intense orgasms (Weiss and Mirin 1987; Grinspoon and Bakalar 1985). These same reports maintain, however, that among long-term addicts, cocaine decreases both sexual desire and performance.

Going further, the crack-sex association involves the need of female crack addicts to pay for their drug. Even this connection has a pharmacological component—crack's rapid onset, extremely short duration of effects, and high addiction liability combine to result in compulsive use and a willingness to obtain the drug through any means. ... Prostitution has long been the easiest, most lucrative, and most reliable means for women to finance drug use (Goldstein 1979).

The combined pharmacological and sociocultural effects of crack use can put female users in severe jeopardy. Because crack makes its users ecstatic and yet is so short-acting, it has an extremely high addiction potential. Use rapidly becomes compulsive use. Crack acquisition thus becomes enormously more important than family, work, social responsibility, health, values, modesty, morality, or self-respect. ...

A benefit of its current criminalization is that since it *is* against the law, it doesn't have widespread availability, so proportionately few people use it.

So where does all of this take us? My point is this. Within the context of reversing the human suffering that crack has helped to exacerbate, what purpose is served by arguing for its legalization? Will legalizing crack make it less available, less attractive, less expensive, less addictive, or less troublesome? Nobody really knows for sure, but I doubt it.

Drugs-Crime Connections

For the better part of this century there has been a concerted belief that addicts commit crimes because they are "enslaved" to drugs, that because of the high prices of heroin, cocaine, and other illicit chemicals on the black market, users are forced to commit crimes in order to support their drug habits. I have often referred to this as the "enslavement theory" of addiction (Inciardi 1986, 147–49; Inciardi 1992, 263–64)....

Research since the middle of the 1970s with active drug users in the streets of New York, Miami, Baltimore, and elsewhere has demonstrated that enslavement theory has little basis in reality, and that the contentions of the legalization proponents in this behalf are mistaken (see Inciardi 1986, 115–43; Johnson et al. 1985; Nurco et al. 1985; Stephens and McBride 1976; McBride and McCoy 1982). All of these studies of the criminal careers of heroin and other drug users have convincingly documented that while drug use tends to intensify and perpetuate criminal behavior, it usually does not initiate criminal careers. In fact, the evidence suggests that among the majority of street drug users who are involved in crime, their criminal careers were well established prior to the onset of either narcotics or cocaine use....

POSTSCRIPT

... [L]et me reiterate the major points I have been trying to make.

The arguments *for* legalization are seemingly based on the fervent belief that America's prohibitions against marijuana, cocaine, heroin, and other drugs impose far too large a cost in terms of tax dollars, crime, and infringements on civil rights and individual liberties. And while the overall argument may be well-intended and appear quite logical, I find it to be highly questionable in its historical, sociocultural, and empirical underpinnings, and demonstrably naive in its understanding of the negative consequences of a legalized drug market. In counterpoint:

1. Although drug-prohibition policies have been problematic, it would appear that they have managed to keep drugs away from most people. High school and general population surveys indicate that most Americans don't use drugs, have never even tried them, and don't know where to get them. Thus, the numbers "at risk" are dramatically fewer than is the case with the legal drugs. Or stated differently, there is a rather large population who might be at risk if illicit drugs were suddenly available.

2. Marijuana, heroin, cocaine, crack, and the rest are not "benign" substances. Their health consequences, addiction liability, and/or abuse potential are considerable.

3. There is extensive physiological, neurological, and anthropological evidence to suggest that people are of a species that has been honed for pleasure. Nearly all people want and enjoy pleasure, and the pursuit of drugs—whether caffeine, nicotine, alcohol, opium, heroin, marijuana, or cocaine—seems to be uni-

versal and inescapable. It is found across time and across cultures. Moreover, history and research has demonstrated that "availability creates demand."

4. Crack cocaine is especially problematic because of its pharmacological and sociocultural effects. Because crack makes its users ecstatic and yet is so short-acting, it has an extremely high addiction potential. *Use* rapidly becomes *compulsive use.* . . .

5. The research literature on the criminal careers of heroin and other drug users have convincingly documented that while drug use tends to intensify and perpetuate criminal behavior, it usually does not initiate criminal careers.

6. There is also a large body of work suggesting that drug abuse is overdetermined behavior. That is, physical dependence is secondary to the wide range of influences that instigate and regulate drug-taking and drug-seeking. Drug abuse is a disorder of the whole person, affecting some or all areas of functioning. In the vast majority of drug offenders, there are cognitive problems, psychological dysfunction is common, thinking may be unrealistic or disorganized, values are misshapen, and frequently there are deficits in educational and employment skills. As such, drug abuse is a response to a series of social and psychological disturbances. Thus, the goal of treatment should be "habilitation" rather than "rehabilitation." Whereas *rehabilitation* emphasizes the return to a way of life previously known and perhaps forgotten or rejected, *habilitation* involves the client's initial socialization into a productive and responsible way of life.

7. The focus on the war on drugs can be shifted. I believe that we do indeed need drug enforcement, but it is stressed far too much in current policy. Cut it in half, and shift those funds to criminal justice-based treatment programs.

8. Drug control should remain within the criminal justice sector for some very good reasons. The Drug Use Forecasting (DUF) program clearly demonstrates that the majority of arrestees in urban areas are drug-involved. Moreover, recent research has demonstrated not only that drug abuse treatment works, but also that coerced treatment works best. The key variable most related to success in treatment is "length of stay in treatment," and those who are forced into treatment remain longer than volunteers. By remaining longer, they benefit more. As such, compulsory treatment efforts should be expanded for those who are dependent on drugs and are involved in drug-related crime.

9. Since the "war on drugs" will continue, then a more humane use of the criminal justice system should be structured. This is best done through treatment in lieu of incarceration, and corrections-based treatment for those who do end up in jails and prisons. . . .

American drug policy as it exists today is not likely to change drastically anytime soon. Given that, something needs to be kept in mind. While the First Amendment and academic freedom enable the scholarly community to continue its attack on American drug policy, verbal assault and vilification will serve no significant purpose in effecting change. Calls for the legalization or decriminalization of marijuana, heroin, cocaine, and other illicit drugs accomplish little more than to further isolate the legalizers from the policy-making enterprise.

Finally, there is far too much suffering as the result of drug abuse that is not being addressed. Many things warrant discussion, debate, and prodding on the steps of Capitol Hill and the White House lawn. More drug abuse treatment slots, a repeal of the statutes designed to prosecute pregnant addicts and prohibit needle-exchange programs, the wider use of treatment as an alternative to incarceration—all of these are worthy of vigorous consideration and lobbying. But not legalizing drugs. It is an argument that is going nowhere.

NO

Thomas Szasz

BLACKS AND DRUGS: CRACK AS GENOCIDE

Crack is genocide, 1990's style.

—Cecil Williams

No one can deny that, in the tragicomedy we call the War on Drugs, blacks and Hispanics at home and Latin Americans abroad play leading roles: They are (or are perceived to be) our principal drug abusers, drug addicts, drug traffickers, drug counselors, drug-busting policemen, convicts confined for drug offenses, and narco-terrorists. In short, blacks and Hispanics dominate the drug abuse market, both as producers and as products.

I am neither black nor Hispanic and do not pretend to speak for either group or any of its members. There is, however, no shortage of people, black and white, who are eager to speak for them. Which raises an important question, namely: Who speaks for black or Hispanic Americans? Those persons, black or white, who identify drugs—especially crack—as the enemy of blacks? Or those, who cast the American state—especially its War on Drugs—in that role? Or neither, because the claims of both are absurd oversimplifications and because black Americans—like white Americans—are not a homogeneous group but a collection of individuals, each of whom is individually responsible for his own behavior and can speak for himself?

BLACK LEADERS ON DRUGS

For the mainline black drug warrior, illegal drugs represent a temptation that African-Americans are morally too enfeebled to resist. This is what makes those who expose them to such temptation similar to slaveholders depriving their victims of liberty. After years of sloganeering by anti-drug agitators, the claim that crack enslaves blacks has become a cliché, prompting the sloganeers to escalate their rhetoric and contend that it is genocide.

Crack as Genocide, Crack as Slavery

The assertion that crack is genocide is a powerful and timely metaphor we ought to clarify, lest we get ourselves entangled in it. Slavery and genocide are the manifestations and the results of the use of force by some people against some other people. Drugs, however, are inert substances unless and until they are taken into the body; and, not being persons, they cannot literally force anyone to do anything. Nevertheless, the claim that black persons are "poisoned" and "enslaved" by drugs put at their disposal by a hostile white society is now the politically correct rhetoric among black racists and white liberals alike. For example, *New York Times* columnist A. M. Rosenthal "denounces even the slightest show of tolerance toward illegal drugs as an act of iniquity deserving comparison to the defense of slavery." Of course, people who want to deny the role of personal agency and responsibility often make use of the metaphor of slavery, generating images of people being enslaved not only by drugs but also by cults, gambling, poverty, pornography, rock music, or mental illness. Persons who use drugs may, figuratively speaking, be said to be the "victims" of temptation, which is as far as one can reasonably carry the rhetoric of victimology. However, this does not prevent Cecil Williams, a black minister in San Francisco, from claiming,

> The crack epidemic in the United States amounts to genocide.... The primary intent of 200 years of slavery was to break the spirit and culture of our people.... Now, in the 1990's, I see substantial similarities between the cocaine epidemic and slavery.... Cocaine is foreign to African-American culture. We did not create it; we did not produce it; we did not ask for it.

If a white person made these assertions, his remarks could easily be interpreted as slandering black people. Being enslaved is something done to a person against his will, while consuming cocaine is something a person does willingly; equating the two denigrates blacks by implying that they are, en masse, so childish or weak that they cannot help but "enslave" themselves to cocaine. Williams's remark that cocaine is foreign to black culture and hence destructive compounds his calumny. Rembrandt's art, Beethoven's music, and Newton's physics are also foreign to black culture. Does that make them all evils similar to slavery?

Another black minister, the Reverend Cecil L. Murray of Los Angeles, repeats the same theme but uses different similes. He refers to drugs as if they were persons and asserts that "drugs are *literally* killing our people." Like other anti-drug agitators, Murray is short on facts and reasoning, and long on bombast and scapegoating. He excoriates proposals to legalize drugs, declaring, "This is a foul breach of everything we hold sacred. To legalize it, to condone it, to market it—that is to put a healthy brand on strychnine.... [W]e cannot make poison the norm."

By now, everyone knows that cigarettes kill more people than illegal drugs. But the point needs to be made again here. "Cigarette smoking," writes Kenneth Warner, a health care economist, "causes more premature deaths than do all of the following together: acquired immunodeficiency syndrome, heroin, alcohol, fire, automobile accidents, homicide, and suicide." Many of the conditions Warner lists affect blacks especially adversely. Both smoking and obesity are unhealthy ("poisonous") but "legal" (not prohibited by the criminal law), yet neither is regarded as the "norm."

Up with Hope, Down with Dope

The Reverend Jesse Jackson is not only a permanent presidential candidate, but is also A. M. Rosenthal's favorite drug warrior. Jackson's trademark incantation goes like this: "Up with hope, down with dope." Better at rhyming than reasoning, Jackson flatly asserts—no metaphor here, at least none that he acknowledges—that "drugs are poison. Taking drugs is a sin. Drug use is morally debased and sick." Poison. Sin. Sickness. Jackson the base rhetorician refuses to be outdone and keeps piling it on: "Since the flow of drugs into the U.S. is an act of terrorism, antiterrorist policies must be applied. . . . If someone is transmitting the death agent to Americans, that person should face wartime consequences. The line must be drawn."

It certainly must. The question, however, is this: Where should we draw it? I believe we ought to draw it by categorizing free trade in agricultural products (including coca, marijuana, and tobacco) as good, and dumping toxic wastes on unsuspecting people in underdeveloped countries as bad; by recognizing the provision of access to accurate pharmacological information as liberating drug education, and rejecting mendacious religiomedical bombast as lamentable political and racial demagogy.

Mayor Marion Barry as Drug Hero

In former days, moral crusaders—especially men of the cloth—thundered brimstone and hellfire at those who succumbed to temptation, typically of the flesh. Why? Because in those benighted pre-Freudian days, moral authorities held people responsible for their behavior. Not any more. And certainly not Jesse Jackson vis-à-vis prominent blacks who use illegal drugs. Foreign drug traffickers are responsible for selling cocaine. Washington, D.C., Mayor Marion Barry is not responsible for buying and smoking it. After the mayor was properly entrapped into buying cocaine and was videotaped smoking it, Jackson pontificated, "Now all of America can learn from the mayor's problems and his long journey back to health." A remarkable disease, this illegal drug use, U.S.A, anno Domini 1990: Caused by being arrested by agents of the state; cured by a "program" provided by agents of the state; its course a "journey"; its prognosis —known with confidence even by priest-politicians without any medical expertise —a return "back to health."

Shamelessly, Jackson used Barry's arrest as an occasion not only for sanctifying the defendant (as if he were accused of a civil rights violation) but also for promoting his own political agenda. A priori, the defendant was a good and great man, "entering the Super Bowl of his career." His accuser—the U.S. government—was, a priori, an evil "political system that can only be described as neocolonial." While thus politicizing drugs, Jackson impudently inveighs against his own practice. "Circumstances like these," he babbles, "remind us that the war on drugs . . . should not be politicized. It is primarily a moral crusade, about values and about health and sickness." Having unburdened himself of his pearls of wisdom about politics, moral values, and sickness and health, Jackson comes to his main point: "Behind these gruesome statistics lies the powerlessness of the people who live in the shadow of a national government from which they are structurally excluded. Now more than ever, it is time to escalate the effort to gain statehood and self-government for the district"— and elect Jesse Jackson senator-for-life-or-until-elected-president. Should we not expect political self-government to be preceded by personal self-government, as it normally is in progressing from disfranchised childhood to enfranchised adulthood? Jackson's envy of and thirst for the power of whites is clear enough. His contention that blacks in Washington, D.C., sell, buy, and use illegal drugs because they are "powerless" is thus but another instance of a drug warrior's fingering a scapegoat in the guise of offering an explanation.

Is Jackson, one of our most prominent anti-drug agitators, trying to protect black Americans from drugs or is he trying to promote his own career? Unlike the Black Muslims committed to an ideology of self-help, self-reliance, and radical separatism, Jackson is playing on the white man's turf, trying to gain power by the "enemy's" methods and rules. The War on Drugs presents him, as it presents his white counterparts, with the perfect social problem: Here is an issue on which Jesse Jackson can join—on common ground, shoulder to shoulder—not only such eminent white liberal-democrats as Mario Cuomo and Kitty Dukakis, but also such eminent white conservative-Republicans as Nancy Reagan and William Bennett. Indeed, on what other issue besides drugs could Jesse Jackson and Nancy Reagan —one a black militant struggling up the social ladder, the other a white conservative standing on its top rung—agree? As pharmarcological agents, dangerous drugs may indeed be toxic for the body anatomic of the individuals who use them; but as a propaganda tool, dangerous drugs are therapeutic for the body politic of the nation, welding our heterogeneous society together into one country and one people, engaged in an uplifting, self-purifying, moral crusade.

THE WAR ON DRUGS: A WAR ON BLACKS

A Martian who came to earth and read only what the newspaper headlines say about drugs would never discover an interesting and important feature of America's latest moral crusade, namely, that its principal victims are black or Hispanic. (I must add here that when I use the world *victim* in connection with the word *drug*, I do not refer to a person who chooses to use a drug and thus subjects himself to its effects, for good or ill. Being his own poisoner—assuming the drug has an ill effect on him—such a person is a victim in a metaphoric sense only. In the conventional use of the term, to which I adhere, a literal or real victim is a person unjustly or tragically deprived of his life, liberty, or property, typically by other people—in our case, as a result of the criminalization of the free market in drugs.)

However, were the Martian to turn on the television to watch the evening news, or look at a copy of *Time* or *Newsweek,* he would see images of drug busts and read stories about drug addicts and drug treatment programs in which virtually all of the characters are black or Hispanic. Occasionally, some of the drug-busting policemen are white. But the drug traffickers, drug addicts, and drug counselors are virtually all black or Hispanic.

Carl Rowan, a syndicated columnist who is black, finally spoke up. "Racist stereotypes," he correctly pointed out, "have crippled the minds of millions of white Americans." Then, rather selectively, Rowan emphasized that "white prejudice on this point has produced a terrible injustice," but chose to remain discreetly silent about the fact that black leaders are the shock troops in this anti-black drug war. "Blacks," complained Rowan, "are being arrested in USA's drug wars at a rate far out of proportion to their drug use." According to a study conducted by *USA Today*, blacks comprise 12.7 percent of the population and make up 12 percent of those who "regularly use illegal drugs"; but of those arrested on drug charges in 1988, 38 percent were blacks.

Other studies indicate that blacks represent an even larger proportion of drug law violators/victims. For example, according to the National Institute on Drug Abuse (NIDA, the leading federal agency on drug abuse research), "Although only about 12% of those using illegal drugs are black, 44% of those who are arrested for simple possession and 57% of those arrested for sales are black." Another study, conducted by the Washington-based Sentencing Project, found that while almost one in four black men of age 20–29 were in jail or on parole, only one in sixteen white men of the same age group were. Clarence Page dramatized the significance of these figures by pointing out that while 610,000 black men in their twenties are in jail or under the supervision of the criminal justice system, only 436,000 are in college. "Just as no one is born a college student," commented Page, "no one is born a criminal. Either way, you have to be carefully taught."

Page does not say who is teaching blacks to be criminals, but I will: The economic incentives intrinsic to our drug laws. After all, although black Americans today are often maltreated by whites, and are in the main poorer than whites, they were *more maltreated and were even poorer* fifty or a hundred years ago, yet fewer young black males chose a criminal career then than do now. This development is far more dangerous for all of us, black and white, than all the cocaine in Columbia. "Under the nation's current approach," a feature report in the *Los Angeles Times* acknowledges, "black America is being criminalized at an astounding rate." Nevertheless, the black community enthusiastically supports the War on Drugs. George Napper, director of public safety in Atlanta, attributes this attitude to "black people... being more conservative than other people. They say: 'To hell with rights. Just kick ass and take names.'" Father George Clements, a Catholic priest who has long been in the forefront of the struggle against drugs in Chicago's black communities, exemplifies this posture: "I'm all for whatever tactics have to be used. If that means they are trampling on civil liberties, so be it." The black leadership's seemingly increasing contempt for civil liberties is just one of the disastrous consequences of drug prohibition. The drug war's impact on poor and poorly educated blacks is equally alarming and tragic. Instead of looking to the free market and the rule of law for self-advancement, the War on Drugs encourages them to look to a race war—or a lottery ticket—as a way out of their misfortune.

Drug Prohibition: Pouring Fuel on the Fire of Racial Antagonism

Clearly, one of the unintended consequences of drug prohibition—far more dangerous to American society than drugs—has been that it has fueled the fires of racial division and antagonism. Many American blacks (whose views white psychiatrists would love to dismiss as paranoid if they could, but happily no longer can) believe that the government is "out to get them" and the War on Drugs is one of its tools: A "popular theory [among blacks] is that white government leaders play a pivotal role in the drug crisis by deliberately making drugs easily available in black neighborhoods." Another consequence of our drug laws (less unintended perhaps) has been that while it is no longer officially permissible to persecute blacks qua blacks, it is permissible to persecute them qua drug law violators. Under the pretext of protecting people—especially "kids"—from dangerous drugs, America's young black males are stigmatized en masse as drug addicts and drug criminals. The possibility that black youths may be more endangered by society's drug laws than by the temptation of drugs surely cannot be dismissed out of hand. It is an idea, however, that only those black leaders who have shaken off the shackles of trying to please their degraders dare to entertain. Thus we now find the Black Muslim minister Louis Farrakhan articulating such a view, much as the martyred Malcolm X did a quarter of a century ago. "There is," says Farrakhan, "a war being planned against black youth by the government of the United States under the guise of a war against drugs." I suspect few educated white persons really listen to or hear this message, just as few listened to or heard what Malcolm X said. And of those who hear it, most dismiss it as paranoid. But paranoids too can have real enemies.

The U.S. Customs Service acknowledges that, to facilitate its work in spotting drug smugglers, the service uses "drug courier" and "drug swallower" profiles developed in the 1970s. Critics have charged that "one characteristic that most of those detained have in common

is their race. 'The darker your skin, the better your chances,' said Gary Trichter, a Houston defense lawyer who specializes in such cases." In a ruling handed down on April 3, 1989, the Supreme Court endorsed the government's use of drug profiles for detaining and questioning airline passengers. Although the Court's ruling addressed only airports, the profiles are also used on highways, on interstate buses, and in train stations. In addition, the Customs Service is authorized to request the traveler, under penalty of being detained or not allowed to enter the country, to submit to an X-ray examination to determine if he has swallowed a condom containing drugs. "In Miami, of 101 X-rays, 67 found drugs. In New York, of 187 X-rays, 90 yielded drugs. In Houston...60 people were X-rayed [and] just 4 were found to be carrying drugs." Although the profiles have proved to be of some value, this does not justify their use unless one believes that the government's interest in finding and punishing people with illegal drugs in their possession deserves more protection than the individual's right to his own body.

What do the statistics about the people stopped and searched on the basis of drug profiles tell us? They reveal, for example, that in December 1989 in Biloxi, Mississippi, of fifty-seven stops on Interstate 10, fifty-five involved Hispanic or black people. On a stretch of the New Jersey Turnpike where less than 5 percent of the traffic involved cars with out-of-state license plates driven by black males, 80 percent of the arrests fitted that description. Topping the record for racially discriminatory drug arrests is the drug-interdiction program at the New York Port Authority Bus Terminal, where 208 out of 210 persons arrested in 1989 were black or Hispanic. Still, the anti-drug bureaucrats insist that "the ratio of arrests reflected a 'reality of the streets,' rather than a policy of racial discrimination."

However, in January 1991 Pamela Alexander, a black judge in Minnesota, ruled that the state's anti-crack law—which "calls for a jail term for first-time offenders convicted of possessing three grams of crack, but only probation for defendants convicted of possessing the same amount of powdered cocaine"—discriminated against blacks and was therefore unconstitutional. Her ruling focuses on the fact that crack cocaine and powdered cocaine are merely two different forms of cocaine, and that blacks tend to use the former, and whites the latter. The law thus addresses a difference in customs, not a difference in drug effects. "Drug policy," Judge Alexander concluded, "should not be set according to anything less than scientific evidence." Unfortunately, this is a very naive statement. There is no scientific basis for any of our "drug policies"—a term that, in this context, is a euphemism for prohibiting pharmaceutical and recreational drugs. Warning people about the risks a particular drug poses is the most that science can be made to justify.

In any case, science has nothing to do with the matter at hand, as the contention of the drug enforcers illustrates. Their rejoinder to Judge Alexander's ruling is that "crack is different." In what way? "The stuff is cheap and... affordable to kids in the school yard who can't afford similar amounts of powdered cocaine." Behind this pathetic argument stand some elementary facts unfamiliar to the public and denied by the drug warriors. Simply put, crack is to powdered cocaine as cigarettes are to chewing tobacco. Smoking introduces drugs into the body via the lungs; snorting and chewing, via the nasal and buccal mucosae. Different classes tend to display different preferences for different drugs. Educated persons (used to) smoke cigarettes and snort cocaine; uneducated persons chew tobacco and smoke crack. (This generalization is rapidly becoming obsolete. In the United States, though much less in Europe, Asia, and Latin America, smoking cigarettes is becoming a lower-class habit.) These facts make a mockery of the Minnesota legislators' disingenuous denunciation of Judge Alexander's decision: "The one thing we never contemplated was targeting members of any single minority group." It remains to be seen whether the Minnesota Supreme Court, to which the case was appealed, will uphold punishing crack smokers more severely than cocaine snorters.

The enforcement of our drug laws with respect to another special population—namely, pregnant women—is also shamefully racist. Many state laws now regard the pregnant woman who uses an illegal drug as a criminal—not because she possesses or sells or uses a drug, but because she "delivers" it to her fetus via the umbilical cord. Ostensibly aimed at protecting the fetus, the actual enforcement of these laws lends further support to the assumption that their real target is the unwed, inner-city, black mother. Although, according to experts, drug use in pregnancy is equally prevalent in white middle-class women, most women prosecuted for using illegal drugs while pregnant have been poor members of racial minorities. "Researchers found that about 15 percent of both the white and the black women used drugs... but that the black women were 10 times as likely as whites to be reported to the authorities."

Drugs and Racism

How do the drug warriors rationalize the racism of the War on Drugs? Partly by ignoring the evidence that the enforcement of drug laws victimizes blacks disproportionately compared to whites; and partly by falling back on a time-honored technique of forestalling the charge by appointing a respected member of the victimized group to a high position in the machinery charged with enforcing the persecutory practice. This is what former drug czar William Bennett did when he picked Reuben Greenberg, a black Jew, as his favorite drug cop. What has Greenberg done to deserve this honor? He chose to prosecute as drug offenders the most defenseless members of the black community. "The tactics Greenberg developed in Charleston [South Carolina]," explained *Time* magazine, "are targeted on the poorest of the poor—the residents of public-housing projects and their neighbors.... The projects were 'the easiest place to start, because that's where the victims are.'" Perhaps so. But, then, it must be safer—especially for a black Jewish policeman in South Carolina—to go after blacks in inner-city housing projects than after whites in suburban mansions.

The evidence supports the suspicion that the professional pushers of drug programs pander precisely to such racial prejudices, with spectacularly hypocritical results. Consider the latest fad in addictionology: a racially segregated drug treatment program for blacks. Because the program is owned by blacks, is operated by blacks for blacks, and offers a service called "drug treatment," its owner-operators have been able to pass it off as a fresh "culturally specific" form of therapy. If whites were to try to do this sort of thing to blacks, it would be decried as racist segregation. When black "for-mer drug abusers" do it to fellow blacks, the insurance money pours in: Soon after opening, the clinic called Coalesce was handling three hundred patients at $13,000 a head per month—not bad pay for treating a nonexisting illness with a nonexisting treatment.

BLACK MUSLIMS ON DRUGS

Mainstream American blacks are Christians, who look for leadership to Protestant priest-politicians and blame black drug use on rich whites, capitalism, and South American drug lords. Sidestream American blacks are Muslims, who look for leadership to Islamic priest-politicians and maintain that drug use is a matter of personal choice and self-discipline.

The Black Muslim supporters of a free market in drugs (though they do not describe their position in these terms) arrive at their conclusion not from studying the writings of Adam Smith or Ludwig von Mises, but from their direct experience with the American therapeutic state and its punitive agents decked out as doctors and social workers. As a result, the Black Muslims regard statist-therapeutic meddling as diminishing the person targeted as needing help, robbing him of his status as a responsible moral agent, and therefore fundamentally degrading; and they see the medicalization of the drug problem—the hypocritical defining of illegal drug use as both a crime and a disease, the capricious law enforcement, the economic incentives to transgress the drug laws, and the pseudotherapeutic drug programs—as a wicked method for encouraging drug use, crime, economic dependency, personal demoralization, and familial breakdown. I have reviewed the enduring Black Muslim principles and policies on drugs, as developed by Malcolm X, elsewhere. Here I shall summarize only what is necessary to round out the theme I developed in this [selection].

Black Muslims demand, on moral and religious grounds, that their adherents abstain from all self-indulgent pleasures, including drugs. Accordingly, it would be misleading to speak of a Black Muslim approach to the "treatment of drug addiction." If a person is a faithful Black Muslim he cannot be an addict, just as if he is an Orthodox Jew he cannot be a pork eater. It is as simple as that. The Muslim perspective on drug use and drug avoidance is—like mine —moral and ceremonial, not medical and therapeutic. Of course, this does not mean that we come to all the same conclusions.

Malcolm X: Triumph Through Resisting Temptation

Malcolm X's passion for honesty and truth led him to some remarkable drug demythologizings, that is, assertions that seemingly fly in the face of current medical dogmas about hard drugs and their addictive powers. "Some prospective Muslims," wrote Malcolm, "found it more difficult to quit tobacco than others found quitting the dope habit." As I noted, for Muslims it makes no difference whether a man smokes tobacco or marijuana; what counts is the habit of self-indulgence, not the pharmacomythology of highs or kicks. Evidently, one good mythology per capita is enough: If a person truly believes in the mythology of Black Muslimism—or Judaism, or Christianity—then he does not need the ersatz mythology of medicalism and therapeutism.

The Muslims emphasize not only that addiction is evil, but also that it is deliberately imposed on the black man by the white man. "The Muslim program began with recognizing that color and addiction have a distinct connection. It is no accident that in the entire Western Hemisphere, the greatest localized concentration of addicts is in Harlem." The monkey on the addict's back is not the abstraction of drug addiction as a disease, but the concrete reality of Whitey. "Most black junkies," explains Malcolm, "really are trying to narcotize themselves against being a black man in the white man's America." By politicizing personal problems (defining self-medication with narcotics as political oppression), the Muslims neatly reverse the psychiatric tactic of personalizing political problems (defining psychiatric incarceration as hospitalization).

Because for Muslims drug use—legal or illegal—is not a disease, they have no use for pretentious drug treatment programs, especially if they consist of substituting one narcotic drug for another (methadone for heroin). Instead, they rely on breaking the drug habit by expecting the drug user to quit "cold turkey." The ordeal this entails helps to dramatize and ritualize the addict's liberation from Whitey. "When the addict's withdrawal sets in," explains Malcolm, "and he is screaming, cursing and begging, 'Just one shot, man!' the Muslims are right there talking junkie jargon to him, 'Baby, knock that monkey off your back!... Kick Whitey off your back!'" Ironically, what Black Muslims tell their adherents is not very different from what white doctors told each other at the beginning of this century. In 1921, writing in the *Journal of the American Medical Association*, Alfred C. Prentice, M. D.—a member of the Committee on Narcotic Drugs of the

American Medical Association—rejected "the shallow pretense that drug addiction is a 'disease'... [a falsehood that] has been asserted and urged in volumes of 'literature' by self-styled 'specialists.'"

Malcolm X wore his hair crew-cut, dressed with the severe simplicity and elegance of a successful Wall Street lawyer, and was polite and punctual. Alex Haley describes the Muslims as having "manners and miens [that] reflected the Spartan personal discipline the organization demanded." While Malcolm hated the white man—whom he regarded as the "devil"—he despised the black man who refused the effort to better himself: "The black man in the ghettoes... has to start self-correcting his own material, moral, and spiritual defects and evils. The black man needs to start his own program to get rid of drunkenness, drug addiction, prostitution."

This is dangerous talk. Liberals and psychiatrists need the weak-willed and the mentally sick to have someone to disdain, care for, and control. If Malcolm had his way, such existential cannibals masquerading as do-gooders would be unemployed, or worse. Here, then, is the basic conflict and contradiction between the Muslim and methadone: By making the Negro self-responsible and self-reliant, Muslimism eliminates the problem and with it the need for the white man and the medicine man; whereas by making the white man and the doctor indispensable for the Negro as permanent social cripple and lifelong patient, medicalism aggravates and perpetuates the problem.

Malcolm understood and asserted—as few black or white men could understand or dared to assert—that white men want blacks to be on drugs, and that most black men who are on drugs want to be on them rather than off them. Freedom and

self-determination are not only precious, but arduous. If people are not taught and nurtured to appreciate these values, they are likely to want to have nothing to do with them. Malcolm X and Edmund Burke shared a profound discernment of the painful truth that the state wants men to be weak and timid, not strong and proud. Indeed, perhaps the only thing Malcolm failed to see was that, by articulating his views as he did, he was in fact launching a religious war against greatly superior forces. I do not mean a religious war against Christianity. The religious war Malcolm launched was a war against the religion of Medicine—a faith other black leaders blindly worship. After all, blacks and whites alike now believe, as an article of faith, that drug abuse is an illness. That is why they demand and demonstrate for "free" detoxification programs and embrace methadone addiction as a cure for the heroin habit. Malcolm saw this, but I am not sure he grasped the enormity of it all. Or perhaps he did and that is why in the end, not long before he was killed, he rejected the Black Muslims as well—to whom, only a short while before, he gave all the credit for his resurrection from the gutter. He converted, one more time, to Orthodox Islam. Then he was murdered.

Do Drug Prohibitionists Protect Blacks?

Not surprisingly, drug prohibitionists systematically ignore the Black Muslim position on drugs. Neither bureaucratic drug criminalizers nor academic drug legalizers ever mention Malcolm X's name, much less cite his writings on drugs. The fact that Louis Farrakhan, the present leader of the Nation of Islam, continues to support Malcolm X's position on drugs does not help to make that position more acceptable to the white establishment. In characteristically statist fashion, instead of seeing drug laws as racist, the drug prohibitionists see the absence of drug laws as racist. If "the legalizers prevail"—James Q. Wilson, a professor of management and public policy at UCLA, ominously predicts—

> then we will have consigned hundreds of thousands of infants and hundreds of neighborhoods to a life of oblivion and disease. To the lives and families destroyed by alcohol we will have added countless more destroyed by cocaine, heroin, PCP, and whatever else a basement scientist can invent. Human character is formed by society.... [G]ood character is less likely in a bad society.

Virtually everything Wilson asserts here is false. Liberty is the choice to do right or wrong, to act prudently or imprudently, to protect oneself or injure oneself. Wilson is disingenuous in selecting alcohol and drugs as the "destroyers" of people. And as for his implying that our present prohibitionist mode of managing drugs has promoted the formation of "good character"—the less said, the better.

Wilson's argument brings us back full circle to the genocidal image of drugs, suggested here by a prominent white academic rather than a black priest-politician. As I observed before, this view casts the individual in a passive role, as victim. But if there are injured victims, there must be injuring victimizers. Wilson knows who they are: us. But he is wrong. Opportunity, choice, temptation do not constitute victimization. Wilson affronts the supporters of liberty by so categorizing them.

Finally, Wilson's explanation leaves no room for why some blacks succeed in not being consigned to what he revealingly calls "a life of oblivion and disease." Nor does Wilson consider the dark possibility that there might, especially for white Americans, be a fate worse than a few thousand blacks selling and using drugs. Suppose every black man, woman, and child in America rejected drugs, chose to emulate Malcolm X, and became a militant black separationist. Would that be better for American whites, or for the United States as a nation?

POSTSCRIPT

Are Blacks Helped by the Drug War?

Are blacks helped by the war on drugs? For some (such as Szasz) the drug war is only part of a larger war on individual freedom. Blacks, according to this reasoning, are simply a convenient conduit for establishing greater legal, medical, and psychological control over citizens. The media and politicians are successful in linking blacks and crime, crime and drugs, and drugs and blacks. This makes a war on drugs and the alleged concomitant loss of basic freedoms for all of us more palpable. Szasz implies that few people understand this other than the medical and criminal justice establishments, especially the former. Moral do-gooders, some black leaders, and criminological scholars, in supporting the drug war and claims of black genocide, unwittingly acquiesce to the charade.

To Szasz, Inciardi's position of calling for treatment over incarceration is dangerous semantics and conceptual surrender to the medical experts, who Szasz sees as grabbing a monopoly on the issue. That is, to define drug use as an illness in need of treatment simply reinforces medical hegemony and maintains the myth that individuals who make drug-related choices are sick and in need of help.

Although Inciardi agrees with Szasz that blacks have been discriminated against in drug arrests, he also feels that arrests do help black communities. Naturally, differential racial arrest rates, if undeserved, should be remedied. For Inciardi, the solution is more rehabilitation programs for everyone. He insists that the drug problem is real and that it is not simply a matter of labeling, as Szasz suggests.

Among Inciardi's many relevant sources are J. Inciardi et al., eds., *The Effectiveness of Innovative Approaches in the Treatment of Drug Abuse* (Greenwood Press, 1997) and J. Inciardi, R. Horowitz, and A. E. Pottieger, *Street Kids, Street Drugs, Street Crime* (Wadsworth Publishing, 1993). Szasz's works include *The Myth of Mental Illness* (Harper & Row, 1961) and *Cruel Compassion: Psychiatric Control of Society's Unwanted* (John Wiley, 1994). Other works are "Differential Punishing of African Americans and Whites Who Possess Drugs," by R. Alexander, Jr., and J. Gyamerah, *Journal of Black Studies* (September 1997); *Making Crime Pay: Law and Order in Contemporary American Politics*, by K. Beckett (Oxford University Press, 1997); and "Race and Criminal Justice," in S. Donziger, ed., *The Real War on Crime* (HarperPerennial, 1996). An excellent source that looks at the media connection is D. Rome's "Stereotyping by the Media: Murders, Rapists, and Drug Addicts," in C. R. Mann and M. S. Zatz, eds., *Images of Color, Images of Crime* (Roxbury Publishing, 1998).

ISSUE 11

Should Jury Nullification Be Used to Reduce Ethnic and Racial Inequities?

YES: Paul Butler, from "Racially Based Jury Nullification: Black Power in the Criminal Justice System," *Yale Law Journal* (December 1995)

NO: Randall Kennedy, from "After the Cheers," *The New Republic* (October 23, 1995)

ISSUE SUMMARY

YES: Paul Butler, an associate professor at the George Washington University Law School, notes that a vastly disproportionate number of blacks in America are under the auspices of the criminal justice system. In order to balance the scales of justice, he argues, black jurors should acquit black defendants of certain crimes, regardless of whether or not they perceive the defendant to be guilty.

NO: Randall Kennedy, a professor at the Harvard Law School, in examining the acquittal of O. J. Simpson, finds it tragic that black jurors would pronounce a murderer "not guilty" just to send a message to white people. He maintains that, although racism among the police and others is deplorable, allowing black criminals to go free does not help minorities, particularly since their victims are likely to be other blacks.

> *The man that is not prejudiced against a horse thief is not fit to sit on a jury in this town.*
>
> —George Bernard Shaw (1856–1950)

The jury system of justice in the United States is considered by many to be sacred. Some 200,000 criminal and civil trials are decided by approximately 2 million jurors each year. Although the vast majority of cases do not go to trial, the symbolic importance of jury trials is great.

In theory, during a trial, the judge decides on correct legal procedures and matters of legal interpretation, while juries decide, based on the evidence, the guilt or innocence of the defendant. Generally, a person accused of a felony (a serious crime) or a misdemeanor in which a sentence of six months or more is possible, could request a jury trial. In all but six states and in the federal courts, juries consist of 12 jurors. In most states, a conviction must be by unanimous decision. Judges can sometimes set aside guilty verdicts that they feel are unfair, but verdicts of not guilty can never be changed.

The jury system is not without its critics. Many have expressed concern that juries do not always consist of the defendant's peers. In many states, for example, women were not allowed to serve on juries until relatively recently. Blacks and other minorities were either directly blocked from serving or were kept off juries by the jury selection process itself. Furthermore, in most states jurors were drawn from voter registrations, which meant that the poor—for whom political elections are frequently not of great concern— were disproportionately underrepresented. In many states, attorneys could exclude blacks from serving on juries. But in *Batson v. Kentucky* (1986), the U.S. Supreme Court ruled that jurors could not be challenged solely on the basis of their race.

Jury nullification—in which a jury acquits a criminal defendant even though guilt has been proven—can be seen throughout U.S. history. Before the Revolutionary War, for example, some juries acquitted men who they felt were being treated unfairly by the British. Many northern juries refused to convict people accused of aiding runaway slaves. And juries have acquitted defendants because they felt that the police or prosecutors were bullying or unfairly treating them. Note that in these examples, the justification for nullification seems to be based on the juries' sense of justice, not on the guilt or innocence of the defendant.

However, not all historical instances of jury nullification are what would likely be considered noble reasons. For instance, until not long ago, very few whites accused of killing blacks were ever found guilty in many parts of the United States. None until the 1960s were ever sentenced to death for killing a black person. Few who participated in black lynchings were even charged with a crime, and the few who were always got off.

In the following selections, Paul Butler—despite jury nullification's checkered past—encourages jurors to acquit black defendants in many cases to remedy past and current discrimination in the criminal justice system. Randall Kennedy argues that the "need to convict a murderer" and the "need to protest the intolerability of official racism" must remain separate if either need is to be met. He maintains that promoting jury nullification as a legitimate way to right racial wrongs will only worsen the crime situation in black communities. As you read this debate consider what unanticipated consequences, both positive and negative, might arise if jury nullification is widely accepted.

YES
Paul Butler

RACIALLY BASED JURY NULLIFICATION: BLACK POWER IN THE CRIMINAL JUSTICE SYSTEM

In 1990 I was a Special Assistant United States Attorney in the District of Columbia. I prosecuted people accused of misdemeanor crimes, mainly the drug and gun cases that overwhelm the local courts of most American cities. As a federal prosecutor, I represented the United States of America and used that power to put people, mainly African-American men, in prison. I am also an African-American man. During that time, I made two discoveries that profoundly changed the way I viewed my work as a prosecutor and my responsibilities as a black person.

The first discovery occurred during a training session for new assistants conducted by experienced prosecutors. We rookies were informed that we would lose many of our cases, despite having persuaded a jury beyond a reasonable doubt that the defendant was guilty. We would lose because some black jurors would refuse to convict black defendants who they knew were guilty.

The second discovery was related to the first but was even more unsettling. It occurred during the trial of Marion Barry, then the second-term mayor of the District of Columbia. Barry was being prosecuted by my office for drug possession and perjury. I learned, to my surprise, that some of my fellow African-American prosecutors hoped that the mayor would be acquitted, despite the fact that he was obviously guilty of at least one of the charges —an FBI videotape plainly showed him smoking crack cocaine. These black prosecutors wanted their office to lose its case because they believed that the prosecution of Barry was racist.

There is an increasing perception that some African-American jurors vote to acquit black defendants for racial reasons, sometimes explained as the juror's desire not to send another black man to jail. There is considerable disagreement over whether it is appropriate for a black juror to do so. I now believe that, for pragmatic and political reasons, the black community is better off when some non-violent lawbreakers remain in the community rather than go to prison. The decision as to what kind of conduct by African Americans ought to be punished is better made by African Americans, based on their understanding of the costs and benefits to their community, than by the traditional criminal justice process, which is controlled by white lawmakers and white law enforcers. Legally, African-American jurors who sit in judgment of African-American accused persons have the power to make that decision. Considering the costs of law enforcement to the black community, and the failure of white lawmakers to come up with any solutions to black antisocial conduct other than incarceration, it is, in fact, the moral responsibility of black jurors to emancipate some guilty black outlaws.

* * *

Why would a black juror vote to let a guilty person go free? Assuming the juror is a rational, self-interested actor, she must believe that she is better off with the defendant out of prison than in prison. But how could any rational person believe that about a criminal?

Imagine a country in which a third of the young male citizens are under the supervision of the criminal justice system—either awaiting trial, in prison, or on probation or parole. Imagine a country in which two-thirds of the men can anticipate being arrested before they reach age thirty. Imagine a country in which there are more young men in prison than in college.

The country imagined above is a police state. When we think of a police state, we think of a society whose fundamental problem lies not with the citizens of the state but rather with the form of government, and with the powerful elites in whose interest the state

exists. Similarly, racial critics of American criminal justice locate the problem not with the black prisoners but with the state and its actors and beneficiaries.

The black community also bears very real costs by having so many African Americans, particularly males, incarcerated or otherwise involved in the criminal justice system. These costs are both social and economic, and they include the large percentage of black children who live in female-headed, single-parent households; a perceived dearth of men "eligible" for marriage; the lack of male role models for black children, especially boys; the absence of wealth in the black community; and the large unemployment rate among black men.

According to a recent *USA Today/CNN/Gallup* poll, 66 percent of blacks believe that the criminal justice system is racist and only 32 percent believe it is not racist. Interestingly, other polls suggest that blacks also tend to be more worried about crime than whites; this seems logical when one considers that blacks are more likely to be victims of crime. This enhanced concern, however, does not appear to translate to black support for tougher enforcement of criminal law. For example, substantially fewer blacks than whites support the death penalty, and many more blacks than whites were concerned with the potential racial consequences of the strict provisions of last year's crime bill. Along with significant evidence from popular culture, these polls suggest that a substantial portion of the African-American community sympathizes with racial critiques of the criminal justice system.

African-American jurors who endorse these critiques are in a unique position to act on their beliefs when they sit in judgment of a black defendant. As jurors, they have the power to convict the accused person or to set him free. May the responsible exercise of that power include voting to free a black defendant who the juror believes is guilty? The answer is "yes," based on the legal doctrine known as jury nullification.

Jury nullification occurs when a jury acquits a defendant who it believes is guilty of the crime with which he is charged. In finding the defendant not guilty, the jury ignores the facts of the case and/or the judge's instructions regarding the law. Instead, the jury votes its conscience.

The prerogative of juries to nullify has been part of English and American law for centuries. There are well-known cases from the Revolutionary War era when American patriots were charged with political crimes by the British crown and acquitted by American juries. Black slaves who escaped to the North and were prosecuted for violation of the Fugitive Slave Law were freed by Northern juries with abolitionist sentiments. Some Southern juries refused to punish white violence against African Americans, especially black men accused of crimes against white women.

The Supreme Court has officially disapproved of jury nullification but has conceded that it has no power to prohibit jurors from engaging in it; the Bill of Rights does not allow verdicts of acquittal to be reversed, regardless of the reason for the acquittal. Criticism of nullification has centered on its potential for abuse. The criticism suggests that when twelve members of a jury vote their conscience instead of the law, they corrupt the rule of law and undermine the democratic principles that made the law.

There is no question that jury nullification is subversive of the rule of law.

Nonetheless, most legal historians agree that it was morally appropriate in the cases of the white American revolutionaries and the runaway slaves. The issue, then, is whether African Americans today have the moral right to engage in this same subversion.

Most moral justifications of the obligation to obey the law are based on theories of "fair play." Citizens benefit from the rule of law; that is why it is just that they are burdened with the requirement to follow it. Yet most blacks are aware of countless historical examples in which African Americans were not afforded the benefit of the rule of law: think, for example, of the existence of slavery in a republic purportedly dedicated to the proposition that all men are created equal, or the law's support of state-sponsored segregation even after the Fourteenth Amendment guaranteed blacks equal protection. That the rule of law ultimately corrected some of the large holes in the American fabric is evidence more of its malleability than its goodness; the rule of law previously had justified the holes.

If the rule of law is a myth, or at least not valid for African Americans, the argument that jury nullification undermines it loses force. The black juror is simply another actor in the system, using her power to fashion a particular outcome. The juror's act of nullification —like the act of the citizen who dials 911 to report Ricky but not Bob, or the police officer who arrests Lisa but not Mary, or the prosecutor who charges Kwame but not Brad, or the judge who finds that Nancy was illegally entrapped but Verna was not—exposes the indeterminacy of law but does not in itself create it.

A similar argument can be made regarding the criticism that jury nullification is anti-democratic. This is precisely why many African Americans endorse it; it is perhaps the only legal power black people have to escape the tyranny of the majority. Black people have had to beg white decision makers for most of the rights they have: the right not to be slaves, the right to vote, the right to attend an integrated school. Now black people are begging white people to preserve programs that help black children to eat and black businesses to survive. Jury nullification affords African Americans the power to determine justice for themselves in individual cases, regardless of whether white people agree or even understand.

* * *

At this point, African Americans should ask themselves whether the operation of the criminal law system in the United States advances the interests of black people. If it does not, the doctrine of jury nullification affords African-American jurors the opportunity to exercise the authority of the law over some African-American criminal defendants. In essence, black people can "opt out" of American criminal law.

How far should they go—completely to anarchy, or is there someplace between here and there that is safer than both? I propose the following: African-American jurors should approach their work cognizant of its political nature and of their prerogative to exercise their power in the best interests of the black community. In every case, the juror should be guided by her view of what is "just." (I have more faith, I should add, in the average black juror's idea of justice than I do in the idea that is embodied in the "rule of law.")

In cases involving violent *malum in se* (inherently bad) crimes, such as murder, rape, and assault, jurors should consider the case strictly on the evidence presented, and if they believe the accused person is guilty, they should so vote. In cases involving non-violent, *malum prohibitum* (legally proscribed) offenses, including "victimless" crimes such as narcotics possession, there should be a presumption in favor of nullification. Finally, for non-violent, *malum in se* crimes, such as theft or perjury, there need be no presumption in favor of nullification, but it ought to be an option the juror considers. A juror might vote for acquittal, for example, when a poor woman steals from Tiffany's but not when the same woman steals from her next-door neighbor.

How would a juror decide individual cases under my proposal? Easy cases would include a defendant who has possessed crack cocaine and an abusive husband who kills his wife. The former should be acquitted and the latter should go to prison.

Difficult scenarios would include the drug dealer who operates in the ghetto and the thief who burglarizes the home of a rich white family. Under my proposal, nullification is presumed in the first case because drug distribution is a non-violent *malum prohibitum* offense. Is nullification morally justifiable here? It depends. There is no question that encouraging people to engage in self-destructive behavior is evil; the question the juror should ask herself is whether the remedy is less evil. (The juror should also remember that the criminal law does not punish those ghetto drug dealers who cause the most injury: liquor store owners.)

As for the burglar who steals from the rich white family, the case is troubling, first of all, because the conduct is so clearly "wrong." Since it is a non-violent *malum in se* crime, there is no presumption in favor of nullification, but it is an option for consideration. Here again, the facts of the case are relevant. For example, if the offense was committed to support a drug habit, I think there is a moral case to be made for nullification, at least until such time as access to drug-rehabilitation services are available to all.

* * *

Why would a juror be inclined to follow my proposal? There is no guarantee that she would. But when we perceive that black jurors are already nullifying on the basis of racial critiques (i.e., refusing to send another black man to jail), we recognize that these jurors are willing to use their power in a politically conscious manner. Further, it appears that some black jurors now excuse some conduct—like murder—that they should not excuse. My proposal provides a principled structure of the exercise of the black juror's vote. I am not encouraging anarchy; rather I am reminding black jurors of their privilege to serve a calling higher than law: justice.

I concede that the justice my proposal achieves is rough. It is as susceptible to human foibles as the jury system. But I am sufficiently optimistic that my proposal will be only an intermediate plan, a stopping point between the status quo and real justice. To get to that better, middle ground, I hope that this [selection] will encourage African Americans to use responsibly the power they already have.

NO

Randall Kennedy

AFTER THE CHEERS

The acquittal of O. J. Simpson brings to an end an extraordinary criminal trial that attracted, like a magnet, anxieties over crime, sex, race and the possibility of reaching truth and dispensing justice in an American courtroom. The verdict is difficult to interpret since juries are not required to give reasons for the conclusions they reach and since, even if jurors do articulate their reasons, there remains the problem of deciphering them and distinguishing expressed views from real bases of decision.

My own view is that the verdict represents a combination of three beliefs. One is that the prosecution simply failed to prove that O. J. Simpson was guilty beyond a reasonable doubt. Reasonable people could come to this conclusion. After all, police investigators displayed remarkable incompetence, the prosecution erred mightily—remember the gloves that did not fit!—and, of course, there was the despicable [police officer] Mark Fuhrman. Even with help given by several questionable judicial rulings before the trial and near the end, the prosecution did permit a reasonable juror to vote to acquit on the basis of the evidence presented. I disagree with that conclusion. But I do concede that it could be reached reasonably and in good faith.

If this belief is what prompted the decision of all twelve of the jurors who acquitted Simpson, their decision has little broader cultural significance than that reasonable jurors sometimes come to different conclusions than those which many observers favor. I doubt, though, that this belief was the only or even the dominant predicate for the acquittal. I say this based on what I have heard many people say and write about the evidence presented at the trial and also on the remarkably short time that the jury deliberated. If the jury was at all representative of the American public, particularly that sector of the public which leaned toward acquittal, it was probably influenced considerably by two other beliefs.

The first is characterized by an unreasonable suspicion of law enforcement authorities. This is the thinking of people who would have voted to acquit O. J. Simpson even in the absence of Mark Fuhrman's racism and the L.A. police department's incompetence and even in the face of evidence that was more incriminating than that which was produced at trial. There is a paranoid, conspiracy-minded sector of the population that would honestly though irrationally have rejected the state's argument virtually without regard to the evidence. One of the things that nourishes much of this community, particularly that part comprised of African Americans, is a vivid and bitter memory of wrongful convictions of innocent black men and wrongful acquittals of guilty white men. A key example of the former were the convictions of the Scottsboro Boys in the 1930s for allegedly raping two white women. Now it is widely believed that these young men were framed. A key example of the latter was the acquittal of the murderers of Emmett Till forty years ago. In the face of overwhelming evidence of guilt, an all-white jury in Sumner, Mississippi, took an hour and seven minutes to acquit two white men who later acknowledged that they had killed Till for having whistled at the wife of one of them. Asked why the jury had taken an hour to deliberate, one of the jurors declared that it would not have taken so long if they hadn't paused for a drink of soda pop. Some readers may find it hard to believe that these despicable events of sixty and forty years ago influence the way that people now evaluate people and events. But just as some in the Balkans remember battles fought 600 years ago as if they happened yesterday, so too do many blacks recall with pained disgust the racially motivated miscarriages of justice that they have helplessly witnessed or been told about. That recollection, refreshed occasionally by more recent outrages, prompts them to regard prosecutions against black men—especially black men accused of attacking white women—with such an intense level of skepticism that they demand more than that which should convince most reasonable people of guilt beyond a reasonable doubt.

A third belief is that to which [defense lawyer] Johnnie Cochran appealed directly in his summation when he pleaded with jurors to help "police the police." This belief animates jury nullification. By nullification, I mean the act of voting for acquittal even though you know that, in terms of the rules laid down by the judge, the evidence warrants conviction. A nullifier votes to acquit not because of dissatisfaction with the evidence but because, in the phrase of choice nowadays, he wants "to send a message." In many locales, black people in particular want to send a message that they are way past tolerating anti-black racism practiced by police and that they are willing to voice their protest in a wide variety of ways, including jury nullification. Frustrated, angry and politically self-aware, some black citizens have decided to take their protest against racism in the criminal justice system to the vital and vulnerable innards of that system: the jury box.

In a certain way, the specter of this sort of jury nullification represents an advance in American race relations. Not too long ago, blacks' dissatisfactions with the criminal justice system could often be largely ignored without significant immediate consequence because whites, on a racial basis, excluded them from decisionmaking. Invisible in courthouses, except as defendants, blacks could safely be permitted to stew in their own resentments. Now, however, because of salutary reforms, blacks are much more active in the administration of criminal justice and thus much more able to influence it.

* * *

Notwithstanding this advance, however, the current state of affairs as revealed by the Simpson case is marked by several large and tragic failures. The first and most important is the failure on the part of responsible officials to clearly, publicly and wholeheartedly abjure racism of the sort that Mark Fuhrman displayed during his hateful career as a police officer. Fuhrman's prejudice and his ability to act on it likely had much to do with O. J. Simpson's acquittal. His bigotry provided a vivid basis for the argument that the police framed Simpson. His bigotry also provided an emotionally satisfying basis upon which to follow Cochran's invitation to "send a message" by voting to acquit. In other words, the state inflicted upon itself a grievous wound when its representatives failed to establish a rigorous, anti-racist personnel policy that might have obviated the problem that ultimately crippled the prosecution most. Perhaps more headway on this front will now be made; practicality and morality dictate a more vigorous push against racism in law enforcement circles.

A second failure has occurred within the ranks of those who cheered the acquittal. I have no objection to cheers based on the assumption that the jury system worked properly, that is, cheers based on an honest and reasonable perception that the acquittal has freed a man against whom there existed too little evidence for a conviction. I get the impression, though, that there are other sentiments being voiced in the celebrations of some observers, including feelings of racial solidarity, yearnings to engage in racial muscle-flexing and a peculiar urge to protect the hero status of a man whose standing within the black community rose precipitously by dint of being charged with murder.

The failure of those moved by these sentiments is two-fold. First, such feelings can only predominate by minimizing the stark fact that two people were brutally murdered and by resisting the claim that *whoever* committed that dastardly deed ought to be legally punished, regardless of his color and regardless of the racism of Mark Fuhrman and company. To subordinate the need to convict a murderer to the need to protest the intolerability of official racism is a moral mistake. Both could have been done and should have been done. Contrary to the logic of Johnnie Cochran's summation, neither jurors nor onlookers were trapped in a situation in which they had to choose one imperative over the other. Second, as a practical matter, it cannot be emphasized too frequently the extent to which the black community in particular needs vigorous, efficient, enthusiastic law enforcement. As bad as racist police misconduct is, it pales in comparison to the misery that criminals (most of whom are black) inflict upon black communities. After all, blacks are four times as likely as whites to be raped, three times as likely to be robbed, twice as likely to be assaulted and seven times as likely to be murdered.

The problem of criminality perpetrated by blacks is the one that many black political leaders appear to have trouble discussing thoroughly. A good many prefer condemning white racist police to focusing on ways to render life in black communities more secure against ordinary criminals. That Simpson allegedly killed two white people makes him in some eyes far easier to rally around than had he allegedly killed two black people. This difference in sympathy based on the race of victims is itself a profoundly destructive racialist impulse, one deeply rooted in our political culture. But there is yet another difficulty with this particular racialist response. Like so much else about the Simpson case, the racial demographics of those who were killed was atypical. Because the more typical scenario features black victims of murder, those who claim to speak on behalf of blacks' interests should be extremely wary of supporting anything that further depresses law enforcement's ability to apprehend and convict those who prey upon their neighbors.

The O. J. Simpson trial is obviously a complicated event that will take years to understand more fully and place into proper perspective. At this point, however, the result, like so much of the trial itself, leaves me—normally an optimist—overcome by a sense of profound gloom.

POSTSCRIPT

Should Jury Nullification Be Used to Reduce Ethnic and Racial Inequities?

Should jury nullification be used to reduce inequities? Can a jury's decision to acquit a guilty person be considered a form of discretion, comparable to a person's decision to dial or not to dial 911 in an emergency or a police officer's deciding whether or not to arrest a potential suspect? Butler says, "Jury nullification affords African Americans the power to determine justice... regardless of whether white people agree or even understand." Is this statement blatantly racist? One critic has suggested that Butler's discussion is actually a satire. Could this be true?

An interesting concept that neither Butler nor Kennedy consider is the possibility of victim, community, or police "nullification." In other words, if many felt that criminals who were minority members would be allowed to go free by sympathetic juries, the probability would be high that even fewer cases would get to trial than currently do: the police, victims' families, or even vigilantes might be driven to administer "neighborhood justice" in order to ensure that criminals are punished.

The acquittal of murder suspect O. J. Simpson on October 3, 1995, revived debate on jury nullification. A thoughtful discussion is J. Q. Wilson, "Reading Jurors' Minds," *Commentary* (February 1996). A radically different analysis is T. Morrison and C. Lacour, eds., *Birth of a Nation'Hood: Gaze, Script, and Spectacle in the O. J. Simpson Case* (Pantheon Books, 1997). A helpful account of the Simpson case is J. T. Gibbs, *Race and Justice: Rodney King and O. J. Simpson in a House Divided* (Jossey-Bass, 1996).

Among the many attackers of Butler's thinking is J. Rosen, in "The Bloods and the Crits," *The New Republic* (December 9, 1996); E. M. Brown, in "The Tower of Babel: Bridging the Divide Between Critical Race Theory and 'Mainstream' Civil Rights Scholarship," *Yale Law Journal* (November 1995); and A. Leipold, in "The Dangers of Race-Based Jury Nullification: A Response to Professor Butler," *UCLA Law Review* (October 1, 1996). Other law journal articles that consider the issue are D. Farnham, "Jury Nullification: History Proves It's Not a New Idea," *Criminal Justice* (Winter 1997); R. Parloff, "Race and Justice: If It Ain't Broke," *The American Lawyer* (June 1, 1997); and D. Brown, "Jury Nullification Within the Rule of Law," *Minnesota Law Review* (May 1, 1997). Also see the Summer 1997 issue of the *John Marshall Law Review*.

For some more recent thoughts by Kennedy, see his *Race, Crime, and the Law* (Pantheon Books, 1997). An iconoclastic view is contained in *Justice Overruled* by B. Katz (Warner Books, 1997).

On the Internet ...

http://www.dushkin.com

Federal Bureau of Investigation
The home page of the FBI leads to the 10 most wanted criminals, uniform crime reports, FBI case reports, major investigations, and more. *http://www.fbi.gov/*

Justice Information Center
A service of the National Criminal Justice Reference Service, the Justice Information Center (JIC) Web site connects to information about corrections, courts, crime prevention, criminal justice, drugs and crime, international justice, juvenile justice, law enforcement, research and evaluation, and victims, as well as the latest statistics, news, and highlights. *http://www.ncjrs.org/*

Sourcebook of Criminal Justice Statistics Online
Data about all aspects of criminal justice in the United States is available at this site, which includes over 655 tables and figures from more than 100 sources. *http://www.albany.edu/sourcebook/*

The Keepers' Voice
The article on this page, "Vindictive Vindications: Crime Causation from the Inmates' Standpoint," by Robert J. Kelly, *The Keepers' Voice,* is based on interviews conducted with and observations of inmates and correction officers. *http://www.acsp.uic.edu/IACO/kv170209.htm*

PART 3

Criminological Research and Public Policy

Although research—in particular, its interpretations and applications—can be highly problematic, it remains a core task for criminologists and criminal justice scholars. Among the most important criminological research findings of the past 25 years is that a relatively small core of criminals commit a disproportionate amount of crime. Also important to criminal justice is the development and utilization of technology, such as DNA technology, computer units in police cars, and innovations in investigation techniques. Yet just how helpful is this research?

Questions addressed in this selection ask, Why haven't increased executions reduced violent crime? Is locking up repeat offenders for life the best policy? and, Are changes in police lineup procedures needed? Perhaps researching crime and then deciding how to use the results is one of criminology's biggest problems.

■ Is Capital Punishment Bad Policy?

■ Does Three Strikes and Other Tough Approaches Work?

■ Should Partial Identifications Be Accepted in Police Lineups?

ISSUE 12

Is Capital Punishment Bad Policy?

YES: David Von Drehle, from "Miscarriage of Justice: Why the Death Penalty Doesn't Work," *The Washington Post Magazine* (February 5, 1995)

NO: Ernest van den Haag, from "The Ultimate Punishment: A Defense," *Harvard Law Review* (May 1986)

ISSUE SUMMARY

YES: David Von Drehle, a writer and the arts editor for the *Washington Post*, examines specific capital punishment cases, statistics, and statements made by U.S. Supreme Court justices and prosecutors reversing their support of the death penalty, and concludes that capital punishment is bad policy.

NO: Ernest van den Haag, a professor of jurisprudence and public policy (now retired), analyzes a number of objections to capital punishment, ranging from its unfair distribution to its excessive costs and its brutal nature. He rejects claims that capital punishment is unfair and barbaric, and he insists that the death penalty does deter criminals and is just retribution for terrible crimes.

In 1968 only 38 percent of all Americans supported the death penalty for certain crimes. In 1972, when the U.S. Supreme Court handed down its decision in *Furman v. Georgia* stating that capital punishment violated the Eighth Amendment, which prohibits cruel and unusual punishment, many Americans were convinced that capital punishment was permanently abolished. After all, even though there were 500 inmates on death row at the time, there had been a steady decline in the number of executions in the United States: In the 1930s there were on average 152 executions per year; in 1962 there were 47 executions; and in 1966 there was 1. Polls in the late 1960s showed that most Americans opposed the death penalty, and virtually every other Western industrial nation had long since eliminated the death sentence or severely modified its use.

Polls taken in the late 1980s and 1990s have shown that 75 to 80 percent of all Americans support capital punishment. Seventy-four executions were carried out in 1997, the most seen in the United States since 1955, when 76 individuals were put to death. These executions took place in 17 states; Texas led the pack with 37. Since 1976, when capital punishment was restored in the United States, 435 inmates have been executed. In the 1990s, 6 juveniles have been executed, and there are currently 63 juveniles on death row. The United

States is one of only six countries that execute juveniles. Also, two women have been executed since 1976. There are now over 3,200 men and women condemned to die, and some of their appeals may take up to 20 years.

What has happened since the 1960s? We will probably never know the full answer to this question, but there are some clues. To begin with, in *Furman v. Georgia*, the Supreme Court did not really ban capital punishment because it was cruel and unusual in itself. It simply argued that it was unconstitutional for juries to be given the right to decide arbitrarily and discriminatorily on capital punishment. Thus, if states can show that capital punishment is not arbitrary or discriminatory and that the sentencing process is performed in two separate stages—first guilt or innocence is established, and *then* the determination of the sentence occurs—then some offenses are legally punishable by death. This was the Supreme Court's ruling in 1976 in *Gregg v. Georgia*, which effectively restored the death penalty.

Since the late 1960s, Americans have become more conservative. Fear of crime has greatly increased, although the number of crimes may not have changed. Moreover, many of the measures taken under the Omnibus Safe Streets Act to reduce crime, speed up judicial processes, and rehabilitate criminals are now viewed by professionals and laypeople alike as failures. The national mood is now solidly behind "getting tough" on criminals, especially drug dealers and murderers. Support and utilization of capital punishment make sense within the logic of the present cultural and political situation.

There is a movement among criminologists to reassess studies done before the 1960s that claimed that states in which capital punishment prevailed had homicide rates that were just as high as those in which it was not a penalty and that executions did not deter others from committing crimes. Isaac Ehrlich, for instance, in an extensive statistical analysis of executions between the years 1933 and 1967, reached very different conclusions. He contends not only that the executions reduced the murder rate but that one additional execution per year between 1933 and 1967 would have resulted in seven or eight fewer murders per year!

Many scholars have bitterly attacked Ehrlich's empirical findings. Most attempt to fault his methods, but others assert that even if he is empirically correct, the trade-off is not worth it. The state should not have the right to extract such a primitive "justice" as the murder of a human being, even a convicted killer. Other scholars emphasize the fact that there have been a disproportionate number of blacks executed (between 1930 and 1967, 2,066 blacks were executed as opposed to 1,751 whites, even though blacks constituted only 10 percent of the total population then). Some counter that this simply indicates that more whites need to be executed as well!

Is capital punishment bad policy? If not, what crimes ought it be reserved for? Murder? Rape? Espionage? Drug dealing? Kidnapping? How should it be carried out?

YES

David Von Drehle

MISCARRIAGE OF JUSTICE: WHY THE DEATH PENALTY DOESN'T WORK

As a boy of 8, the son of good, poor parents, James Curtis "Doug" McCray had limitless dreams; he told everyone he met that someday he would be president of the United States. Soon enough, he realized that poor black children did not grow up to be president, but still he was a striver. At Dunbar High School in Fort Myers, Fla., he was an all-state receiver on the football team, an all-conference guard in basketball and the state champion in the 440-yard dash. He made the honor roll, and became the first and only of the eight McCray kids to attend college.

His was a success story, but for one flaw. McCray had a drinking problem. He washed out of college and joined the Army. A year and a half later, the Army gave him a medical discharge because he had been found to suffer from epilepsy. McCray married, fathered a son, tried college again; nothing took. He wound up back home, a tarnished golden boy.

On an October evening in 1973, an elderly woman named Margaret Mears was at home in her apartment, picking no trouble, harming no one, when someone burst in, stripped and raped her, then beat her to death. A bloody handprint was matched to Doug McCray's. He insisted that he had no memory of the night in question, and his jury unanimously recommended a life sentence. But McCray had the bad fortune to be tried by Judge William Lamar Rose.

... To him, the murder of Margaret Mears was precisely the type of savagery the law was intended to punish: committed in the course of another felony, and surely heinous, surely atrocious, surely cruel. Rose overruled the jury and banged the gavel on death.

* * *

When McCray arrived at Florida State Prison in 1974, nine men awaited execution and he made 10. His case entered the appeals process, and as the years went by, McCray wept for his best friend on death row, John Spenkelink, who became the first man in America executed against his will under modern death penalty laws. He watched as a young man named Bob Graham became

From David Von Drehle, "Miscarriage of Justice: Why the Death Penalty Doesn't Work," *The Washington Post Magazine* (February 5, 1995). Copyright © 1995 by *The Washington Post*. Reprinted by permission.

governor of Florida and led the nation in executing criminals. Eight years later, he watched Gov. Bob Martinez take Graham's place and sign 139 death warrants in four years. McCray saw the infamous serial killer Ted Bundy come to the row, and almost 10 years later saw him go quietly to Old Sparky.

Living on death row, McCray saw men cut, saw men burned, even saw a man killed. He saw inmates carried from their cells after committing suicide, and others taken away after going insane. He saw wardens and presidents come and go. Death row got bigger and bigger. By the time Spenkelink was executed in May 1979, Jacksonville police officers printed T-shirts proclaiming "One down, 133 to go!" ...

Doug McCray watched as death row doubled in size, and grew still more until it was not a row but a small town, Death Town, home to more than 300 killers. Nationwide, the condemned population climbed toward 3,000. The seasons passed through a sliver of dirty glass beyond two sets of bars outside McCray's tiny cell on the row, which was very cold in the winter and very hot in the summer, noisy at all times and stinking with the odor of smoking, sweating, dirty, defecating men. Four seasons made a year, and the years piled up: 5, 10, 15, 16, 17 ...

All this time, Doug McCray was sentenced to death but he did not die. Which makes him the perfect symbol of the modern death penalty.

People talk a great deal these days about getting rid of government programs that cost too much and produce scant results. So it's curious that one of the least efficient government programs in America is also among the most popular. Capital punishment is favored by more

than three-quarters of American voters. And yet, in 1994, the death row population nationwide exceeded 3,000 for the first time ever; out of all those condemned prisoners, only 31 were executed. There are hundreds of prisoners in America who have been on death row more than a decade, and at least one—Thomas Knight of Florida—has been awaiting execution for 20 years. Every cost study undertaken has found that it is far more expensive, because of added legal safeguards, to carry out a death sentence than it is to jail a killer for life. Capital punishment is the principal burden on the state and federal appellate courts in every jurisdiction where it is routinely practiced. The most efficient death penalty state, Texas, has a backlog of more than 300 people on its death row. It manages to execute only about one killer for every four newly sentenced to die—and the number of executions may drop now that the U.S. Supreme Court has ordered Texas to provide lawyers for death row inmate appeals. Overall, America has executed approximately one in every 20 inmates sentenced to die under modern death penalty laws.

This poor record of delivering the punishments authorized by legislatures and imposed by courts has persisted despite a broad shift to the right in the federal courts. It has resisted legislative and judicial efforts to streamline the process. It has outlasted William J. Brennan Jr. and Thurgood Marshall, the Supreme Court's strongest anti-death penalty justices. It has endured countless campaigns by state legislators and governors and U.S. representatives and senators and even presidents who have promised to get things moving. If New York reinstates the death penalty this year, as Gov. George Pataki has promised, there is no reason to believe things will change; New York is unlikely to see another execution in this century. Congress extended the death penalty to cover more than 50 new crimes last year, but that bill will be long forgotten before Uncle Sam executes more than a handful of prisoners.

Most people like the death penalty in theory; virtually no one familiar with it likes the slow, costly and inefficient reality. But after 20 years of trying to make the death penalty work, it is becoming clear that we are stuck with the reality, and not the ideal.

* * *

To understand why this is, you have to understand the basic mechanics of the modern death penalty. The story begins in 1972.

For most of American history, capital punishment was a state or even a local issue. Criminals were tried, convicted and sentenced according to local rules and customs, and their executions were generally carried out by town sheriffs in courthouse squares. Federal judges took almost no interest in the death penalty, and even state appeals courts tended to give the matter little consideration.

Not surprisingly, a disproportionate number of the people executed under these customs were black, and the execution rate was most dramatically skewed for the crime of rape. As sensibilities became more refined, however, decent folks began to object to the spectacle of local executions. In Florida in the 1920s, for example, a coalition of women's clubs lobbied the legislature to ban the practice, arguing that the sight of bodies swinging in town squares had a brutalizing effect on their communities. Similar efforts around the country led to the centralizing

of executions at state prisons, where they took place outside the public view, often at midnight or dawn.

Still, the death penalty remained a state matter, with the federal government extremely reluctant to exert its authority. Washington kept its nose out of the death chambers, just as it steered clear of the schools, courtrooms, prisons and voting booths. All that changed, and changed dramatically, in the 1950s and '60s, when the Supreme Court, in the era of Chief Justice Earl Warren, asserted more vigorously than ever that the protections of the U.S. Constitution applied to actions in the states. For the first time, federal standards of equality were used to strike down such state and local practices as school segregation, segregation of buses and trains, poll taxes and voter tests. The lengthened arm of the federal government reached into police stations: For example, in *Miranda v. Arizona*, the Supreme Court required that suspects be advised of their constitutional rights when arrested. The long arm reached into the courtrooms: In *Gideon v. Wainwright*, the high court declared that the federal guarantee of due process required that felony defendants in state trials be provided with lawyers.

Opponents of capital punishment urged the courts to reach into death rows as well. Anthony Amsterdam, at the time a Stanford University law professor, crafted arguments to convince the federal courts that the death penalty violated the Eighth Amendment (which bars "cruel and unusual punishments") and the 14th Amendment (which guarantees "equal protection of the laws"). Amsterdam's arguments won serious consideration in the newly aggressive federal courts, and on January 17, 1972, the greatest of Amsterdam's lawsuits, *Furman v. Georgia,* was heard in the Supreme Court.

Amsterdam delivered a brilliant four-pronged attack on capital punishment. He began by presenting statistical proof that the death penalty in America was overwhelmingly used against the poor and minorities. Next, Amsterdam argued that the death penalty was imposed arbitrarily, almost randomly. Judges and juries meted out their sentences without clear standards to guide them, and as a result men were on death row for armed robbery, while nearby, murderers served life, or less. Discretion in death sentencing was virtually unfettered. Amsterdam's third point was his most audacious, but it turned out to be crucial: The death penalty was so rarely carried out in contemporary America that it could no longer be justified as a deterrent to crime. In the years leading up to Amsterdam's argument, use of the death penalty had steeply declined. What made this argument so daring was that the sharp drop in executions was partly a result of Amsterdam's own legal campaign to abolish the death penalty. He was, in effect, challenging a state of affairs he had helped to create.

In closing, Amsterdam argued that the death penalty had become "unacceptable in contemporary society," that the "evolving standards" of decent behavior had moved beyond the point of legal killing. This was the weakest of his arguments, because nearly 40 states still had death penalty laws on the books, but previous Supreme Court decisions suggested that the shortest route to abolishing the death penalty would be to convince a majority of the justices that "standards of decency" had changed. Amsterdam had to try.

Behind closed doors, the nine justices of the court revealed a wide range of reactions to Amsterdam's case—from Brennan and Marshall, the court's liberal stalwarts, who voted to abolish capital punishment outright, to Justice William H. Rehnquist, the new conservative beacon, who rejected all of the arguments. Justice William O. Douglas was unpersuaded by the notion that standards of decency had evolved to the point that capital punishment was cruel and unusual punishment, but he agreed the death penalty was unconstitutionally arbitrary. Chief Justice Warren E. Burger and Justice Harry A. Blackmun both expressed personal opposition to capital punishment—if they were legislators, they would vote against it—but they believed that the language of the Constitution clearly left the matter to the states. That made three votes to strike down the death penalty, and three to sustain it.

Justice Lewis F. Powell Jr. also strongly objected to the court taking the question of the death penalty out of the hands of elected legislatures. This would be an egregious example of the sort of judicial activism he had always opposed. Though moved by Amsterdam's showing of racial discrimination, Powell believed this was a vestige of the past, and could be rectified without a sweeping decision in Furman. Powell's vote made four to sustain the death penalty. Justice Potter Stewart, painfully aware of the more than 600 prisoners whose lives were dangling on his vote, moved toward Douglas's view that the death penalty had become unconstitutionally arbitrary. Stewart's vote made four to strike down the death penalty as it existed.

That left Justice Byron R. White, known to observers of the court as a strict law-and-order man. In his brusque opinions, White backed prosecutors and police at almost every turn. But he was deeply impressed by Amsterdam's presentation; he told his law clerks that it was "possibly the best" oral argument he had ever heard. The point that had won White was Amsterdam's boldest: that the death penalty was applied too infrequently to serve any purpose. White cast the deciding vote to strike down the death penalty not because he wanted to see an end to capital punishment, but because he wanted to see more of it.

The product of these deliberations was one of the most difficult decisions in the history of the U.S. Supreme Court. The broad impact of *Furman v. Georgia*, striking down hundreds of separate laws in nearly 40 separate jurisdictions, was unprecedented. Rambling and inchoate—nine separate opinions totaling some 50,000 words—it remains easily the longest decision ever published by the court. But for all its wordy impact, Furman was almost useless as a precedent for future cases. It set out no clear legal standards. As Powell noted in his stinging dissent:

"Mr. Justice Douglas concludes that capital punishment is incompatible with notions of 'equal protection' that he finds 'implicit' in the Eighth Amendment... Mr. Justice Brennan bases his judgment primarily on the thesis that the penalty 'does not comport with human dignity'... Mr. Justice Stewart concludes that the penalty is applied in a 'wanton' and 'freakish' manner... For Mr. Justice White it is the 'infrequency' with which the penalty is imposed that renders its use unconstitutional... Mr. Justice Marshall finds that capital punishment is an impermissible form of punishment because it is 'morally unacceptable' and 'excessive'...

"I [will not] attempt to predict what forms of capital statutes, if any, may avoid condemnation in the future under the variety of views expressed by the collective majority today."

In other words, totally missing from the longest Supreme Court decision in history was any clear notion of how the death penalty might be fixed.

* * *

That painfully splintered 5-to-4 vote turned out to be a high-water mark of the Supreme Court's willingness to intervene in the business of the states. In Furman, the justices were willing to abolish the death penalty as it existed. But the justices were not willing to forbid executions forever. They kicked the question of whether the death penalty was "cruel and unusual" back to the state legislatures. For nearly 20 years, the states—especially the Southern states—had felt pounded by the Supreme Court. Rarely did they get the chance to answer. The court did not ask what they thought about school desegregation, or voting rights, or the right to counsel. But *Furman v. Georgia* invited the states to respond to a hostile Supreme Court decision.

Florida was the first state to craft an answer, after calling its legislature into special session. Blue-ribbon panels appointed by the governor and legislature struggled to make sense of Furman—but how? On the governor's commission, legal advisers unanimously predicted that no capital punishment law would ever satisfy the high court, but the membership turned instead to a nugget from Justice Douglas's opinion. Douglas wrote that the problem with the pre-Furman laws was that "under these laws no standards govern the selection of the penalty." Douglas seemed to be saying that judges and juries needed rules to guide their sentencing.

The legislative commission reached a different conclusion, simply by seizing on a different snippet from the Furman ruling. Figuring that Byron White was the most likely justice to change his position, commission members combed his opinion for clues. White had complained that "the legislature authorizes [but] does not mandate the penalty in any particular class or kind of case..." That phrase seemed crucial: "Authorizes but does not mandate." Apparently, White would prefer to see death made mandatory for certain crimes.

Furman was as cryptic as the Gnostic gospels. Robert Shevin, Florida's attorney general at the time, was just as confused. He summoned George Georgieff and Ray Marky, his two top death penalty aides, to explain the ruling. "I've been reading it since it came out," Marky told his boss, "and I still have no idea what it means."

Gov. Reubin Askew refused to go along with mandatory sentences—he considered them barbaric. And so it was that while rank-and-file lawmakers made interminable tough-on-crime speeches, in the last month of 1972 Florida's power brokers hashed out a deal behind closed doors. Their new law spelled out "aggravating" circumstances—such as a defendant's criminal record and the degree of violence involved in the crime—which, if proven, would make a guilty man eligible for the death penalty. The law also spelled out "mitigating" circumstances, such as a defendant's age or mental state, that might suggest a life sentence instead. After a defendant was found guilty of a capital offense, the jury would hear evidence of aggravating and mitigating factors. By majority vote, the jurors would recommend either life in prison or the death penalty. Then the judge would be required to reweigh the aggravating and mitigating factors and impose the sentence, justifying it in writing. As a final safeguard, the sentence would be reviewed by the state's highest court. In this way, perhaps, they could thread the Furman needle: setting standards, limiting discretion, erasing caprice—all while avoiding mandatory sentences.

They were a few men in a back room, trading power and guessing over an incoherent Supreme Court document. It was not a particularly promising effort. Nevertheless, their compromise passed overwhelmingly, giving America its first legislative answer to Furman. Immediately, officials from states across the country began calling Florida for advice and guidance. And very soon, lawyers and judges began to discover that the law drafted in confusion and passed in haste was going to be hell to administer.

* * *

The problem was that underneath the tidy, legalistic, polysyllabic, etched-in-marble tone of the new law was a lot of slippery mishmash. The aggravating and mitigating factors sounded specific and empirical, but many of them were matters of judgment rather than fact. A murderer was more deserving of the death penalty, for example, if his actions involved "a great risk of death to many persons"—but where one judge might feel that phrase applied to a drive-by killer who sprays a whole street with gunfire, another might apply it to a burglar who stabs a man to death while the victim's wife slumbers nearby. How much risk makes a "great" risk, and what number of persons constitutes "many"?

Another aggravating circumstance was even harder to interpret—"especially heinous, atrocious or cruel." The idea was to identify only the worst of the hundreds of murders each year in Florida. But wasn't the act of murder itself "heinous, atrocious or cruel"? Again, this aggravating circumstance was very much in the eye of the beholder: To one judge, stabbing might seem more cruel than shooting, because it involved such close contact between killer and victim. Another judge, however, might think it crueler to place a cold gun barrel to a victim's head before squeezing the trigger. One jury might find it especially heinous for a victim to be killed by a stranger, while the next set of jurors might find it more atrocious for a victim to die at the hands of a trusted friend. And so forth. It was an attempt to define the undefinable.

The imprecision was even more obvious on the side of mitigation, where it weighed in a defendant's favor if he had no "significant history" of past criminal behavior. How much history was that? "The age of the defendant" was supposed to be considered under the new law— but where one judge might think 15 was old enough to face the death penalty, another might have qualms about executing a man who was "only" 20. What about elderly criminals? Was there an age beyond which a man should qualify for mercy— and if so, what was it?

Clearly, a lot of discretion was left to the judge and jury. Even more discretion was allowed in tallying the aggravating versus the mitigating circumstances, and still more in deciding what weight to give each factor. The jury was supposed to render an "advisory" opinion on the proper sentence, death or life in prison, but how much deference did the judge have to pay to that advice? The law said

nothing. After the judge imposed a death sentence, the state supreme court was required to review it. But what standards was the court supposed to apply? The law said nothing.

These questions might have seemed tendentious and picayune, except for the fact that Doug McCray and dozens of others were quickly sent to death row, and these seemingly trivial questions became the cruxes of life-and-death litigation. The law, shot through with question marks, became a lawyer's playground. After all, laws were supposed to be clear and fixed; they were supposed to mean the same thing from day to day, courtroom to courtroom, town to town. And given that their clients were going to be killed for breaking the law, it seemed only fair for defense lawyers to demand that simple degree of reliability.

In 1976, when the U.S. Supreme Court returned to the question of capital punishment, the justices agreed that the laws must be reliable. By then some 35 states had passed new death penalty laws, many of them modeled on Florida's. In a string of rulings the high court outlawed mandatory death sentences and affirmed the complex systems for weighing specified factors in favor of and against a death sentence.

But in striking down mandatory sentences, the court made consistency a constitutional requirement for the death penalty; the law must treat "same" cases the same and "different" cases differently. The thousands of capital crimes committed each year in America raised a mountain of peculiarities—each criminal and crime was subtly unique. Somehow the law must penetrate this mountain to discern some conceptual key that would consistently identify cases that were the "same" and cull ones that were "different." Furthermore, the court decided, the Constitution requires extraordinary consistency from capital punishment laws. "The penalty of death is qualitatively different from a sentence of imprisonment, however long," Justice Potter Stewart wrote. "Because of that qualitative difference, there is a corresponding difference in the need for reliability . . ."

Each year, some 20,000 homicides are committed in America, and the swing justices expected the death penalty laws to steer precisely and consistently through this carnage to find the relatively few criminals deserving execution. Somehow, using the black-and-white of the criminal code, the system must determine the very nature of evil. King Solomon himself might demur.

"The main legal battle is over," declared the New York Times in an editorial following the 1976 decisions. In fact, the battles were only beginning.

* * *

After Doug McCray was sentenced to die in 1974, his case went to the Florida Supreme Court for the required review. . . . In October 1980, the Florida Supreme Court agreed that Doug McCray should die. The following year the U.S. Supreme Court declined to review the state court's decision.

Through all this, McCray continued to insist that he had no memory of murdering Margaret Mears. He passed a lie detector test, and though such tests are not admissible in court, there was another reason to believe what he said. It was possible that McCray's epilepsy, which had first emerged in several powerful seizures during his Army basic training, was the type known as "temporal lobe seizure disorder." This disease often emerges in late adolescence; it is known

to cause violent blackouts; and it can be triggered by alcohol. The possibility had not come out at McCray's trial, nor was it properly researched in preparation for his hearing on executive clemency. The hearing, held on December 16, 1981, went badly for McCray. An attorney, Jesse James Wolbert, had been appointed to represent him, but Wolbert did not bother to read the trial record, let alone prepare a compelling case for mercy. Perhaps he had other things on his mind: By the time McCray's death warrant was signed three months later, Wolbert had drained another client's trust fund and become a federal fugitive.

Wolbert's disappearance turned out to be a blessing for McCray, because an anti-death penalty activist named Scharlette Holdman persuaded Bob Dillinger of St. Petersburg to take the case, and Dillinger was a damn good lawyer. He filed a hasty appeal in the Florida Supreme Court asking for a stay of execution. The result was amazing: Having affirmed McCray's death sentence 18 months earlier, the justices now ordered a new trial. The sentence, they ruled, had been based on the theory that the murder had been committed in conjunction with a rape. "Felony murder," this is called—murder coupled with another felony. In 1982, the Florida Supreme Court, by a vote of 4 to 3, declared that the underlying felony, rape, had not been proven beyond a reasonable doubt. Eight years after the original sentence, Doug McCray was going back to trial.

Except that something even more amazing happened a few weeks later. The state supreme court granted the prosecution's request for a rehearing, and Justice Ray Ehrlich abruptly changed his mind. His vote made it 4 to 3 in favor of upholding McCray's death sentence.

In the course of six months, Ehrlich had gone from believing McCray's sentence was so flawed that he should have a new trial to believing that his sentence was sound enough to warrant his death. The court contacted the company that publishes all its decisions and asked that the first half of this flip-flop—the order for a new trial—be erased from history.

Gov. Bob Graham signed a second death warrant on May 27, 1983. By this time, Bob Dillinger had located his client's ex-wife in California, where she lived with her son by Doug McCray. The son was what his father had once been: bright as a whip, interested in current events, a devourer of books, good at games. The ex-wife, Myra Starks, was mystified by the course her husband's life had taken. They had been high school sweethearts, and she had married him certain that he was upward bound. When McCray had left school to join the Army, Starks had clung to that vision, picturing a steady string of promotions leading to a comfortable pension. Then came the seizures and the medical discharge, and her husband's behavior changed horribly. He drank heavily, and sometimes when he was drunk he struck out at her violently—though after each of these outbursts, he insisted he remembered nothing. Myra Starks did not make a connection between the medical discharge and the change in her man; instead, she packed up their baby boy and moved out. Within a year, McCray was on trial for murder.

In addition to locating Starks, Bob Dillinger also arranged for a full-scale medical evaluation of his client, and the doctor concluded that McCray indeed suffered from temporal lobe seizure disorder. It all came together: the violent blackouts, triggered by drink. In prison,

after a number of seizures, McCray was put on a drug regimen to control his disease: Dilantin, a standard epilepsy treatment, in the mornings, and phenobarbital, a sedative, at night. When Dillinger arranged for Myra Starks to see her ex-husband, after a decade apart, she exclaimed, "He's just like the old Doug!"

But he was scheduled to die. Following established procedure, Dillinger returned to the Florida Supreme Court. It was the fifth time the court had considered McCray's case. This time, the justices concluded that the new medical evidence might be important in weighing whether death was the appropriate sentence. They ordered the trial court to hold a hearing and stayed the execution while this was done.

Doug McCray had lived on death row nine years....

In all that time, though, his case had not moved past the first level of appeals. The Florida Supreme Court had weighed and reweighed his case, and with each weighing the justices had reached a different conclusion.

* * *

McCray's case was far from unusual. Every death penalty case winds up on spongy ground, even the most outrageous. It took nearly a decade for Florida to execute serial killer Ted Bundy, and even longer for John Wayne Gacy to reach the end in Illinois. The courts routinely reverse themselves, then double back again. The same case can look different with each fresh examination or new group of judges. Defenders have learned to exploit every possible advantage from the tiniest detail to the loftiest constitutional principle. A conscientious defense attorney has no choice—especially if any question remains as to whether the condemned man actually committed the crime for which he was sentenced. The effort involves huge expenditures of time and resources, and results are notoriously uncertain. . . .

* * *

By the time Doug McCray's case returned to the trial court for a new sentence in 1986, the hanging judge, William Lamar Rose, was gone. So many years had passed. But in his place was another stern man who was no less outraged at the enormity of McCray's crime. . . .

McCray had, over the years, become a favorite of death penalty opponents, because he seemed so gentle and redeemable. Frequently, they argued that not all death row prisoners are "like Ted Bundy," and McCray was the sort of prisoner they were talking about. The harshest word in his vocabulary was "shucks." He read every book he could get his hands on. There was a poignant vulnerability to him.

But the new judge focused, as the old one had done, on the crime: A defenseless, innocent, helpless woman alone, terrorized, apparently raped, then killed. He sentenced McCray to death once more. And the case returned to the Florida Supreme Court for a sixth time. In June 1987, after a U.S. Supreme Court decision in favor of another Florida inmate, the justices sent McCray's case back because the judge had overruled the jury's advisory sentence. What was his justification? The judge's justification was an elderly woman savagely murdered. Once again, he imposed the death sentence.

So the case of Doug McCray returned for the seventh time to the Florida Supreme Court. Did he deserve to die? Four times, a trial judge insisted

that he did. Twice, the state's high court agreed. And four times, the same court expressed doubts. A single case, considered and reconsidered, strained and restrained, weighed and reweighed. A prism, a kaleidoscope, a rune of unknown meaning. The life of a man, viewed through the lens of a complex, uncertain, demanding law. Should he live or die?

In May 1991, after weighing his case for the seventh time in 17 years, the Florida Supreme Court reversed McCray's death sentence and imposed a sentence of life in prison. For 17 years, two courts had debated—the trial court and the state supreme court. No liberal outsiders stalled the process, no bleeding hearts intervened. Even the lawyers added little to the essential conundrum, which was in the beginning as it was in the end: Doug McCray, bad guy, versus Doug McCray, not-quite-so-bad guy. The case was far from aberrant. It was one of hundreds of such cases.

* * *

Some politicians and pundits still talk as if the confusion over the death penalty can be eliminated by a healthy dose of conservative toughness, but among the people who know the system best that explanation is losing steam. More than 20 years have passed since *Furman v. Georgia*; courts and legislatures have gotten tougher and tougher on the issue—but the results have remained negligible. The execution rate hovers at around 25 or 30 per year, while America's death row population has swelled past 3,000. It makes no real difference who controls the courts, as California voters learned after they dumped their liberal chief justice in 1986. The court turned rightward, but 7 1/2 years later, California had executed just two of the more than 300 prisoners on its death row. (One of the two had voluntarily surrendered his appeals.) No matter how strongly judges and politicians favor capital punishment, the law has remained a mishmash.

It is hard to see a way out. The idea that the death penalty should not be imposed arbitrarily—that each case should be analyzed by a rational set of standards —has been so deeply woven into so many federal and state court rulings that there is little chance of it being reversed. Courts have softened that requirement, but softening has not solved the problem. Proposals to limit access to appeals for death row inmates have become staples of America's political campaigns, and many limits have been set. But it can take up to a decade for a prisoner to complete just one trip through the courts, and no one has proposed denying condemned inmates one trip.

... [E]ven the most vicious killers... cannot be executed quickly. Gerald Stano, who in the early 1980s confessed to killing more than two dozen women, is alive. Thomas Knight, who in 1980 murdered a prison guard while awaiting execution for two other murders, is alive. Jesus Scull, who in 1983 robbed and murdered two victims and burned their house around them, is alive. Howard Douglas, who in 1973 forced his wife to have sex with her boyfriend as he watched, then smashed the man's head in, is alive. Robert Buford, who in 1977 raped and beat a 7-year-old girl to death, is alive. Eddie Lee Freeman, who in 1976 strangled a former nun and dumped her in a river to drown, is alive. Jesse Hall, who in 1975 raped and murdered a teenage girl and killed her boyfriend, is alive. James Rose, who in 1976 raped and murdered an 8-year-old girl in Fort Lauderdale, is alive. Larry Mann, who in 1980 cut a little girl's throat and clubbed her to death as she crawled away, is alive.

And that's just in Florida. The story is the same across the country.

In 1972, Justice Harry Blackmun cast one of the four votes in favor of preserving the death penalty in *Furman v. Georgia,* and he voted with the majority to approve the new laws four years later. For two decades, he stuck to the belief that the death penalty could meet the constitutional test of reliability. But last year Blackmun threw up his hands. "Twenty years have passed since this Court declared that the death penalty must be imposed fairly and with reasonable consistency or not all," he wrote."... In the years following Furman, serious efforts were made to comply with its mandate. State legislatures and appellate courts struggled to provide judges and juries with sensible and objective guidelines for determining who should live and who should die... Unfortunately, all this experimentation and ingenuity yielded little of what Furman demanded...It seems that the decision whether a human being should live or die is so inherently subjective, rife with all of life's understandings, experiences, prejudices and passions, that it inevitably defies the rationality and consistency required by the Constitution... I feel morally and intellectually obligated simply to concede that the death penalty experiment has failed."

Also last year, an admiring biography of retired Justice Lewis Powell was published. Powell was one of the architects of the modern death penalty. As a swing vote in 1976, he had helped to define the intricate weighing system that restored capital punishment in America. Later, as the deciding vote in a 1987 case, *McCleskey v. Kemp,* Powell had saved the death penalty from the assertion that racial disparities proved the system was still arbitrary. Now Powell was quoted as telling his biographer, "I have come to think that capital punishment should be abolished." The death penalty "brings discredit on the whole legal system," Powell said, because the vast majority of death sentences are never carried out. Biographer John C. Jeffries Jr. had asked Powell if he would like to undo any decisions from his long career. "Yes," the justice answered. "McCleskey v. Kemp."

No one has done more than Ray Marky to make a success of the death penalty. As a top aide in the Florida attorney general's office, he worked himself into an early heart attack prosecuting capital appeals. Eventually, he took a less stressful job at the local prosecutor's office, where he watched, dispirited, as the modern death penalty—the law he had helped write and had struggled to enforce—reached its convoluted maturity. One day a potential death penalty case came across his new desk, and instead of pushing as he had in the old days, he advised the victim's mother to accept a life sentence for her son's killer. "Ma'am, bury your son and get on with your life, or over the next dozen years, this defendant will destroy you, as well as your son," Marky told her. Why put the woman through all the waiting, the hearings and the stays, when the odds were heavy that the death sentence would never be carried out? "I never would have said that 15 years ago," Marky reflected. "But now I will, because I'm not going to put someone through the nightmare. If we had deliberately set out to create a chaotic system, we couldn't have come up with anything worse. It's a merry-go-round, it's ridiculous; it's so clogged up only an arbitrary few ever get it.

"I don't get any damn pleasure out of the death penalty and I never have," the prosecutor said. "And frankly, if they abolished it tomorrow, I'd go get drunk in celebration."

NO

Ernest van den Haag

THE ULTIMATE PUNISHMENT:
A DEFENSE

In an average year about 20,000 homicides occur in the United States. Fewer than 300 convicted murders are sentenced to death. But because no more than thirty murderers have been executed in any recent year, most convicts sentenced to death are likely to die of old age.[1] Nonetheless, the death penalty looms large in discussions: it raises important moral questions independent of the number of executions.

The death penalty is our harshest punishment. It is irrevocable: it ends the existence of those punished, instead of temporarily imprisoning them. Further, although not intended to cause physical pain, execution is the only corporal punishment still applied to adults. These singular characteristics contribute to the perennial, impassioned controversy about capital punishment.

I. DISTRIBUTION

Consideration of the justice, morality, or usefulness, of capital punishment is often conflated with objections to its alleged discriminatory or capricious distribution among the guilty. Wrongly so. If capital punishment is immoral *in se*, no distribution among the guilty could make it moral. If capital punishment is moral, no distribution would make it immoral. Improper distribution cannot affect the quality of what is distributed, be it punishments or rewards. Discriminatory or capricious distribution thus could not justify abolition of the death penalty. Further, maldistribution inheres no more in capital punishment than in any other punishment.

Maldistribution between the guilty and the innocent is, by definition, unjust. But the injustice does not lie in the nature of the punishment. Because of the finality of the death penalty, the most grievous maldistribution occurs when it is imposed upon the innocent. However, the frequent allegations of discrimination and capriciousness refer to maldistribution among the guilty and not to the punishment of the innocent.

From Ernest van den Haag, "The Ultimate Punishment: A Defense," *Harvard Law Review,* vol. 99 (May 1986). Copyright © 1986 by The Harvard Law Review Association. Reprinted by permission.

Maldistribution of any punishment among those who deserve it is irrelevant to its justice or morality. Even if poor or black convicts guilty of capital offenses suffer capital punishment, and other convicts equally guilty of the same crimes do not, a more equal distribution, however desirable, would merely be more equal. It would not be more just to the convicts under sentence of death.

Punishments are imposed on persons, not on racial or economic groups. Guilt is personal. The only relevant question is: does the person to be executed deserve the punishment? Whether or not others who deserved the same punishment, whatever their economic or racial group, have avoided execution is irrelevant. If they have, the guilt of the executed convicts would not be diminished, nor would their punishment be less deserved. To put the issue starkly, if the death penalty were imposed on guilty blacks, but not on guilty whites, or, if it were imposed by a lottery among the guilty, this irrationally discriminatory or capricious distribution would neither make the penalty unjust, nor cause anyone to be unjustly punished, despite the undue impunity bestowed on others.

Equality, in short, seems morally less important than justice. And justice is independent of distributional inequalities. The ideal of equal justice demands that justice be equally distributed, not that it be replaced by equality. Justice requires that as many of the guilty as possible be punished, regardless of whether others have avoided punishment. To let these others escape the deserved punishment does not do justice to them, or to society. But it is not unjust to those who could not escape.

These moral considerations are not meant to deny that irrational discrimina-tion, or capriciousness, would be inconsistent with constitutional requirements. But I am satisfied that the Supreme Court has in fact provided for adherence to the constitutional requirement of equality as much as possible. Some inequality is indeed unavoidable as a practical matter in any system.[2] But, *ultra posse neo obligatur.* (Nobody is bound beyond ability.)

Recent data reveal little direct racial discrimination in the sentencing of those arrested and convicted of murder. The abrogation of the death penalty for rape has eliminated a major source of racial discrimination. Concededly, some discrimination based on the race of murder victims may exist; yet, this discrimination affects criminal victimizers in an unexpected way. Murderers of whites are thought more likely to be executed than murderers of blacks. Black victims, then, are less fully vindicated than white ones. However, because most black murderers kill blacks, black murderers are spared the death penalty more often than are white murderers. They fare better than most white murderers. The motivation behind unequal distribution of the death penalty may well have been to discriminate against blacks, but the result has favored them. Maldistribution is thus a straw man for empirical as well as analytical reasons.

II. MISCARRIAGES OF JUSTICE

In a recent survey Professors Hugo Adam Bedau and Michael Radelet found that 7000 persons were executed in the United States between 1900 and 1985 and that 25 were innocent of capital crimes. Among the innocents they list Sacco and Vanzetti as well as Ethel and Julius Rosenberg. Although their data may be questionable, I do not doubt that, over a long enough period, miscarriages of justice will occur even in capital cases.

Despite precautions, nearly all human activities, such as trucking, lighting, or construction, cost the lives of some innocent bystanders. We do not give up these activities, because the advantages, moral or material, outweigh the unintended losses. Analogously, for those who think the death penalty just, miscarriages of justice are offset by the moral benefits and the usefulness of doing justice. For those who think the death penalty unjust even when it does not miscarry, miscarriages can hardly be decisive.

III. DETERRENCE

Despite much recent work, there has been no conclusive statistical demonstration that the death penalty is a better deterrent than are alternative punishments. However, deterrence is less than decisive for either side. Most abolitionists acknowledge that they would continue to favor abolition even if the death penalty were shown to deter more murders than alternatives could deter. Abolitionists appear to value the life of a convicted murderer or, at least, his nonexecution, more highly than they value the lives of the innocent victims who might be spared by deterring prospective murderers.

Deterrence is not altogether decisive for me either. I would favor retention of the death penalty as retribution even if it were shown that the threat of execution could not deter prospective murderers not already deterred by the threat of imprisonment.[3] Still, I believe the death penalty, because of its finality, is more feared than imprisonment, and deters some prospective murderers not deterred by the threat of imprisonment. Sparing the lives of even a few prospective victims by deterring their murderers is more important than preserving the lives of convicted murderers because of the possibility, or even the probability, that executing them would not deter others. Whereas the lives of the victims who might be saved are valuable, that of the murderer has only negative value, because of his crime. Surely the criminal law is meant to protect the lives of potential victims in preference to those of actual murderers.

Murder rates are determined by many factors; neither the severity nor the probability of the threatened sanction is always decisive. However, for the long run, I share the view of Sir James Fitzjames Stephen: "Some men, probably, abstain from murder because they fear that if they committed murder they would be hanged. Hundreds of thousands abstain from it because they regard it with horror. One great reason why they regard it with horror is that murderers are hanged." Penal sanctions are useful in the long run for the formation of the internal restraints so necessary to control crime. The severity and finality of the death penalty is appropriate to the seriousness and the finality of murder.

IV. INCIDENTAL ISSUES: COST, RELATIVE SUFFERING, BRUTALIZATION

Many nondecisive issues are associated with capital punishment. Some believe that the monetary cost of appealing a capital sentence is excessive. Yet most comparisons of the cost of life imprisonment with the cost of execution, apart from their dubious relevance, are flawed at least by the implied assumption that life prisoners will generate no judicial costs during their imprisonment. At any rate, the actual monetary costs are trumped by the importance of doing justice.

Others insist that a person sentenced to death suffers more than his victim suffered, and that this (excess) suffering is undue according to the *lex talionis* (rule of retaliation). We cannot know whether the murderer on death row suffers more than his victim suffered; however, unlike the murderer, the victim deserved none of the suffering inflicted. Further, the limitations of the *lex talionis* were meant to restrain private vengeance, not the social retribution that has taken its place. Punishment—regardless of the motivation—is not intended to revenge, offset, or compensate for the victim's suffering, or to be measured by it. Punishment is to vindicate the law and the social order undermined by the crime. This is why a kidnapper's penal confinement is not limited to the period for which he imprisoned his victim; nor is a burglar's confinement meant merely to offset the suffering or the harm he caused his victim; nor is it meant only to offset the advantage he gained.[4]

Another argument heard at least since Beccaria is that, by killing a murderer, we encourage, endorse, or legitimize unlawful killing. Yet, although all punishments are meant to be unpleasant, it is seldom argued that they legitimize the unlawful imposition of identical unpleasantness. Imprisonment is not thought to legitimize kidnapping; neither are fines thought to legitimize robbery. The difference between murder and execution, or between kidnapping and imprisonment, is that the first is unlawful and undeserved, the second a lawful and deserved punishment for an unlawful act. The physical similarities of the punish-ment to the crime are irrelevant. The relevant difference is not physical, but social.[5]

V. JUSTICE, EXCESS, DEGRADATION

We threaten punishments in order to deter crime. We impose them not only to make the threats credible but also as retribution (justice) for the crimes that were not deterred. Threats and punishments are necessary to deter and deterrence is a sufficient practical justification for them. Retribution is an independent moral justification. Although penalties can be unwise, repulsive, or inappropriate, and those punished can be pitiable, in a sense the infliction of legal punishment on a guilty person cannot be unjust. By committing the crime, the criminal volunteered to assume the risk of receiving a legal punishment that he could have avoided by not committing the crime. The punishment he suffers is the punishment he voluntarily risked suffering and, therefore, it is no more unjust to him than any other event for which one knowingly volunteers to assume the risk. Thus, the death penalty cannot be unjust to the guilty criminal.

There remain, however, two moral objections. The penalty may be regarded as always excessive as retribution and always morally degrading. To regard the death penalty as always excessive, one must believe that no crime—no matter how heinous—could possibly justify capital punishment. Such a belief can be neither corroborated nor refuted; it is an article of faith.

Alternatively, or concurrently, one may believe that everybody, the murderer no less than the victim, has an imprescriptible (natural?) right to life. The law therefore should not deprive anyone of life. I share Jeremy Bentham's view that any such "natural and imprescriptible rights" are "nonsense upon stilts."

Justice Brennan has insisted that the death penalty is "uncivilized," "inhuman," inconsistent with "human dignity" and with "the sanctity of life," that it "treats members of the human race as nonhumans, as objects to be toyed with and discarded," that it is "uniquely degrading to human dignity" and "by its very nature, [involves] a denial of the executed person's humanity." Justice Brennan does not say why he thinks execution "uncivilized." Hitherto most civilizations have had the death penalty, although it has been discarded in Western Europe, where it is currently unfashionable probably because of its abuse by totalitarian regimes.

By "degrading," Justice Brennan seems to mean that execution degrades the executed convicts. Yet philosophers, such as Immanuel Kant and G. F. W. Hegel, have insisted that, when deserved, execution, far from degrading the executed convict, affirms his humanity by affirming his rationality and his responsibility for his actions. They thought that execution, when deserved, is required for the sake of the convict's dignity. (Does not life imprisonment violate human dignity more than execution, by keeping alive a prisoner deprived of all autonomy?)

Common sense indicates that it cannot be death—or common fate—that is inhuman. Therefore, Justice Brennan must mean that death degrades when it comes not as a natural or accidental event, but as a deliberate social imposition. The murderer learns through his punishment that his fellow men have found him unworthy of living; that because he has murdered, he is being expelled from the community of the living. This degradation is self-inflicted. By murdering, the murderer has so dehumanized himself that he cannot remain among the living. The social recognition of his self-degradation is the punitive essence of execution. To believe, as Justice Brennan appears to, that the degradation is inflicted by the execution reverses the direction of causality.

Execution of those who have committed heinous murders may deter only one murder per year. If it does, it seems quite warranted. It is also the only fitting retribution for murder I can think of.

NOTES

1. Death row as a semipermanent residence is cruel, because convicts are denied the normal amenities of prison life. Thus, unless death row residents are integrated into the prison population, the continuing accumulation of convicts on death row should lead us to accelerate either the rate of executions or the rate of commutations. I find little objection to integration.

2. The ideal of equality, unlike the ideal of retributive justice (which can be approximated separately in each instance), is clearly unattainable unless all guilty persons are apprehended, and thereafter tried, convicted and sentenced by the same court, at the same time. Unequal justice is the best we can do; it is still better than the injustice, equal or unequal, which occurs if, for the sake of equality, we deliberately allow some who could be punished to escape.

3. If executions were shown to increase the murder rate in the long run, I would favor abolition. Sparing the innocent victims who would be spared, *ex hypothesi*, by the nonexecution of murderers would be more important to me than the execution, however just, of murderers. But although there is a lively discussion of the subject, no serious evidence exists to support the hypothesis that executions produce a higher murder rate. Cf. Phillips, *The Deterrent Effect of Capital Punishment: New Evidence on an Old Controversy*, 86 AM. J. Soc. 139 (1980) (arguing that murder rates drop immediately after executions of criminals).

4. Thus restitution (a civil liability) cannot satisfy the punitive purpose of penal sanctions, whether the purpose be retributive or deterrent.

5. Some abolitionists challenge: if the death penalty is just and serves as a deterrent, why not televise executions? The answer is simple. The death even of a murderer, however well-deserved,

should not serve as public entertainment. It so served in earlier centuries. But in this respect our sensibility has changed for the better, I believe. Further, television unavoidably would trivialize executions, wedged in, as they would be, between game shows, situation comedies and the like. Finally, because televised executions would focus on the physical aspects of the punishment, rather than the nature of the crime and the suffering of the victim, a televised execution would present the murderer as the victim of the state. Far from communicating the moral significance of the execution, television would shift the focus to the pitiable fear of the murderer. We no longer place in cages those sentenced to imprisonment to expose them to public view. Why should we so expose those sentenced to execution?

POSTSCRIPT

Is Capital Punishment Bad Policy?

One of the most striking elements about the issue of capital punishment is that most of the public, the politicians, and even many criminological scholars do not seem to be fazed by empirical evidence. Each side ritualistically marshalls empirical evidence to support its respective position. Opponents of capital punishment often draw from Thorsten Sellin's classic study *The Penalty of Death* (Sage Publications) to "prove" that the number of capital offenses is no lower in states that have the death penalty as compared to states that have abolished executions.

In the 1992 presidential election, both George Bush and Bill Clinton indicated support for the death penalty. In fact, most political candidates seem to support capital punishment nowadays. Supporters of capital punishment draw from numerous studies, including I. Ehrlich's "The Deterrent Effect of Capital Punishment," *American Economic Review* (vol. 65, 1975), pp. 397–417, and his "Capital Punishment and Deterrence: Some Further Thoughts and Additional Evidence," *Journal of Political Economy* (vol. 85, 1977), pp. 741–788. They also draw from W. Berns's *For Capital Punishment: Crime and the Morality of the Death Penalty* (Basic Books, 1979).

Generally, the empirical research indicates that the death penalty cannot conclusively be proven to deter others from committing homicides and other serious crimes. Entire scientific commissions have been charged with the responsibility of determining the deterrent effects of the death penalty (for example, the National Academy of Sciences in 1975). The gist of their conclusions was that the value of the death penalty as a deterrent "is not a settled matter."

As is typical with most aspects of human behavior, including crime and crime control, the issue is filled with much irony, paradox, and contradiction. First, clashing views over capital punishment rely largely on emotion. The public's attitudes, politicians' attitudes, and even scholarly attitudes are frequently shaped more by sentiment and preconceived notions than by rational discourse. As F. Zimring and G. Hawkins indicate in *Capital Punishment and the American Agenda* (Cambridge University Press, 1986), very few scholars have ever changed their opinions about capital punishment.

As we rapidly approach the twenty-first century, capital punishment should be a dead issue. Yet it is still with us and may continue into the next century. For dissenting views, see "The Death Penalty Dinosaur," by R. C. Dieter, *Commonweal* (January 15, 1988); *Challenging Capital Punishment: Legal and Social Scientific Approaches* edited by K. Haas and J. Inciardi (Sage

Publications, 1988); and "The Symbolic Death of Willie Darden," *U.S. News and World Report* (March 28, 1988).

A remarkable work that almost puts you into the death chamber and is the best description of the bureaucratization if not the trivialization of executions is R. Johnson's *Death Watch: A Study of the Modern Execution Process* (American Correctional Association, 1990). Two books of interest are *The Death Penalty in America: Current Research* edited by R. M. Bohm (Anderson, 1991) and R. Paternoster's *Capital Punishment in America* (Lexington Books, 1992). Both Bohm and Paternoster have written extensively on capital punishment.

A more recent book, written by a Catholic nun who counsels death row inmates, is H. Prejean's *Dead Man Walking: Eyewitness Account of the Death Penalty* (Random House, 1993). Two provocative works that take the death penalty to task are K. Miller, *Executing the Mentally Ill* (Sage Publications, 1993) and M. Radelet et al., *In Spite of Innocence: Erroneous Convictions in Capital Cases* (Northeastern University Press, 1993).

Two studies of the deterrence issue are "Capital Punishment and the Deterrence of Violent Crime in Comparable Countries," by D. Cheatwood, *Criminal Justice Review* (August 1993) and "Deterrence or Brutalization?" by J. Cochran et al., *Criminology* (February 1994). For a survey of the attitudes toward capital punishment among politicians, see M. Sandys and E. McGarrell, "Attitudes Toward Capital Punishment Among Indiana Legislators," *Justice Quarterly* (December 1994). A popular media account of a death penalty sentence given to a mentally impaired individual is "Untrue Confessions," by J. Smolowe, *Time* (May 22, 1995). An interesting comparison of the effects of publicized executions on whites and blacks is "The Impact of Publicized Executions on Homicide," by S. Stack, *Criminal Justice and Behavior* (June 1995). The *Bureau of Justice Statistics Bulletin* routinely updates death penalty statistics. For an outstanding description of death row, see Von Drehle's *Among the Lowest of the Dead: The Culture of Death Row* (Times Books, 1995).

L. K. Gillespie's *Dancehall Ladies: The Crimes and Executions of America's Condemned Women* (University Press of America, 1997) is a solid historical discussion. D. A. Cabana's *Death at Midnight: The Confessions of an Executioner* (Northeast University Press, 1996) is an insightful insider's account. A helpful legal overview is *Death Penalty Cases: Leading U.S. Supreme Court Cases on Capital Punishment* by B. Latzer (Butterworth-Heinemann, 1998). Finally, two outstanding articles that provide both historical and theoretical background for understanding violence and capital punishment as an extension of inequalities maintenance are Roberta Senechal de la Roche, "Collective Violence as Social Control," *Sociological Forum* (March 1996) and "The Sociogenesis of Lynching," in W. F. Brundae, ed., *Under Penalty of Death: Essays on Lynching in the South* (University of North Carolina Press, 1997).

ISSUE 13

Does Three Strikes and Other Tough Approaches Work?

YES: Eugene H. Methvin, from "Mugged by Reality," *Policy Review* (July/August 1997)

NO: David Shichor, from "Three Strikes as a Public Policy: The Convergence of the New Penology and the McDonaldization of Punishment," *Crime and Delinquency* (September 1997)

ISSUE SUMMARY

YES: Eugene H. Methvin, senior editor for *Reader's Digest*, contends that a very small number of juveniles and adults commit the majority of serious crimes. The main solution to the crime problem, then, is to identify them as early as possible and increase the punishments each time they offend, eventually incarcerating the repeat offenders.

NO: Professor of criminal justice David Shichor argues that the "three-strikes" policy is permeated with negative unanticipated consequences and that it is costly, inefficient, unfair, and does little to reduce crime.

The traditional approaches to crime are retribution (sometimes conceptually couched as vengeance or justice), deterrence, and incapacitation. Many criminologists and liberal politicians have called for incarceration during the twentieth century. For a variety of reasons, including increasing fear of crime, significant increases in violent crimes in many areas, a shrinking economy, and the election in 1980 of a conservative president, there has been a decisive paradigmatic shift. Current constructions of the crime problem and responses to crime policies seem to ignore rehabilitation as a goal of incarceration.

"Criminals need to be locked up," many say these days, because they deserve to be punished, to deter others from doing the same thing, and to get bad people off the streets. Structural or environmental factors, with their concomitant theoretical response modalities, are forgotten by many. That is, racism, blocked opportunities, lack of education, poverty, and the like as theorized causes of crime implying a need for rehabilitation (such as job training, education, and improved opportunities) are seemingly receding rapidly into distant criminological memory.

Initially framed as federal law, now being replicated in different variants in 24 states, three-strikes criminal justice ideologically "makes sense" within the current weltanschauungen (world view). If an individual has already committed two serious felonies and now commits a third one, defenders argue, what can be more rational than making sure that he gets a very long sentence for his third crime? Studies show that a hard core of offenders, if taken off the streets, would save taxpayers hundreds of thousands of dollars a year. A life prison sentence would clearly incapacitate them. Individuals, then, would be deterred from committing their third crime, and general deterrence would result from others being afraid of being imprisoned for the remainder of their lives.

Supporters of tough sentencing laws also say, if criminals have already done terrible things and are obviously still doing them, justice would be served better by separating them from you and me. After all, what good has "rehabilitation" done them if they are still committing crimes?

In the second selection, David Shichor attempts to counter much of this by applying to penology four key concepts—efficiency, calculability, prediction, and control—derived from social theorist George Ritzer's "McDonaldization of society" theory. What distinguishes modern, industrial societies from all others is the bureaucratization of social and economic life. According to classic theorist Max Weber (1864–1920), who both Shichor and Ritzer draw from, modernity necessitates increased rational behavior that is oriented to economic values over family and personal ones. Both market and social life are increasingly routinized, controlled, planned, and calculated. This enables increased productivity and industrial survival. However, as Weber warned with his prophecy of the "iron cage of the future" consequence, there is a tremendous cost: Life becomes more routinized and regimented. People and policies run the risk of becoming robot-like. Ritzer extends this argument to suggest that with increased technological efficiency comes a curvilinear relationship (a U-shaped curve). That is, after certain points, the "efficiency" and "savings" backfire, or become counterproductive and irrational.

As you wrestle with this important debate, notice Eugene H. Methvin's classifications of the types of offenders in the first selection. Which does he seem to be addressing? What does he see as the causes of crime? Are they sometimes contradictory? How often does Shichor actually prove that three strikes does not work as opposed to speculating that it *could* be a problem?

YES

Eugene H. Methvin

MUGGED BY REALITY

The most serious offenders against people and property in this country generally hit their criminal peak between 16 and 18 years of age. The hard-core young thug-to-be starts stealing from mama's purse before he's 10. By the fourth and fifth grades, he is skipping school. As he enters his teens, he's gangbanging—and on the track to prison or an early violent death. Typically he is committing burglaries at about 15, armed robberies at 16, and often killing by 18—and sometimes much younger. After years of effort to contain the crime committed by these hoodlums, we know what works and what doesn't. At long last, we have all the knowledge we need to design an effective strategy for the prevention of crime.

1. Most serious crime is committed by a violent minority of predatory recidivists.

Criminologist Marvin Wolfgang compiled records of all of the 9,945 males born in 1945 and attending school in Philadelphia between the ages of 10 and 18. A mere 627—just under 7 percent—were chronic offenders, with five or more arrests by age 18. These so-called Dirty Seven Percenters committed more than half of all offenses and two-thirds of the violent crimes, including all the murders, that were committed by the entire cohort.

Wolfgang followed his "Class of '45" through its 30th year in 1975. Shockingly few offenders were incarcerated. Even the 14 murderers among them spent an average of only four years behind bars for these crimes. Worse, these hardcore criminals admitted in interviews that, for each arrest, they typically got away with 8 to 11 other serious crimes. Wolfgang found that 70 percent of juveniles arrested three times committed a fourth offense; of those, 80 percent not only committed a fifth offense, but kept at it through 20 or more. If the city's judges had sent each Dirty Seven Percenter to prison for just a year after his *third* offense, Wolfgang calculated, Philadelphians would have suffered 7,200 fewer serious crimes while they [were] off the streets.

Wolfgang's findings electrified the law-enforcement world. At the request of U.S. Attorney General Edward Levi, Wolfgang repeated the study on the 13,160 Philadelphian males born in 1958. The proportion of chronic offenders was virtually the same: 982 young men (7.5 percent) collected five or more arrests before age 18. But the crimes committed by the "Class of '58" were

From Eugene H. Methvin, "Mugged by Reality," *Policy Review: The Journal of American Citizenship* (July/August 1997). Copyright © 1997 by *Policy Review: The Journal of American Citizenship*. Reprinted by permission.

bloodier and far more frequent. Compared with the Class of '45, these youths were twice as likely to commit rape and aggravated assault, three times more likely to murder, and five times more likely to commit robbery. They were, concluded Wolfgang, "a very violent criminal population of a small number of nasty, brutal offenders. They begin early in life and should be controlled equally early."

Other studies with different methodologies corroborated Wolfgang's approximate finding of 7 percent in places as different as London; Copenhagen; Orange County, California; Racine, Wisconsin; Columbus, Ohio; Phoenix, Arizona; and Salt Lake City, Utah.

2. A minority of this minority is extraordinarily violent, persistent, or both.

They are "Super Predators," far more dangerous than the rest. Researchers for Rand questioned 2,190 prisoners convicted of robbery in California, Texas, and Michigan. Nearly all admitted to many more crimes than those for which they were jailed. But a tiny fraction of these career criminals proved to be *extraordinarily* frequent offenders. The least active 50 percent of burglars averaged a little under six burglaries a year, while the most prolific 10 percent averaged more than 230. The least active 50 percent of the robbers committed five robberies a year on average, but the top 10 percent averaged 87. The distribution of drug-dealing offenses was even more skewed: Half of these convicts did 100 deals a year on average, while the highest tenth averaged 3,251.

Sociologist Delbert S. Elliott of the University of Colorado has tracked a nationally representative sample of 1,725 boys and girls who were between 11 and 17 years old in 1976. By 1989, 369 of them had committed one or more serious, violent offenses. But only 32 were high-rate offenders. Year after year, those in this small group committed an average of 30 violent crimes each and hundreds of lesser crimes. Just under 2 percent of the whole, they accounted for half the serious crimes committed by the entire group. These Super Predators distinguish themselves by their arrest records, by the early age at which they first tangle with the law, and by the seriousness of their early offenses. Nationally, we can crudely estimate the current crop of young "super felons" at about 500,000 of our 26.7 million 11- to 17-year-olds.

3. Most of these persistent predators are criminal psychopaths, and we now have a scientifically valid instrument to identify them with reasonable accuracy.

Psychopaths are responsible for more than half of all serious crimes. The normal criminal has an internalized set of values, however warped, and he feels guilt whenever he violates his standards. The psychopath doesn't even know what guilt is, because he has never experienced it. But he is good at *faking* it.

Even within prison populations, psychopaths stand out because their antisocial and illegal behavior is more varied and frequent than that of ordinary criminals. In prisons and mental hospitals, they are generally the nastiest inmates. They are more resistant to treatment, more likely to try to escape, and more violent with other inmates and the staff. After they are released, they reoffend at four to five times the rate of other criminals. Psychopaths constitute an estimated 1 to 2 percent of the population—and 20 to 25 percent of our prison population. This means the United States has at least 2 *million* psychopaths.

After 25 years of research, psychologist Robert D. Hare of the University of British Columbia developed a reliable instrument for diagnosing psychopathy: the Hare Psychopathy Check List [PCL]. After interviewing relatives and associates and studying criminal and other records, a trained clinician interviews the subject and scores him on 20 personality traits and behaviors characteristic of this personality disorder. Is the person glib, manipulative, a liar, sexually promiscuous, grandiose in his sense of self-worth, impulsive, averse to boredom, incapable of remorse? Was he trouble from an early age? Does he have a juvenile and adult arrest record? Has he had many short-term marital relationships? And so on.

Hare, in his 1993 book *Without Conscience: The Disturbing World of Psychopaths Among Us,* says: "Psychopaths are social predators who charm, manipulate, and ruthlessly plow their way through life, leaving a broad trail of broken hearts, shattered expectations, and empty wallets. Completely lacking in conscience and feelings for others, they selfishly take what they want and do as they please, violating social norms and expectations without the slightest sense of guilt or regret."

Studies of Canadian and American convicts released from prison show that only about 20 percent of the low scorers on the PCL are re-arrested within three years, but 80 percent of the high scorers end up back behind bars.

The PCL can be a powerful tool for prison administrators, parole boards, judges, and others who must cope with this extraordinarily destructive population. High scorers are poor risks for probation or parole and good candidates for maximum sentences in higher security institutions. Maryland prison officials have used the PCL to assess some 10,00 inmates. It has enabled them to divert low scorers from costly maximum-security facilities into lower-cost units or parole, freeing up 1,100 prison beds a day, which yields $19.8 million in savings a year. Moreover, the state has avoided an estimated $55 million in new prison construction. Canada, New Zealand, the United Kingdom, and most American states are now using the PCL in their prison systems.

4. Savvy police, prosecutors, and judges can identify and isolate high-rate violent predators.

In Miami, sociologist James A. Inciardi used a "snowballing" interview technique to find them. He sent researchers into high-crime neighborhoods to talk to youngsters about "who's doing drugs" and "who's into crime." They found 611 youngsters ages 12 to 17 who admitted to multiple crimes and repeated drug use. Ninety percent of them had been arrested, an equal proportion had been thrown out of school, and almost half had been incarcerated. Typically they began to use alcohol at age seven and turned to crime and drugs at 11; almost two-thirds had participated in a robbery by the age of 13. The interviewees confessed to a total of 429,136 criminal acts during the year prior to their interviews—more than 700 each, or nearly two a day. Of these acts, 18,477, or 30 apiece, were major felonies, including 6,269 robberies and 721 assaults. Nearly 18 percent had committed armed robberies, as young as 14, and 90 percent carried weapons most of the time. Among this violent crowd, 361 committed the 6,269 robberies—an average of 17 each—and two-thirds of them robbed before the age of 13.

If sociologists can find the Super Predators, police can, too. William Bratton proved it, first in New York City's subway system in 1990, then citywide after Mayor Rudolph Giuliani named him police commissioner in 1994. By 1990, the New York subway had become a lawless jungle. Riders were deserting by the tens of thousands. An estimated 180,000 fare evaders jumped the turnstiles every day, costing the system $65 million a year. Vandals jammed coin slots and opened exit doors; aggressive panhandlers threatened riders on the cars; muggers stole their tokens and money. Violent teenagers prowled the subways in "wolfpacks."

As the chief of New York's 4,000 transit police offices, Bratton created strategies for winnowing out the criminal minority. He ordered uniformed officers to enforce all subway rules. He planted plainclothes teams to arrest fare evaders. Each of them was searched; one in 14 was arrested for packing illegal guns, and one out of seven was wanted on previous criminal warrants. Whenever detectives caught one mugger, they extracted information about other wolfpack members. They also tracked down a group of about 75 hard-core graffiti vandals. Bratton insisted that his officers act on bench warrants for subway crimes within 24 hours. Their apprehension rate rose sharply to more than 60 percent. The hunters became the hunted. Bratton's strategies cut subway crime by two-thirds—and robberies by three-fourths. Fare evaders were reduced by two-thirds, too. Riders returned by the ten of thousands. By 1994 New York's subways were the scene of fewer than 20 felonies a day, down 64 percent in five years.

Named in 1994 to head the whole police department, Bratton and his deputy

commissioner, Jack Maple, implemented a strategy of "relentless pursuit." Bratton personally urged officers to cite citizens for "quality of life" offenses such as drinking beer in pubic, smoking marijuana, or urinating in the street, and to frisk offenders for illegal weapons at the slightest suspicion. Maple launched a campaign to remind officers to interrogate every arrestee. Talented interrogators created a three-day "verbal judo" course at the police academy to teach officers how to extract information from suspects. New York's cops responded enthusiastically, and with dramatic results. A topless dancer arrested for prostitution fingered the bouncer at her Brooklyn club in an unsolved murder. A car thief turned in a fence, who then turned in a father-son gun-dealing team. A parolee arrested for failing to report turned out to have been the only eyewitness to a drug-related murder.

This campaign produced "a miracle happening before our eyes," says Jeffrey Fagan, the director of Columbia University's Center for Violence Research and Prevention. From 1994 to 1996, New York City's murders declined by 49 percent, robberies 43 percent, burglaries 39 percent, and grand larcenies 32 percent. In 1995, the city accounted for 70 percent of the heralded national decline in serious crimes.

5. *The rehabilitation ideal of the juvenile-court system leads to costly coddling of serious and persistent offenders.*

Studies show that youths who land in juvenile court a second time will likely become chronic offenders. Howard N. Snyder, a researcher with the National Council of Family and Juvenile Court Judges, analyzed the records of 48,311 boys who went through juvenile courts in

Utah and Arizona. More than half never returned after the first trip. But most of those who landed in court a second time before their 16th birthdays became persistent repeaters, and the earlier their first prosecution, the more likely they were to be violent chronics.

It is important to note that a troublesome youngster typically has 10 to 12 contacts with the criminal-justice system and many more undiscovered offenses before he ever receives any formal "adjudication," or finding of guilt, from a judge. He quickly concludes that he will never face any serious consequences for his delinquency. For each young chronic offender who comes before him, a juvenile-court judge typically moves toward more severe punishments and costly interventions in five or more small steps. Snyder recommends that judges impose upon second-time convicts stiffer penalties and the more intense (and costly) rehabilitation programs. Waiting until the fourth or fifth offense to do so only wastes court time and money—and looses serious crime upon the public.

In Richmond, Virginia, a juvenile-court psychologist estimated that court costs, rehabilitation efforts, and incarceration for just 14 defendants who cycled through her court regularly totaled more than $2 million. Welfare, food stamps, court-appointed lawyers, and other services over the years swelled their cost to taxpayers to more than $5 million. She tracked 56 young men locked in the youth-detention center over one five-day period. On average, they were 15 years old and had compiled 12 arrests apiece for crimes of escalating severity. Social-service agencies had intervened in their lives at an average age of nine, and their criminal activity began four years later, on average, though some started as early

as age seven. Their offenses ranged from curfew violation to rape and murder. A year later, one-third had graduated to adult prisons. Three-fourths were still incarcerated or faced new charges or warrants. Almost all those older than 15 who had been released faced new charges.

6. Punishment works—and the United States has barely tried it.

Psychologist Sarnoff A. Mednick of the University of Southern California studied the records of thousands of Danish criminals and discovered that punishment is very effective in deterring crime. He compared the criminal histories of thousands of offenders in Copenhagen and Philadelphia who had exactly four or five arrests. Those who received four punishments in a row for their crimes were unlikely to have a fifth arrest. But those who had been punished irregularly after the earlier arrests were more likely to be arrested again.

Mednick studied 28,879 males born in Copenhagen between 1944 and 1947 who lived there through age 26. He found that 6,579 had at least one arrest. The third of arrestees who were not punished went on to commit far more crimes. Mednick found 3,809 offenders were punished after every single arrest, while 2,793 were not. Those who escaped punishment committed three times as many crimes as those consistently punished. Punishment delivered after every offense significantly reduced later offenses. But an offender who was punished for early crimes and received none for later offenses resumed criminal activity at the higher rates.

It made little difference whether the punishment was fines, probation, or incarceration. Consistent delivery of sanctions was more effective than intermittent sanctions, and criminal recidivism recovered when punishment was discontinued. Severity of sanction also made little difference: Longer jail terms, higher fines, and longer probations did not decrease subsequent offenses more than lighter sanctions did.

"Punishment is very effective in suppressing crime, and it does not have to be severe if you get on them early enough," says Mednick. "The way to reduce prison populations is to punish offenders from their first offense with graduated, increasingly severe and certain sanctions. But the records show we do not do that in America." Mednick compared the Danish criminals to those in Marvin Wolfgang's Philadelphia cohort studies. The Philadelphia figures confirmed the effectiveness of punishment, but he also found that only 14 percent of the four- and five-time offenders in the Philadelphia cohorts were punished, compared with 60 percent of those in Denmark.

"The big problem with our handling of criminals in America is that they're not punished," he wrote. "People are usually surprised to hear that, because of all our prisons. But the fact is by the time a guy makes his way to jail, that's very often his first punishment. And he usually has committed 15 offenses by then. He might have been arrested 10 times. In Philadelphia, the kids committed huge numbers of offenses, and serious ones, and nothing happened. They just laughed. Our laws provide severe punishments, but . . . they deter not the criminals but the judges. They don't want to throw a kid who's done some little thing in jail, so they just let him go."

7. *Prisons work, and they are a relative bargain.*

Critics of incarceration claim it has failed because about two-thirds of those released soon land back behind bars. But these studies begin with a batch of released convicts, and each batch contains a high proportion of repeaters who cycle through the revolving doors of justice. Moreover, criminologists have found that these hard-core repeaters get away with a dozen or more serious crimes for every arrest. But two-thirds to three-fourths of criminals sent to prison for the first time never return.

One study that tracked the careers of 6,310 California prisoners released in 1962–63 revealed a shocking picture. These were hard-core criminals: 56 percent had been in prison before, and 44 percent served time for violent crimes, burglary, or robbery. Over the next 26 years, these convicts were arrested 30,464 times, and were probably responsible for more than a quarter-million unsolved crimes. More than half the arrests were nuisance offenses such as parole violations, drunk driving, and disorderly conduct. But the ex-cons were also arrested for about 10,000 serious crimes, including 184 homicides, 2,084 assaults, 126 kidnappings, 144 rapes, 2,756 burglaries, 655 auto thefts, and 1,193 robberies. California could have kept all 5,192 second-termers locked away for an estimated cost of only $2.1 billion—a real bargain in public safety.

Patrick A. Langan, a statistician at the U.S. Department of Justice, calculates that, by doubling the number of criminals in prison from 1973 to 1982, the United States reduced reported crime by 10 to 20 percent. This amounted to 66,000 to 190,000 fewer robberies and 350,000 to 900,000 fewer burglaries in 1982 alone. By tripling the prison population from 1975 to 1989, Langan estimates, we prevented 390,000 murders, rapes, robberies, and aggravated assaults just in 1989.

California tripled its prison population in the decade after 1984—and achieved a significant drop in the rates of reported crime from its peak in 1980–81. Bucking nationwide trends, by 1993 California had reduced murders by 10.4 percent, rapes by 36 percent, and burglaries by a whopping 43 percent. By the 1990s, that meant nearly 1,000 fewer murders, 16,000 fewer robberies, and a quarter of a million fewer burglaries yearly. The overall serious crime rate fell 14 percent.

The American public is catching on. In 1990, Oregon voters passed, by a margin of three to one, an anti-crime initiative that requires a criminal convicted of a second violent offense to serve his entire sentence with no parole. In November 1993, voters in Washington state passed by a similar margin a "three strikes and you're out" law, which imposes automatic life sentences for three-time felony convicts. Within two years, 14 states altogether and Congress had adopted such laws.

California has been a leader in the "three strikes" movement. The state automatically doubles the sentence for a felon with a prior conviction for a serious or violent felony. A third felony of any sort can trigger a life sentence, with eligibility for parole after 25 years. Philip J. Romero, Governor Pete Wilson's chief economist, estimates that the new law will add an extra 8,300 convicts a year to the state's prison population and will cost $6.5 billion for new prisons in the first five years—but will save society $23 billion net in crime prevented. A Rand study concluded that the new California law, if fully implemented, will cut serious felonies committed by adults between 22 and 34 percent.

In 1994, the American Legislative Exchange Council, the largest bipartisan association of state legislators, published a stunning analysis of prison populations and crime rates in all 50 states. The 10 states that increased their prison populations the most in relation to serious crimes between 1980 and 1992 cut their crime rates by an average of 19 percent. Meanwhile, the 10 states with the smallest increases in incarceration rates saw their crime rates go up by 9 percent on average.

In the 1980s, New Hampshire's legislature executed one of the sharpest policy reversals in the nation. For 20 years, legislators had added little new prison capacity, and the imprisonment rate—the number of prisoners per 1,000 crimes—declined by more than 80 percent, the third sharpest decline of any state. Meanwhile crime had soared by 579 percent, the highest increase in the nation.

All that changed after convicted killer Edward Coolidge, while serving a prison sentence of 25 to 40 years, was released after 18 years with "time off for good behavior." Coolidge had murdered Pamela Mason, a teenaged baby-sitter, and left her abused body in a snow bank. Outraged at his early release, Mason's family started a statewide petition drive for a "truth in sentencing" law to require convicts to serve their minimum sentences in full. Legislators passed the law in 1984 and appropriated $65 million for new prison construction. As a result, New Hampshire increased its incarceration rate between 1980 and 1992 more than any state. In the meantime, crime declined by 34 percent, the steepest drop in the nation.

8. Families are the first line of defense, and we now know how to target and help children raised in our "cradles of crime."

Experts agree that criminal behavior patterns crystallize by the age of eight, and sometimes much sooner. After age eight, youngsters are less likely to respond to correctional treatment as they gravitate toward truancy, street gangs, violent crime, and prison or early death. In Bellingham, Washington, Detective Steve Lance, who directs a police unit that targets serious habitual offenders who are juveniles, echoes: "If we wait until they're eight, it's too late. We've got to get them when they're *two*."

Dozens of scientific studies back up the cop's street wisdom. For 60 years, criminologists and psychologists have tracked thousands of youngsters from early childhood into their adult years, identifying the risk factors and early warning signs of delinquency and persistent crime. In recent decades, they have carefully evaluated various early interventions and correctional treatments, comparing treated youngsters to matched groups of untreated ones, winnowing what works and what doesn't. Today we know that the typical "cradles of crime" are households headed by poor unwed mothers who bore their first children as teenagers and live on welfare, usually in public housing with others like them, with few law-abiding, employed male role models among them. Seventy percent of the juvenile offenders in our state reform institutions grew up in a household with only one parent or no parent at all. Children whose mothers are teenagers when they are born have a 10.3 percent chance of landing in jail as juveniles, triple that of children whose mothers bore them between the ages of 20 and 23.

A number of early-childhood intervention programs have been shown to knock many high-risk youngsters off the track to crime, prison, and possible early violent death:

New York. Syracuse University's Family Development Research Program experimented with a concentrated five-year child-care program for the group at highest risk for child-abuse and neglect complaints: poor, mostly single, pregnant teenagers who had not completed high school. Sixty-five of the women received prenatal health care and two years of weekly home visits by specialists who taught parenting skills, provided counseling in employment and education, and encouraged friends and family to help. Until their children entered public school, they received free day care at the University Children's Center, which aims to develop children's intellectual abilities.

At age 15, the delinquency rate of these kids was 89 percent lower than that of a control group. Moreover, the few who had tangled with the law committed less serious and fewer offenses than their counterparts. The untreated youngsters had cost the criminal-justice system alone —excluding injuries or property losses to victims—$1,985 apiece, compared with $186 per treated child.

Michigan. David Weikart, a University of Michigan doctoral candidate, randomly chose for a two-year enrichment program 58 three- and four-year-old black children from a poor Ypsilanti neighborhood with a terrible school failure rate. The program kids attended daily two-hour classes in small groups with a specialist in the teaching of language through play. Counselors visited their homes weekly to reinforce class activities and to teach the mothers parenting skills.

By the time they turned 27, the preschooled group earned higher grades and were more likely to have graduated, found well-paying jobs, and formed stable families than those in a control group. Even more sensational, the preschooled group averaged half the arrests of the control group, and only a fifth as many had been arrested five or more times. For every $1 spent on early enrichment, taxpayers realized $7.16 in benefits, mostly in savings from crimes prevented.

Quebec. Richard Trembley, a psychologist from the University of Montreal, tracked 104 of the most disruptive boys from 53 kindergartens. He gave 46 of the boys and their families two years of special training. Parents on average took part in 20 one-hour sessions in how to monitor their children's behavior, praise and punish effectively, and handle family crises. Their boys got 19 sessions in how to make friends, invite others to play, handle anger, respond to rejection and teasing, and follow rules. Five years later, when the boys were 12, the proportion of those who had been involved in gang mischief, a precursor of serious delinquency, was one-tenth that of the untreated youths.

The popular "Head Start" program was also modeled on the Ypsilanti experiment's successes. But, says James Q. Wilson, a political scientist at UCLA, bureaucrats and policymakers "stripped it down to the part that was the most popular, least expensive, and easiest to run, namely, preschool education. Absent from much of Head Start are the high teacher-to-child caseloads, the extensive home visits, and the elaborate parent training—the very things that probably account for much of the success of these programs."

A NATIONAL STRATEGY

In outline, a strategy for reducing crime through prevention and punishment would look like this: We should identify the families—mostly households started by unwed teenage mothers—that are likely to be "cradles of crime." For a modest investment, we can sharply reduce the likelihood that their children will engage in persistent criminality by providing educational enrichment, parenting advice, and training in disciplined behavior. In pre-school or first or second grades, we can apply screening techniques at school to find those youngsters with a high risk of troubled futures. At the first contact with police, we should begin keeping permanent records. At the second offense, at the latest, we should bring to bear our best efforts at intensive supervision and family intervention, and impose the first of a series of unequivocal and escalating sanctions. Jailing serious three-time offenders would be a prudent alternative to suffering the millions of crimes habitual criminals perpetrate each year. We should insist that police and prosecutors learn to identify and pursue repeat offenders aggressively. We should hold judges and parole boards accountable for sentencing and incarcerating those felons for whom intervention has come too late, and we should not shrink from investing in the prison space needed to keep recidivists off the streets for good.

It is both humane and smart to turn delinquent youngsters away from a path of crime early, but in cases where all these efforts ultimately fail, in the words of the late sociologist Robert Martinson, "Lock 'em up and weld the door shut!" Our crime rates will plummet.

NO

David Shichor

THREE STRIKES AS A PUBLIC POLICY

This article analyzes the theoretical principles of the recently legislated "three strikes and you're out" laws. In many respects, these are related to the "new penology" that shifted the focus of criminological and penological interest from the individual offender toward the control of aggregates. Furthermore, the analysis relates the three-strikes measures to the cultural model of the "McDonaldization" of society in which the principles of the fast-food restaurant dominate many aspects of American society. These principles include efficiency, calculability, predictability, and control mainly by nonhuman technology. The analysis in this article, which focuses especially on the three-strikes law in California, suggests that three-strikes laws can be viewed as a part of the McDonaldization trend.

INTRODUCTION

Street crime has become one of the major public concerns in the United States during the past two decades. In response to it, several "war on crime" campaigns have been waged since the 1970s, and there is a growing public demand to get "tough on crime" and to get even tougher on violent and repeating criminals.... In the spring of 1994, the U.S. prison population passed the 1 million mark and the nation gained the dubious honor of having the highest incarceration rate in the world. By 1996, the U.S. jail and prison population was around the 1.5 million mark.

... [T]he Violent Crime Control and Law Enforcement Act, also known as the Federal Crime Bill, was enacted by Congress [in 1994]. Among other things, this law "mandates life in prison for criminals convicted of three violent felonies or drug offenses if the third conviction is a federal crime." It became labeled, using the popular baseball lingo, as the "three strikes and you're out" law. Several states followed suit and enacted similar measures. One of those mentioned most often was the California mandatory sentencing law, which came into effect in March 1994 and prescribes that "felons found guilty of a third serious crime be locked up for 25 years to life." ...

From David Shichor, "Three Strikes as a Public Policy: The Convergence of the New Penology and the McDonaldization of Punishment," *Crime and Delinquency*, vol. 43, no. 4 (September 1997). Copyright © 1997 by Sage Publications, Inc. Reprinted by permission. Notes and some references omitted.

This article focuses on the "three-strikes" laws in general with particular emphasis on the California measure because that law has been the most scrutinized and quoted in the professional literature so far. Although there are differences in some of details among the various three-strikes laws, their main aims and principles are similar.

Several scholars maintain that recent penal thinking and the ensuing policies have gone through a major paradigm change. According to them, a "new penology" has emerged shifting the traditional penological concern that focused on the individual offender to an actuarial model focusing on the management of aggregates....

The analysis to follow examines three-strikes laws in relation to the new penology and in relation to their connections to a more general sociocultural orientation, identified by Ritzer (1993) as the "McDonaldization" of society, based on the rationalization process suggested by Max Weber (one of the pioneers of sociological thought), that is embodied in the model of fast-food restaurants....

THREE STRIKES AND THE NEW PENOLOGY

...The change from penal policies aimed at punishment and rehabilitation of individuals to the management and control of certain categories of people has followed the pessimism expressed about the criminal justice system's ability to change offenders, making them into law-abiding citizens. In this vein, Bottoms noted that "the abandonment of the rehabilitative ethic has led to a widespread abandonment of hope" because the idea of rehabilitation was an expression of optimism about human nature and about the ability of social organizations to bring out the positive in people. The new penology takes for granted that a high level of criminal behavior will continue to occur, and its concern is how to manage the criminal justice system efficiently rather than to effect major changes in crime rates or to bring about rehabilitation of a significant number of offenders.

The new penology has rekindled the historical notion of "dangerous classes" that traditionally has been linked to the urban poor. Feeley and Simon (1992) claimed that the new penology is oriented toward the management of a "permanently dangerous population." Their description of this population parallels Wilson's (1987) depiction of the "underclass," which, because of the social realities of capitalist industrial societies in which production is based on a high level of technology and a reduction of manual labor, became a marginal population, unemployable, lacking in adequate education and marketable skills, and without any real prospects or hope to change its situation....

The new penal approach, focusing on the control and management of specific aggregates, has made increasing use of actuarial methods that rely heavily on statistical decision theory, operations research techniques, and system analysis to devise and implement penal policies. These reflect the positivist orientation in criminology that concentrates on "methods, techniques, or rules of procedure" rather than on "substantive theory or perspectives."...

Three-strikes laws have historical roots in American penology.... They are based on the penal principle of incapacitation.... In theory, three-strikes laws were meant to target repeating violent and dangerous felons, similar to "selective incapacitation" strategies....

Simon and Feeley (1994) criticized the three-strikes measures, stating, "This spate of three-strikes laws as well as other types of mandatory sentences can easily be characterized as mindless 'spending sprees' or 'throwing money at a problem' without likelihood of benefit."...

THE MCDONALDIZATION OF PUNISHMENT

In a recent book, Ritzer (1993) used the analogy of fast-food establishments to characterize and analyze the social and cultural ethos of modern technological societies, particularly that of the United States. He defined McDonaldization as "the process by which the principles of the fast-food restaurant are coming to dominate more and more sectors of American society as well as the rest of the world." This process also has a major impact on the social control policies of these societies. The theoretical underpinnings of the three-strikes measures, their definitions of strikeable offenses, and the wide-scale public support of these types of legislation are closely related to, and are influenced by, McDonaldazation.

In this model, which is based on the Weberian concept of "formal rationality" (Weber 1968), there are four basic dimensions of the fast-food industry: efficiency, calculability, predictability, and control. Efficiency refers to the tendency to choose the optimum means to a given end, calculability is identified as the tendency to quantify and calculate every product and to use quantity as a measure of quality, predictability has to do with the preference to know what to expect in all situations at all times, and control involves the replacement of human technology with nonhuman technology in a way that goods, services, products, and workers are better controlled. Ritzer (1993) suggested that there are various degrees of McDonaldization and that some phenomena are more McDonaldized than others. As mentioned previously, the contention of this article is that three-strikes laws are promoting punishment policies in accordance with this model....

THE IRRATIONAL CONSEQUENCES OF MCDONALDIZATION IN PENOLOGY

Three-strikes laws and McDonaldization are phenomena of modernization that put a high value on rationality. However, although McDonaldization represents rationalism (i.e., scientific approach, positivism, modernity), it also leads to irrational consequences. Borrowing from Weber's concept of the "iron cage of rationality," Ritzer referred to these consequences as the "irrationality of rationality." In the case of McDonaldization, irrationalities may result in inefficiency, incalculability, unpredictability, and lack of control, which may have serious effects on penal policies and practices.

Inefficiency
One of the inefficiencies of fast-food sites is that although they are meant to be "fast," often long lines of people have to wait to be served (Ritzer 1993). In the criminal justice system, three-strikes laws contribute to the clogging up of courts and the overcrowding of confinement facilities. The measure also seems to have had a major impact on the number of cases that go to trial. In California before the new law came into effect in March

1994, about 90% to 94% of all criminal cases were settled through plea bargaining. But in the summer of that year, Santa Clara County projected a 160% increase in the number of criminal trials. In an assessment of the preliminary impacts of the three-strikes implementation for the first eight months, the California Legislative Analyst's Office (1995b) found a 144% increase in jury trials in Los Angeles County. In San Diego County, it is expected that there will be a 300% increase in jury trials. The decline in plea bargaining is the result of the mandatory aspect of the three-strikes law. Many offenders feel that they cannot gain much from a negotiated settlement under the new law and that it is preferable to exercise their constitutional right to jury trials without increasing their risks of substantially more severe sentences. The increase in the number of trials not only has affected the three-strikes cases but also has caused delays in nonstrike criminal and civil cases. For example, Los Angeles district attorney transferred a large number of attorneys who previously were handling white-collar cases to work on three-strikes offenses.

The growing backlog in the courts also has had an impact on county jails because more suspects are detained for longer periods of time prior to their trials....

Another efficiency issue is concerned with the type of offenders handled by the three-strikes law. This law was enacted to curb violent crime, or at least "serious" crime, through the incapacitation of "dangerous" and violent criminals. However, early findings in California indicate that most offenders prosecuted and convicted under this measure have been brought into the system for nonviolent offenses. Furthermore, this measure inevitably will increase the numbers of elderly inmates in prisons because of the long terms mandated in this legislation. In 1994, inmates age 50 years or older represented about 4% of the California prison population, but it was estimated that by 2005 they will constitute around 12% of the inmates....

According to all indications, the three-strikes law will increase considerably the cost of criminal justice operations because (a) more people will be detained in jails, (b) the increase in the number of trials will necessitate the building of more courts and the hiring of more judges and other court personnel, (c) the number of long-term prisoners will grow and so more prisons will have to be built, (d) the growing number of elderly prisoners will need additional (and more expensive) health care than prisons usually provide, and (e) welfare agencies will have to support a larger number of dependents of incarcerated felons for longer periods of time than ever before.

... Greenwood et al. (1994) projected that, in California, "to support the implementation of the law, total spending for higher education and other services would have to fall by more than 40 percent over the next 8 years."

Incalculability

The outcomes of three-strikes cases, which were supposedly easily calculable, often are not so....

For example, because of overcrowding of jails by detainees who were reluctant to plea bargain, many minor offenders have been released early from jail, and a large number of misdemeanants have not even been prosecuted. Thus, the calculability of punishment for minor offenders has been neglected and even sacrificed for that of three-strikes offenders. In other instances, some arrests that could have been qualified as three-strikes cases have been processed as parole violations rather than new offenses and, thus, were not considered as felonies. In other cases, prosecutors and judges have ignored some previous felonies or redefined them as nonstrike offenses....

[L]ittle concern has been paid to the concept of justice that requires a balance between the seriousness of the crime and the severity of punishment. In 1994, a California offender was sentenced to prison for 25 years to life for grabbing a slice of pepperoni pizza from a youngster (this sentence was reduced in January 1997, and he will be released by 1999). Another offender received 30 years to life for stealing a video recorder and a coin collection. Still another three-striker got 25 years to life for stealing a package of meat worth $5.62, apparently to feed his family. More recently, a heroin addict with a record of previous theft-related offenses was sentenced to 25 years to life for stealing two pair of jeans worth $80 from a store.... Similarly, another aspect of justice, equal treatment, is being neglected because three-strikes measures focus almost exclusively on street crimes that usually are committed by poor offenders. Meanwhile, crimes of the middle and upper classes either are not affected or will be handled even more leniently than before because the criminal justice system that is overoccupied by predatory street crimes will have diminishing resources to deal with them.... Thus, the implementation of this measure will increase perceptions, which already are pervasive among many, that the criminal justice system is biased, discriminatory, and unjust.

Another factor that adds to the incalculability of this measure is that it is not applied uniformly. Data pertaining to the first six months of implementation compiled by the Los Angeles Public Defender's Office indicate that minorities with criminal histories comparable to those of White offenders were being charged under the three-strikes law at 17 times the rate of Whites....

Unpredictability

Several of the issues concerning predictability resemble those that emerged in relation to efficiency and calculability. For various reasons, the outcomes of three-strikes cases are not as clearly predictable as they were intended to be, based on this law's mandatory and determinate nature. For example, in some instances victims refuse to testify when the convictions would carry sentences of long-term incarceration under the three-strikes law. In other cases, juries may fail to convict for the same reason....

[B]ecause of jail overcrowding caused by the growing numbers of detainees waiting for trials, many sheriff departments release minor offenders early to ease the situation. Sometimes this is done because of court orders that limit facility crowding. According to court sources, in Los Angeles County, misdemeanor offenders sentenced to one year in jail are serving on the average only 19 days. Thus, the implementation of the three-strikes law, instead of increasing the predictability of punishment, may have an opposite impact in nonstrike cases. Moreover,... the outcome of a case under this law may be entirely different from what was foreseen because juries may refuse to convict, authorities may refuse to press a felony charge, or the courts may not count previous felonies. Also, by decreasing considerably the number of plea bargains and by increasing the number of jury trials, a larger number of outcomes may become unpredictable.

Although plea bargaining should not be considered as the best method of dispensing justice, it does provide a certain level of predictability....

[T]hree-strikes laws cannot predict, and are not interested in predicting, the effects of the punishment on individual convicts, and they may waste a great deal of money, time, and effort on false positives by keeping those who would not cause further harm to society incarcerated for long periods of time.... Three-strikes legislation was based on the assumption that the high rate of criminal behavior of "dangerous" offenders already has been proven; however, many times it is dependent on how the offenders' criminal records are being used by the prosecution and the courts....

Lack of Control
Rational systems often can spin out of the control of those who devise and use them (Ritzer 1993). Sentencing based on an almost automatic decision-making system drastically reduces the court's authority to consider particular circumstances of offenses and individual differences among offenders. However, there are experts who maintain that to render a high quality of justice, a certain degree of judicial discretion is essential....

There also is the issue of "hidden discretion"; that is, whereas the court's decision-making power in the imposition of punishment is severely curtailed, the discretion of law enforcement, and especially that of the prosecution, increases greatly. The charges brought against a suspect will be determined by these agencies. The major discretionary decision in many instances will be whether a case should be filed as a misdemeanor or a felony, which bears directly on the ap-

plication of three-strikes laws.... [T]he ability of the judicial system to control the imposition and administration of the law will be affected. In many instances, the lack of control will stem not from the latitude in sentencing but rather from the growing discretionary powers given to agencies in the pretrial stages of the criminal justice process. Because of the reduced visibility of decision making in the determination of charges, in many cases sentencing disparities among jurisdictions may become even greater in spite of the promise of increased control over such differences under three-strikes laws.

...Many three-strikes cases involve property offenders and drug abusers rather than vicious, violent criminals....

CONCLUSION

The three-strikes laws that have spread recently in the United States are a reaction to a moral panic that has swept the country since the late 1970s. On the public policy level, these measures can be viewed as being related to the new penology trend. They are based on the concern for managing aggregates of "dangerous" people rather than being concerned with rendering justice, protecting the community, or attempting to rehabilitate individual offenders. The emphasis is on rational criminal justice operations that apply management methods based on statistical estimates of patterns of crimes and future inmate populations, risk indicators of future criminal behavior, operations research, and system analysis.

Three-strikes laws also are in line with the modern sociocultural ethos of McDonaldization (Ritzer 1993), a model built on the principles of rationality embodying an attitude that "it is possible to calculate and purposively manipulate the environment." However, the quest for extreme rationality can lead to irrationalities in the practical workings of this model. Often, the application of three-strikes laws results in inefficiency of the criminal justice process, punishments are not always clearly calculable, predictability of outcomes may be negatively affected by rational procedures, and the system may lose control over the nature of punishment. In short, as is the case with many other public policies, three-strikes laws could lead to a host of unintended consequences that may defeat the purposes for which they were intended. Probably, the greatest irrationality of the penal policy represented by three-strikes laws is their tremendous economic cost.... In sum, it seems that, as Ritzer claimed, modern contemporary society is locked into the "iron cage of rationality," which is characterized by policies made on a rational basis that lead to irrational consequences. This is demonstrated in current penal policies.

REFERENCES

Greenwood, Peter W., C. Peter Rydell, Allan F. Abrahamse, Jonathan P. Caulkins, James Chiesa, Karyn E. Model, and Stephen P. Klein. 1994 *Three Strikes and You're Out: Estimated Benefits and Costs of California's New Mandatory Sentencing Law.* Santa Monica, CA: RAND.

Irwin, John and James Austin. 1994. *It Is About Time: America's Imprisonment Binge.* Belmont, CA: Wadsworth.

Kramer, John H. and Jeffery T. Ulmer. 1996. "Sentencing Disparity and Departures From Guidelines." *Justice Quarterly* 13:81–105.

McCarthy, Nancy. 1995. "A Year Later, '3 Strikes' Clogs Jails, Slows Trials." *California Bar Journal,* March: 1, 6–7.

Ritzer, George. 1993. *The McDonaldization of Society.* Newbury Park, CA: Pine Forge.

Saint-Germain, Michelle A. and Robert A. Calamia. 1996. "Three Strikes and You're In: A Streams and Windows Model Incremental Policy Change." *Journal of Criminal Justice* 24:57–70.

Shichor, David and Dale K. Sechrest. 1996. "Three Strikes as Public Policy: Future Implications." Pp. 265–77 in *Three Strikes and You're Out: Vengeance as Public Policy,* edited by D. Shichor and D. K. Sechrest. Thousand Oaks, CA: Sage.

Turner, Michael G., Jody L. Sundt, Brandon K. Applegate, and Francis T. Cullen. 1995. " 'Three Strikes and You're Out' Legislation: A National Assessment." *Federal Probation* 59 (3): 16–35.

Weber, Max. 1968. *Economy and Society.* Totowa, NJ: Bedminster.

POSTSCRIPT

Does Three Strikes and Other
Tough Approaches Work?

Before three strikes, most states already had provisions for enhancing sentences for those with prior serious convictions. However, with the passage of three strikes, life or lengthy sentences after a third violent felony conviction became mandatory. However, exactly which felonies are "third strikeable"; the number of inmates incarcerated under this mandate; negative consequences such as jail overcrowding due to offenders opting to go to trial instead of plea bargaining, which would automatically result in life or lengthy sentences with no hope of parole; and the reluctance of prosecutors to charge offenders who might face life after committing a relatively minor felony are remarkably inconsistent from state to state.

The two states that initially passed three strikes, Washington and California, have had radically different experiences. For example, Washington has had only 86 inmates incarcerated under this provision, while California has had over 26,000. The issue of fairness of law is self-evident from these statistics as well as racial, economic, and other disparities identified by Shichor. Yet defenders of three strikes point out that in a democracy, citizens have a right to pass legislation that they feel will protect them. Even if there are extreme cases, such as receiving a life sentence for stealing a slice of pizza, people still have that right.

Some suggest that criminologists who ridicule the severity of assaults are being arrogant by trivializing possible harms experienced by those whose personal space was invaded. Moreover, the examples that Methvin cites of horrible crimes committed by individuals with several prior, equally terrible felonies—who, if three strikes had been applied, could not have done additional harm—can easily be multiplied. They would probably far exceed the examples that Shichor gives of life sentences resulting from "minor" acts of violence.

Two striking cases involving repeat offenders include the 1994 murder of 7-year-old Megan Kanga by two-time convicted offender Jesse Timmendequas and the 1978 case in which violent felon Lawrence Singleton chopped off a 15-year-old California girl's arms after raping her. He served less than 10 years and was recently convicted of first-degree murder in Florida. These cases are troubling. What may be equally troubling, however, as Shichor illustrates, is that a significant number of "striked" criminals (at least in California) were not convicted on their third offense of *violent* felonies. Moreover, thus far it is unclear whether or not the policy has resulted in a net lowering of crime rates. Most studies indicate that the law, its applications, and its consequences are uneven.

Excellent overviews of this topic are "Three Strikes and You're Out: A Review of State Legislation," by J. Clark et al., *National Institute of Justice* (September 1997); "Striking Out: The Crime Control Impact of 'Three-Strikes' Laws," by V. Schiraldi and T. Ambrosio, *The Justice Policy Institute* (March 1997); *Three Strikes and You're Out: Vengeance as Public Policy* edited by D. Shichor and E. K. Sechrest (Sage Publications, 1996); and *The Tough-On-Crime Myth* by P. Elikann (Plenum, 1996).

Another helpful study is "Assessing Public Support for Three-Strikes-and-You're-Out Laws," by F. Cullen et al., *Crime and Delinquency* (October 1996). Sources agreeing with Methvin are B. Jones, "California's Three-Strikes Law Has Made Big Cuts in Crime," *The New York Times* (April 20, 1995) and *Body Count* by J. DiIulio, Jr., et al. (Simon & Schuster, 1996). An earlier study often cited and highly critical of the cost factor is *Three Strikes and You're Out* by P. W. Greenwood et al. (Rand, 1994). For a critique of mandatory sentencing, see *A Rage to Punish: The Unintended Consequences of Mandatory Sentencing* by L. Forer (W. W. Norton, 1994). For a critique of the get-tough movement, see "Science and the Punishment/Control Movement," by T. Clear, *Social Pathology* (Spring 1996). For an update of his thesis, see G. Ritzer's *The McDonaldization Thesis: Explorations and Extensions* (Sage Publications, 1998). For charges that the National Institute of Justice (NIJ) censored a critical study of the three-strikes policy, see S. Glass, "Anatomy of a Policy Fraud," *The New Republic* (November 17, 1997).

ISSUE 14

Should Partial Identifications Be Accepted in Police Lineups?

YES: A. M. Levi and Noam Jungman, from "The Police Lineup: Basic Weaknesses, Radical Solutions," *Criminal Justice and Behavior* (December 1995)

NO: Michael R. Leippe and Gary L. Wells, from "Should We Be Partial to Partial Identification? Commentary on the Levi-Jungman Proposal," *Criminal Justice and Behavior* (December 1995)

ISSUE SUMMARY

YES: A. M. Levi and Noam Jungman, of the Division of Identification and Forensic Sciences at the Israel Police Headquarters in Jerusalem, identify several serious flaws in existing police lineup procedures and propose novel remedies, including the allowance of partial identifications.

NO: Psychological researcher Michael R. Leippe and psychologist Gary L. Wells applaud efforts to improve existing procedures but reject key aspects of the proposal as being unrealistic and untested.

For years moralists, writers, and criminologists have worried about how many innocent people have been incarcerated or, worse, executed. A 1987 study indicated that between 1905 and 1974, at least 23 innocent people were executed in the United States. The writer Edward Radin, drawing from a judge's estimate that 5 percent of all people sentenced are innocent, concluded in 1964 that 14,000 people are wrongfully convicted each year.

C. Ronald Huff et al. more recently updated Radin's and others' works. Utilizing extremely conservative estimates, they suggested that 99.5 percent of all those found guilty are indeed guilty. However, the seemingly insignificant 0.5 percent is misleading. For instance, in 1993, 2,848,400 U.S. citizens were charged with serious crimes. Probably 70 percent of them were convicted (1,993,880). This means that just under 10,000 innocent people were found guilty (0.5 percent of 1,993,880)! Most agree that the main source of error leading to unjust arrests, indictments, and convictions results from eyewitness identification mistakes. Indeed, Huff et al. conclude from an analysis of several published studies on the issue that such mistakes occur about 52 percent of the time.

No one knows how many people are investigated, charged, found guilty, and sentenced for crimes they did not commit. It is, like the real rate of crime itself, unknowable. However, just as we can discern trends and changes in crime and evaluate some crime control policies, so too can we get a rough fix on major sources of conviction errors. Certainly, in addition to witness mistakes, there are police errors, technological errors, court errors (especially those made by prosecutors), and intentional errors. This latter category includes police officers' framing disliked suspects, lying under oath in court ("testilying"), and fudging data, as well as district attorneys' being overzealous, if not overly ambitious.

Yet the most common source of error by far appears to lie in mistaken identification by witnesses. This, too, often results from criminal justice complicity, such as investigators' coaching witnesses during a lineup or utilizing improper lineup techniques. Moreover, witnesses themselves sometimes deliberately lie.

An important decision was handed down in 1967 in *United States v. Wade*. It was ruled that a defendant, after being indicted, was entitled to have his attorney present at police lineups in which the defendant was participating. While that case applied to federal courts, *Gilbert v. California* (1967) extended the decision to state cases. Other relevant court decisions include *United States v. Toney* (1971), in which it was ruled that even if a witness cannot identify a defendant from a photograph, the testimony is still admissible; *Simmons v. United States* (1968), which allowed the use of photographs for pretrial identification; and *United States v. Asch* (1973), which said that defendants do not have a right for an attorney to be present when witnesses make photo identifications.

The terms *lineup* and *showup* are sometimes used interchangeably. However, the former usually applies to a situation involving a defendant and several others, including additional suspects or foils (known innocents) or both. A showup usually involves one person (the suspect) being viewed by a witness (or witnesses). Generally, with some exceptions, showups are impermissible. Also, if a witness has indicated that the perpetrator of the crime was wearing a long jacket, for example, it is impermissible to have the suspect wear such a jacket to a lineup while others in the lineup do not. Furthermore, police or prosecutors at a lineup are not allowed to make suggestions to witnesses or to prompt them on who the "right" suspect is. Ideally for the prosecution, a positive identification of the suspect will be made, although a case may procede without one, allowing that the witness could be traumatized or simply unable to say for certain. Confessions, fingerprints, DNA evidence, and so on can be sufficient to obtain a conviction.

There are many permutations and combinations of the police lineup— who is in it, its format, its lighting, and so on. Although rarely discussed in criminology and even criminal justice textbooks, it remains an important tool for police and prosecutors. Yet it is admittedly a flawed tool.

As you read the following selections by A. M. Levi and Noam Jungman and by Michael R. Leippe and Gary L. Wells, consider the many delineated problems with lineups. Pay attention to the proposed solutions and their criticisms. Which do you think might be workable and fair?

YES

A. M. Levi and Noam Jungman

THE POLICE LINEUP: BASIC WEAKNESSES, RADICAL SOLUTIONS

Police lineups are an essential tool of justice but remain dangerous. Six problems still to be dealt with sufficiently are (a) the overbelief in lineup "identifications," (b) the all-or-none nature of the lineup, (c) similarity of the foils to the suspect, (d) similarity of innocent suspects to the offender, (e) failures to choose the offender, and (f) the small size of the lineup. This article discusses these problems and suggests a radical departure in procedure. The proposed method would have witnesses view more than a hundred foils, have them choose foils by their own judgment of similarity to the offender, and allow multiple choices from the lineup.

The police lineup is both the critical means of presenting eyewitness identification in court and one of the most dangerous tools of justice (Brooks, 1983). This pernicious combination has resulted in its continued use despite the recognized dangers to innocent suspects in being mistakenly chosen in the lineup. At most, the British commission headed by Lord Devlin (1976), appointed to investigate two such miscarriages of justice, recommended that the lineup not be the sole source of evidence against an accused.

A recent famous case was the trial of John Demanjuk in Israel. Demanjuk was accused of being Ivan the Terrible, a notoriously sadistic guard at one of Hitler's extermination camps. The judges were certain that Demanjuk had been a guard, but the only evidence identifying him as Ivan the Terrible was the eyewitness testimony of several survivors of the camp. He was found guilty and escaped execution on appeal only on the basis of newly discovered documentary evidence. Somehow, despite their knowledge of numerous misidentifications, three of Israel's most respected judges almost sent a man to his death.

It is small wonder, then, that jurors often err. Somehow, jurors and judges alike give undue weight to lineup identifications, convicting with little supporting evidence, no supporting evidence, or even in the face of conflicting evidence (e.g., in the cases reviewed by the Devlin Commission and the

From A. M. Levi and Noam Jungman, "The Police Lineup: Basic Weaknesses, Radical Solutions," *Criminal Justice and Behavior*, vol. 22, no. 4 (December 1995). Copyright © 1995 by Sage Publications, Inc. Reprinted by permission. Notes and references omitted.

Demanjuk case). Less discussed but also a serious problem is the failure to identify a guilty suspect from a lineup.

THE BASIC WEAKNESSES

Six sources of danger exist that have yet to be addressed sufficiently in lineup procedure: (a) the overbelief in lineup "identifications," (b) the all-or-none nature of the lineup, (c) the degree of similarity of the foils to the suspect, (d) the degree of similarity of innocent suspects to the offender, (e) failures to choose the offender, and (f) the size of the lineup. This article will suggest a radical departure from present practice to deal with them.

Overbelief in Lineup "Identification"

Judges know, and jurors can be told, that witnesses can mistakenly choose an innocent suspect in a lineup, yet both often believe the mistaken witness. Brandon and Davies (1973) listed 70 such cases of mistaken identification and pointed out that they were merely the "tip of a much larger iceberg." After all, such cases come to light only by the chance appearance of new evidence. The police do not usually search for evidence on a crime for which a suspect already has been convicted. Experimental evidence confirms a tendency to believe "identifying" witnesses, regardless of their accuracy (Wells & Leippe, 1981; Wells, Lindsay, & Ferguson, 1979).

Why is this so? Let us first remind ourselves what an "identification" actually entails. Identification requires a comparison between a mental image of the offender and a suspect who, even if he is the offender, cannot be absolutely identical to the person the witness saw. He likely will be dressed differently, have a different expression on his face, have more or less facial hair, and so on. The memory image of the face may itself change. Small wonder that we err at times in identifying even familiar people (Young, Hay, & Ellis, 1985).

Witnesses must, then, compare an image in their heads to each person in the lineup and decide whether the similarity is great enough for concluding identity (what Tulving, 1981, termed *ecphoric similarity*). Error would be reduced if we could get the witness to choose only when there was a very high degree of ecphoric similarity. A number of methods are available to influence the witness against choosing too easily, such as giving unbiased instructions (Buckhout, 1980; Hall & Ostrom, 1975; Malpass & Devine, 1981) and presenting the lineup members sequentially (Lindsay, Lea, & Fulford, 1991; Lindsay, Lea, Nosworthy, et al., 1991; Lindsay & Wells, 1985).

However, given the uncertain effect of our efforts on any particular witness (Fleet, Brigham, & Bothwell, 1987; Hilgendorf & Irving, 1978), we should be wary of pushing the witness to adopt a criterion that is too strict. Such a criterion will cause the witness to fail to choose the offender. We are faced with the problem of balancing the need to protect the innocent suspect with the need to convict the guilty one.

In addition, we have very little control over many factors that cause the witness to choose (Clifford & Davies, 1989; Malpass & Devine, 1984). Witnesses may believe, despite unbiased instructions, that the police would not bother with a lineup unless they were fairly sure that they had caught the offender (a very reality-based belief), or they may have a strong desire for revenge. Doob and Kirshenbaum (1973) suggested that the witness may act like "good" participants in psychological experiments (Orne, 1962), trying to please the police.

In sum, witnesses do not identify suspects in lineups. They choose the suspect. As Navon (1990) pointed out, "An identification of the suspect merely indicates that the suspect resembles the perpetrator" (p. 510). Surely the probability that the suspect is the perpetrator is greater if the suspect is chosen than if he is not, but we have little idea how much greater.

If this view was firmly in the mind of the triers of fact when they evaluated an eyewitness identification, they would view it with greater skepticism. Why is it not? We suggest that a major problem lies in the term *identification*. Witnesses *choose* suspects, yet we say they identify them. The Pocket Oxford dictionary defines "to identify" as to "establish absolute sameness." When witnesses testify that they have identified the suspect as the offender, judge and jury alike are led to an entirely different mental model of identification than previously discussed, a model of establishment of precise sameness. This model has a strong base in our personal experience.

Although we all make mistaken identifications, we do so rarely. We hardly ever try to identify a stranger, as witnesses do. Furthermore, as Wells et al. (1979) argued, social situations are such that if we believe that we recognize another person, it is practically nondisconfirmable. We also usually have a feeling of certainty attached to our identification. As Leippe (1980) noted, we are unaware of the degree to which recognition of faces uses a reconstructive process involving the integration of sensory information with pre-existing ideas and memories. Inferences occur so quickly that they do not enter consciousness. Thus, when a witness makes an identification claim, then the triers of fact, consulting their personal experiences, tend to believe the witness.

This belief in the witness is further strengthened by the aura of scientific accuracy attached to the lineup. The memory of the witness was tested, after all, with the suspect appearing alongside foils. An inaccurate witness would more likely choose a foil. The triers of fact neglect, it would seem, to calculate that in an eight-person lineup the suspect would be chosen by chance alone one out of eight times, or $p = .125$ (O'Hagan, 1993).

We may warn the jury. To date, instructions to the jury seem to have failed in this task (Cutler, Dexter, & Penrod, 1990; Greene, 1988), because they come too late (O'Hagan, 1993) or the proper format has yet to be devised. More to the point, our goal is not simply to increase jury skepticism of eyewitness identifications (Woocher, 1986). Achieving that goal would, in addition to decreasing the dangers to innocent suspects, allow more guilty ones to go free.

Expert testimony, on the other hand, may have some effect in sensitizing the trier of fact to the factors that influence eyewitness memory, so that only the innocent would be protected (Cutler, Dexter, & Penrod, 1989; Cutler, Penrod, & Dexter, 1989; Wells, 1986). The problem, however, is that the more we learn about those factors, the less the expert can testify with confidence. Elliott (1993) has pointed out, in the latest of the contributions to the debate on expert testimony (e.g., Loftus, 1986; McCloskey, Egeth, & McKenna, 1986), that new research evidence has increased doubts about both the reliability and validity of the results that experts have been presenting in court. Even if certain facts are true, their impact on eyewitness accuracy may be so small as to render expert testimony either quite misleading or useless. Wells (1986), in the one study that had mock jurors judge the testimony of actual "witnesses," found that even after expert testimony, 45% of the jurors believed inaccurate witnesses.

Finally, the studies testing the effectiveness of expert witnesses included only an expert for the defense. If both sides provide contesting experts, each might very well cancel out the effect of the other (McCloskey & Egeth, 1983).

The All-or-None Nature of the Lineup

A different approach might be to escape the present all (identification) or nothing (no choice or foil chosen) format of the present lineup. The present format reinforces our natural tendency to believe witnesses, even against our better judgment. The basic logic of the lineup is based on the assumption that either the eyewitness is able to identify definitely the suspect as the offender, thus choosing him or her in the lineup, or cannot identify him or her, leading to either no choice or a false choice of one of the foils. Thus a positive identification carries great weight.

In fact, of course, a positive identification can reflect anything from a chance guess to an accurate certainty. In between lies a wide range of accuracy. This range is defined by the ability of the witness to choose the offender from among foils more or less similar to the offender. An extremely accurate witness would be able to choose the offender over his twin. A less accurate witness would not, but still could choose him from a set of quite similar foils. A still less accurate one would require the foils to be rather dissimilar.

We note that in any but a chance guess an identification has some probative value, even if minor. It increases by some finite amount the probability that the suspect is the offender. However, there is quite a difference in probative value between an identification of a suspect from among quite similar foils than from quite dissimilar ones (assuming that it was not a guess). The difference is based on the likelihood that the offender is someone other than the suspect. If the witness is able to choose the suspect from quite similar foils, there are fewer people left who might be the real offender if the suspect is actually innocent.

The present lineup, however, does not differentiate between these identifications. Indeed, the range of similarity of foils can vary widely from one lineup to another. The triers of fact are given no indication of how accurate the witness is. Indeed, they are given no indication that there can be a variation in accuracy. The all-or-none nature of the lineup biases them toward viewing an identification as an all-or-none affair.

We require the possibility of demonstrating instances of less than perfect identification. These would vary in their probative value relative to the ability of a particular witness to differentiate the suspect from similar foils. The court could then be provided in some instances with near-perfect identification when witnesses chose the suspect over quite similar-looking foils, no identification when they failed to choose the suspect, and a degree of partial identification that depended on their ability to differentiate the suspect from various foils.

Lineup evidence would thus, when necessary, be presented in a manner that emphasizes that the witness's choice of the suspect was an ecphoric similarity judgment rather than an identification. We might thereby manage to reduce the weight of identification evidence to its proper size without destroying altogether its valid credibility. A proposal for accomplishing this will be proposed after other issues are discussed.

Similarity of the Foils to the Suspect

Luus and Wells (1991) argued that a fair lineup requires that all foils be selected according to their similarity to the witness's description of the culprit, not for their similarity to the suspect. The suspect often is chosen because he or she fits the description, but usually many people fit it. The purpose of the lineup is to determine whether the witness can discriminate the suspect from these others. Indeed, including foils who are similar to the suspect may reduce identifications of the guilty suspect (Lindsay, Nosworthy, Martin, & Martynuck, 1994) and even increase false choices of the innocent one (Wogalter, Marwitz, & Leonard, 1992; Wogalter, Van't Slot, & Kalsher, 1991).

Including foils who are similar to the suspect suffers from two weaknesses. On the one hand, there is no way to determine the optimal degree of specificity. Clones of the suspect, at the extreme, would make identification of a guilty suspect impossible. On the other hand, there is no way to specify which aspects of the infinite potential descriptors of the suspect should be used to select the foils.

Wells, Rydell, and Seelau (1993) recently have provided compelling evidence for the witness-description criterion. They compared it with the similarity-to-suspect method and found that although the two methods were equally effective in protecting the innocent suspect, the latter reduced identifications of the guilty one. The latter find-

ing is explained easily by the fact that the witness with poorer memory has difficulty distinguishing the offender from the similar-looking foils in the similarity-to-suspect method and therefore often chooses one of the foils instead of the offender. This same problem faces that witness in the offender-absent condition. Unable to distinguish between the similar lineup members, his choice of the innocent suspect is essentially at chance, $1/N$, where N is the number of lineup members.

The situation facing that witness in a witness-description lineup is different, but the result is the same. In most cases, at least one of the foils will be more similar to the offender than the innocent suspect is. Because the lineup members are not so similar to each other, the witness notices that the foil is most similar to the offender and chooses him or her. This is caused by the witness's tendency to choose the most similar lineup member (the principle of relative judgment; Wells, 1984). However, by chance, $1/N$ times the innocent suspect will be the most similar, and therefore he or she will be chosen. Indeed, in both conditions in Wells et al. (1993) the rate of false identifications was almost $1/N$.

Despite these points, the criterion of witness description has its adversaries. Wogalter et al. (1992) summed up the problems as follows:

> People are not fluent in describing faces and the resulting descriptions are poor (Ellis, Shepherd, & Davies, 1980; Laughery, Duval, & Wogalter, 1986; Navon, 1990; Shepherd, Davies, & Ellis, 1978).... In addition, the witness may not be thinking clearly shortly after a crime incident and may inadvertently omit or misdescribe crucial information in the verbal description. Another source of error comes from interpretation of

the witness description by other persons (e.g., police officers)... to form a lineup. Additionally, lineups may be conducted for reasons not based on a witness's verbal description. (p. 451)

We might add that there is no relationship between quality of description and identification accuracy (Pigott & Brigham, 1985). A witness may be able to recognize the offender but give a very poor description. In addition, Wogalter et al. (1992) pointed out that it may be difficult to convince the court of the fairness of a lineup in which many foils only remotely resembled the suspect. An innocent suspect who only vaguely resembled the offender might then be chosen because the rest of the lineup members looked even less like the offender. We want to protect the innocent suspect from the witness whose memory is so unclear as to be unable to note the difference. By contrast, in a similar-to-suspect lineup, that same witness would have much greater difficulty distinguishing the innocent suspect from the foils, and the suspect thus would be protected more.

One also might argue that if the suspect is actually the offender, the lineup is also unfair if the foils are very dissimilar. If the guilty suspect is chosen simply because he happened to be in the lineup instead of one of many potential innocent suspects or foils, the factual basis for the identification becomes quite strained. Put conceptually, as stated in the previous section, the witness-description method is a less stringent test of the witness's ability to discriminate between the offender and others. Thus its probative value may be considerably lower.

There is a third possibility for resolving the controversy between the two methods of foil selection, which we will detail later: Have witnesses themselves choose the foils based on their own judgment of the foils' similarity to the offender. If this can actually be done, we should escape both the problems of using the suspect as a reference point (similarity to suspect) and the problems of foils too different from the suspect (witness description).

Similarity of the Innocent Suspect to the Offender

We have noted that, in a lineup of N members, the probability that an innocent suspect will be the most similar is $1/N$, where N is the number of lineup members. With a presently respectable lineup of eight, this chance is .125, a rather high risk for an innocent suspect.

The actual risk may, of course, be less, because the witness need not choose anyone. We already have noted that we cannot calculate the relative probabilities that the witness actually will decide to choose an innocent suspect rather than decide to choose no one. Wells et al. (1993), for example, found approximately 12% false identifications with $N = 6$, for both similarity-to-suspect and witness-description lineups.

In contrast to the usual lineup, in which the witness views all members simultaneously and can directly compare them, a sequential lineup has each member viewed separately in turn. The witness then must use an absolute judgment strategy, that is, to decide for each member separately whether or not he or she is the offender. Because this method reduces the potential for using relative judgment, mistaken identifications of innocent suspects are significantly reduced (Lindsay, Lea, & Fulford, 1991; Lindsay, Lea, Nosworthy, et al., 1991; Lindsay & Wells, 1985).

Lindsay, Lea, Nosworthy, et al. (1991, Experiment 3) demonstrated that a sequential lineup reduces the effects of similarity of foils on mistaken choice of an innocent suspect. Indeed, the rate of false identification was identical for "low" and "highly similar" foils. If the innocent suspect bears only a general similarity to the offender, Lindsay, Lea, Nosworthy et al.'s finding makes excellent sense: When witnesses are forced by the sequential method to make an absolute judgment, an innocent suspect matching only the general description of the offender is no more likely to be chosen no matter what the other foils look like.

However, what if by chance the innocent suspect actually looks enough like the witness's image of the offender as to cause potential confusion, so that with appropriate motivation the witness may choose the innocent suspect? In that case, the sequential lineup will not save the suspect.

A semantic difficulty might lead us to conclude that the Lindsay, Lee, Nosworthy, et al. (1991) study already has disproved this hypothesis. They stated that "all lineup members were highly similar or only the innocent suspect was highly similar" (p. 798) to the offender. If the innocent suspect was indeed highly similar to the offender, then it would seem that the conditions of our hypothetical example have been met: Despite such high similarity, their witnesses were not confused and did not choose the innocent suspect. Unfortunately, there is no clear standardization of the quantitative meaning of highly similar, and studies tend to use the term to describe quite different similarities. Lindsay, Lea, Nosworthy, et al. (1991) chose their foils and innocent sus-

pect to be somewhat more similar to the offender than witness description but not much more: About 16 photos were chosen that fitted the "witness description," and the 8 most similar ones were chosen for the lineup (R. C. L. Lindsay, personal communication, February, 1993). We can imagine cases in which the innocent suspect was more similar to the offender, similar enough to cause confusion.

Indeed, we have every reason to expect that innocent suspects who are similar enough to the offender will be chosen by mistake in a sequential lineup. Such a lineup, after all, is very similar to testing in classical face recognition experiments. Such experiments involve showing participants slides of a number of faces (targets), and then testing their recognition of these targets when shown in a sequence that also includes new (previously unseen) ones. Any false alarm in such an experiment (i.e., mistakenly identifying a new face as a target) is a case of a participant (witness) mistaking a new (foil or innocent suspect) for an original target (offender). Goldstein, Stephenson, and Chance (1977) demonstrated that certain new faces were far more likely to be chosen, and others (Davies, Shepherd, & Ellis, 1979b; Laughery, Fessler, Lenorovitz, & Yoblick, 1974; Patterson & Badeley, 1977) have found that new faces more similar to the targets are more likely to be chosen.

The Davies et al. (1979b) study also demonstrated that the confusion between the offender and an innocent suspect does not require a very high degree of similarity. They based their study on only a hundred photos, which was not a very large sample to define high similarity between them. Although we know of no formal research on the topic, we have found (Levi, Jungman, Ginton,

Aperman, & Nobel, in press) that even the most similar photos in our experimental collection of more than 1,200 are often not very similar subjectively. Indeed, in the Davies et al. (1979b) study, examples of similarity clusters were "young men with long, thin faces and straight, short, tidy hair" and "older men with square chins, lined complexions, fat faces and short, tidy, receding hair" (p. 510).

Lindsay et al. (1994) reported similar results. Their definition of similarity was Caucasian race; age approximately 23; average body build; short, dark hair; and no facial hair or glasses—a very general, average description. When searching for the "offender" in a set of 200 photos, witnesses made more false identifications from a set of similar photos than from a random set.

We should remind ourselves, in this context, that such not-so-similar photos do not cause most witnesses confusion. The problem is that the minority who err is still too many. This is demonstrated by the sequential lineup experiments themselves (Lindsay, Lea, & Fulford, 1991; Lindsay, Lee, Nosworthy, et al., 1991; Lindsay & Wells, 1985). The median false identifications of the innocent suspect was 6.7%.

Such a risk seems at first glance to be satisfactory protection of the innocent suspect. After all, a probability of .067 is almost acceptable as a standard alpha for rejecting the null hypothesis. However, the practical risk in a standard experiment is the publication of results that will be later discredited through failure to replicate. If the dangers of error are greater, as in testing new drugs, even the .01 level would be considered too risky. When an innocent suspect is falsely identified, the increased danger of incarceration and severe social stigma

can be significant. Therefore, we would wish to set as strict an alpha as is feasible, certainly much lower than .067.

Even the .067 figure is likely an optimistic estimate of the risk, when we consider the relationship between the quality of the memory and similarity judgments. The research paradigm of Lindsay and his colleagues creates rather optimal memory conditions, with the offender engaging the witness in conversation and establishing eye contact before committing the offense and with the lineup taking place typically right afterward. However, real-life witness situations are extremely variable, often with less optimal viewing conditions and always with a longer delay. Both factors should result in some deterioration in the image (Shapiro & Penrod, 1986) and therefore decrease the ability of witnesses to differentiate between less objectively similar faces (i.e., faces that would be judged less similar if they were viewed simultaneously). With poorer memory, foils and innocent suspects need look less like the offender in order to be chosen erroneously. Thus the potential for witnesses confusing a foil or an innocent suspect with the offender may be significantly greater than the studies of sequential lineups indicate.

It would seem, then, that the sequential lineup eliminates the effect of witnesses with rather poor memory choosing an innocent suspect only superficially resembling the offender simply because he or she was the most similar among dissimilars. However, it does not seem able to deal completely with the problem of an innocent suspect who actually could be confused with the offender.

Failures to Choose the Offender

The danger of failing to choose the guilty suspect is not less critical. The sequential lineup is particularly vulnerable. An essential feature of such lineups is that the sequence ends once the witness chooses a suspect. Any foil who causes a false alarm and precedes the guilty suspect results in the lineup being terminated before the witness has a chance to see the offender. Choosing foils who are similar to the suspect could then be a dangerous tactic, because the witness could easily choose one of the similar-looking foils before seeing the (guilty) suspect.

The sequential experiments (Lindsay, Lea, & Fulford, 1991; Lindsay, Lee, Nosworthy, et al., 1991; Lindsay & Wells, 1985) do not address directly that question. Their experimental procedure diverged from operational requirements by showing each witness the entire lineup regardless of the witness's choices. However, Lindsay and Wells (1985) report that 2.5% of their witnesses chose a foil that appeared before the guilty suspect, whereas Lindsay, Lea, and Fulford (1991, Experiment 1) found that 6.7% of their witnesses did the same (R. C. L. Lindsay, personal communication, June 28, 1994). The difference in rates between the two experiments can be attributed to the earlier placement of the suspect in the Lindsay and Wells (1985) study (third or fifth position), compared with the eighth position in the later study. With more previous foils, there was more opportunity for mistakenly identifying a foil.

It would seem that the authors of the original sequential lineup article (Lindsay & Wells, 1985) do not believe that its advent has rendered the simultaneous lineup obsolete. Both have since authored articles featuring the simultaneous lineup (Nosworthy & Lindsay, 1990; Wells et al., 1993).

Size of Lineup

One of the most basic tenets of experimental methodology calls for the establishment of an acceptable risk of mistakenly rejecting the null hypothesis. Although at times, for exploratory purposes, we find references to alpha = .10, the minimum is usually, of course, .05. We have noted, however, that an innocent suspect deserves as much protection against chance error as we can provide, certainly more than 5 false identifications in 100.

In the case of the lineup, the null hypothesis is that the suspect is in fact innocent, and therefore the chance of the witness identifying the suspect if the witness chooses someone at random is no greater than choosing a foil. With a fair lineup, this probability is simply $1/N$, where N is the number of people in the lineup (Luus & Wells, 1991). A very respectable size of a police lineup today is eight, resulting in alpha = $1/8$ = .125.

We have noted above that the actual risk may, of course, be less, because the witness need not choose anyone. However, in a series of experiments following the same general research paradigm (Lindsay, Lea, & Fulford, 1991; Lindsay, Lee, Nosworthy, et al., 1991; Lindsay & Wells, 1980, 1985; Wells, 1984), witnesses did choose someone fairly often: The median choices in a suspect-absent lineup were 58% of witnesses in a simultaneous lineup, and 25% in a sequential one. If we take the latter figure, the chances of choosing the innocent suspect purely randomly in an eight-person lineup would be $1/8 \times 1/4$ = .03. The median false identifications for the sequential case was .05 in those experiments.) This would seem far too great a risk for an innocent suspect.

Although the logic of the above is elementary, we must confront the paradox of the results of Nosworthy and Lindsay (1990), on the basis of which they suggested that a lineup as small as four should be sufficient. Their experiments demonstrated that simultaneous lineups that small produced no more false identifications than lineups more than twice that size. Their experiment created very special conditions, which should not be expected to generalize to normal lineups. They selected foils that were even more similar to the offender than required by witness description, so much so that some of them were more similar to the offender than the innocent suspect was. Thus, despite the fact that a median of 33% witnesses in the offender-absent lineups chose someone in the lineup, a median of .04 false identifications of the innocent suspect were made: The foils drew the bulk of the choices, with one foil getting a full 29%.

We note also the relative low number of choices, compared to the 58% of previous experiments using a similar general paradigm. It seems that some witnesses, faced with a number of foils looking equally similar to the offender, preferred not to choose. In sum, with only .07 witnesses falsely identifying the innocent suspect in a four-person lineup, compared to a chance choice of $1/4 = .25$, there remained no room for improvement with larger lineups.

In general, the event used in all of these experiments of Lindsay and his colleagues is not quite appropriate for testing the problem of lineup size as related to alpha. We have noted that the logic of

the null hypothesis is based on a witness randomly choosing and is most appropriate for poor eyewitness conditions. We also noted that the aforementioned experiments took care to create a near-optimal (Deffenbacher, 1980) situation for identifying the offender: The offender sat with the witnesses for a few minutes, and took care to establish eye contact with them while talking to them. The witnesses then viewed the photo lineup right after the "crime." Clearly, the chances of choosing an innocent suspect decrease to the degree that the witness has a better memory of the perpetrator. It would seem, then, that we need more experimental results before adopting the counterintuitive conclusion that lineup size does not affect false identifications.

In summary, lineup practice is conflicted over the value of choosing foils similar to the suspect or fitting witness description. The sequential lineup, the state-of-the-art solution to the problem of relative similarity choices, results in too many choices of innocent suspects and causes failures to choose the guilty one. The small size of the lineup exacerbates the former problem by increasing the likelihood that by chance the innocent suspect will be the lineup member most similar to the offender and by increasing the chances that a witness with poor memory will randomly choose the innocent suspect. These factors are just some examples of why it is unreasonable to assume that a lineup identification can be considered an all-or-nothing decision. (If the witness selects the suspect, he or she is guilty.) Yet, that is what the present methods, in its all-or-nothing (selection or no selection) determination, leads the court to believe.

RADICAL SOLUTIONS

A radically different lineup will now be described to confront these various problems. The informed reader is begged to have patience with what may seem its patent absurdities until later, when they will be analyzed with care. In the proposed approach, witnesses would be told that they are to search for the offender among photos that will be presented to them on a computer screen. Their primary task is, of course, to choose the offender. However, if the offender does not appear on a particular screen, the witness is to pick photos that look the most similar to the offender from the various photos on the screen. (The optimum wording requires experimental exploration.)

The photos shown at first to the witness would be a set of photos that fits the witness's verbal description of the offender. Such photos would continue to be shown in the next sets until the witness chose at least one photo. The computer would now choose, based on its similarity network of the photos, those most similar to the photo(s) chosen by the witness. Each additional choice by the witness would continue to modify the photos displayed in the next set. The search process would not necessarily end when the witness chose an offender. Rather, the witness would be given an opportunity to choose one or more additional photos. Additional sets might be shown until it becomes obvious that all photos similar to the offender have been displayed, or a set maximum have been seen.

Let us first note the departures from current lineup practice: Although the first photos are selected as in the witness description method, the witnesses themselves, in their similarity and identification choices, select most of the photos. The witnesses view many more photos than in a standard lineup and are allowed to choose as many "identical" photos as they wish. A live lineup is no longer feasible, because we cannot gather so many foils for such a lineup. The format of the lineup is a combination of a simultaneous and sequential lineup, because more than one photo is viewed at a time but more than one screen is viewed.

Two major questions come to mind regarding this new lineup: (a) Can it be done? (b) Should it be done? We will discuss each in turn.

Our research (Levi et al., in press) indicates that it can be done. We developed a new procedure for conducting a mug shot search. The mug shot search is the most important investigative tool of the police when they have a witness but no suspect. The witness is shown photos (mug shots) from the police collection of past offenders (the police album) and is requested to choose the perpetrator. Its greatest problem is how to help the witness select a small enough set of photos to view. Albums have grown too large for every one to be viewed.

The core of the new method is similarity judgments. For the Levi et al. (in press) experiments, more than a thousand photos were coded by the senior author with respect to their overall similarity to each other. The resulting similarity network between the photos served as the infrastructure of the search process.

As in the proposed lineup, the photos first were ordered in terms of their fit to the witness's verbal description, and the 24 fitting it best were displayed on a computer screen. Witnesses were instructed to choose from each set of 24 photos on the screen those that were similar to the target. Each time a photo was chosen, the computer increased the weight of each photo in the album that was similar to it, using the similarity network. Each consecutive screen consisted of the 24 photos with the largest weights. If the similarity network was in agreement with the witness's judgment, the target was among the photos whose weights were increased, and therefore the target appeared relatively quickly. This usually occurred. Naturally, photos similar to the target appeared along with it.

Additional improvements have been added since the reported research was conducted. The computer itself now codes the photos by factor analyzing the faces (the actual pixels of the digitized image; Turk & Pentland, 1991). Minor modifications are required to fit the proposed lineup. We require a library of foils instead of mug shots. Larger weighting of photos chosen as identical should be added. We may want to program the procedure so that the suspect appears along with a specified group of foils at a particular point in the lineup regardless of the witness's choices. We might want to plant a photo very similar to the suspect in a screen before the suspect. We might want, in general, to ensure that photos similar to the suspect appear regardless of the witness's choices. Aside from these minor changes, the system is ready to accommodate the proposed lineup.

Overbelief Identification

We submit that the proposed lineup solves the six problems previously discussed while creating few and less serious new ones. The overbelief in the identification will be destroyed as soon as a witness identifies more than one

person. To identify more than one person as the same offender is, of course, a contradiction.

A present danger is that the court would jump to the opposite conclusion, that the identification is worthless. If a witness is given the opportunity to select the most relevant photos from a foil library of more than a thousand photos and chooses only one photo in addition to the suspect, the probability that the suspect is the offender is certainly considerably greater than if the witness failed to choose the suspect at all.

Judges and juries alike may require some educational input to assimilate the notion of a *partial identification*. Israeli experience suggests that the police officer introducing the evidence might be the best source of such input, although expert witnesses could be used when needed and when possible. Such identification evidence, reduced to its proper size, can then be evaluated by the court along with the other evidence to reach a decision as to the suspect's guilt or innocence.

We do not wish to minimize resistance to the new procedure. It is hard to evaluate how difficult an adjustment to the idea of a partial identification might be. A major factor is the degree to which the trier of fact is attuned to the problems attached to the notion of full identification. The more one is aware of the uncertain value of an identification in a classic lineup, the more open one would be to an alternative approach.

Another potential barrier is the law. Certain aspects of the new method may be illegal in certain countries. Some reviewers have claimed, for example, that choosing more than one person from a lineup is illegal in countries that have inherited British law. This is not so in at least one such country, Israel. We have consulted with local legal authorities and have encountered no objections to the method. However, such opinions must be gathered separately in each country. Moreover, the ultimate test is in court. Fortunately, laws change in the face of scientific progress. Until a law is changed, it might be possible simply to refrain from defining the procedure as a lineup, but rather refer to it as a new identification method.

The All-or-None Nature of the Lineup

The new method simply does away with this aspect of the lineup, by providing for partial identifications. We do not want to give the impression that partial identifications will become so common as to seriously affect eyewitness identification. We have noted earlier that very similar people are relatively rare. A library of a thousand photos need not present a witness with a good memory too difficult a challenge in discriminating an offender from the offender's most similar foils. How many witnesses tend to have a good memory is an issue that we finally will be able to determine.

The courts' attitude toward partial identifications may be influenced by their relative frequency. If they turn out to be very rare, for example, courts may find it easier to discount them. Wells et al. (1993) found that when witnesses were faced with a traditional offender-present lineup with similar foils, many chose a foil instead of the offender. The same foils in our method likely would have led to partial identifications. Thus, to judge by Wells et al.'s results, partial identifications could be quite frequent. However, Wells et al. made special efforts to find foils similar to the offender, and therefore their finding may not be typical.

Similarity of the Foils to the Suspect

The controversy between choosing foils by witness description or similarity to the suspect is sidestepped by enabling the witnesses themselves to choose the vast majority of the foils, based on the criterion of similarity to the offender. We no longer are concerned with the dangers of foils too similar to the offender once we allow the witness more than one choice. Indeed, the method actually seeks out those who are most similar, because we wish to provide witnesses with a stringent test of their ability to discriminate the suspect (if the suspect is chosen) from look-alikes. If a clone were indeed among the photos, the court, provided with the chosen photos, easily would see that the inability of the witness to differentiate between the suspect and the clone detracted very little from the identification evidence.

Similarity of the Suspect to the Offender

This problem also is much mitigated by this new approach. If indeed, due to somewhat faulty memory, witnesses confuse the suspect with the offender, they will have available a large number of foils, among which some will be found that cause similar confusion and that also will be chosen. In general, the more faulty the memory, the more foils will have to be chosen to choose the suspect as well, and with them the probative value of the identification naturally will decrease.

Allowing for multiple choices increases the chance that an innocent suspect will be chosen. However, with the larger number of photos viewed by witnesses, chosen by them from an even greater number of potential foils, the danger is much decreased. If an innocent suspect is actually similar to the offender, the suspect may be protected more. Instead of being the only one chosen, the suspect is protected by the additional choices. The larger number of photos increases the chances of even more similar foils being present and chosen instead.

Failures to Choose the Offender

The issue also is now less serious. With the possibility of more than one choice, the witness is no longer in danger of missing the offender in a sequential lineup by choosing a similar-looking foil first. Of course, if the witness chooses at least one foil in addition to the offender (and our method increases that possibility), the value of the identification will be less than if only the offender were chosen. Thus the offender also may be protected more. However, the protection offered by the new method is what the offender fairly deserves. If a witness confuses the suspect with many foils, the court should be made aware of the limited value of the identification evidence.

Size of Lineup

The problem of the limited size of the lineup is resolved by the fact that its size has been increased significantly. We must, of course, distinguish between the size of the foil library (more than a thousand) and the size of the lineup—the number of photos the witness actually will view —which will be less, but certainly more than a hundred. The chances of choosing only the innocent suspect have been reduced significantly.

If, on the other hand, the witness chooses from more than a thousand photos the suspect and only the suspect, the court will have stronger evidence than presently available that the suspect is indeed guilty. The new lineup method is not, then, simply a strategy for increasing skepticism in identification evidence. Rather, it differentiates various degrees of probative value. Indeed, the strategy is one of increasing similarity of foils within the bounds of their natural occurrence to provide a stringent test of the witness's ability to differentiate the suspect, if the suspect is the offender, from others. This technique is similar to many tests of skill that are purposely made difficult to differentiate various levels of proficiency.

Is it realistic to expect any witness to manage to differentiate the guilty suspect from more than a thousand other photos while viewing a few hundred of them? Indeed, has the witness a fair chance of even choosing the guilty suspect? Regarding the ability to differentiate, it will depend on both the witness's memory and the similarity of the photos, with the distinctiveness of the offender playing a role. Lindsay et al. (1994) found that few false identifications were made in mug shot searches, despite instructions that encouraged such choices. We (Levi & Jungman, 1994) found even fewer with, as Lindsay et al. (1994) found, the vast majority of incorrect choices being made by very few witnesses. However, both studies used albums much smaller than operational ones. It may be that in field conditions, with poorer memory conditions and the greater likelihood of more similar-looking photos being available, fewer witnesses will be able to differentiate the guilty suspect from all others.

Regarding the effect of seeing a few hundred photos on identifying the suspect, we are much more optimistic despite certain empirical evidence. Laughery, Alexander, and Lane (1971) found reductions in identifications of a target if it was placed in the 140th position of what was essentially a sequential photo lineup, compared to the 40th place. Davies, Shepherd, and Ellis (1979a) reported reductions in identifications of targets between the 100th position and the 136th, compared to targets placed up to the 34th position. That evidence indicates that the suspect should not be placed much further than the 40th position (Brooks, 1983). However, although Lindsay et al. (1994) found reductions from the 100th to the 500th position, they did not find such reductions from the 100th to the 300th. Similarly, Ellis, Shepherd, Flin, Shepherd, and Davies (1989) obtained reductions from the 97th to the 649th position, but not to the 353rd.

This latter evidence suggests that the reductions found to date may be a function of the experimental methods used. What might happen, for example, if witnesses were given a rest break after each set of 50 pictures? What might happen if witnesses were required, in addition to choosing the offender, to choose photos that were similar to the offender? What would be the effect of varying the number of photos viewed per screen? In our test of the latter two questions, we (Levi & Jungman, 1994) found that either requesting witnesses to choose photos similar to the offender or having them view 24 photos per screen instead of 1 per screen eliminated the difference in identifications between the target in the 50th versus 300th position.

The issue has relevance to the extent that we might prefer allowing the suspect to appear later in the lineup. There is no problem technically in ensuring that the suspect appears relatively early, regardless of the choices of the witness. We also could ensure that particular other photos appear on the same screen to avoid any chance of the suspect standing out (Wogalter et al., 1992). We even could ensure that the witness views photos that the computer considers to be similar to the suspect. With the possibility of multiple choices, we no longer fear making the task too difficult.

Live lineups of more than a hundred are, of course, totally impractical; therefore, lineups would have to be photo or video lineups. However, despite official guidelines to the contrary (Brooks, 1983), police usually use photos already (Wogalter, Malpass, & Burger, 1993).

Reviews of the evidence indicate that little or nothing is lost in accuracy when photos and video are used (Clifford & Davies, 1989; Shepherd, Ellis, & Davies, 1982). Yuille and Cutshall (1984) found no differences among live, video, or photo lineups. Egan, Pittner, and Goldstein (1977) and Turnbull and Thompson (1984) reported live lineups to be better than photo lineups, and Cutler and Fisher (1990), Cutler, Fisher, and Chicvara (1989), and Cutler, Penrod, and Martins (1988) found comparable performance between live lineups and videotaped ones, with both being superior to photos. Dent and Gray (1975) and Dent (1977) reported three projected color slides of each lineup member to be superior to live lineups.

If the police continue to use photos, the new method will make life easier for them. The mug shot album provides a very large collection of potential foils. The computer takes over once an appropriate set of foils has been chosen (i.e., those who cannot be suspected of committing the particular crime) and the suspect has been added.

We noted that some research indicates that video lineups are superior to photo lineups. It is possible to envision that further technological advances will enable police forces to store on computer video clips of each past offender, thus improving mug file searches. Once that occurs, they also will have available a pool of video foils organized in a similarity network.

Another potential problem is the rate of choosing. If this grew with lineup size, the value of the larger lineup could be lessened. Fortunately, the evidence suggests that this does not happen (Davies et al., 1979a; Ellis et al., 1989; Laughery et al., 1971; Lindsay et al., 1994). Davies et al. and Lindsay et al. even found decreased choices among later photos.

Other Issues

In addition to those already mentioned, a number of interesting research questions are raised by the proposed new method. Research is needed to determine the best instructions for achieving the best balance between our desire for the optimal probative value (choosing only the guilty suspect) and the danger that, with too strict a choice criterion, the witness may miss the guilty suspect by not choosing anyone at all.

Other issues involve the issue of what weight the court should give to various identifications, in terms of (a) similarity between the foils and the suspect and (b) number of foils. Should any weight be given to the differing degree of confidence of a witness to various choices? (e.g., a witness may first hesitatingly pick a foil but then later reject the foil once the suspect appears, claiming great confidence that the suspect, and no other, is the offender).

These issues, however, are essentially related to fine-tuning the procedure. Unless the new method has some Achilles' heel that is hidden from the authors, it should warrant serious attention as an alternative to present lineup procedure.

NO

Michael R. Leippe
and Gary L. Wells

SHOULD WE BE PARTIAL TO PARTIAL IDENTIFICATION?

Eyewitness identification of criminal suspects from lineups and photospreads is the largest single cause of false imprisonment in the United States. Research programs have outlined experimentally proven techniques to reduce the dangers. Levi and Jungman have proposed a radial technique in which eyewitnesses choose several people from a large set of photos based on their similarity to the culprit. They argue that this will help solve many problems, including the tendency for courts to overbelieve eyewitnesses. Some problems and prospects for this new technique are discussed.

When investigation of a crime turns up both an eyewitness and a suspect, the next legal step is an identification test. Typically, the investigating police detectives will construct either a live or a photo lineup that includes the suspect and perhaps four to six known-innocent "foils." These foils, theoretically, are chosen because they match the verbal description of the perpetrator given by the eyewitness and/or because they resemble the suspect. In turn, the eyewitness is asked to examine the lineup and to indicate whether he or she recognizes any member of the lineup as the "one who did it." If the eyewitness claims such recognition of the suspect, the police have a positive identification and proceed with an arrest and charges.

There are well-documented risks of mistaken identification with this traditional lineup identification test, and procedures and techniques for minimizing such risks have been studied and proposed by a number of eyewitness researchers (see Wells, 1993, for an extensive review and discussion). Levi and Jungman... have proposed an intriguing new procedure for collecting eyewitness identification evidence that they believe would advance even further the cause of validly using eyewitness evidence. Their technique differs dramatically from the traditional lineup. Not only would the proposed technique "radically" change the task that confronts an eyewitness at the police

From Michael R. Leippe and Gary L. Wells, "Should We Be Partial to Partial Identification? Commentary on the Levi-Jungman Proposal," *Criminal Justice and Behavior*, vol. 22, no. 4 (December 1995). Copyright © 1995 by Sage Publications, Inc. Reprinted by permission. References omitted.

station, but it also would alter what the eyewitness would convey to a judge and a jury in a courtroom. Instead of viewing a limited number of faces in a lineup and making a discrete, "all-or-none" decision, the eyewitness would examine up to hundreds of faces (including that of the suspect) on a computer screen and choose any and all faces that resemble his or her memory trace of the criminal. Triers of fact, in turn, would be apprised of the quality of the eyewitness's "partial identification," which is based on such factors as whether the suspect was among the chosen, how many other faces were chosen (the fewer chosen, the stronger is the memory evidence), and how many faces were viewed in total.

This is a fascinating idea. In particular, we applaud the application of fast-developing video and computer technology to the problem of judging eyewitness memory, and we trust that the practical and scientific merit of the technique can only improve as psycholegal investigators turn their attention to it. Beyond their "radical solution," Levi and Jungman also present an important set of arguments concerning the dangers of mistaken identification and the impossibility (as they see it) of controlling those dangers *without* abandoning conventional identification procedures. Although we agree with many of the arguments and premises of Levi and Jungman, we feel that it is important to note some points of contention and to qualify some of the claims that are made about the magnitude, as well as the controllable sources, of the dangers of false identification. In addition, we have questions about the practicality and the legal status of the partial identification method.

THE "ALL-OR-NONE" ISSUE

To be sure, a lineup identification involves an all-or-none decision. The witness either does or does not "identify" a lineup member as the culprit. But does the all-or-none procedure lead jurors, police officers, and other fact finders to believe that memory is an all-or-none matter? We doubt it. Although it seems pretty clear from research that people, on average, have some faulty beliefs about how memory works and how certain variables affect eyewitness memory, and tend to overbelieve eyewitness identifications, this does not mean that they assume that all identifications are created equally valid, or that they fail to appreciate that the "match" witnesses make is between the face they see before them and their *more-or-less* clear and accurate memory image of the culprit. We know of no research on this specific question, so we would not automatically rule out that jurors are so exceptionally naive. However, neither should Levi and Jungman, without data, assume that they are. We need only look to Western common law and legal thinking in this century to see a clear appreciation that eyewitness reports vary on a continuum of likely accuracy. Consider, for instance, the *Neil v. Biggers* U.S. Supreme Court case of 1972. Although the Court's ruling can and has been faulted for the criteria that were discussed in trying to determine the likely accuracy of eyewitness identification evidence (see Wells & Murray, 1983), the very fact that criteria were discussed at all is an indication that the Court believes that not all testimony is created equally valid or invalid. Also, pattern jury instructions that are based on the same belief about witness memory abound in the U.S. states and jurisdictions. Thus there at least seems to be no legal naïveté about the all-or-none assumption.

Even if all the actors in a criminal case did subscribe to the all-or-none assumption, it is not clear that the partial identification procedure would dispel this belief or the problems it creates. Choosing the suspect as the offender may be enough for the police and prosecution to conclude definitively that "we've got our guy," even if the choosing eyewitness also picks out some other faces that "are similar to" the offender or "could be" the offender. Indeed, we can readily imagine police, prosecutors, and jurors jumping to the assumption of a "full identification" when the witness picks the suspect and a half-dozen innocents as "could bes" out of several hundred pictures. If the all-or-none belief about recognition is part of human metamemory, it will be invoked by human fact finders until the false alarms become really substantial.

THE DANGER AND THE PROCESS OF MISTAKEN IDENTIFICATION

Probability and Proper Base Rates

Levi and Jungman note that the likelihood that an innocent suspect is more similar to the actual culprit than are the other lineup members is $1/N$, where N is the number of lineup members. Hence, they argue, if a lineup identification is nothing more than a choice of the person who most looks like the culprit relative to the other members, there is an unacceptable chance (e.g., nearly 17% in a six-person lineup) of a mistaken identification. They qualify this appropriately by noting that this does not take into account that a witness need not choose anyone. However, there are other qualifications that also must be made if we are to assume that the $1/N$ figure is related meaningfully to false identification rates in actual cases. Actual probabilities of mistaken identification are highly dependent on the base rate likelihood that the sole suspect in the lineup is the actual culprit or not. Imagine, for instance, 100 lineups in which the lineup's sole suspect is the true culprit 90% of the time and is an innocent suspect only 10% of the time. In 90% of these cases, the person who is most similar to the culprit is in fact the culprit. Therefore, only 10% of the time would the suspect be innocent, and of this 10% only $1/N$ (e.g., 17%) would qualify as the most similar person. At this point, then, we have only 1.7% of the original 100 lineups for which we have to worry about the possibility that an innocent suspect will be chosen merely because the suspect is the most similar to the culprit. This 1.7% would then be further reduced by whatever proportion of witnesses make no choice or somehow decide that the actual culprit is not in the lineup. Hence it should not go unnoticed that Levi and Jungman's portrayal of the dangers of lineups is predicated on the assumption that witnesses are viewing a lineup in which the suspect is innocent. This assumption (that the actual culprit is not in the lineup) is not in itself an improper supposition on which to make a number of important observations about lineup identification dangers. However, one cannot extrapolate from this supposition to statements about the likelihood of mistaken identification in real cases without knowing the base rate likelihoods for the supposition being true in real-world cases. In fact, Wells (1993) has argued that the base rate for placing innocent versus guilty suspects in lineups may be the most critical determinant of the likelihood of false identification and that one of the key ways to lower false identification rates in real cases is to require that there be probable cause for believing that the suspect is guilty *prior* to subjecting a suspect to the risk of lineup identification.

Relative Judgments

We think that there is now good evidence to support the contention that identifications are governed at least in part by relative judgment processes, as described originally by Wells (1984). The relative judgment idea simply states that witnesses tend to choose the person who most looks like their memory of the culprit relative to the other lineup members. Levi and Jungman, however, risk leaving the impression on readers that the process is *entirely* relative. The decision on the part of the witnesses to choose someone cannot be entirely a relative judgment, however, because witnesses sometimes indicate that the culprit is not in the lineup. Because there is always someone in the lineup who looks more like the culprit than do others in the lineup, there must also be some level at which identification decisions operate on something other than this purely relative process. Accordingly, it must also be the case that an identification is more than merely a statement that someone looks like the culprit more than someone else does. There must be some criterion of sufficiency that extends beyond the mere comparison of one lineup member to another and that involves some kind of "ecphoric similarity threshold." This in no sense nullifies Levi and Jungman's general claims or speaks against the idea of their solution. Nevertheless, it would be misleading to depict lineup identifications as being nothing more than relative judgments among the options in the lineup itself, when we know that rejections of entire lineups are made frequently by both real-world and staged-crime eyewitnesses.

THE PROCEDURE

Levi and Jungman are surely not presenting a finished product for our consideration. They make it quite clear that the partial identification procedure is still very experimental, if not exploratory, and they themselves often present their ideas for the procedure more as questions to be answered (of the "what if we did this?" variety) than as data-based answers. Recognizing this early stage of development, we offer the following observations as matters that require careful consideration as development continues.

Instructional Sets and Witness Motivation

It is not at all clear just how the judgment task will be presented to witnesses. Is the witness to be instructed to pick out the offender, pick out all faces that could be the offender, or pick out all faces that resemble their image of the offender? Or all three of these? Clarity and specificity here are very important, as we know from signal detection and other memory studies that both the number of faces picked and the number of misses can be strongly affected by instructional variations. As one especially important example, consider variation in how the stringency of the criteria for picking faces is presented by the police officer administering the task. A lax standard will produce many choices of similar others, whereas a stricter standard will produce fewer selections. Yet the number of choices made is seen as one of the critical indexes for deciding just how partial—and therefore trustworthy—the eyewitness's identification is. This is problematic, of course, to the extent that instructions will vary from one police station to the next—and from one police officer to the next—making it difficult to disentangle this influence from the strength of the witness's memory. Instructions would need to be standardized. However, an open question is whether they *can* be equated for such a task, given the complexity of the task (relative to a lineup) and variations in the facial distinctiveness of the offender (see below), among other matters.

Another issue regarding instructions is their legal status, or rather, the legal status of the responses they evoke. It may be most desirable, based on the logic of the procedure, for witnesses to be prohibited from making identification. After all, once an identification is made, we are right back to the all-or-none assumption the method is designed to sidestep; moreover, the witness's decision criteria for choosing similar faces before and after making a choice are apt to be different. If specific identifications are disallowed, however, a legal question arises: Is it evidence that the suspect, now defendant, was among 20 faces that were all chosen as merely *resembling* the offender?

There is also the issue of witness motivation. If an offender can be (procedurally), and is, chosen, how motivated will the confident and retribution-minded witness be to continue to choose similar faces (and thus weaken the impact of his or her identification) relative to the witness who is less confident or not especially hell-bent on getting someone "to pay for this crime"?

Similarity and Distinctiveness
An important claim of the Levi-Jungman procedure is that an innocent suspect benefits because "instead of being the only one chosen, the suspect is protected by the additional choices" (p. 365). However, if an innocent suspect happens to both closely resemble the offender and share a highly distinctive face with the offender, such "safety in numbers" is unlikely. Few additional choices will be made under these circumstances. In effect, the same danger inherent in traditional lineups is also a danger here. Paradoxically, though, the danger to the distinctive innocent suspect is potentially *greater* with the Levi-Jungman procedure. In this case, not only do the police and jurors receive a positive identification, but they also, at the extreme, could be informed that the witness chose "from over 1,000 photos the suspect and only the suspect." As Levi and Jungman point out (and themselves believe is appropriate), this will be perceived by jurors as stronger evidence of guilt.

As it stands, the efficacy and fairness of the procedure depend in great measure on having a pool of photographed foils that is large and diverse enough to include decently sized subsets of faces that are highly similar to *any* suspect. To the extent that this is not feasible, it would seem that a means of measuring distinctiveness should be devised and that distinctiveness (as measured) be factored into a metric that weights the informational values of the number of foils chosen.

Police Behavior
Inherent problems of the lineup per se are not the only—or perhaps even the major—causes of false identifications. Systems variables involving police behavior are significant culprits as well, including poor interviewing techniques for securing a witness description, pre-lineup procedures (e.g., excessive mug shot view-

ing, showups, leaking suggestions from other witnesses), construction of poor lineups, biased lineup instructions, and postidentification bolstering of the eyewitness's confidence. Levi and Jungman do not really acknowledge that the danger associated with these factors probably overwhelms the danger inherent in a well-constructed, high-functional-size lineup. More important, they do not address how their procedure could lessen these dangers (e.g., is it *less* dependent on having a clear and complete witness description? Would any unconscious "demand" to choose someone emanating from a conscientious detective be inherently less with their procedure?). In a way, the Levi-Jungman procedure may win a battle against mistaken identifications, but it may be only a small victory far away from the center of the war.

In particular, we wonder what, if any, features of this procedure help control for the confidence malleability problem discussed originally by Leippe (1980) and dramatically demonstrated in a recent experiment by Luus and Wells (1994). The phenomenon is one in which an identification (or "choice" as Levi and Jungman prefer) is made initially with little confidence but is then inflated later by other information about the person who was chosen. This malleability is bidirectional, such that information from other sources that indicates the chosen person is probably innocent serves to lower eyewitness confidence just as information that the person is probably guilty serves to raise confidence (Luus & Wells, 1994). In U.S. jurisdictions, police are free to inform the witness (after the identification) of the status of the person(s) identified. Telling the witness which person among those chosen is the suspect would serve to increase the

witness's confidence in that choice and lower confidence in the other choices. With such dynamics allowed to operate, what can be made of the eyewitness's in-court statements of confidence that the suspect was a better match to his or her memory of the culprit than were the foils? At that point, the witness knows which persons were foils and which was the suspect. We admit that this problem is not unique to the method advanced by Levi and Jungman, but it illustrates our point that detailed procedures and well-defined safeguards are essential to the acceptability of any procedure.

Decision Quality Across Faces and Time

The matters of when the suspect's face appears and how many total faces are viewed seem, so far, to have been considered far too inadequately. Invariably, putting the suspect among the earlier presentations raises the question of the usefulness of proceeding beyond the suspect if he or she is not chosen, as well as questions of how much further to go and the meaning of postsuspect choices if the suspect is chosen. According to Levi and Jungman, the total number of choices is a critical determinant of the likelihood that the (also chosen) suspect is the offender. However, as we have noted, the threshold for choosing others is apt to change if the suspect is "recognized." In addition, regardless of the authors' optimism, there is empirical evidence that the "quality" of choices will decline as the number of faces viewed mounts. Here again, perhaps a weighting scheme will be required, with choices weighted as a function of whether they precede or follow the suspect and according to their numerical position in the sequence.

REALISM, PRACTICALITY, AND LEGALITY

Levi and Jungman depict their solution to the identification problem as radical. We agree with this depiction and we applaud the introduction of new ideas into the literature. We are especially pleased and encouraged about the fact that this radical idea comes not from academic researchers, who are often credited with proposing unrealistic or naive solutions to real-world problems, but from professionals operating within the Israeli police system. Somehow, though, we feel that this would have never been proposed by someone invested in the American police system. Interestingly, we now find ourselves in an unusual position. Our own research programs have proposed many new ways for police and courts to approach the design, procedure, and interpretation of eyewitness evidence. These proposals have always been well grounded in critical experimental tests and have included such ideas as the sequential lineup, the dual lineup, the high-functional-size lineup, and so on. Over a period of many years, we have had to contend with arguments that these ideas are unrealistic, or impractical for police, or somehow would prove unacceptable to the courts. We find it awkward, therefore, to hear ourselves argue that Levi and Jungman's proposal is unrealistic. Nevertheless, we have a hard time imagining what American courts would do with a witness who takes the stand, points to the defendant, and says, "That's him... yes... that is the guy who *looks* like the guy who robbed me." We can only imagine the field day that defense attorneys in American courts would have with a witness who had selected several people from photos, only one of whom is the defendant. In fact, many attorneys will be sure to make the not unreasonable point that choosing the defendant as, say 1 of 10 people who could be the culprit manifestly *increases* reasonable doubt that the defendant is guilty (because the witness has provided at least nine instances of confusing the offender with an innocent person).

Levi and Jungman argue that this is how it should be because it would serve to diminish the unrealistic and dangerous assumption that an identification is anything other than a statement about similarity between the accused and the actual culprit. We partially agree with this argument, but we note that such a change would require profound mutations in the doctrine and dogma of the American courts, the same courts that still have not accepted basic arguments for simple unbiased instructions to eyewitnesses or the fundamental point that all lineup members should match the witness's description of the culprit. Surely, therefore, Levi and Jungman's proposal is well off the map of realism in terms of what would be considered practical and acceptable to the courts.

Beyond practicality and acceptance, we wonder how easy it would be to truly educate jurors about the procedure. For example, what information would help jurors counterargue a defense attorney's claim of reasonable doubt that we noted earlier? And what could we tell jurors regarding how many choices of similar-looking faces constitute more partial or more complete memory? Like other laypeople, jurors are not fond of or good at statistical thinking. Yet, it seems that explaining partial identification to them would require more than a few numbers, base rates, and the like.

We see the Levi and Jungman proposal as something that may be more practical as an investigatory tool than as something that is practical in terms of "courtroom-quality" evidence. The distinction between the investigative value of a procedure and the probative evidentiary value of a procedure has been laid out clearly in certain other domains of American legal evidence procedure. The use of hypnosis with witnesses to aid their recall is one example of where American courts have largely ruled that the technique of hypnotic induction is acceptable as an investigative tool but that testimonial evidence based on hypnosis is not acceptable in court. Similarly, U.S. courts generally have held that the use of the polygraph is acceptable as an investigative device but that the results cannot constitute evidence in court.

A CALL FOR EMPIRICAL DATA

One of our concerns with the Levi and Jungman proposal is that it lacks any form of comparison data (or even a clear demonstration of the procedure) at this point. Although many aspects of the proposed procedure seem straightforward, implementation requires making some decisions that are apparent only when one begins to operationalize the procedure. Comparison data are particularly critical here. Levi and Jungman make some plausible arguments, but there have been many plausible arguments that have been raised over the years in the eyewitness area that do not hold up to empirical tests. In the case of the procedure proposed by Levi and Jungman, for instance, we see a need to test directly the suppositions contained in their procedure. Minimally, we need to know what happens when the target is not in the entire set of photos that are shown to the witness. As has been argued with lineups, the critical test of whether a procedure is able to operate successfully in real-world conditions depends in large part on its ability to distinguish between situations in which the suspect is among the options available to the witness or is not a part of the set of options at all. The existence of a database on lineups with staged crimes for which target-absent lineups were used is what allows Levi and Jungman to note that even the best procedures produce false identification rates that may be too high. However, the challenge is not to generate a better idea per se but to actually prove, by setting up critical empirical tests, that the proposed procedure is better than the ones developed to date.

CONCLUSION

Ultimately, empirical tests will determine whether Levi and Jungman's idea is a good one. Whether and how the idea will be usable, however, will depend on answers to issues such as those we have presented here. At the very least, however, if their proposal stimulates new thinking about how to improve our ability to asses the likely veracity of eyewitness identification, Levi and Jungman will have done us a service by putting their radical solution out there for all to consider.

POSTSCRIPT

Should Partial Identifications Be Accepted in Police Lineups?

Levi and Jungman certainly provide an extensive plan for revising the process for identifying culprits. If there had been eyewitnesses to Nicole Simpson's murder and they had partially identified O. J. Simpson as the murder, what do you think defense attorney Johnnie Cochran would have done to their testimony? Should eyewitness accounts be zero-sum, or "all or nothing"? Would it make sense to assign weight to degrees of certitude? That is, based on some of Levi and Jungman's ideas, should a scale be developed? Or are Leippe and Wells correct that, legally, these ideas would not hold up? We need empirical testing of them, at the very least. Yet, in a sense, courts already allow partial identifications (e.g., on the witness stand during cross-examination, the degree of certainty of witnesses is roughly established as attorneys attempt to poke holes in testimony). Also, witnesses are allowed to provide testimony based on courtroom observation even after they have failed to pick out the suspect from photos.

Currently, it is impermissible for two or more witnesses to sort through photographs of suspects at the same time. However, is it possible that group discussions and identifications might be stronger? That is, people who have witnessed or been victims of the same crime may actually help each other remember more accurately. Does the idea of neutral eyewitness experts who testify solely to clarify identification issues for the court make sense? Or might this preempt the defense's making its own case by selecting its own preferred experts? These are a few relevant aspects of the issue waiting to be addressed. Do partial identifications merit a try?

For Levi and Jungman's response to Leippe and Wells, see "No to the Lineup, Yes to Further Research," *Criminal Justice and Behavior* (December 1995). Two less controversial discussions are *Eyewitness Testimony: Civil and Criminal* by E. F. Loftus and J. Doyle (Lexis Law Publishing, 1997) and "Accuracy of Eyewitness Identification in Show-up and Lineup," by A. Yarmey, *Law and Human Behavior* (August 1996). For a helpful reader dealing with issues such as other race effects, voice identifications, and elderly witnesses, see *Psychological Issues in Eyewitness Identification* edited by S. L. Sporer et al. (Lawrence Erlbaum, 1996). For an alternative lineup modality, see "Police Practice Detection Dog Lineups," by G. J. Hargreaves, *FBI Law Enforcement Bulletin* (January 1996).

An outstanding book on the subject is C. R. Huff et al.'s *Convicted but Innocent: Wrongful Conviction and Public Policy* (Sage Publications, 1996). Also see the earlier works *The Innocents* by E. Radin (William Morrow, 1964) and

W. E. Ringel, *Identification and Police Line-ups* (Gould Publications, 1968). For a discussion of children as witnesses, see the special issue "International Perspectives on Children's Testimony," *Criminal Justice and Behavior* (June 1996).

On the Internet . . .

Crime-Free America
Crime-Free America is a grassroots, nonprofit group dedicated to ending the crime epidemic that it feels has gripped the United States during the last four decades. This site links to the Bureau of Justice Statistics, crime forums, and crime watch profiles.
http://www.announce.com/cfa/cfa.htm

Violent Criminal Apprehension Program
The Violent Criminal Apprehension Program (VICAP) is a nationwide data information center that collects, collates, and analyzes crimes of violence—specifically murder. A program of the FBI's National Center for the Analysis of Violent Crime, its mission is to aid cooperation, communication, and coordination among law enforcement agencies and to provide support for their efforts.
http://www.fbi.gov/vicap/vicap.htm

Gun Owners of America
Gun Owners of America is a gun lobby organization based in Springfield, Virginia. Their site links to current national alerts and state-wide alerts about gun owners' rights, proposed gun-control legislation, and other gun-related information. *http://www.gunowners.org/*

Handgun Control, Inc.
Handgun Control, Inc., is a nonpartisan, not-for-profit organization that lobbies in favor of commonsense gun regulations at both state and national levels. This site offers action alerts, information on gun laws and legislation, and advice on how to avoid becoming a victim of handgun violence. *http://www.handguncontrol.org/*

PART 4

Future Trends

In the field of criminal justice, forecasting is an important device that entails extrapolating from present trends and projecting solutions to organizational problems. Criminologists supply the needed data, including the rates, frequencies, and distributions of crime. Yet even if we indeed know who commits what crimes, where, when, how, and why with any real certainty, there is no guarantee that this knowledge will hold true a few years from now. Moreover, as debatable as current policy proposals are, what we should do in the future is even more so. Drugs and gun control have been subjects of controversy for generations now, and they will more than likely be part of crime debates into the twenty-first century. By contrast, while both euthanasia and variants of police crackdowns have been around for years, they have been peripheral to criminological and legal dialogue until recently. Now the issues of physician-assisted suicide and increased local crime control are being widely debated. Finally, over 50 years after the Holocaust and 25 years after the victories of the civil rights movement, widespread violations of human rights are once again assuming a prominent place both on the world scene and within criminal justice. The past becomes the future as crime control is once again debated, this time on an international scale and with human rights as the focus.

■ Will Gun Control Reduce Crime?

■ Should Euthanasia Be a Crime?

■ Does Increased Crime Control Make New York Safer?

■ Are Human Rights Basic to Justice?

■ Does the International Drug War Encourage Human Rights Violations?

ISSUE 15

Will Gun Control Reduce Crime?

YES: Josh Sugarmann, from "The NRA Is Right: But We Still Need to Ban Handguns," *The Washington Monthly* (June 1987)

NO: James D. Wright, from "Ten Essential Observations on Guns in America," *Society* (March/April 1995)

ISSUE SUMMARY

YES: Josh Sugarmann, formerly with the National Coalition to Ban Handguns, identifies several problems with legal handguns, including what he describes as unacceptably high rates of suicides with guns, family homicides, and accidents.

NO: Sociologist James D. Wright offers ten "fundamental truths" about guns. While he acknowledges that there is widespread disagreement over interpretations of the facts, he concludes that most gun control laws are unfair and ineffective.

According to some estimates, one in every two households in the United States contains a gun. And because of the growing fear of crime, many citizens express increased unwillingness to give up their guns. Guns are seen as necessary to protect home and family. An excellent example of this is the complicated situation that the nationally syndicated columnist Carl Rowan confronted. A well-known supporter of strict firearm controls, he was allegedly threatened by an intruder in his own backyard. Rowan quickly produced a pistol and shot the intruder. While conservatives (who consistently support the right to bear arms and oppose most kinds of gun control) jeered Rowan for his hypocrisy, other Americans were sympathetic. Rowan was later acquitted of criminal charges in the incident. He, like approximately 50 million other Americans, continues to possess a handgun.

This reflects another paradox in our society. On the one hand, many, if not most, Americans support handgun control. On the other hand, most also feel that law-abiding citizens should have the right to possess a gun, at least inside their own homes, and to use it to protect themselves and their families. The argument is that weapons are needed for simple protection.

Simple assault is the most common crime of violence, followed by aggravated assault, which is the use of or threat of a weapon to inflict bodily harm. Other than robbery, most violent crimes are not committed with a gun. Knives, fists, and blunt instruments are more likely to be the weapons of choice. Homicide is the least frequent form of assault in the United States.

However, for most years between 1960 and 1985, violent crimes as reported to the police increased. In the late 1970s and in the 1982–1984 period, there was a slight decrease, but between 1984 and 1985 there was about a 4 percent increase. According to the U.S. Bureau of Justice Statistics, the number of attempted violent crimes increased by approximately 11 percent between 1990 and 1991. Currently, over 6 million violent crimes are committed each year. (Although the rate has come down since the peak year of 1981, when 6.6 million violent crimes were reported, as compared to 6.4 million in 1991.) There are over 20,000 murders per year, and in approximately 62 percent of all murders, guns are used in the commission of the crime. Six percent of gun assaults result in death; by comparison, 1.8 percent of knife assaults are fatal, and .05 percent of fights result in death.

Traditionally, the debate over gun control has centered largely around the control of, if not the elimination of, "Saturday night specials" (inexpensive, .22-caliber pistols). However, the issue has become more complicated in the 1990s. Not only is the fear and frustration over assaults and homicides being fueled by the significant numbers of young people being arrested for possession of arms, use of arms, and threats with arms, but the power of the weapons on the streets and the types of weapons available have changed dramatically. Uzis, AK-47 assault rifles, MAC-11 assault pistols, .357 Magnums, .45-caliber semiautomatics, and other semiautomatic weapons are frequently being used in deadly assaults. The consequences are an increase of public fear and an increase in fatalities because these weapons, newer to the criminal street scene, are far deadlier than "mere" Saturday night specials.

Gun control is now very much part of the cultural war landscape. Reminiscent (only in reverse) of the charges in the 1920s that Prohibition (of alcohol) was the triumph of the conservative, mean-spirited, rural religious right over the fun-loving, ethnically diverse, liberal city dwellers, some charge today that gun control laws represent the efforts of urban politicians and scholars to suppress rural hunters and other Americans. Many gun owners nowadays interpret gun control as a deliberate attempt to export to America's heartland the violence and chaos of the cities. Certainly such sentiments pervade far right militants who openly call for war on various government agencies. It seems that this issue is spreading and growing uglier.

In the following selections, Josh Sugarmann of the National Coalition to Ban Handguns acknowledges that the issue is complex, but he still recommends banning handguns. Sociologist James D. Wright asserts that neither empirically nor morally can some Americans demand other Americans to give up their guns.

Do *you* own a handgun? Would you willingly give it up if a law were passed? If a burglar has been working your neighborhood, would you still forgo purchasing one? Would you be willing to be a close friend of someone who has handguns? Why, or why not? Are folks with guns safer than those without them?

YES   Josh Sugarmann

THE NRA IS RIGHT: BUT WE STILL NEED
TO BAN HANDGUNS

One tenet of the National Rifle Association's faith has always been that hand-gun controls do little to stop criminals from obtaining handguns. For once, the NRA is right and America's leading handgun control organization is wrong. Criminals don't buy handguns in gun stores. That's why they're criminals. But it isn't criminals who are killing most of the 20,000 to 22,000 people who die from handguns each year. We are.

This is an ugly truth for a country that thinks of handgun violence as a "crime" issue and believes that it's somehow possible to separate "good" handguns (those in our hands for self-defense) from "bad" handguns (those in the hands of criminals).

Contrary to popular perception, the most prevalent form of handgun death in America isn't murder but suicide. Of the handgun deaths that occur each year, approximately 12,000 are suicides. An additional 1,000 fatalities are accidents. And of the 9,000 handgun deaths classified as murders, most are not caused by predatory strangers. Handgun violence is usually the result of people being angry, drunk, careless, or depressed—who just happen to have a handgun around. In all, fewer than 10 percent of handgun deaths are felony-related.

Though handgun availability is not a crime issue, it does represent a major public health threat. Handguns are the number one weapon for both murder and suicide and are second only to auto accidents as the leading cause of death due to injury. Of course there are other ways of committing suicide or crimes of passion. But no means is more lethal, effective, or handy. That's why the NRA is ultimately wrong. As several public health organizations have noted, the best way to curb a public health problem is through prevention—in this case, the banning of all handguns from civilian hands.

THE ENEMY IS US

For most who attempt suicide, the will to die lasts only briefly. Only one out of every ten people attempting suicide is going to kill himself no matter what.

The success or failure of an attempt depends primarily on the lethality of the means. Pills, razor blades, and gas aren't guaranteed killers, and they take time. Handguns, however, lend themselves well to spontaneity. Consider that although women try to kill themselves four times as often as men, men succeed three to four times as often. For one reason: women use pills or less lethal means; men use handguns. This balance is shifting, however, as more women own or have access to handguns. Between 1970 and 1978 the suicide rate for young women rose 50 percent, primarily due to increased use of handguns.

Of course, there is no way to lock society's cupboard and prevent every distraught soul from injuring him or herself. Still, there are ways we can promote public safety without becoming a nation of nannies. England, for instance, curbed suicide by replacing its most common means of committing suicide—coal stove gas—with less toxic natural gas. Fifteen years after the switch, studies found that suicide rates had dropped and remained low, even though the number of suicide *attempts* had increased. "High suicide rates seem to occur where highly lethal suicidal methods are not only available, but also where they are culturally acceptable," writes Dr. Robert Markush of the University of Alabama, who has studied the use of handguns in suicide.

Most murders aren't crime-related, but are the result of arguments between friends and among families. In 1985, 59 percent of all murders were committed by people known to the victim. Only 15 percent were committed by strangers, and only 18 percent were the result of felonious activity. As the FBI admits every year in its *Uniform Crime Reports,* "murder is a societal problem over which law enforcement has little or no control." The FBI doesn't publish separate statistics on who's killing whom with handguns, but it is assumed that what is true of all murders is true of handgun murders.

CONTROLLING THE VECTOR

Recognizing that eliminating a disease requires prevention, not treatment, health professionals have been in the forefront of those calling for a national ban on handguns. In 1981, the Surgeon General's Select Panel for the Promotion of Child Health traced the "epidemic of deaths and injuries among children and youth" to handguns, and called for "nothing short of a total ban." It is estimated that on average, one child dies from handgun wounds each day. Between 1961 and 1981, according to the American Association of Suicidology, the suicide rate for 15- to 24-year-olds increased 150 percent. The report linked the rise in murders and suicides among the young to the increased use of firearms—primarily handguns. In a 1985 report, the Surgeon General's Workshop on Violence and Public Health recommended "a complete and universal ban on the sale, manufacture, importation, and possession of handguns (except for authorized police and military personnel)." ...

Comparing the relationship between handguns and violence to mosquitos and malaria, Stephen P. Teret, co-director of the Johns Hopkins Injury Prevention Center, says, "As public health professionals, if we are faced with a disease that is carried by some type of vehicle/vector like a mosquito, our initial response would be to control the vector. There's no reason why if the vehicle/vector is a handgun, we should not be interested in controlling the handgun."

The NRA refers to handgun suicides, accidental killings, and murders by acquaintances as "the price of freedom." It believes that handguns right enough wrongs, stop enough crimes, and kill enough criminals to justify these deaths. But even the NRA has admitted that there is no "adequate measure that more lives are saved by arms in good hands than are lost by arms in evil hands." Again, the NRA is right.

A 1985 NCBH study found that a handgun is 118 times more likely to be used in a suicide, murder, or fatal accident than to kill a criminal. Between 1981 and 1983, nearly 69,000 Americans lost their lives to handguns. During that same period there were only 583 justifiable homicides reported to the FBI, in which someone used a handgun to kill a stranger—a burglar, rapist, or other criminal. In 1982, 19 states reported to the FBI that not once did a private citizen use a handgun to kill a criminal. Five states reported that more than 130 citizens were murdered with handguns for each time a handgun was justifiably used to kill a criminal. In no state did the number of self-defense homicides approach the murder toll. Last year, a study published in the *New England Journal of Medicine* analyzing gun use in the home over a six-year period in the Seattle, Washington area, found that for every time a firearm was used to kill an intruder in self-defense, 198 lives ended in murders, suicides, or accidents. Handguns were used in more than 70 percent of those deaths.

Although handguns are rarely used to kill criminals, an obvious question remains: How often are they used merely to wound or scare away intruders? No reliable statistics are available, but most police officials agree that in a criminal confrontation on the street, the handgun-toting civilian is far more likely to be killed or lose his handgun to a criminal than successfully use the weapon in self-defense. "Beyond any doubt, thousands more lives are lost every year because of the proliferation of handguns than are saved," says Joseph McNamara, chief of police of San Jose, who has also been police chief in Kansas City, a beat cop in Harlem, and is the author of a book on defense against violent crime. Moreover, most burglaries occur when homes are vacant, so the handgun in the drawer is no deterrent. (It would also probably be the first item stolen.)

Faced with facts like these, anti-control advocates often turn to the argument of last resort: the Second Amendment. But the historic 1981 Morton Grove, Illinois, ban on handgun sale and possession exploded that rationale. In 1983, the U.S. Supreme Court let stand a lower court ruling that stated, "Because the possession of handguns is not part of the right to keep and bear arms, [the Morton Grove ordinance] does not violate the Second Amendment."

CRIMINAL EQUIVOCATION

Unfortunately, powerful as the NRA is, it has received additional help from the leading handgun control group. Handgun Control Inc. (HCI) has helped the handgun lobby by setting up the perfect strawman for the NRA to shoot down. "Keep handguns out of the wrong hands," HCI says. "By making it more difficult for criminals, drug addicts, etc., to get handguns, and by ensuring that law-abiding citizens know how to maintain their handguns, we can reduce handgun violence," it promises. Like those in the NRA, HCI chairman Nelson

T. "Pete" Shields "firmly believe[s] in the right of law-abiding citizens to possess handguns... for legitimate purposes."

In its attempt to paint handgun violence solely as a crime issue, HCI goes so far as to sometimes ignore the weapon's non-crime death tally. In its most recent poster comparing the handgun murder toll in the U.S. with that of nations with strict handgun laws, HCI states: "In 1983, handguns killed 35 people in Japan, 8 in Great Britain, 27 in Switzerland, 6 in Canada, 7 in Sweden, 10 in Australia, and 9,014 in the United States." Handguns *killed* a lot more than that in the United States. About 13,000 suicides and accidents more.

HCI endorses a ban only on short-barrelled handguns (the preferred weapon of criminals). It advocates mandatory safety training, a waiting period during which a background check can be run on a purchaser, and a license to carry a handgun, with mandatory sentencing for violators. It also endorses mandatory sentencing for the use of a handgun in a crime. According to HCI communications director Barbara Lautman, together these measures would "attack pretty much the heart of the problem."

HCI appears to have arrived at its crime focus by taking polls. In his 1981 book, *Guns Don't Die—People Do*, Shields points out that the majority of Americans don't favor a ban on handguns. "What they do want, however, is a set of strict laws to control the easy access to handguns by the criminal and the violence prone—*as long as those controls don't jeopardize the perceived right of law-abiding citizens to buy and own handguns for self defense* [italics his]." Shields admits "this is not based on any naive hope that criminals will obey such laws. Rather, it is based on the willingness of the rest

of us to be responsible and accountable citizens, and the knowledge that to the degree we are, we make it more difficult for the criminal to get a handgun." This wasn't always HCI's stand. Founded in 1974 as the National Council to Control Handguns, HCI originally called a ban on private handgun possession the "most effective" solution to reducing violent crime rapidly and was at one time a member of NCBH. Michael Beard, president of NCBH, maintains that HCI's focus on crime "started with a public relations concern. Some people in the movement felt Americans were worried about crime, and that was one way to approach the problem. That's the problem when you use public opinion polls to tell you what your position's going to be. And I think a lot of the handgun control movement has looked at whatever's hot at the time and tried to latch onto that, rather than sticking to the basic message that there is a relationship between the availability of handguns and the handgun violence in our society.... Ultimately, nothing short of taking the product off the market is really going to have an effect on the problem."

HCI's cops and robbers emphasis has been endlessly frustrating to many in the anti-handgun movement. HCI would offer handgun control as a solution to crime, and the NRA would effectively rebut their arguments with the common-sensical observation that criminals are not likely to obey such laws. I can't help but think that HCI's refusal to abandon the crime argument has harmed the longterm progress of the movement.

SATURATED DRESSER DRAWERS

In a nation with 40 million handguns—where anyone who wants one can get one

—it's time to face a chilling fact. We're way past the point where registration, licensing, safety training, waiting periods, or mandatory sentencing are going to have much effect. Each of these measures may save some lives or help catch a few criminals, but none—by itself or taken together—will stop the vast majority of handgun suicides or murders. A "controlled" handgun kills just as effectively as an "uncontrolled" one.

Most control recommendations merely perpetuate the myth that with proper care a handgun can be as safe a tool as any other. Nothing could be further from the truth. A handgun is not a blender.

Those advocating a step-by-step process insist that a ban would be too radical and therefore unacceptable to Congress and the public. A hardcore 40 percent of the American public has always endorsed banning handguns. Many will also undoubtedly argue that any control measure—no matter how ill-conceived or ineffective—would be a good first step. But after more than a decade, the other foot hasn't followed.

In other areas of firearms control there has been increasing recognition that bans are the most effective solution. The only two federal measures passed since the Gun Control Act of 1968 have been bans. In each case, the reasoning was simple: the harm done by these objects outweighed any possible benefit they brought to society. In 1986, Congress banned certain types of armor-piercing "cop-killer" bullets. There was also a silver lining to last year's NRA-McClure-Volkmer handgun "decontrol" bill, which weakened the already lax Gun Control Act of 1968, making it legal, for instance, for people to transport unloaded, "not readily accessible" handguns interstate. A last-minute amendment added by pro-control forces banned the future production and sale of machine guns for civilian use.

Unfortunately, no law has addressed the major public health problem. Few suicides, accidental killings, or acquaintance murders are the result of cop-killer bullets or machine guns.

Outlawing handguns would in no way be a panacea. Even if handgun production stopped tomorrow, millions would remain in the dresser drawers of America's bedrooms—and many of them would probably stay there. Contrary to NRA fantasies, black-booted fascists would not be kicking down doors searching for handguns. Moreover, the absolute last segment of society to be affected by any measure would be criminals. The black market that has fed off the legal sale of handguns would continue for a long while. But by ending new handgun production, the availability of illegal handguns can only decrease.

Of course, someone who truly wants to kill himself can find another way. A handgun ban would not affect millions of rifles and shotguns. But experience shows that no weapon provides the combination of lethality and convenience that a handgun does. Handguns represent only 30 percent of all the guns out there but are responsible for 90 percent of firearms misuse. Most people who commit suicide with a firearm use a handgun. At minimum, a handgun ban would prevent the escalation of killings in segments of society that have not yet been saturated by handgun manufacturers. Further increases in suicides among women, for example, might be curtailed.

But the final solution lies in changing the way handguns and handgun violence are viewed by society. Public health campaigns have changed the way Americans look at cigarette smoking and drunk driving and can do the same for handguns.

For the past 12 years, many in the handgun control movement have confined their debate to what the public supposedly wants and expects to hear— not to reality. The handgun must be seen for what it is, not what we'd like it to be.

NO

James D. Wright

TEN ESSENTIAL OBSERVATIONS ON GUNS IN AMERICA

Talk of "gun control" is very much in the air these days. Emboldened by their successes in getting the Brady Act enacted, the pro-control forces are now striking on a number of fronts: bans on various so-called assault weapons, mandatory gun registration, strict new laws against juvenile acquisition and possession of guns, and on through the list. Much current gun-control activity springs from a recent and generally successful effort to redefine gun violence mainly as a public health issue rather than a criminal justice issue.

Increasingly, the ammunition of the gun control war is data. Pro-control advocates gleefully cite studies that seem to favor their position, of which there is no shortage, and anti-control advocates do likewise. Many of the "facts" of the case are, of course, hotly disputed; so too are their implications and interpretations. Here I should like to discuss ten essential facts about guns in America that are not in dispute—ten fundamental truths that all contestants either do or should agree to—and briefly ponder the implications of each for how the problem of guns and gun violence perhaps should be approached. These facts and their implications derive from some twenty years of research and reflection on the issues.

1. *Half the households in the country own at least one gun.* So far as I have been able to determine, the first question about gun ownership asked of a national probability sample of U.S. adults was posed in 1959; a similar question asking whether anyone in the household owns a gun has since been repeated dozens of times. Over the ensuing thirty-five years, every survey has reported more or less the same result: Just about half of all U.S. households own one or more guns. This is probably not the highest gun ownership percentage among the advanced industrial societies (that honor probably goes to the Swiss), but it qualifies as a very respectable showing. We are, truly, a "gun culture."

Five important implications follow more or less unambiguously from this first essential observation.

The percentage of households owning guns has been effectively constant for nearly four decades; at the same time, the total number of guns in circulation has increased substantially, especially in the last two decades. The

From James D. Wright, "Ten Essential Observations on Guns in America," *Society* (March/April 1995). Copyright © 1995 by Transaction Publishers. Reprinted by permission.

evident implication is that the increasing supply of guns has been absorbed by population growth, with newly formed households continuing to arm themselves at the average rate, and by the purchase of additional guns by households already owning one or more of them. In fact there is fairly solid evidence that the average number of guns owned by households owning any has increased from about three in the late 1970s to about four today.

The second implication is thus that many (and conceivably nearly all) of the new guns coming into circulation are being purchased by people who already own guns, as opposed to first-time purchases by households or individuals who previously owned no guns. I think it is also obvious that from the viewpoint of public safety, the transition from N to N + 1 guns is considerably less ominous than the transition from no guns to one gun. If this second implication is correct, it means that *most of the people in the gun shops today buying new guns already own at least one gun*, a useful point to keep in mind when pondering, for example, the alleged "cooling off" function to be served by waiting periods imposed at the point of retail sale.

Furthermore, it is frequently argued by pro-control advocates that the mere presence of guns causes people to do nutty and violent things that they would otherwise never even consider. In the academic literature on "guns as aggression-eliciting stimuli," this is called the "trigger pulls the finger" hypothesis. If there were much substance to this viewpoint, the fact that half of all U.S. households possess a gun would seem to imply that there ought to be a lot more nuttiness "out there" than we actually observe. In the face of widespread alarm about the sky-

rocketing homicide rate, it is important to remember that the rate is still a relatively small number of homicides (ten to fifteen or so) per hundred thousand people. If half the households own guns and the mere presence of guns incites acts of violence, then one would expect the bodies to be piled three deep, and yet they are not.

Fourth, gun ownership is normative, not deviant, behavior across vast swaths of the social landscape. In certain states and localities, it would be an odd duck indeed who did not own a gun. Surveys in some smaller southern cities, for example, have reported local gun ownership rates in excess of 90 percent.

And finally, to attempt to control crime or violence by controlling the general ownership or use of guns among the public at large is to attempt to control the behaviors of a very small fraction of the population (the criminally or violently inclined fraction) by controlling the behaviors and activities of roughly half the U.S. population. Whatever else might be said about such an approach, it is certainly not very efficient.

2. *There are 200 million guns already in circulation in the United States*, give or take a few tens of millions. It has been said, I think correctly, that firearms are the most commonly owned piece of sporting equipment in the United States, with the exception of pairs of sneakers. In any case, contestants on all sides of the gun debate generally agree that the total number of guns in circulation is on the order of 200 million—nearly one gun for every man, woman, and child in the country.

It is not entirely clear how many acts of gun violence occur in any typical year. There are 30–35,000 deaths due to guns each year, perhaps a few hundred thousand nonfatal but injurious firearms accidents, maybe 500,000 or 600,000 chargeable gun crimes (not including crimes of illegal gun possession and carrying), and God knows how many instances in which guns are used to intimidate or prey upon one's fellow human beings. Making generous allowances all around, however, the total number of acts of accidental and intentional gun violence, whether fatal, injurious, or not, cannot be more than a couple of million, at the outside. This implies that the 200 million guns now in circulation would be sufficient to sustain roughly another century of gun violence at the current rates, even assuming that each gun was used once and only once for some nefarious purpose and that all additions to the gun supply were halted permanently and at once. Because of the large number of guns already in circulation, the violence-reductive effects of even fairly Draconian gun-control measures enacted today might well not be felt for decades.

Many recent gun-control initiatives, such as the Brady Act, are aimed at the point of retail sale of firearms and are therefore intended to reduce or in some way disrupt the flow of new guns into the domestic market. At the outside, the number of new guns coming into the market yearly is a few million, which adds but a few percent to the existing supply. If we intend to control gun violence by reducing the availability of firearms to the general public, as many argue we should, then we have to find some workable means to confront or control the vast arsenal of guns already circulating through private hands.

Various "amnesty," "buyback," and "please turn in your guns" measures have been attempted in various jurisdictions all over the country; in one well-publicized effort, teenagers could swap guns for Toys R Us gift certificates. The success of these programs has been measured in units of several dozen or at most a few hundred relinquished firearms; the net effect on the overall supply of guns is far too trivial to even bother calculating.

3. *Most of those 200 million guns are owned for socially innocuous sport and recreational purposes.* Only about a third of the guns presently in circulation are handguns; the remainder are rifles and shotguns. When one asks gun owners why they own guns, various sport and recreational activities dominate the responses—hunting, target shooting, collecting, and the like. Even when the question is restricted to handgun owners, about 40 percent say they own the gun for sport and recreational applications, another 40 percent say they own it for self-protection, and the remaining 20 percent cite their job or occupation as the principal reason for owning a gun.

Thus for the most part, gun ownership is apparently a topic more appropriate to the sociology of leisure than to the criminology or epidemiology of violence. Many pro-control advocates look on the sporting uses of guns as atavistic, barbaric, or just plain silly. But an equally compelling case could be made against golf, which causes men to wear funny clothes, takes them away from their families, and gobbles up a lot of pretty, green, open space that would be better used as public parks. It is, of course, true that golf does not kill 35,000 people a year (although middle-aged men drop dead on the golf course quite regularly), but it is also true that the sport and recreational use of guns does not kill 35,000 people a year. There are fewer than a thousand fatal hunting accidents annually; death from skeet shooting, target practice, and such is uncounted but presumably very small. It is the violent or criminal *abuse* of guns that should concern us, and the vast majority of guns now in circulation will never be used for anything more violent or abusive than killing the furry creatures of the woods and fields.

Unfortunately, when we seek to control violence by controlling the general ownership and use of firearms among the public at large, it at least *looks* as though we think we have intuited some direct causal connection between drive-by shootings in the inner city and squirrel hunting or skeet shooting in the hinterland. In any case, this is the implication that the nation's squirrel hunters and skeet shooters often draw; frankly, is it any wonder they sometimes come to question the motives, not to mention the sanity, of anyone who would suggest such a thing?

4. *Many guns are also owned for self-defense against crime, and some are indeed used for that purpose; whether they are actually any safer or not, many people certainly seem to feel safer when they have a gun.* There is a fierce debate raging in gun advocacy circles these days over recent findings by Gary Kleck that Americans use guns to protect themselves against crime as often as one or two million times a year, which, if true, is hard to square with the common assumption of pro-control advocates that guns are not an efficacious defense against crime. Whatever the true number of self-defensive uses, about a quarter of all gun owners and about 40 percent of handgun owners cite defense against crime as the main reason they own a gun, and large percentages of those who give some other main reason will cite self-defense as a secondary reason. Gun owners and gun advocates insist that guns provide real

protection, as Kleck's findings suggest; anti-gun advocates insist that the sense of security is more illusory than real.

But practically everything people do to protect themselves against crime provides only the illusion of security in that any such measure can be defeated by a sufficiently clever and motivated criminal. Dogs can be diverted or poisoned, burglar bars can be breached, home alarm systems can be subverted, chains and deadbolt locks can be cut and picked. That sales of all these items have skyrocketed in recent years is further proof—as if further proof were needed—that the fear of crime is real. Most people have also realized, correctly, that the police cannot protect them from crime. So people face the need to protect themselves and many choose to own a gun, along with taking many other measures, for this purpose. Does a society that is manifestly incapable of protecting its citizens from crime and predation really have the right or moral authority to tell people what they may and may not do to protect themselves?

Since a "sense of security" is inherently a psychological trait, it does no good to argue that the sense of security afforded by owning a gun is "just an illusion." Psychological therapy provides an *illusion* of mental wellness even as we remain our former neurotic selves, and it is nonetheless useful. The only sensible response to the argument that guns provide only an illusion of security is, So what?

5. *The bad guys do not get their guns through customary retail channels.* Research on both adult and juvenile felons and offenders has made it obvious that the illicit firearms market is dominated, overwhelmingly, by informal swaps, trades, and purchases among family members,

friends, acquaintances, and street and black-market sources. It is a rare criminal indeed who attempts to acquire a gun through a conventional over-the-counter transaction with a normal retail outlet. It is also obvious that many or most of the guns circulating through criminal hands enter the illicit market through theft from legitimate gun owners. (An aside of some possible significance: Large numbers of legitimate gun owners also obtain guns through informal "street" sources.)

As I have already noted, many efforts at gun control pertain to the initial retail sale of weapons, for example, the prohibition against gun purchases by people with felony records or alcohol or drug histories contained in the Gun Control Act of 1968, the national five-day waiting period, or various state and local permit and registration laws. Since felons rarely obtain guns through retail channels, controls imposed at the point of retail sale necessarily miss the vast majority of criminal firearms transactions. It is thus an easy prediction that the national five-day waiting period will have no effect on the acquisition of guns by criminals because that is not how the bad guys get their guns in the first place.

Having learned (now more than a decade ago) that the criminal acquisition of guns involves informal and intrinsically difficult-to-regulate transfers that are entirely independent of laws concerning registration and permits, average gun owners often conclude (whether rightly or wrongly) that such measures must therefore be intended primarily to keep tabs on them, that registration or permit requirements are "just the first step" toward outright confiscation of all privately held firearms, and that mandated registration of new gun purchases is thus an unwarranted "police state" intrusion on law-abiding citizens' constitutional rights. Reasoning in this vein often seems bizarre or even psychotic to proponents of registration or permit laws, but it is exactly this reasoning that accounts for the white-hot ferocity of the debate over guns in America today.

And similar reasoning applies to the national waiting period: Since it is well known that the bad guys do not generally obtain guns through normal retail channels, waiting periods enforced at the point of retail sale can only be aimed at thwarting the legitimate intentions of the "good guys." What conceivable crime-reductive benefit will a national five-day waiting period give us? If the answer is "probably very little," then the minds of average gun owners are free to speculate on the nefarious and conspiratorial intentions that may be harbored, consciously or not, by those who favor such a thing. The distinction between ill-considered and evil is quickly lost, and the debate over guns in America gets hotter still.

That the illicit gun market is supplied largely through theft from legitimate owners erodes any useful distinction between legitimate and illegitimate guns. Any gun that can be owned legitimately can be stolen from its legal owner and can end up in criminal hands. The effort to find some way to interdict or interfere with the criminal gun market while leaving legitimate owners pretty much alone is therefore bootless. So long as anybody can have a gun, criminals will have them too, and it is useful to remember that there are 200 million guns out there—an average of four of them in every second household.

6. *The bad guys inhabit a violent world; a gun often makes a life-or-death difference to them.* When one asks felons—either adult

or juvenile—why they own and carry guns, themes of self-defense, protection, and survival dominate the responses. Very few of the bad guys say they acquire or carry guns for offensive or criminal purposes, although that is obviously how many of them get used. These men live in a very hostile and violent environment, and many of them have come to believe, no doubt correctly, that their ability to survive in that environment depends critically on being adequately armed. Thus the bad guys are highly motivated gun consumers who will not be easily dissuaded from possessing, carrying, and using guns. If sheer survival is the issue, then a gun is a bargain at practically any price. As James Q. Wilson has argued, most of the gun violence problem results from the wrong kinds of people carrying guns at the wrong time and place. The survival motive among the bad guys means exactly that the "wrong kinds of people" will be carrying guns pretty much all the time. The evident implication is that the bad guys have to be disarmed on the street if the rates of gun violence are to decline, and that implies a range of intervention strategies far removed from what gun control advocates have recently urged on the American population.

7. *Everything the bad guys do with their guns is already against the law.* That criminals will generally be indifferent to our laws would seem to follow from the definitions of the terms, but it is a lesson that we have had to relearn time and time again throughout our history. So let me stress an obvious point: Murder is already against the law, yet murderers still murder; armed robbery is against the law, yet robbers still rob. And as a matter of fact, gun acquisition by felons, whether from retail or private sources, is also already illegal, yet felons still acquire guns. Since practically everything the bad guys do with their guns is already against the law, we are entitled to wonder whether there is any new law we can pass that would persuade them to stop doing it. It is more than a little bizarre to assume that people who routinely violate laws against murder, robbery, or assault would somehow find themselves compelled to obey gun laws, whatever provisions they might contain.

8. *Demand creates it own supply.* That "demand creates its own supply" is sometimes called the First Law of Economics, and it clearly holds whether the commodity in demand is legal or illegal. So long as a demand exists, there will be profit to be made in satisfying it, and therefore it will be satisfied. In a capitalist economy, it could scarcely be otherwise. So long as people, be they criminals or average citizens, want to own guns, guns will be available for them to own. The vast arsenal of guns already out there exists in the first instance because people who own guns like guns, the activities that guns make possible, and the sense of security that guns provide. "Supply side" approaches to the gun problem are never going to be any more effective than "supply side" approaches to the drug problem, which is to say, not at all. What alcohol and drug prohibition should have taught us (but apparently has not) is that if a demand exists and there is no legal way to satisfy it, then an illegal commerce in the commodity is spawned, and we often end up creating many more problems than we have solved.

Brazil and several European nations manufacture small arms; the Brazilian lines are relatively inexpensive but decent guns. In fundamental respects, the question whether we can disarm the

American criminal population amounts to asking whether an organized criminal enterprise that successfully illegally imports hundreds of tons of Colombian cocaine into the U.S. market each year would not find the means to illegally import hundreds of tons of handguns from Brazil. And if this is the case, then it seems more or less self-evident that the supply of firearms to the criminal population will never be reduced by enough to make an appreciable difference.

9. *Guns are neither inherently good nor inherently evil; guns, that is, do not possess teleology.* Benevolence and malevolence inhere in the motives and behaviors of people, not in the technology they possess. Any firearm is neither more nor less than a chunk of machined metal that can be put to a variety of purposes, all involving a small projectile hurtling at high velocity downrange to lodge itself in a target. We can only call this "good" when the target is appropriate and "evil" when it is not; the gun itself is immaterial to this judgment.

Gun-control advocates have a long history of singling out "bad" guns for policy attention. At one time, the emphasis was on small, cheap handguns—"Saturday Night Specials"—which were thought to be inherently "bad" because no legitimate use was thought to exist for them and because they were thought to be the preferred firearm among criminals. Both these thoughts turned out to be incorrect. Somewhat later, all handguns, regardless of their characteristics, were singled out (as by the National Coalition to Ban Handguns); most recently, the so-called military-style assault weapons are the "bad guns of the month."

Singling out certain types of guns for policy attention is almost always justified on the grounds that the type of gun in question "has no legitimate use" or "is designed only to kill." By definition, however, all guns are "designed to kill" (that is, to throw a projectile downrange to lodge in a target), and if one grants the proposition that self-defense against predation and plunder is a legitimate reason to own a gun, then all guns, regardless of their type or characteristics, have at least some potentially "legitimate" application. It seems to me, therefore, that the focus in gun-control circles on certain "bad" guns is fundamentally misplaced. When all is said and done, it is the behavior of people that we should seek to control. Any gun can be used legitimately by law-abiding people to hunt, shoot at targets, or defend themselves against crime; and likewise, any gun can be used by a criminal to prey upon and intimidate other people. Trying to sort firearms into "inherently bad" and "inherently good" categories seems fundamentally silly.

10. *Guns are important elements of our history and culture.* Attempts to control crime by regulating the ownership or use of firearms are attempts to regulate the artifacts and activities of a culture that, in its own way, is as unique as any of the myriad other cultures that comprise the American ethnic mosaic. This is the American gun culture, which remains among the least understood of any of the various subcultural strands that make up modern American society.

There is no question that a gun culture exists, one that amply fulfills any definition of a culture. The best evidence we have on its status as a culture is that the single most important predictor of whether a person owns a gun is whether his or her father owned one, which means that gun owning is a tradition transmitted across generations. Most gun owners report that there were firearms in their homes when they were growing up; this is true even of criminal gun users.

The existence and characteristics of the American gun culture have implications that rarely are appreciated. For one, gun control deals with matters that people feel strongly about, that are integral to their upbringing and their worldview. Gun-control advocates are frequently taken aback by the stridency with which their seemingly modest and sensible proposals are attacked, but from the gun culture's viewpoint, restrictions on the right to "keep and bear arms" amount to the systematic destruction of a valued way of life and are thus a form of cultural genocide.

Guns evoke powerful, emotive imagery that often stands in the way of intelligent debate. To the pro-control point of view, the gun is symbolic of much that is wrong in American culture. It symbolizes violence, aggression, and male dominance, and its use is seen as an acting out of our most regressive and infantile fantasies. To the gun culture's way of thinking, the same gun symbolizes much

that is right in the culture. It symbolizes manliness, self-sufficiency, and independence, and its use is an affirmation of man's relationship to nature and to history. The "Great American Gun War," as Bruce-Briggs has described it, is far more than a contentious debate over crime and the equipment with which it is committed. It is a battle over fundamental and equally legitimate sets of values.

Scholars and criminologists who speculate on the problem of guns, crime, and violence would thus do well to look at things, at least occasionally, from the gun culture's point of view. Hardly any of the 50 million or so American families that own guns have ever harmed anyone with their guns, and virtually none ever intend to. Nearly everything these families will ever do with their firearms is both legal and largely innocuous. When, in the interests of fighting crime, we advocate restrictions on their rights to own guns, we are casting aspersions on their decency, as though we somehow hold them responsible for the crime and violence that plague this nation. It is any wonder they object, often vociferously, to such slander?

POSTSCRIPT

Will Gun Control Reduce Crime?

In spite of the National Rifle Association's powerful lobbying efforts and media campaigns in support of gun ownership without restrictions, most Americans support some form of gun control. Yet the issue is confusing to many, in spite of the obvious evidence of the deadliness of gun assaults. One gun control fad that's catching on involves programs run by municipalities and even private organizations to buy back guns from gun owners in order to reduce the number in circulation. Symbolically, these actions strike a responsive chord. Citizens like to think something is being done about violent crime. However, empirical data suggests that the gun bounties may have little effect.

On a more positive note, local police are stepping up efforts to constitutionally identify and locate criminals who are illegally carrying guns. University of Maryland criminologist Lawrence W. Sherman is assisting urban police in developing such patrols. Meanwhile, both "what works" and "what is fair" in gun control remains highly problematic partly because the average individual who assaults with a gun, as well as the average victim, seems to be becoming younger and younger.

One factor not considered by Sugarmann or Wright is the rapid movement toward adding safety features to guns, such as trigger locks, combination locks, and cable locks. In October 1997 nine major U.S. gun manufacturers promised to include locks with new guns sold within the country. A study reported in the same month in the *Journal of the American Medical Association* revealed that in states that have child access prevention (CAP) laws, accidental deaths were down 23 percent compared with states that did not have these safety measures. However, negative factors not considered by the authors include the $10 billion annual weapons sales to military dictatorships abroad. In addition, unregulated guns remain readily available in the United States. Hence, any anticipated positive effects of gun registration laws and safety precautions may be diminished.

On another front, the city of Philadelphia, Pennsylvania, is considering a first-of-its-kind lawsuit against America's four dozen gun manufacturers. If successful, the manufacturers would be held liable for damages done by the guns they make and distribute. Such legal action would resemble the recent successful lawsuits against tobacco companies.

For an early discussion of the effectiveness of gun control laws, see J. Wright and P. Rossi's *Armed and Considered Dangerous: A Survey of Felons and Their Firearms* (Aldine de Gruyter, 1986) and D. McDowall, B. Wiserema, and C. Loftin's "Did Mandatory Firearm Ownership in Kennesaw Really Prevent

Burglaries?" *Sociology and Social Research* (October 1989). For a thoughtful overview of the issue, see Cook and Moore, "Gun Control," in J. Wilson and J. Petersilia, eds., *Crime* (ICS Press, 1995).

Current discussions from a cultural war perspective include "The Fight to Bear Arms," by G. Witkin et al., and "The Gun Lobby," by Ted Gest, both in *U.S. News and World Report* (May 22, 1995). Also see "Extreme Prejudice: How the Media Misrepresent the Militia Movement," by M. Tanner, *Reason* (July 1995). A seminal study that challenges supporters of gun control is G. Kleck's *Point Blank: Guns and Violence in America* (Aldine de Gruyter, 1991). Two articles from the same point of view are D. Kates, Jr.'s "Shot Down" and J. D. Wright's "Bad Guys, Bad Guns," both in *National Review* (March 6, 1995). Also challenging gun control laws but for different reasons is D. Polsby's "The False Promise of Gun Control," *The Atlantic Monthly* (March 1994).

Canada's recent legislation controlling guns has generated widespread responses. For several sides of this debate, see *Canadian Journal of Criminology* (April 1995) and "Fighting Back: Canadians Against Gun Control," by M. Nemeth, *Maclean's* (June 5, 1995). For a legalistic article that looks at melting down guns, see T. Funk's "Gun Control and Economic Discrimination," *Journal of Criminal Law and Criminology* (Winter 1995).

A recent book by J. D. Wright and J. Sheley is *In the Line of Fire: Youth, Guns, and Violence in Urban America* (Aldine de Gruyter, 1995). For another side of the issue, see L. Fingerhut and J. Kleinman's *Firearm Mortality Among Children and Youth* (U.S. National Center for Health Statistics, 1989). A summary of the sad finding that many adolescent suicides and accidental deaths result from guns can be found in H. Hendin, *Suicide in America* (W. W. Norton, 1995).

For another study that is sympathetic to Wright, see "Guns, Germs, and Science: Public Health Approaches to Gun Control," by D. Kopel, *Journal of the Medical Association of Georgia* (June 1995). A recent book by Gary Kleck, a recognized gun researcher, is *Targeting Guns: Firearms and Their Control* (Aldine de Gruyter, 1997). A discussion of gun checks can be found in D. Manson and D. Gilliard, "Presale Handgun Checks, 1996," *Bureau of Justice Statistics Bulletin* (September 1997). A useful delineation of the global arms market problem is "Guns 'R' Us," by M. Honey, *The Sentinel* (November 1997). For a chilling account of the potential problems of Louisiana's law allowing carjack victims to shoot to kill, see "Is It OK to Kill for a Car?" by A. S. Lewis, *USA Weekend* (October 24–26, 1997). On the Internet, see the home page of the pro-gun organization Independence Institute, which contains extensive studies, at http://i2i.org.

Finally, see N. A. Lewis, "N.R.A. Takes Aim at Study of Guns as Public Health Risk," *The New York Times* (August 27, 1995), which describes the National Rifle Association's attempts to eliminate a study of firearms as a public health issue being conducted by the Centers for Disease Control.

ISSUE 16

Should Euthanasia Be a Crime?

YES: Paul R. McHugh, from "The Kevorkian Epidemic," *The American Scholar* (Winter 1997)

NO: Ronald Dworkin et al., from "Assisted Suicide: The Philosophers' Brief," *The New York Review of Books* (March 27, 1997)

ISSUE SUMMARY

YES: Paul R. McHugh, director of the Department of Psychiatry and Behavioral Sciences at the Johns Hopkins University School of Medicine, contends that many patients who indicate that they want to die are actually mentally depressed individuals who should be counseled, not helped to die.

NO: Professor of jurisprudence Ronald Dworkin and five fellow moral philosophers, in a brief filed in two cases before the Supreme Court, maintain that individuals have a moral and constitutional right to determine their own life's value.

The word *euthanasia* is a combination of the Greek prefix *eu*, which means "good," and *thanatos*, meaning "death." Euthanasia therefore implies "easy death." Webster's New Collegiate Dictionary defines it as "the act or practice of killing individuals (such as persons or domestic animals) that are hopelessly sick or injured for reasons of mercy."

The legal aspect currently challenging America is physician-assisted suicide. This issue was largely brought to a head by Dr. Jack Kevorkian's helping over 85 people to die (since 1990) and the 1994 vote in Oregon (which was reaffirmed in November 1997) to allow physician-assisted suicide. Past legal decisions regarding euthanasia had to do with doctors' ceasing to provide necessities to keep patients alive—patients that were often comatose or in a persistent vegetative state (PVS)—or the patient's right to die and to not be forceably treated. Physician-assisted suicide is far more complicated. In Oregon physicians may legally prescribe lethal doses of drugs to terminally ill patients. This law is federally supported: the Supreme Court has upheld the right of states to provide their own guidelines in this area. Kevorkian is a critic of the Oregon measure, which precludes physicians' directly administering death, such as through a lethal injection. He and others claim that pills and other medicines often do not work or take hours, in contrast to his methods, which enable patients to die in minutes.

The issue, simply in terms of death-inducing strategies, has moved well beyond one of "should we pull the plug on a patient who has been unconscious for two years with no hope of resuscitation?" Of the estimated 30,000 suicides committed annually in the United States, less than 3 percent are by terminally ill people, and a very small fraction of that number are likely to have been assisted suicides. However, the number of patients who die because family members and physicians elected to withhold medicines or other life-sustaining supplies or simply failed to revive them is considerably larger. Meanwhile, proponents of physician-assisted suicide maintain that such "passive" measures are similar to when abortions were illegal and many women had to use wire hangers and other horrible techniques to induce abortion. They claim that many terminally ill patients who want to die are forced to suffocate themselves with plastic bags or use other crude means to kill themselves since neither physicians nor family and friends are allowed to assist them legally.

Compounding the issue of euthanasia, already laden with symbolic and emotional implications, is the fact that modern medical staffs can often prolong the lives of the severely injured and the elderly far longer than they used to. However, this is at fantastic economic as well as emotional cost (e.g., relatives seeing loved ones in a comatose or vegetative state). Also, people are living far longer on average than in the past, though sometimes under very uncomfortable medical circumstances. Thus, the potential pool of candidates for euthanasia is vast and growing. Many worry that the "slippery slope" may result in an epidemic of involuntary euthanasia—that is, doctors would allow very sick poor people or unconscious patients to die or even hasten their deaths through medical injections without their knowledge or consent. Observers of the experience in the Netherlands, where physician-assisted suicide has been legal for years, claim that this practice is widespread.

As you read the following selections by Paul R. McHugh and Ronald Dworkin et al., try to develop a typology (classification) of types of euthanasia (e.g., voluntary, involuntary, passive, active, ethically/legally acceptable, and unacceptable). Also consider types of safeguards that could be put into effect to minimize unanticipated negative consequences of physician-assisted suicides.

YES

Paul R. McHugh

THE KEVORKIAN EPIDEMIC

Dr. Jack Kevorkian of Detroit has been in the papers most days this past summer and autumn [1997] helping sick people kill themselves. He is said to receive hundreds of calls a week. Although his acts are illegal by statute and common law in Michigan, no one stops him. Many citizens, including members of three juries, believe he means well, perhaps thinking: Who knows? Just maybe, we ourselves shall need his services some day.

To me it looks like madness from every quarter. The patients are mad by definition in that they are suicidally depressed and demoralized; Dr. Kevorkian is "certifiable" in that his passions render him, as the state code specifies, "dangerous to others"; and the usually reliable people of Michigan are confused and anxious to the point of incoherence by terrors of choice that are everyday issues for doctors. These three disordered parties have converged, provoking a local epidemic of premature death.

* * *

Let me begin with the injured hosts of this epidemic, the patients mad by definition. At this writing, more than forty, as best we know, have submitted to Dr. Kevorkian's deadly charms. They came to him with a variety of medical conditions: Alzheimer's disease, multiple sclerosis, chronic pain, amyotrophic lateral sclerosis, cancer, drug addiction, and more. These are certainly disorders from which anyone might seek relief. But what kind of relief do patients with these conditions usually seek when they do not have a Dr. Kevorkian to extinguish their pain?

Both clinical experience and research on this question are extensive—and telling. A search for death does not accompany most terminal or progressive diseases. Pain-ridden patients customarily call doctors for remedies, not for termination of life. Physical incapacity, as with advanced arthritis, does not generate suicide. Even amyotrophic lateral sclerosis, or Lou Gehrig's disease, a harrowing condition I shall describe presently, is not associated with increased suicide amongst its sufferers. Most doctors learn these facts as they help patients and their families burdened by these conditions.

But we don't have to rely solely upon the testimonies of experienced physicians. Recently cancer patients in New England were asked about their attitudes toward death. The investigators—apparently surprised to discover a will to live when they expected to find an urge to die—reported in the *Lancet* (vol. 347, pp. 1805–1810, 1996) two striking findings. First, that cancer patients enduring pain were not inclined to want euthanasia or physician-assisted suicide. In fact, "patients actually experiencing pain were more likely to find euthanasia or physician-assisted suicide unacceptable." Second, those patients inclined toward suicide—whether in pain or not—were suffering from depression. As the investigators noted: "These data indicate a conflict between attitudes and possible practices related to euthanasia and physician-assisted suicide. These *interventions* were approved of for terminally ill patients with unremitting pain, but these are not the patients most likely to request such *interventions*.... There is *some* concern that with legislation of euthanasia or physician-assisted suicide non-psychiatric physicians, who generally have a poor ability to detect and treat depression, may allow life-ending *interventions* when treatment of depression may be more appropriate." (Italics added to identify mealymouthed expressions: *interventions* means homicides, and *some* means that we investigators should stay cool in our concerns—after all, it's not we who are dying.)

None of this is news to psychiatrists who have studied suicides associated with medical illnesses. Depression, the driving force in most cases, comes in two varieties: symptomatic depression found as a feature of particular diseases—that is, as one of the several symptoms of that

disease; and demoralization, the common state of mind of people in need of guidance for facing discouraging circumstances alone. Both forms of depression render patients vulnerable to feelings of hopelessness that, if not adequately confronted, may lead to suicide.

* * *

Let me first concentrate on the symptomatic depressions because an understanding of them illuminates much of the problem. By the term *symptomatic*, psychiatrists mean that with some physical diseases suicidal depression is one of the condition's characteristic features. Careful students of these diseases come to appreciate that this variety of depression is not to be accepted as a natural feeling of discouragement provoked by bad circumstances—that is, similar to the downhearted state of, say, a bankrupt man or a grief-stricken widow. Instead the depression we are talking about here, with its beclouding of judgment, sense of misery, and suicidal inclinations, is a symptom identical in nature to the fevers, pains, or loss of energy that are signs of the disease itself.

A good and early example of the recognition of symptomatic depression is found in George Huntington's classical (1872) description of the disorder eventually named after him: Huntington's disease. Huntington had first seen the condition when he was a youth visiting patients with his father, a family doctor on Long Island. He noted that one of the characteristic features of the condition was "the tendency to... that form of insanity which leads to suicide." Even now between 7 and 10 percent of nonhospitalized patients with Huntington's disease do succeed in killing themselves. Psychiatrists and neurologists have perceived that Parkinson's disease, multiple sclerosis, Alzheimer's disease, AIDS dementia, and some cerebral-vascular strokes all have this same tendency to provoke "that form of insanity which leads to suicide."

That these patients are insane is certain. They are overcome with a sense of hopelessness and despair, often with the delusional belief that they are in some way useless, burdensome, or even corrupt perpetrators of evil. One of my patients with Huntington's disease felt that Satan was dwelling within her and that she acted in accordance with his wishes. These patients lose their capacity to concentrate and reason, they have a pervasive and unremitting feeling of gloom, and a constant, even eager willingness to accept death. These characteristics of symptomatic depression recur in all the diseases mentioned above. Multiple Sclerosis (MS) patients are frequently afflicted by it. Some five or six of Dr. Kevorkian's patients had MS.

The problematic nature of symptomatic depression goes beyond the painful state of mind of the patient. Other observers—such as family members and physicians—may well take the depressive's disturbed, indeed insane, point of view as a proper assessment of his or her situation. It was this point that Huntington, long before the time of modern anti-depressant treatment, wished to emphasize by identifying it as an insanity. He knew that failure to diagnose this feature will lead to the neglect of efforts to treat the patient properly and to protect him or her from suicide until the symptom remits.

Such neglect is a crucial blunder, because, whether the underlying condition is Huntington's disease, Alzheimer's disease, MS, or something else, mod-

ern anti-depressant treatment is usually effective at relieving the mood disorder and restoring the patient's emotional equilibrium. In Michigan and in Holland, where physician-assisted suicide also takes place, these actions to hasten death are the ultimate neglect of patients with symptomatic depression; they are, really, a form of collusion with insanity.

The diagnosis of symptomatic depression is not overly difficult if its existence is remembered and its features systematically sought. But many of its characteristics—such as its capacity to provoke bodily pains—are not known to all physicians. The fact that such depression occurs in dire conditions, such as Huntington's disease, may weigh against its prompt diagnosis and treatment. Again and again, kindly intended physicians presume that a depression "makes sense"—given the patient's situation—and overlook the stereotypic signs of the insanity. They presume justifiable demoralization and forget the pharmacologically treatable depressions.

* * *

Over the last decade, at least among psychiatrists, the reality of symptomatic depressions has become familiar and treatment readiness has become the rule. Yet not all sick patients with life-threatening depression have symptomatic depressions. Many physically ill patients are depressed for perfectly understandable reasons, given the grueling circumstances of their progressive and intractable disease. Just as any misfortune can provoke grief and anxiety, so can awareness of loss of health and of a closed future.

Well-titled *demoralization*, this depression, too, has a number of attributes. It waxes and wanes with experiences and events, comes in waves, and is worse at certain times—such as during the night, when contemplating future discomforts and burdens, and when the patient is alone or uninstructed about the benefits that modern treatments can bring him.

In contrast to the symptomatic depressions that run their own course almost independent of events, demoralization is sensitive to circumstances and especially to the conduct of doctors toward the patient. Companionship, especially that which provides understanding and clear explanations of the actions to be taken in opposing disease and disability, can be immensely helpful in overcoming this state and sustaining the patient in a hopeful frame of mind.

The obverse is also true. If faced by inattentive physicians—absentee physicians most commonly—patients can become more discouraged and utterly demoralized by what they assume is their physician's resignation from a hopeless battle. All patients afflicted with disease —curable or incurable—are susceptible to bleak assumptions about their future and their value. These susceptibilities can be magnified or diminished by the behavior of their physicians.

The therapeutic implication here is that despairing assumptions wither if directly combated and shown to be an inaccurate analysis of the situation. Demoralization is an eminently treatable mental condition. Hopeless doctors, however, ready to see patients as untreatable, produce hopeless patients. The combination of the two produces a zeal for terminating effort. "What's the point?" becomes the cry of both patient and doctor.

This is the point: Depression, both in the form of a symptomatic mental state and in the form of demoralization, is the result of illness and circumstances combined and is treatable just as are other effects of illness. These treatments are the everyday skills of many physicians, but particularly of those physicians who are specialists in these disorders and can advance the treatments most confidently.

Most suicidally depressed patients are not rational individuals who have weighed the balance sheet of their lives and discovered more red than black ink. They are victims of altered attitudes about themselves and their situation, which cause powerful feelings of hopelessness to abound. Doctors can protect them from these attitudes by providing information, guidance, and support all along the way. Dr. Kevorkian, however, trades upon the vulnerabilities and mental disorders of these patients and in so doing makes a mockery of medicine as a discipline of informed concern for patients.

* * *

Let us turn to Dr. Kevorkian, the agent of this epidemic in Michigan, and consider why I think that he is "certifiably" insane, by which I mean that he suffers from a mental condition rendering him dangerous to others.

Without question, Dr. Kevorkian has proven himself dangerous, having participated in killing more than forty people already, with no end in sight. Dr. Kevorkian, by the way, does not shy from the word *killing.* He prescribes it and even coined a term for this practice—*medicide,* that is: "the termination of life performed by ... professional medical personnel (such as a doctor, nurse, paramedic, physician's assistant, or medical technologist)." [Kevorkian, J., *Prescription: Medicide,* Prometheus Books, Buffalo, New York, 1991, page 202.] (Note his sense of a whole industry of killing to come, with much of it to be carried out by technicians because the doctors are busy.)

The question is whether his behavior is a product of a mental disorder. Not everyone agrees on an answer. Indeed the *British Medical Journal (BMJ)* described Dr. Kevorkian as a "hero."

His champions see no discernible motive for Dr. Kevorkian other than that he believes his work is fitting. The *BMJ* notes that greed for money or fame or some sadistic urge does not motivate Dr. Kevorkian. They make much of the fact that he does not charge a fee for killing.

Because of the absence of such motives, the editors presume that he is a hero among doctors since it is only a "personal code of honor that admits of no qualification" that leads him into action.

But let us look rather more closely at "personal codes that admit no qualification." We have seen a few of them before and not all were admirable. As Dr. Kevorkian motors around Michigan carrying cylinders of carbon monoxide or bottles of potassium chloride to dispatch the sick, his is the motivation of a person with an "overvalued idea," a diagnostic formulation first spelled out by the psychiatrist Carl Wernicke in 1906. Wernicke differentiated overvalued ideas from obsessions and delusions. Overvalued ideas are often at the motivational heart of "personal codes that admit no qualification" and certainly provide a drive as powerful as that of hunger for money, fame, or sexual gratification.

An individual with an overvalued idea is someone who has taken up an idea shared by others in his milieu or culture and transformed it into a ruling passion or "monomania" for himself. It becomes the goal of all his efforts and he is prepared to sacrifice everything—family, reputation, health, even life itself—for it.

He presumes that what he does in its service is right regardless of any losses that he or others suffer for it. He sees all opposition as at best misguided and at worst malevolent.

For Dr. Kevorkian, people may die before their time and the fabric of their families may be torn apart, but it's all for the good if he can presume they were "suffering pain unnecessarily" and he has eliminated it. He scorns all opposition —in particular constitutional democratic opposition—as resting on bad faith or ignorance. Empowered by his idea, he feels free to disregard the law and any of its officers.

An overvalued idea has three characteristics: (1) it is a self-dominating but not idiosyncratic opinion, given great importance by (2) intense emotional feelings over its significance, and evoking (3) persistent behavior in its service. For Dr. Kevorkian, thinking about how to terminate the sick has become his exclusive concern. His belief in the justice of his ideas is intense enough for him to starve himself if thwarted by law.

Dr. Kevorkian thinks that all opposition to him is "bad faith" and thus worthy of contempt—a contempt he expresses with no reservation. He is fond of saying that the judicial system of our country is "corrupt," the religious members of our society are "irrational," the medical profession is "insane," the press is "meretricious."

He considers his own behavior "humanitarian." Dr. Kevorkian holds himself beyond reproach, even after killing one patient he believed had multiple sclerosis but whose autopsy revealed no evidence of that disease and another patient with the vague condition of "chronic fatigue syndrome" in whom no pathological process could be found at autopsy—

only Kevorkian's poison. He acts without taking a careful medical history, trying alternative treatments, or reflecting on how his actions affect such people as surviving family members.

Dr. Kevorkian's is a confident business. As the news reports flow out of Michigan, it appears that his threshold for medicide is getting lower. Physician-assisted suicide that had previously demanded an incurable disease such as Alzheimer's is now practiced upon patients with such chronic complaints as pelvic pain and emphysema, whose life expectancy cannot be specified. He can justify the active termination of anyone with an ailment —which is just what might be expected once the boundary against active killing by doctors has been breached. What's to stop him now that juries have found his actions to be de facto legal in Michigan?

A crucial aspect of overvalued ideas is that, in contrast to delusions, they are not idiosyncratic. They are ideas that can be found in a proportion of the public —often an influential proportion. It is from such reservoirs of opinion that the particular individual harnesses and amplifies an idea with the disproportionate zeal characteristic of a ruling passion. That Dr. Kevorkian can find people in the highest places—even within the medical profession—to support his ideas and say that they see heroism in his actions is not surprising, given the passion of the contemporary debate over euthanasia. In this way the person with the overvalued idea may be seen, by those who share his opinion but not his self-sacrificing zeal, as giving expression to their hopes —disregarding the slower processes of democracy, filled with prejudice against all who resist, and pumped up with a sense of a higher purpose and justice.

People such as Dr. Kevorkian have found a place in history. With some, with the passage of time, we come to agree with the idea if not the method by which the idea was first expressed. Such was John Brown, the abolitionist, ready to hack five anonymous farmers to death in the Pottowatomi massacre to advance his cause. With others we may come to tolerate some aspect of the idea but see its expression in actual behavior as ludicrous. Such was Carry Nation, the scourge of Kansas barkeeps and boozers, who went to jail hundreds of times for chopping up saloons with a small hatchet in the cause of temperance. Finally, for some, we come to recognize the potential for horror in an overvalued idea held by a person in high authority. Such was Adolf Hitler.

* * *

But how is it that anxieties and confusions about medical practice and death can so afflict the judicious people of Michigan as to paralyze them before the outrageous behavior of Dr. Kevorkian and thus generate an environment for this epidemic? In Michigan these states of mind derive from conflicting concerns over medical decisions. The citizens—like any inexpert group—are relatively uninformed about what doctors can do for patients, even in extreme situations. Conflicting goals and unfamiliar practices—common enough around medical decisions—produce anxiety and confusion every time.

No one thinks happily about dying, especially dying in pain. Death is bad; dying can be worse. Anyone who says he does not fear dying—and all the pain and suffering tied to it—has probably not experienced much in life.

This concern, though, certainly has been exaggerated in our times, even though now much can be done to relieve the heaviest burdens of terminally ill patients. Yet through a variety of sources —such as movies, newspapers, and essays—all the negative aspects of dying have been emphasized, the agonies embellished, and the loss of control represented by disease accentuated. Horror stories feed upon one another, and rumors of medical lack of interest grow into opinions that doctors both neglect the dying and hold back relief. Doctors are regularly accused of surrendering to professional taboos or to legal advice to avoid risk of malpractice or prosecution—and in this way are presumed ready to sacrifice their patients out of selfish fear for themselves.

On the contrary, most doctors try to collaborate with patients and do listen to their wishes, especially when treatments that carry painful burdens are contemplated. As Dr. Kevorkian can demonstrate—with videotapes, no less—the patients he killed asked him repeatedly for help in dying rather than for help in living. Do not they have some right to die at their own hands steadied by Dr. Kevorkian? Is not the matter of assisted suicide simply a matter of rights and wants to which any citizen of Michigan is entitled?

The idea of a right to suicide provokes most psychiatrists. Psychiatry has worked to teach everyone that suicide is not an uncomplicated, voluntary act to which rights attach. It has shown that suicide is an act provoked, indeed compelled, by mental disorder—such as a disorienting depression or a set of misdirected, even delusionary, ideas. In that sense psychiatry taught that suicidal people were not "responsible" for this behavior—no matter what they said or wrote

in final letters or testaments—any more than they would be for epileptic seizures.

This idea—generated from the careful study of the clinical circumstances and past histories of suicidal patients—gradually prevailed in civil law and even in the canon law of churches. As a result, laws against suicide were repealed—not to make suicide a "right" but to remove it from the status of a crime.

We psychiatrists thought we had done a worthy thing for our society, for families of patients, and even for patients themselves. We were not saying, not for a moment, that we approved of suicide. Far from it. We knew such deaths to be ugly and misguided—misguided in particular because the disposition to die, the wish for suicide, was, on inspection, often a symptom of the very mental disorders that psychiatry treats. Suicide in almost all cases is as far from a rational choice based on a weighing of the balance books of life as is responding to hallucinated voices or succumbing to the paranoid ideas of a charismatic madman such as Jim Jones, who at Jonestown directed a gruesome exhibition of mass assisted suicide.

Psychiatrists were united in their views about suicide and shook their heads when contemplating past traditions when suicides were considered scandalous. We did not think too deeply into the consequences of our actions. For, after suicide ceased to be a crime, it soon became a right and, conceivably under some circumstances, such as when costs of care grow onerous, an obligation. Psychiatrists, who had worked for decades demonstrating that suicides were insane acts, are now recruited in Holland to assure that requests for suicide made by patients offered "no hope of cure" by their doctors are "rational."

What had begun as an effort at explanation and understanding of the tragic act of suicide has developed into complicity in the seduction of vulnerable people into that very behavior. The patients are seduced just as the victims in Jonestown were—by isolating them, sustaining their despair, revoking alternatives, stressing examples of others choosing to die, and sweetening the deadly poison by speaking of death with dignity. If even psychiatrists succumb to this complicity with death, what can be expected of the lay public in Michigan?

* * *

At the heart of the confusion lies the contention that if the aim of medicine is to eliminate suffering and if only the killing of the patient will relieve the suffering, then killing is justified. On this logic rests Dr. Kevorkian's repeatedly successful defense before the juries of Michigan.

Yet the aim of medicine cannot simply be to prevent suffering. Not only would that be an impossible task, given the nature of human life, but it would diminish the scope of human potential —almost all of which demands some travail. The elimination of suffering is a veterinary rather than a medical goal. But veterinarians eliminate their animal subjects for other reasons than suffering. This fact can occasionally startle us.

When the race horse Cavonnier, second in the 1996 Kentucky Derby, pulled up lame during the Belmont Stakes later in the year, everyone watching on television feared that he must have broken a bone in his leg, with the inevitable consequences. His trainer provided brief comfort when he came on television to describe what had turned out to be a ligamentous rather than a bony injury

to the animal. "This will probably end his racing career," he noted, "but it is not a life-threatening injury." He then paused, before adding, "However, he *is* a gelding." An ominous comment for Cavonnier and one worth remembering when anyone says, in defense of killing infirm people, "They shoot horses, don't they?" They do, but for many reasons other than just to protect horses from suffering. Sometimes it's to save money. Are we ready for the Cavonnier test for ourselves?

* * *

The idea that diseases herald only mortality and death, to be hurried along if their burdens are overwhelming, is not only an ethical error but a fundamental misunderstanding of contemporary medical science. Contemporary physician/scientists do not think of diseases as "entities," "things," "maledictions," and, in this sense, signposts to the grave, but as processes in life for which the body has ways of compensating and resisting, even if only temporarily. Diseases, in this way, are construed as forms of life under altered circumstances rather than as modes of death.

Because diseases are processes rather than entities, efforts to sustain life, alleviate symptoms, and moderate impairments represent collaborations with nature itself. These efforts remain the essence of doctoring, the whole reason for investing in the study of diseases and the body's responses to them. Physician-assisted suicide and euthanasia attack the very premises on which medical science and practices are progressing today and do so by denying the life that scientific conceptions of disease represent. Life with dignity—not death with dignity—is what doctors aim for in their practice and in their science.

* * *

Medicine is one of the practical arts —a fact old enough to be known to Aristotle—among which are included navigation, economics, and architecture and for which the goal is usually obvious and unquestioned. For medicine, actions to prevent, alleviate, and cure are aimed at the obvious goal of sustaining the life and health of patients. Technical progress through scientific discoveries assists these actions, rendering them more effective. But modern techniques can seem in some circumstances to forestall the inevitable, prolong suffering, deny reality with little or no gain to the patient. Dr. Kevorkian writes and disseminates stories on this theme to justify his actions and to bolster his support. Allow me to present a story in which the conflict between preserving life and surrendering to disease was resolved by doctors who recognized their limits while striving to facilitate and extend a person's best experiences.

Nelson Butters was one of America's most distinguished neuropsychologists of the last twenty-five years. He died in 1995 at age fifty-eight after suffering for just under three years from the nightmare known as Lou Gehrig's disease. This disease is a relentless and progressive wasting of the body because of an atrophic degeneration of the nerves that innervate the muscles. As the body wastes away over the course of months, the mind is customarily unaffected and witnesses these depredations. It anticipates further weakness and ultimate death from a loss of strength to breathe. Such an affliction you would not wish on your worst enemy. Dr. Jack Kevorkian lives to termi-

nate—the earlier the better—any patient smitten by it.

My colleague and friend Nelson Butters saw it through to its natural end. In so doing—without making it his mission— he rebuked those who cannot (or will not) differentiate incurable diseases, of which there are many, from untreatable patients, of which there are few.

Nelson was a great scientist and an indomitable man. He took on all of life's challenges, personal and professional, with vigor and courage. But when he learned that he had Lou Gehrig's disease, he was shaken and responded with a most natural discouragement. "I'd rather die than be helpless," he said several times to his doctors. Yet he proved willing to try the assistance they offered him at each of the bad patches in his course, so that he could continue to enjoy what remained despite his illness. He had neurologists aiding him with his growing weakness, and he had psychiatrists and psychologists ready to assist him when he was tormented by his prospects.

He had bad times. They came mostly when some partial surrender to the disease was required—accepting a wheelchair, retreating to bed, undergoing a tracheostomy to facilitate breathing—but after each procedure, and despite its implicit indication that his condition was progressing, he recovered his cheer as he found himself more comfortable and able to continue his work with students and colleagues and his life with his family.

Like Stephen Hawking, Nelson toward the end made use of computers to communicate and work. This permitted him to edit a major journal in neuropsychology, even when he could move only one finger and then only one toe. With these small movements he used E-mail to write to colleagues everywhere—usually on professional matters, but also to transmit amusing academic gossip.

Eventually, Nelson lost all his strength. He was left with only eye-blinking signals, breathing with the help of a machine. Then he asked his doctors, with his family around him, that the ventilator cease breathing for him. This was done, and on a weekend he slipped into a coma and died—thirty-four months after his symptoms began.

Nelson, his family, and his doctors had achieved much together. They fought to enable him to sustain purposeful life as long as possible. They weathered distressing, powerfully painful portions of his clinical course. The doctors never suggested a poison to shorten his life. When there was still something to do, they encouraged him to try to do it and helped allay his reluctance at the prospect. And in the end they surrendered to the illness without betraying their mission or letting contemporary technology drag them along.

It was grim. Everyone who knew him was saddened to think that Nelson had to suffer so. But everyone also was struck by how he overcame the disease by staying purposeful, lively, and wittily intelligent right through to the end, teaching much to all of us.

* * *

I tell this story because many believe that permitting a progressive infirmity to continue right out to its natural end is cruel and pointless. It certainly is tough. Any gains need to be identified. In fact, the gains for Nelson Butters were several.

Most obvious among them was the continuation of Nelson's work as a scientist, an editor, and a teacher for many months, despite his illness. This was no trivial gain, for he was an inventive scientist with deep insight into his discipline. He continued to function effectively and to enjoy his work and the accomplishments of his students.

Another gain was an extended duration of Nelson's company to his family and his friends. Again, no trivial matter, for he was a lovable person. One of his daughters decided to help nurse him through his trials, and after his death, reflecting on all she had seen and done, decided to take up a career in nursing incapacitated people.

Finally, there was the appreciation—to the point of amazement—on the part of his doctors of the value he fashioned from their efforts to help him. They told me how he had taken what they offered and made more of it—more than they expected and more in the form of continuing work and personal life—than they thought could be achieved. This was as true of the neurologists who offered means to offset his physical impairments as it was of the psychiatrists who at times of particular discouragement helped him keep going.

These gains were made easier because Nelson was such a good man and had such a good family to support him. Yet I sensed the awe felt by the doctors themselves for what had been accomplished in the end. Almost despite themselves and their own feelings about this awful disease, they had been partners with Nelson in a great achievement. They had carried out excellently the task set before doctors —help the patient encounter and resist the chaos of disease for as long as possible—and thus preserve the purposeful character of life to its end.

In Nelson's life a set of interwoven but distinct purposes—husband, father, teacher, scientist—were sustained by him with the help of several doctors. And this happened despite the depredations of a crushing disease and the recurrent waves of discouragement that naturally accompany the loss of vitality and the realization of impending death.

* * *

But there was something more in Nelson's story. For all that he was surrounded by devoted nurses, technicians, family, and physicians, death came to him alone just as it will to each of us. Its approach confronts us all with the challenge to decide what moves us, what matters most, what we love. Nelson loved life. He wanted as much of it as he could have. Through this love he won a victory over death—for himself, for his family, for all who knew him.

This is really what distinguishes him from Dr. Kevorkian, his sad victims, and those who support his cause. None of them love life the way Nelson did —not enough, certainly, to work hard and suffer much for it, not enough to appreciate it throughout its course, when it flickers just as much as when it glows. And certainly not enough to realize that sometimes we need help to protect it so that we don't throw it away.

To be on the side of life provides a source of sanity. Be on the side of life

and your course is clear, your efforts concentrated, the rules coherent. Bad patches can then be overcome, and even bad luck such as befell my friend Nelson Butters can be turned into something good. Be on the side of death and things fall apart, chaos reigns, and the fearful passions evoked by conflicting aims make malice, misdirection, sentiment, and compassion all look the same.

* * *

One can think of ways to combat the deadly convergence of madnesses in Michigan and to deter the spread of this local epidemic to other regions of our country. The suicidal patients certainly should be treated for their depressive vulnerabilities by doctors able to assist them with their underlying illnesses. Dr. Kevorkian, the agent of their extinction, should be stopped by whatever means the state has at its disposal to stay dangerous men. And the people of Michigan should be taught about the capacities of modern medicine. With this information, the hope is, they will emerge from their anxious confusions, accept mortality for what it is rather than for what they imagine, and, at last, end their support for this insanity.

NO

Ronald Dworkin et al.

ASSISTED SUICIDE: THE PHILOSOPHERS' BRIEF

INTRODUCTION

... The laws of all but one American state now forbid doctors to prescribe lethal pills for patients who want to kill themselves. These cases began when groups of dying patients and their doctors in Washington State and New York each sued asking that these prohibitions be declared unconstitutional so that the patients could be given, when and if they asked for it, medicine to hasten their death. The pleadings described the agony in which the patient plaintiffs were dying, and two federal Circuit Courts of Appeal... agreed with the plaintiffs that the Constitution forbids the government from flatly prohibiting doctors to help end such desperate and pointless suffering.

Washington State and New York appealed these decisions to the Supreme Court, and a total of sixty amicus briefs were filed.... The justices repeatedly cited two versions—one theoretical, the other practical—of the "slippery slope" argument: that it would be impossible to limit a right to assisted suicide in an acceptable way, once that right was recognized.

The theoretical version of the argument denies that any principled line can be drawn between cases in which proponents say a right of assisted suicide is appropriate and those in which they concede that it is not.... Why should it be denied to dying patients who are so feeble or paralyzed that they cannot take pills themselves and who beg a doctor to inject a lethal drug into them? Or to patients who are not dying but face years of intolerable physical or emotional pain, or crippling paralysis or dependence? But if the right were extended that far, on what ground could it be denied to anyone who had formed a desire to die—to a sixteen-year-old suffering from a severe case of unrequited love, for example?

* * *

The philosophers' brief answers these questions in two steps. First, it defines a very general moral and constitutional principle—that every competent person has the right to make momentous personal decisions which invoke fundamental religious or philosophical convictions about life's value for himself. Second, it recognizes that people may make such momentous decisions impulsively or out of emotional depression, when their act does not reflect their enduring convictions; and it therefore allows that in some circumstances a state has the constitutional power to override that right in order to protect citizens from mistaken but irrevocable acts of self-destruction. States may be allowed to prevent assisted suicide by people who—it is plausible to think—would later be grateful if they were prevented from dying.

That two-step argument would justify a state's protecting a disappointed adolescent from himself. It would equally plainly not justify forcing a competent dying patient to live in agony a few weeks longer. People will of course disagree about the cases in between these extremes....

The practical version of the slippery slope argument is more complex. If assisted suicide were permitted in principle, every state would presumably adopt regulations to insure that a patient's decision for suicide is informed, competent, and free. But many people fear that such regulations could not be adequately enforced, and that particularly vulnerable patients—poor patients dying in overcrowded hospitals that had scarce resources, for example—might be pressured or hustled into a decision for death they would not otherwise make. The evidence suggests, however, that such patients might be better rather than less well protected if assisted suicide were legalized with appropriate safeguards.

More of them could then benefit from relief that is already available—illegally —to more fortunate people who have established relationships with doctors will-

ing to run the risks of helping them to die. The current two-tier system—a chosen death and an end of pain outside the law for those with connections and stony refusals for most other people—is one of the greatest scandals of contemporary medical practice. The sense many middle-class people have that if necessary their own doctor "will know what to do" helps to explain why the political pressure is not stronger for a fairer and more open system in which the law acknowledges for everyone what influential people now expect for themselves....

* * *

The most important benefit of legalized assisted suicide for poor patients however, might be better care while they live. For though the medical experts cited in various briefs disagreed sharply about the percentage of terminal cases in which pain can be made tolerable through advanced and expensive palliative techniques, they did not disagree that a great many patients do not receive the relief they could have. The Solicitor General who urged the Court to reverse the lower court judgments conceded in the oral argument that 25 percent of terminally ill patients actually do die in pain. That appalling figure is the result of several factors, including medical ignorance and fear of liability, inadequate hospital funding, and (as the Solicitor General suggested) the failure of insurers and health care programs to cover the cost of special hospice care....

According to several briefs, moreover, patients whose pain is either uncontrollable or uncontrolled are often "terminally sedated"—intravenous drugs (usually barbiturates or benzodiazepenes) are injected to induce a pharmacologic coma during which the patient is given neither water nor nutrition and dies sooner than he otherwise would. Terminal sedation is widely accepted as legal, though it advances death. But it is not subject to regulations nearly as stringent as those that a state forced to allow assisted suicide would enact, because such regulations would presumably include a requirement that hospitals, before accepting any request for assistance in suicide, must demonstrate that effective medical care including state-of-the-art pain management had been offered. The guidelines recently published by a network of ethics committees in the Bay Area of California, for example, among other stringent safeguards, provide that a primary care physician who receives a request for suicide must make an initial referral to a hospice program or to a physician experienced in palliative care, and certify in a formal report filed in a state registry, signed by an independent second physician with expertise in such care, that the best available pain relief has been offered to the patient....

* * *

So neither version of the slippery slope argument seems very strong. It is nevertheless understandable that Supreme Court justices are reluctant, particularly given how little experience we have so far with legalized assisted suicide, to declare that all but one of the states must change their laws to allow a practice many citizens think abominable and sacrilegious. But as the philosphers' brief that follows emphasizes, the Court is in an unusually difficult position. If it closes the door to a constitutional right to assisted suicide it will do substantial damage to constitutional practice and precedent, as well as to thousands of people in great suffering. It would face a dilemma in justifying any

such decision, because it would be forced to choose between the two unappealing strategies that the brief describes.

The first strategy—declaring that terminally ill patients in great pain do not have a constitutional right to control their own deaths, even in principle—seems alien to our constitutional system.... It would also undermine a variety of the Court's own past decisions, including the carefully constructed position on abortion set out in its 1993 decision in *Casey*....

[S]everal justices suggested a "common-sense" distinction between the moral significance of acts, on the one hand, and omissions, on the other. This distinction, they suggested, would justify a constitutional distinction between prescribing lethal pills and removing life support; for, in their view, removing support is only a matter of "letting nature take its course," while prescribing pills is an active intervention that brings death sooner than natural processes would.

The discussion of this issue in the philosophers' brief is therefore particularly significant. The brief insists that such suggestions wholly misunderstand the "common-sense" distinction, which is not between acts and omissions, but between acts or omissions that are designed to cause death and those that are not. One justice suggested that a patient who insists that life support be disconnected is not committing suicide. That is wrong: he is committing suicide if he aims at death, as most such patients do, just as someone whose wrist is cut in an accident is committing suicide if he refuses to try to stop the bleeding. The distinction between acts that aim at death and those that do not cannot justify a constitutional distinction between assisting in suicide and terminating life support. Some doctors, who stop life support only because the patient so demands, do not aim at death. But neither do doctors who prescribe lethal pills only for the same reason, and hope that the patient does not take them. And many doctors who terminate life support obviously do aim at death, including those who deny nutrition during terminal sedation, because denying nutrition is designed to hasten death, not to relieve pain.

* * *

There are equally serious objections, however, to the second strategy the philosophers' brief discusses. This strategy concedes a general right to assisted suicide but holds that states have the power to judge that the risks of allowing any exercise of that right are too great. It is obviously dangerous for the Court to allow a state to deny a constitutional right on the ground that the state lacks the will or resource to enforce safeguards if it is exercised, particularly when the case for the practical version of the "slippery slope" objection seems so weak and has been little examined. As Justice Rehnquist... observed,... "[I]f we assume a liberty interest but nevertheless say that, even assuming a liberty interest, a state can prohibit it entirely, that would be rather a conundrum." ...

—Ronald Dworkin

THE BRIEF OF THE AMICI CURIAE

Introduction and Summary of Argument

These cases do not invite or require the Court to make moral, ethical, or religious judgments about how people should approach or confront their death or about when it is ethically appropriate to hasten one's own death or to ask others for help in doing so. On the contrary, they ask the Court to recognize that individuals have a constitutionally protected interest in making these grave judgments for themselves, free from the imposition of any religious or philosophical orthodoxy by court or legislature. States have a constitutionally legitimate interest in protecting individuals from irrational, ill-informed, pressured, or unstable decisions to hasten their own death. To that end, states may regulate and limit the assistance that doctors may give individuals who express a wish to die. But states may not deny people in the position of the patient-plaintiffs in these cases the opportunity to demonstrate, through whatever reasonable procedures the state might institute—even procedures that err on the side of caution—that their decision to die is indeed informed, stable, and fully free. Denying that opportunity to terminally ill patients who are in agonizing pain or otherwise doomed to an existence they regard as intolerable could only be justified on the basis of a religious or ethical conviction about the value or meaning of life itself. Our Constitution forbids government to impose such convictions on its citizens.

Petitioners [i.e., the state authorities of Washington and New York] and the amici who support them offer two contradictory arguments. Some deny that the patient-plaintiffs have any constitutionally protected liberty interest in hastening their own deaths. But that liberty interest flows directly from this Court's previous decisions. It flows from the right of people to make their own decisions about matters "involving the most intimate and personal choices a person may make in a lifetime, choices central to personal dignity and autonomy." *Planned Parenthood v. Casey* (1992).

The Solicitor General, urging reversal in support of Petitioners, recognizes that the patient-plaintiffs do have a constitutional liberty interest at stake in these cases. *See* Brief for the United States as Amicus Curiae Supporting Petitioners at 12, *Washington v. Vacco* [hereinafter Brief for the United States] ("The term 'liberty' in the Due Process Clause... is broad enough to encompass an interest on the part of terminally ill, mentally competent adults in obtaining relief from the kind of suffering experienced by the plaintiffs in this case, which includes not only severe physical pain, but also the despair and distress that comes from physical deterioration and the inability to control basic bodily functions.")....

The Solicitor General nevertheless argues that Washington and New York properly ignored this profound interest when they required the patient-plaintiffs to live on in circumstances they found intolerable. He argues that a state may simply declare that it is unable to devise a regulatory scheme that would adequately protect patients whose desire to die might be ill-informed or unstable or foolish or not fully free, and that a state may therefore fall back on a blanket prohibition. This Court has never accepted that patently dangerous rationale for denying protection altogether to a conceded fundamental constitutional interest. It would be a serious mistake to do so now. If that rationale were accepted, an interest acknowledged to be constitutionally protected would be rendered empty.

Argument

I. The Liberty Interest Asserted Here Is Protected by the Due Process Clause

The Due Process Clause of the Fourteenth Amendment protects the liberty interest asserted by the patient-plaintiffs here.

Certain decisions are momentous in their impact on the character of a person's life—decisions about religious faith, political and moral allegiance, marriage, procreation, and death, for example. Such deeply personal decisions pose controversial questions about how and why human life has value. In a free society, individuals must be allowed to make those decisions for themselves, out of their own faith, conscience, and convictions. This Court has insisted, in a variety of contexts and circumstances, that this great freedom is among those protected by the Due Process Clause as essential to a community of "ordered liberty." In its recent decision in *Planned Parenthood v. Casey* (1992), the Court offered a paradigmatic statement of that principle:

> matters [] involving the most intimate and personal choices a person may make in a lifetime, choices central to a person's dignity and autonomy, are central to the liberty protected by the Fourteenth Amendment.

That declaration reflects an idea underlying many of our basic constitutional protections....

A person's interest in following his own convictions at the end of life is so central a part of the more general right to make "intimate and personal choices" for himself that a failure to protect that particular interest would undermine the general right altogether. Death is, for each of us, among the most significant events of life. As the Chief

Justice said in *Cruzan v. Missouri* (1990), "[t]he choice between life and death is a deeply personal decision of obvious and overwhelming finality." Most of us see death—whatever we think will follow it—as the final act of life's drama, and we want that last act to reflect our own convictions, those we have tried to live by, not the convictions of others forced on us in our most vulnerable moment.

Different people, of different religious and ethical beliefs, embrace very different convictions about which way of dying confirms and which contradicts the value of their lives. Some fight against death with every weapon their doctors can devise. Others will do nothing to hasten death even if they pray it will come soon. Still others, including the patient-plaintiffs in these cases, want to end their lives when they think that living on, in the only way they can, would disfigure rather than enhance the lives they had created. Some people make the latter choice not just to escape pain. Even if it were possible to eliminate all pain for a dying patient—and frequently that is not possible—that would not end or even much alleviate the anguish some would feel at remaining alive, but intubated, helpless, and often sedated near oblivion.

None of these dramatically different attitudes about the meaning of death can be dismissed as irrational. None should be imposed, either by the pressure of doctors or relatives or by the fiat of government, on people who reject it. Just as it would be intolerable for government to dictate that doctors never be permitted to try to keep someone alive as long as possible, when that is what the patient wishes, so it is intolerable for government to dictate that doctors may never, under any circumstances, help someone to die who believes that further life means only

degradation. The constitution insists that people must be free to make these deeply personal decisions for themselves and must not be forced to end their lives in a way that appalls them, just because that is what some majority thinks proper.

II. This Court's Decisions in Casey and Cruzan Compel Recognition of a Liberty Interest Here

A. Casey supports the Liberty Interest Asserted Here In *Casey*, this Court, in holding that a state cannot constitutionally proscribe abortion in all cases, reiterated that the Constitution protects a sphere of autonomy in which individuals must be permitted to make certain decisions for themselves. The Court began its analysis by pointing out that "[a]t the heart of liberty is the right to define one's own concept of existence, of meaning, of the universe, and of the mystery of human life." Choices flowing out of these conceptions, on matters "involving the most intimate and personal choices a person may make in a lifetime, choices central to personal dignity and autonomy, are central to the liberty protected by the Fourteenth Amendment." ...

The analysis in *Casey* compels the conclusion that the patient-plaintiffs have a liberty interest in this case that a state cannot burden with a blanket prohibition. Like a woman's decision whether to have an abortion, a decision to die involves one's very "destiny" and inevitably will be "shaped to a large extent on [one's] own conception of [one's] spiritual imperatives and [one's] place in society." Just as a blanket prohibition on abortion would involve the improper imposition of one conception of the meaning and value of human existence on all individuals, so too would a blanket prohibition on assisted suicide. The liberty interest asserted here cannot be rejected without undermining the rationale of *Casey*....

B. Cruzan Supports the Liberty Interest Asserted Here   We agree with the Solicitor General that this Court's decision in "*Cruzan*...supports the conclusion that a liberty interest is at stake in this case." Petitioners, however, insist that the present cases can be distinguished because the right at issue in *Cruzan* was limited to a right to reject an unwanted invasion of one's body. But this Court repeatedly has held that in appropriate circumstances a state may require individuals to accept unwanted invasions of the body. [For example,] extraction of blood sample from individual suspected of driving while intoxicated, notwithstanding defendant's objection, does not violate privilege against self-incrimination or other constitutional rights....

The liberty interest at stake in *Cruzan* was a more profound one. If a competent patient has a constitutional right to refuse life-sustaining treatment, then, the Court implied, the state could not override that right. The regulations upheld in *Cruzan* were designed only to ensure that the individual's wishes were ascertained correctly. Thus, if *Cruzan* implies a right of competent patients to refuse life-sustaining treatment, that implication must be understood as resting not simply on a right to refuse bodily invasions but on the more profound right to refuse medical intervention when what is at stake is a momentous personal decision, such as the timing and manner of one's death....

Cruzan also supports the proposition that a state may not burden a terminally ill patient's liberty interest in determining the time and manner of his death by prohibiting doctors from terminating life support. Seeking to distinguish *Cruzan*, Petitioners insist that a state may nevertheless burden that right in a different way by forbidding doctors to assist in the suicide of patients who are not on life-support machinery. They argue that doctors who remove life support are only allowing a natural process to end in death whereas doctors who prescribe lethal drugs are intervening to cause death....

This argument is based on a misunderstanding of the pertinent moral principles. It is certainly true that when a patient does not wish to die, different acts, each of which foreseeably results in his death, nevertheless have very different moral status. When several patients need organ transplants and organs are scarce, for example, it is morally permissible for a doctor to deny an organ to one patient, even though he will die without it, in order to give it to another. But it is certainly not permissible for a doctor to kill one patient in order to use his organs to save another. The morally significant difference between those two acts is not, however, that killing is a positive act and not providing an organ is a mere omission, or that killing someone is worse than merely allowing a "natural" process to result in death. It would be equally impermissible for a doctor to let an injured patient bleed to death, or to refuse antibiotics to a patient with pneumonia—in each case the doctor would have allowed death to result from a "natural" process—in order to make his organs available for transplant to others. A doctor violates his patient's rights whether the doctor acts or refrains from acting, against the patient's wishes, in a way that is designed to cause death.

When a competent patient does want to die, the moral situation is obviously different, because then it makes no sense to appeal to the patient's right not to be killed as a reason why an act designed to cause his death is impermissible. From the patient's point of view, there is no morally pertinent difference between a doctor's terminating treatment that keeps him alive, if that is what he wishes, and a doctor's helping him to end his own life by providing lethal pills he may take himself, when ready, if that is what he wishes—except that the latter may be quicker and more humane. Nor is that a pertinent difference from the doctor's point of view. If and when it is permissible for him to act with death in view, it does not matter which of those two means he and his patient choose. If it is permissible for a doctor deliberately to withdraw medical treatment in order to allow death to result from a natural process, then it is equally permissible for him to help his patient hasten his own death more actively, if that is the patient's express wish.

It is true that some doctors asked to terminate life support are reluctant and do so only in deference to a patient's right to compel them to remove unwanted invasions of his body. But other doctors, who believe that their most fundamental professional duty is to act in the patient's interests and that, in certain circumstances, it is in their patient's best interests to die, participate willingly in such decisions: they terminate life support to cause death because they know that is what their patient wants. *Cruzan* implied that a state may not absolutely prohibit a doctor from deliberately causing death, at the patient's request, in that way and for that reason. If so, then a state may not prohibit doctors from deliberately us-

ing more direct and often more humane means to the same end when that is what a patient prefers. The fact that failing to provide life-sustaining treatment may be regarded as "only letting nature take its course" is no more morally significant in this context, when the patient wishes to die, than in the other, when he wishes to live. Whether a doctor turns off a respirator in accordance with the patient's request or prescribes pills that a patient may take when he is ready to kill himself, the doctor acts with the same intention: to help the patient die.

The two situations do differ in one important respect. Since patients have a right not to have life-support machinery attached to their bodies, they have, in principle, a right to compel its removal. But that is not true in the case of assisted suicide: patients in certain circumstances have a right that the state not forbid doctors to assist in their death, but they have no right to compel a doctor to assist them. The right in question, that is, is only a right to the help of a willing doctor.

III. State Interests Do Not Justify a Categorical Prohibition on All Assisted Suicide

The Solicitor General concedes that "a competent, terminally ill adult has a constitutionally cognizable liberty interest in avoiding the kind of suffering experienced by the plaintiffs in this case." He agrees that this interest extends not only to avoiding pain, but to avoiding an existence the patient believes to be one of intolerable indignity or incapacity as well. The Solicitor General argues, however, that states nevertheless have the right to "override" this liberty interest altogether, because a state could reasonably conclude that allowing doctors to assist in suicide, even under the most stringent regulations and procedures that could be devised, would unreasonably endanger the lives of a number of patients who might ask for death in circumstances when it is plainly not in their interests to die or when their consent has been improperly obtained.

This argument is unpersuasive, however, for at least three reasons. *First*, in *Cruzan*, this Court noted that its various decisions supported the recognition of a general liberty interest in refusing medical treatment, even when such refusal could result in death. The various risks described by the Solicitor General apply equally to those situations. For instance, a patient kept alive only by an elaborate and disabling life-support system might well become depressed, and doctors might be equally uncertain whether the depression is curable: such a patient might decide for death only because he has been advised that he will die soon anyway or that he will never live free of the burdensome apparatus, and either diagnosis might conceivably be mistaken. Relatives or doctors might subtly or crudely influence that decision, and state provision for the decision may (to the same degree in this case as if it allowed assisted suicide) be thought to encourage it.

Yet there has been no suggestion that states are incapable of addressing such dangers through regulation. In fact, quite the opposite is true. In *McKay v. Bergstedt* (1990), for example, the Nevada Supreme Court held that "competent adult patients desiring to refuse or discontinue medical treatment" must be examined by two nonattending physicians to determine whether the patient is mentally competent, understands his prognosis and treatment options, and appears free of coercion or pressure in making

his decision. See also: *id.* (in the case of terminally-ill patients with natural life expectancy of less than six months, [a] patient's right of self-determination shall be deemed to prevail over state interests, whereas [a] non-terminal patient's decision to terminate life-support systems must first be weighed against relevant state interests by trial judge); [and] *In re Farrel* (1987) ([which held that a] terminally-ill patient requesting termination of life-support must be determined to be competent and properly informed about [his] prognosis, available treatment options and risks, and to have made decision voluntarily and without coercion). Those protocols served to guard against precisely the dangers that the Solicitor General raises....

Indeed, the risks of mistake are overall greater in the case of terminating life support. *Cruzan* implied that a state must allow individuals to make such decisions through an advance directive stipulating either that life support be terminated (or not initiated) in described circumstances when the individual was no longer competent to make such a decision himself, or that a designated proxy be allowed to make that decision. All the risks just described are present when the decision is made through or pursuant to such an advance directive, and a grave further risk is added: that the directive, though still in force, no longer represents the wishes of the patient. The patient might have changed his mind before he became incompetent, though he did not change the directive, or his proxy may make a decision that the patient would not have made himself if still competent. In *Cruzan*, this Court held that a state may limit these risks through reasonable regulation. It did not hold—or even suggest—that a state may avoid them through a blanket prohibition that, in effect, denies the liberty interest altogether.

Second, nothing in the record supports the [Solicitor General's] conclusion that no system or rules and regulations could adequately reduce the risk of mistake. As discussed above, the experience of states in adjudicating requests to have life-sustaining treatment removed indicates the opposite. The Solicitor General has provided no persuasive reason why the same sort of procedures could not be applied effectively in the case of a competent individual's request for physician-assisted suicide.

Indeed, several very detailed schemes for regulating physician-assisted suicide have been submitted to the voters of some states and one has been enacted. In addition, concerned groups, including a group of distinguished professors of law and other professionals have drafted and defended such schemes. The weakness of the Solicitor General's argument is signaled by his strong reliance on the experience in the Netherlands which, in effect, allows assisted suicide pursuant to published guidelines. The Dutch guidelines are more permissive than the proposed and model American statutes, however. The Solicitor General deems the Dutch practice of ending the lives of people like neo-nates who cannot consent particularly noteworthy, for example, but that practice could easily and effectively be made illegal by any state regulatory scheme without violating the Constitution.

[T]he question here is... whether a state has interests sufficiently compelling to allow it to take the extraordinary step of altogether refusing the exercise of a liberty interest of constitutional dimension. In those circumstances, the burden is plainly on the state to demonstrate that the risk of mistakes is very high.... Neither of the Petitioners has made such a showing.

Nor could they. The burden of proof on any state attempting to show this would be very high. Consider, for example, the burden a state would have to meet to show that it was entitled altogether to ban public speeches in favor of unpopular causes because it could not guarantee, either by regulations short of an outright ban or by increased police protection, that such speeches would not provoke a riot that would result in serious injury or death to an innocent party. Or that it was entitled to deny those accused of crime the procedural rights that the Constitution guarantees, such as the right to a jury trial, because the security risk those rights would impose on the community would be too great....

Third, it is doubtful whether the risks the Solicitor General cites are even of the right character to serve as justification for an absolute prohibition on the exercise of an important liberty interest. The risks fall into two groups. The first is the risk of medical mistake, including a misdiagnosis of competence or terminal illness. To be sure, no scheme of regulation, no matter how rigorous, can altogether guarantee that medical mistakes will not be made. But the Constitution does not allow a state to deny patients a great variety of important choices, for which informed consent is properly deemed necessary, just because the information on which the consent is given may, in spite of the most strenuous efforts to avoid mistake, be wrong. Again, these identical risks are present in decisions to terminate life support, yet they do not justify an absolute prohibition on the exercise of the right.

The second group consists of risks that a patient will be unduly influenced by considerations that the state might deem it not in his best interests to be swayed by, for example, the feelings and views of close family members. But what a patient regards as proper grounds for such a decision normally reflects exactly the judgments of personal ethics—of why his life is important and what affects its value—that patients have a crucial liberty interest in deciding for themselves. Even people who are dying have a right to hear and, if they wish, act on what others might wish to tell or suggest or even hint to them, and it would be dangerous to suppose that a state may prevent this on the ground that it knows better than its citizens when they should be moved by or yield to particular advice or suggestion in the exercise of their right to make fateful personal decisions for themselves. It is not a good reply that some people may not decide as they really wish—as they would decide, for example, if free from the "pressure" of others. That possibility could hardly justify the most serious pressure of all—the criminal law which tells them that they may not decide for death if they need the help of a doctor in dying, no matter how firmly they wish it....

Of course, a state has important interests that justify regulating physician-assisted suicide. It may be legitimate for a state to deny an opportunity for assisted suicide when it acts in what it reasonably judges to be the best interests of the potential suicide, and when its judgment on that issue does not rest on contested judgments about "matters involving the most intimate and personal choices a person may make in a lifetime, choices central to personal dignity and autonomy."...

Even in the case of terminally ill patients, a state has a right to take all reasonable measures to insure that a patient requesting such assistance has made an informed, competent, stable and uncoerced decision. It is plainly legitimate for a state to establish procedures through which professional and administrative judgments can be made about these matters, and to forbid doctors to assist in suicide when its reasonable procedures have not been satisfied. States may be permitted considerable leeway in designing such procedures. They may be permitted, within reason, to err on what they take to be the side of caution. But they may not use the bare possibility of error as justification for refusing to establish any procedures at all and relying instead on a flat prohibition.

CONCLUSION

Each individual has a ... right to exercise some control over the time and manner of one's death.

The patient-plaintiffs in these cases were all mentally competent individuals in the final phase of terminal illness and died within months of filing their claims.

Jane Doe described how her advanced cancer made even the most basic bodily functions such as swallowing, coughing, and yawning extremely painful....

George A. Kingsley, in advanced stages of AIDS which included, among other hardships, the attachment of a tube to an artery in his chest which made even routine functions burdensome and the development of lesions on his brain, sought advice from his doctors regarding prescriptions which could hasten his impending death.

Jane Roe, suffering from cancer since 1988, had been almost completely bedridden since 1993 and experienced constant pain which could not be alleviated by medication. After undergoing counseling for herself and her family, she desired to hasten her death by taking prescription drugs....

James Poe suffered from emphysema which caused him " a constant sensation of suffocating" as well as a cardiac condition which caused severe leg pain. Connected to an oxygen tank at all times but unable to calm the panic reaction associated with his feeling of suffocation even with regular doses of morphine, Mr. Poe sought physician-assisted suicide.

A state may not deny the liberty claimed by the patient-plaintiffs in these cases without providing them an opportunity to demonstrate, in whatever way the state might reasonably think wise and necessary, that the conviction they expressed for an early death is competent, rational, informed, stable, and uncoerced.

Affirming the decisions by the Courts of Appeals would establish nothing more than that there is such a constitutionally protected right in principle. It would establish only that some individuals, whose decisions for suicide plainly cannot be dismissed as irrational or foolish or premature, must be accorded a reasonable opportunity to show that their decision for death is informed and free. It is not necessary to decide precisely which patients are entitled to that opportunity. If, on the other hand, this Court reverses the decisions below, its decision could only be justified by the momentous proposition—a proposition flatly in conflict with the spirit and letter of the Court's past decisions—that an American citizen does not, after all, have the right, even in principle, to live and die in the light of his own religious and ethical beliefs, his own convictions about why his life is valuable and where its value lies.

POSTSCRIPT

Should Euthanasia Be a Crime?

Clearly, the issue of euthanasia is replete with complications, ranging from the moral to the macabre. It reiterates the difficulty of separating the objective, or clearly "factual," from the subjective, or constructed, interpreted aspects of human existence. What could be more factual than death? Yet death has been redefined in the United States since the 1950s and continues to be. Prior to 1968 the human heart had to stop beating for death to occur. However, an ad hoc committee of the Harvard Medical School contributed to the new definition, which calls for the patient to only be brain-dead (i.e., the heart can still be beating). Brain death legitimizes turning off a respirator and/or removing needed tissues for medical research. At another level of analysis, 56 criminals were executed in 1995—more than twice the number of patients that Dr. Jack Kevorkian had assisted in dying to that point. However, the *meaning* of the respective deaths for most is quite different.

Does McHugh's relatively happy scenario of the demise of his friend, Nelson Butters, ring true? How many terminal patients have scores of knowledgeable others helping them to write manuscripts, revise books, and intelligently discuss their condition? How many patients receive the same respect and attention that Butters received from the hospital's medical staff? Moreover, are there any guidelines in place to protect the terminally ill from being wrongly assisted in suicide?

The literature on euthanasia is vast. A concise discussion of previous euthanasia cases is "What *Quinlan* Can Tell Kevorkian About the Right to Die," by M. L. T. Stevens, *The Humanist* (March/April 1997). An excellent article that is sympathetic toward euthanasia but critical of Dworkin et al. is "A Right to Choose Death?" by F. M. Kamm, *Boston Review* (Summer 1997). An outstanding work by a critic of euthanasia is H. Hendin's *Seduced by Death: Doctors, Patients and the Dutch Cure* (W. W. Norton, 1997). Also see his *Suicide in America* (W. W. Norton, 1996). Among the many religious perspectives are *Denial of the Soul: Spiritual and Medical Perspectives on Euthanasia and Mortality* by M. S. Peck (Harmony Books, 1997) and Episcopal Church, Diocese of Washington, Committee on Medical Ethics, *Assisted Suicide and Euthanasia: Christian Moral Perspectives* (Morehouse Publishers, 1997). For a legal discussion, see *Voluntary Euthanasia and the Common Law* by M. Otlowski (Clarendon Press, 1997).

ISSUE 17

Does Increased Crime Control Make New York Safer?

YES: Paul Ruffins, from "How the Big Apple Cut to the Core of Its Crime Problem," *Crisis* (July 1997)

NO: David N. Dinkins, from "Does Quality-of-Life Policing Diminish Quality of Life for People of Color?" *Crisis* (July 1997)

ISSUE SUMMARY

YES: Writer Paul Ruffins traces the "miracle" of New York City's crime reduction to efforts in the late 1980s to increase community policing and to halt petty street crimes.

NO: Former New York mayor David N. Dinkins maintains that crime control in the city has gotten out of control, making the streets unsafe for citizens, especially citizens of color, who he insists are often harmed by the police.

In 1997 Frederick Siegel published *The Future Once Happened Here: New York, D.C., L.A., and the Fate of America's Big Cities* (Free Press), in which the author provides an obituary of New York City. At the same time, others were hailing that city's success story. Impressive statistics showing a dramatic reduction in homicides and other serious crimes since 1989 have prompted police chiefs and politicians from around the United States to scramble to institute crime control policies resembling those of New York.

Felonies in New York have gone down 80 percent since 1990; the homicide rate is the lowest it has been in that city in 30 years; and, according to FBI statistics, it ranks safest among America's cities with 1 million people or more. Mayor Rudolph Giuliani, along with former commissioner William Bratton and current commissioner Howard Safir, could easily gloat. After all, there has been a renewal of the tourist industry, a flood of residents are returning to a city that thousands had given up on (driving real estate prices skyward), and polls show that New Yorkers feel safer than they have for years.

From a scholarly perspective there are few, if any, more dramatic empirical cases of sound criminological theories guiding practitioners to the successful solution of a major crime problem. The primary theory is largely derived from the controlling-crime-from-the-bottom-up thesis of James Q. Wilson and George Kelling. This was spelled out clearly in a 1982 *Atlantic Monthly* article entitled "Broken Windows." Instead of worrying about organized crime, the Mafia, white-collar crime, or even underlying structural causes of crime,

Wilson and Kelling theorized that once neighborhood deterioration began (e.g., neglected properties, unrepaired damages, and broken windows), the neighborhood would quickly become infested with petty criminals. Their crimes would be largely public order and nuisance, such as public urination, talking or playing radios loudly into the night, drug use, prostitution, and trespassing. The trick is to have police concentrate on these petty problems. This would alert communities that police care and enable residents to regain a sense of pride, safety, and stability in their own blocks.

In 1971, long before Wilson and Kelling's article, New York had initiated a "cop of the block" model community policing policy in most of its 76 precincts. However, it was not until the early 1990s—when Transit Authority chief William Bratton carried out a "zero tolerance" policy on New York's subway system, which quickly spilled over into the streets—that the "broken window" thesis was put into effect. Bratton insisted that those who jumped the gate instead of paying for a subway ride be arrested. Also, loiterers and others were required to show identification. Such sweeps resulted in the arrests of thousands of people who turned out to be wanted or in possession of illegal weapons or drugs.

Several other criminological insights were also drawn from efforts to control crime. One was the blanketing of hot spots, or areas of heavy criminal activity. Professor of criminology Lawrence Sherman and others have documented the value of such policing. Another innovation was the use of advanced technology and computers, such as Compstat (computer comparison statistics). This enables police to quickly pinpoint clusters of crimes in any of the 76 precincts and to readily identify types of crime, exact times of incidents, and so on. Weekly meetings with precinct commanders became a staple, and commanders who could not control escalating problem areas and crimes were put under the threat of dismissal. Hence, theories emphasizing the importance of information, technology, and leadership were also drawn from and utilized.

New York City's crime control efforts seem to be successful. However, in the second selection of this debate, former mayor David N. Dinkins accuses New York police officers of abusing and harassing citizens, especially poorer racial and ethnic minority ones. He asks, are abuses occurring on a regular basis and, if so, how can we possibly argue that the crime control "successes" are worth it? Others assert that improvements in crime rates have little or nothing to do with police policies, draconian or otherwise.

In the first selection, Paul Ruffins, while acknowledging that there are some cases of overzealous officers, notes that several black politicians are thankful that the body count of young blacks has been significantly reduced. Overall, the changes in police style have netted greater citizen safety, he says.

YES

Paul Ruffins

HOW THE BIG APPLE CUT TO THE CORE OF ITS CRIME PROBLEM

The miracle started far underground in the gritty, grimy confines of the New York City subway system. In 1989, when David Dinkins became the city's first black mayor, he shook up its law enforcement command structure by hiring two outsiders who were the nation's smartest cops. Houston's Lee Brown, who virtually pioneered community policing, became head of the overall New York Police Department (NYPD). Boston's William Bratton was chosen to lead the city's transit police. One of Bratton's first moves was to vigorously prosecute fare-beaters who would simply jump over the turnstiles or rush through exit gates. These scofflaws infuriated honest commuters who often had to endure long lines to buy tokens. Sometimes these incidents took place in clear sight of transit police officers, who ignored them rather than put in the effort and paperwork involved in chasing down fare-beaters over a nonviolent offense worth less than a dollar.

But Bratton ordered his officers to apprehend, search and question fare-beaters. This strategy yielded some amazing findings, as well as results. Virtually all fare-beaters had enough money to pay. Many committed this obvious crime while out on parole, or while carrying firearms, drugs, or wads of cash. Rather than being a crime of economic necessity, fare-beating was really a way to say: "I'm just too cool to go along with your rules like everyone else." The transit police began enforcing the basic rules of civilized behavior with a particular emphasis on tracing guns and making weapons charges stick. Within six months, felonies in the transit system fell 50%.

The strategy of focusing on "quality-of-life offenses" has spread to the entire city, helping to reduce its crime rate faster than anywhere else in the country, from 2,245 murders in 1990 to 984 in 1996—a decline of 56%. By comparison, during the same period, Chicago only experienced a 7% reduction in crime, and while crime is down 11% across the country, in Washington, D.C., Miami, and Atlanta, murders actually increased between 1995 and 1996.

"I think that the average person on the streets of Harlem or Brooklyn feels safer," declares New York *Newsday* columnist Les Payne. "There are places where shots were being fired every night where you don't hear gunfire anymore."

New York's falling crime rate has been the subject of intense debate. However, as other cities try to import its success, it is very important that they do not make the same mistake as the Mayor of Washington, D.C., who concluded that New York's secret was simply making a lot of arrests for small crimes.

This is a dangerous oversimplification. The Los Angeles police, for example, are notorious for stopping and arresting minority men on the slightest of pretexts. Yet, years of harassment and brutality in LA did not result in a 56% decline in its murder rate.

THE POLITICS OF REFORM

New York's dramatic gains in public safety are the result of a complex combination of political reform, ethnic politics, and police accountability. Dinkins was elected mayor after voters rejected the pervasive corruption of the Democratic machine headed by Ed Koch, and demanded real changes in city government agencies. Several major politicians were indicted, and one, Queens Borough President Donald Manes, committed suicide rather than face jail.

In addition, organized crime in New York suffered a major blow when the infamous Mafia boss John Gotti received a tough jail sentence. When former federal prosecutor Rudy Giuliani became mayor in 1993, he continued the pressure on the mob, confronting its influence at the Fulton Street Fish Market and loosening its grip on the city's convention center. He also sent an important message to corrupt cops by busting more than

a dozen drug-dealing cops in Harlem's "Dirty" Thirtieth Police Precinct.

A BIG SHIFT IN BLACK ATTITUDES

"Law and order" has long been the rallying cry of the right wing. However, it was liberal Dave Dinkins who made this promise: "Most of all, we must reaffirm the rule of law, and fight back against the pushers and muggers, and take back our streets and subways and our parks ... Let me say what I said so often during the campaign: I intend to be the toughest mayor on crime this city has ever seen."

Dinkins' statement reflected an important shift in black opinion. Despite an ongoing sympathy for the accused, African-Americans were beginning to realize they could no longer afford to tolerate or glorify violence or lawlessness. As Congressman John Lewis notes, poverty causes crime but crime also causes poverty. This attitude change was also reflected in the Million Man March, and in the growing opposition to Gangsta Rap spearheaded by C. Delores Tucker, with strong support from New York minister Calvin Butts.

As New York Congressman Floyd Flake noted, "For too long people talked as if thousands of young black men were just magically waking up in prison. Well, myself and a lot of other ministers have tried to preach a reality check to young folks—pointing out that their own behavior was creating a whole lot of jobs in the prison industry upstate."

This change in opinion was what led New York's black communities to at least grudgingly tolerate, if not welcome, an intensive level of policing that it might have resisted only a few years earlier. Congressman Major Owens of Brooklyn explains it this way: "My constituents distrust the police, but they are just totally fed up with the violence and intimidation they experienced from criminals."

Analyzing this shift in ethnic politics is central to understanding what happened in New York and appreciating the critical role African-American leaders have played in reducing crime nationwide. In three of the four cities with the largest reductions: New York, Houston (54%), San Diego (46%) and Dallas (45%), the change coincided with the selection of a black mayor and/or chief of police. New York had both.

The ethnic politics of crime are not limited to African-Americans. New York's Italian-American community has largely supported Giuliani's attacks on the Mafia because it trusts him and realizes that other Italian-Americans are the most likely victims of mob violence.

The bottom line is that, although they can make a lot of arrests and brutalize suspects, police departments cannot significantly reduce crime without some cooperation from the community. Otherwise, witnesses and victims can refuse to testify; angry jurors can nullify a prosecution; and bystanders can riot when police make arrests.

Dinkins had both the wisdom and the luck to institute police tactics in a way that quickly paid off for poor and minority citizens. Many Blacks and Hispanics had to endure more frequent interactions with the police—but in return, they got a much safer transit system, rather than just hassles and brutality.

If James Q. Wilson's "Broken Window" theory is true and disorder itself breeds crime, the subways were the perfect test case. Just as Giuliani later benefited from the thousands of additional police hired by Dinkins, Dinkins gained from the Metropolitan Transit Authority's innovative techniques which included repairing everything any time a subway car went out of service, rather than simply making quick fixes. The time between failures rose from 6,000 to 66,000 miles. Riders experienced the whole system becoming safer, cleaner and more reliable.

Equally important, the transit police focused on deliberate illegal acts like smoking, which actually undermined the quality of life for all passengers. This is very different from troopers pulling over a car for a broken taillight—which might just mean the driver was too poor to fix his car.

Dinkins, and later Giuliani, also shifted police emphasis from drugs to guns. Years of the drug war put thousands of black men behind bars, but largely failed to make neighborhoods any safer. Without professional help, addicts simply can not stop consuming drugs. Thus, the laws of economics dictate that there will always be suppliers, often abetted by corrupt cops sharing in the astronomical profits. In addition, many African-Americans do not support the drug war because they feel it is racist. For example, George Washington University professor Paul Butler uses the disproportionate sentences imposed on non-violent black crack dealers as the primary moral justification for jury nullification.

By contrast, strict gun laws have wide support in New York City. In addition, taking guns off the street brings the self-interests of African-Americans and Hispanics closer into line with those of police officers, who may have little incentive to fight drugs, but who fear being shot. New York proves that if you want an immediate drop in violence, reducing guns on the street is a lot more productive than concentrating on drugs.

Therefore, it is ironic that New York's most unsung hero lives in Virginia. Former Governor Douglas Wilder championed that state's law which restricts handgun purchases to one a month. Modeled on a South Carolina statute, it is probably the most politically sophisticated gun control legislation ever crafted. Law-abiding Virginians can still purchase handguns for sport or self-defense. Yet, the law rapidly changed Virginia's status as the largest, most convenient source for guns smuggled north into New York, Massachusetts and other states with stronger gun controls.

POLICE ACCOUNTABILITY

Perhaps the biggest change in the NYPD is that it is now being held accountable for reducing crime. This may seem obvious, but within law enforcement circles, it was widely known that police chiefs were usually fired after widely-publicized scandals or brutality incidents, not because crime went up. As Bratton explained, "... in [most] police departments, the focus is on reacting to crimes that have already been committed... Success is measured by response times, arrest rates, and clearance rates—all after-the-fact measurements. The [real] job is to keep crime from happening."

Hiring and mobilizing thousands of police may not fit the traditional civil rights preference for reducing crime by providing jobs or improving schools. However, it is much less harmful than waiting until people have already been victimized, and then giving the perpetrators severe prison sentences on the theory that young black men are so inherently criminal they can only be deterred by being locked away.

Using intense policing supports the environmental view of crime that even normal adolescents can get into serious trouble if the police do not have the inclination nor the resources to maintain order. Without adequate police protection, even "good kids" can feel the need to carry weapons in self-defense.

Focusing on police mismanagement marks another welcome development in the crime debate. Conservatives are often unwilling to critique any aspect of police behavior, and most liberals focus on brutality, corruption or the lack of affirmative action. Besides criminologists, few people examine police inefficiency, laziness or bad-management, partly because mayors and chiefs tenaciously resist public scrutiny of how they deploy their resources.

Bratton explains that, "In New York, we discovered that our warrant investigators, once they'd read the papers and had their morning coffee, weren't hitting the streets until 10 or 11 a.m. We started sending them out at 3 a.m., when their targets were more likely to be home. Apprehensions of those with outstanding warrants tripled in two years."

Pointing out another example of mismanagement, Congressman Owens observes that, "You used to see busloads of police officers, with a starting salary of $35,000 including benefits, putting out the wooden horses for parades. I always wondered why trained officers were wasted on jobs that could have been done by a laborer."

WEIGHING THE COSTS AND BENEFITS

Has the sharp increase in police activity really left black folks any safer? It depends on whom you ask. According to *New York Times* reporter Alan Finder, "Giuliani argues that the greatest beneficiaries are the hundreds, if not thousands, of young black and Hispanic men who would have been killed if things hadn't changed." Conversely, Dinkins believes the police are dangerously out of control. Bratton feels that in a city with 7.5 million residents and visitors, 5,000 complaints against police officers is a reasonable trade-off for 240,000 fewer victims.

Others who are less partisan seem to have more mixed feelings. Political observer Gloria Dulan-Wilson feels the media exaggerates the violence in black communities. "Now the police have a Gestapo mentality," she asserts. "The only good thing is that youngsters are more likely to heed older people's warnings to stay out of trouble to avoid the police." Les Payne believes that the real downside of "qualify-of-life-arrests" is higher unemployment, as more black men are saddled with police records for trivial offenses.

So far, many black citizens would probably agree with Congressman Flake's assessment that despite some troubling incidents, the overall impact has been positive. "An undercover cop started calling me a nigger until he saw my Congressional license plate," he explains. "It was humiliating. On the other hand, I and most of my constituents are very grateful we're no longer finding dead teenagers scattered through South Jamaica. I don't think that aggressive policing has become too abusive yet. The trick to making it work will be making sure the cops don't cross that line."

NO
David N. Dinkins

DOES QUALITY-OF-LIFE POLICING DIMINISH QUALITY OF LIFE FOR PEOPLE OF COLOR?

While crime is down in New York City, many residents feel less safe than they did a few years ago—because they fear our cops. In fact, not since the heyday of the Klan have African-American men been at more serious personal risk.

Some suspects have been shot in the back. An innocent young man was killed when he was put into an illegal choke hold by an officer after his football struck a police car. Another was shot as a result of an argument with an off-duty officer. These are not isolated cases, but symptoms of a very real disease.

And while we see reports of abusive and corrupt cops in the news all too often, public outrage fades with the headlines.

Whenever I speak of our police force, I am reminded that the women and men of the NYPD are by and large hardworking people who put their lives on the line very day for the rest of us. They have a tough and dangerous job.

But civilian complaints against police for excessive force rose by 61.9 percent in 1995 compared to 1993. Abuse of authority allegations soared by 86.2 percent, and allegations of illegal searches skyrocketed by 135 percent. That this particular kind of complaint has risen the most is likely a reflection of increased brutality and illegal arrests. Complaint figures for 1996 are similarly high.

We are told that such increases are the inevitable result of more arrests and a more assertive assault on quality-of-life offenses. Even if that were true, the police department would still be dangerously close to adopting the philosophy that, "The end justifies the means." But aggressive policing is not the cause of the increase in complaints, as anyone can discover by reading Civilian Complaint Review Board (CCRB) reports. They reveal that the majority of abuse allegations involve officers on routine patrol, in incidents that never result in arrests.

These complainants are not even charged with any crimes. Eighty-eight percent of the complaints come from people who are not only not arrested, but not even ticketed. In past years, only thirty percent of civilian complaints involved no arrest. Clearly, complainants are largely innocent bystanders who get caught up in illegal police behavior.

Another disturbing statistic shows that more than half the complainants whose race is known are African-American. About another 25 percent are Latino. Altogether, 80 percent of complaints are registered by people of color.

A properly funded and staffed CCRB could save the city money by sending a message to cops about brutality. The city's civil suit payments to the victims of police malfeasance have risen dramatically. The total for fiscal year 1994 was twenty-five million dollars—and the comptroller tells us that a deluge of new cases is now being filed.

Complaints are so backlogged that, in many instances, by the time the investigation is completed, the eighteen-month statute of limitations has run out.

In many cases in which investigators do finish their inquiry, substantiate allegations, and recommend action to the board in a timely fashion, the board fails to follow the recommendation. And when the board does vote to adopt the recommendation, it must pass the findings on to the police commissioner for action—unless a crime has been committed, in which event the district attorney has jurisdiction. The police commissioner then has but two options: suspension for thirty days or dismissal—nothing in between.

So, in many cases, no action at all is taken against abusive officers. In the first six months of last year, 159 substantiated cases were referred to the department for possible disciplinary action. Charges were filed against only one officer. A second officer was subjected to "command discipline," which generally means loss of vacation time. One case was dismissed and 26 cases were dropped for lack of evidence. Seven cases were dropped last year, and 43 the year before, because the statute of limitations ran out. The rest are pending.

While the statistics about brutality paint a deeply troubling picture, the individual suffering of the victims of brutality is even more distressing.

Consider the young man whom an officer kicked so hard in the groin that the victim had to have a testicle surgically removed. The officer was found guilty at a departmental trial. His penalty? Thirty days suspension without pay. He was also put on probation for one year.

When the Bronx District Attorney found out about the case, he had the officer indicted for felonious assault. If convicted, he will have to be dismissed —which should have been the penalty imposed in the first place.

Nevertheless, independent oversight and command accountability must be established. Officers must obey the law, and their Commissioner and their Mayor must send a clear message that lawlessness among cops will not be tolerated. Offenders must be fairly tried, and punished. Police integrity must be fostered from the day cops enter the academy to the day they return their badges and guns.

And, a city residency requirement for officers is essential—so that fewer officers view the communities in which they work as alien, and fewer residents view the police in that same light. Today in New York, over forty percent of our thirty-eight thousand member police force reside outside the city.

Encouraging cops to be more assertive against crime can be good. But fostering an environment in which they feel they can ride roughshod over the rights of the innocent only erodes safety and people's trust in the law.

POSTSCRIPT

Does Increased Crime Control Make New York Safer?

On August 9, 1997, a black Haitian immigrant, after his arrest outside a Brooklyn nightclub, was allegedly sodomized with the handle of a toilet plunger by four NYPD officers. He experienced a ruptured colon and bladder, requiring two months of hospitalization. Apparently, other officers were aware of the assault and did nothing. He is suing the city.

Mayor Rudolph Giuliani, long known for his loyal support of New York officers and his reservations about the Civilian Complaint Review Board (CCRB), immediately demanded an investigation. He and virtually all other city leaders registered shock and outrage. Many maintain that the act, as horrendous as it was, in no way reflects the NYPD. It is unfair, they say, to judge either the police or their crime control policies by this aberrant event. They maintain that 98 percent of New York's 38,000 police officers are good.

The number of police brutality complaints in New York has tripled over the past 10 years. Between 1996 and 1997, 2,735 complaints were filed. Moreover, since 1993 only about 180 NYPD officers have been disciplined, many with a gentle slap on the wrist. A 72-page Amnesty International report (1996) documented regular abuses of blacks and Latinos. Commissioner Howard Safir and Mayor Giuliani ridiculed the report.

Many warn that a "war on crime" can be really a war on the poor and minorities. Others contend that the initial thesis that "grime leads to crime by attracting slime" and that quality of life could be protected by attacking petty criminals is, at best, dubious. At worst, it legitimizes police doing terrible things.

Among the proliferating analyses of the New York experiment are "Restore Order and You Reduce Crime," by G. Kelling, and "New York Story: More Luck Than Policing," by R. Moran, both in *The Washington Post* (February 9, 1997). For a critical article, see "Broken Windows: Prevention Strategy or Cracked Policy?" by S. Henry et al., *Critical Criminologist* (Fall 1997).

An excellent source developing the theory of crime reduction as a result of changing drug markets is H. Brownstein, *The Rise and Fall of a Violent Crime Wave* (Harrow & Heston Press, 1996). Other books include *Crime Is Not the Problem: Lethal Violence in America* by F. Zimring and G. Hawkins (Oxford University Press, 1997) and *Forces of Deviance: Understanding the Dark Side of Policing*, 2d ed., by V. Kappeler, R. D. Sluder, and G. P. Alpert (Waveland Press, 1996).

ISSUE 18

Are Human Rights Basic to Justice?

YES: Rhoda E. Howard, from "Human Rights and the Necessity for Cultural Change," *Focus on Law Studies* (Fall 1992)

NO: Vinay Lal, from "The Imperialism of Human Rights," *Focus on Law Studies* (Fall 1992)

ISSUE SUMMARY

YES: Sociology professor Rhoda E. Howard argues that human rights are both universal and basic for justice. Although she makes some allowances for "weak cultural relativism," she nevertheless insists that justice largely depends on a general acceptance of basic rights.

NO: Vinay Lal, a professor of humanities, dismisses human rights as a tool used by Western nations to legitimize brutal tactics that maintain their power over weaker nations and regions. Focusing primarily on the international level, Lal proposes that, in practice, human rights have been used as little more than a cover for injustice.

The philosophes such as Rousseau, Montesquieu, and Voltaire, the writers and thinkers of the eighteenth-century French Enlightenment, argued that women and men were the measure of all things, not religion or the state. The influence of their ideas permanently altered the West. Their thinking formed the foundation of most modern legal and political systems, including the U.S. Declaration of Independence and the U.S. Constitution. The idea that all people had the right to "life, liberty, and the pursuit of happiness" was indeed revolutionary.

Unfortunately, from the very beginning of the U.S. government, there were built-in contradictions and hypocrisies. Slaves, for instance, simply were not entitled to any rights or freedoms. Women, too, were disenfranchised: they could not vote until 1920. The Bill of Rights itself was not viewed as applicable at the state level (where most legal action takes place) until the late 1800s. The idea of "due process" within America's criminal justice system was an alien concept until well into the twentieth century. This was often equally true in British and other European legal systems.

Yet, beginning with the ideas of the French philosophes and as written into such documents as the U.S. Constitution, the foundation and form for the establishment and respect of individual rights as the basis of justice and law were there.

While many intellectuals in the early twentieth century embraced human rights and the legal ideals of the West, others criticized Western missionaries and jingoists ("my country, right or wrong"; "America, love it or leave it") for superimposing their own views of morality on other countries, and a reaction against universal cultural standards set in. Influential American anthropologists such as Franz Boas (1858–1942) advocated what they called cultural relativism. This is the doctrine that any society's structures should be understood in terms of the functions they perform within that society, not by Western standards of correct conduct. The ethical corollary is ethical relativism, which can be broadly interpreted to mean anything is permissible when viewed within the context of a groups' values; there is no universal right or wrong.

Canadian sociologist Rhoda E. Howard maintains that human rights are necessary for positive cultural changes. Reflecting the economist Walter Rostow's notion of prerequisites needed for developing societies to pass through stages of growth before they reach a "taking off" point, she points out that democracy and justice, predicated on human rights, are necessary for change. Although she defends universal values, including specific legal rights, she also concedes that some elements of justice are more important than others. For instance, she would allow for a "weak cultural relativism" in certain areas where local traditions are supported.

Vinay Lal of Columbia University dismisses human rights as not only an imperfect ideal but also a tool used by the United States at the international level to unfairly attack others and advance its own cause.

While dwelling primarily at the international level in his discussion of human and legal rights, Lal also reflects an expanded understanding of rights. Traditionally, human rights (as Howard presents them) primarily had political and civil (legal) dimensions. Lal, though, argues for the inclusion of *social* rights as well (such as economic support of education, health, and employment). Since Lal and Howard's debate, reprinted here, reports of inhumane actions by criminal justice agencies around the world as well as by soldiers and private citizens have been widely publicized. Officials in Honduras are searching for bodies of dissenters as the civilian government there claims hundreds were killed by CIA-trained and financed Honduran army units in the 1980s. Police trained by the U.S. government in several other countries have been linked directly with both the brutalization of civilians and drug running. In Bosnia genocide is used as a solution to the "Muslim problem," according to the Yugoslav War Crimes Tribunal. Canadian soldiers were recently charged with the brutal murder of several Somalian teens. And perhaps the most tragic violation of human rights continues to occur in Rwanda. In 1994, 500,000 unarmed civilians were slaughtered in less than six months.

As you read the selections by Howard and Lal, who would you say is more pessimistic? Why? Who seems to have a more consistent respect for the concept of human rights? Why? Do you agree that respect for human rights is necessary for justice? Why, or why not?

YES

Rhoda E. Howard

HUMAN RIGHTS AND THE NECESSITY FOR CULTURAL CHANGE

Many critics of the concept of human rights argue that it undermines indigenous cultures, especially in the underdeveloped world (Cobbah, 1987; Pollis and Schwab, 1980; Renteln, 1990). I agree that the concept of human rights often undermines cultures. Cultural rupture is often a necessary aspect of the entrenchment of respect for human rights. Culture is not of absolute ethical value; if certain aspects of particular cultures change because citizens prefer to focus on human rights, then that is a perfectly acceptable price to pay.

Human rights are rights held by the individual merely because she or he is human, without regard to status or position. In principle, all human beings hold human rights equally. These rights are claims against the state that do not depend on duties to the state, although they do depend on duties to other citizens, e.g., not to commit crimes. They are also claims that the individual can make against society as a whole. Society, however, may have cultural preconceptions that certain types of individuals ought not to be entitled to such rights. Thus, culture and human rights come into conflict. The concept of cultural relativism recognizes this, but does not consider the possibility that, in such instances, perhaps the better path to choose is to change the culture in order to promote human rights.

Cultural relativism is a method of social analysis that stresses the importance of regarding social and cultural phenomena from the "perspective of participants in or adherents of a given culture" (Bidney, 1968). Relativism assumes that there is no one culture whose customs and beliefs dominate all others in a moral sense. Relativism is a necessary corrective to ethical ethnocentrism. But it is now sometimes taken to such an extreme that any outsider's discussions of local violations of human rights are criticized as forms of ideological imperialism.

In effect, this extreme position advocates not cultural relativism but cultural absolutism. Cultural absolutists posit particular cultures as of absolute moral value, more valuable than any universal principle of justice. In the left-right/North-South debate that permeates today's ideological exchanges,

From Rhoda E. Howard, "Human Rights and the Necessity for Cultural Change," *Focus on Law Studies*, vol. 8, no. 1 (Fall 1992). Copyright © 1992 by The American Bar Association. Reprinted by permission.

cultural absolutists specifically argue that culture is of more importance than the internationally accepted principles of human rights.

Cultural absolutists argue that human rights violate indigenous cultures because they are Western in origin. But the origins of any idea, including human rights, do not limit its applicability. The concept of human rights arose in the West largely in reaction to the overwhelming power of the absolutist state; in the Third World today, states also possess enormous power against which citizens need to be protected. As societies change, so ideals of social justice change.

Cultures are not immutable aspects of social life, ordained forever to be static. Cultures change as a result of structural change: secularism, urbanization and industrialism are among the chief causes of cultural change both in the West since the eighteenth century and in the underdeveloped world today (Howard, 1986, chapter 2). Cultures can also be manipulated by political or social spokespersons in their own interest. Culturalism is frequently an argument that is used to "cover" political repression, as when Kenyan President Daniel arap Moi told a female environmental activist not to criticize his policies because it is "against African tradition" for women to speak up in public. This does not mean that all aspects of culture must necessarily be ruptured in order that human rights can be entrenched. Many aspects of culture, such as kinship patterns, art or ritual, have nothing to do with human rights and can safely be preserved, even enhanced, when other rights-abusive practices are corrected. Many aspects of public morality are similarly not matters of human rights. The existence or abolition of polygamous marriage, for example, is not an international human rights issue, despite objections to it in the West. Nor is the proper degree of respect one should show to one's elders, or the proper norms of generosity and hospitality. The apparent Western overemphasis on work at the expense of family is a cultural practice that Third World societies can avoid without violating human rights. Many other such matters, such as whether criminal punishment should be by restitution or imprisonment, can be resolved without violating international human rights norms.

Jack Donnelly argues that "weak" cultural relativism is sometimes an appropriate response to human rights violations. Weak cultural relativism would "allow occasional and strictly limited local variations and exceptions to human rights," while recognizing "a comprehensive set of prima facie universal human rights" (Donnelly, 1989, p. 110). This is an appropriate position if the violation of a human right is truly a cultural practice that no political authority and no socially dominant group initiates or defends. Consider the case of female genital operations in Africa and elsewhere. Governments do not promote these violations; indeed, through education about their detrimental health consequences, they try to stop them. Nevertheless there is strong popular sentiment in favour of the operations, among women as well as (if not more so than) men (Slack, 1988). Similarly, child betrothal, officially a violation of international human rights norms, is popularly accepted in some cultures (Howard, 1986, chapter 8). And certain forms of freedom of speech, such as blasphemy and pornography, are deeply offensive to popular sentiment in many cultures, whether or not the government permits or prohibits them.

Although a weak cultural relativist stance is appropriate in some instances as a protection of custom against international human rights norms, to implement human rights does mean that certain cultural practices must be ruptured. One obvious example is the universal subordination of women as a group to men as a group, backed up by men's collective economic, political and physical power over women. If women have achieved greater access to human rights in North America since the second wave of feminism began about 1970, it is largely because they have challenged cultural stereotypes of how they ought to behave. Feminist activists no longer believe that women ought to be deferential to men or wives subordinate to their husbands. Nor do they any longer hold to the almost universal cultural belief that women's divinely ordained purpose in life is to bear children. Feminists in other parts of the world such as India or Africa are making similar challenges to their cultures in the process of asserting their rights (on women's rights as human rights, see Bunch, 1990, and Eisler, 1987.)

Many critics of human rights find them overly individualistic; they point to the selfish materialism they see in Western (North American) society. But the individualism of Western society reflects not protection but neglect of human rights, especially economic rights (Howard, "Ideologies of Social Exclusion," unpublished). In the United States, certain economic rights are regarded as culturally inappropriate. A deeply ingrained belief exists that everyone ought to be able to care for himself and his family. Since the U.S. is or was the land of opportunity (at least for white people), anyone who lives in poverty is personally responsible for his being in that state. Thus the U.S. has the worst record of

provision of economic rights of any major Western democratic state. The right to health is not acknowledged, nor is the right to housing or food. Before such rights are acknowledged and provided in the U.S., the cultural belief in the virtues of hard work and pulling oneself up by one's bootstraps will have to be replaced by a more collectivist vision of social responsibility. The culturally ingrained belief that blacks are inferior people not deserving of the respect and concern of whites will also need to be ruptured.

Critics of human rights sometimes argue that cultures are so different that there is no possibility of shared meanings about social justice evolving across cultural barriers. The multivocality of talk about rights precludes any kind of consensus. The very possibility of debate is rejected. Indeed, debate, the idea that people holding initially opposing views can persuade each other through logic and reason of their position, is rejected as a form of thought typical of rationalist and competitive Western society. Western thought, it is argued, silences the oppressed.

Yet it is precisely the central human rights premises of freedom of speech, press and assembly that all over the world permit the silenced to gain a social voice. Human rights undermine constricting status-based categorizations of human beings: they permit people from degraded social groups to demand social change. Rational discourse about human rights permits degraded workers, peasants, untouchables, women and members of minority groups to articulate and consider alternate social arrangements than those that currently oppress them (see also Teson, 1985).

Human rights are "inauthentic" in many cultures because they challenge the ingrained privileges of the ruling classes, the wealthy, the Brahmin, the patriarch, or the member of a privileged ethnic or religious group. The purpose of human rights is precisely to change many culturally ingrained habits and customs that violate the dignity of the individual. Rather than apologizing that human rights challenge cultural norms in many societies, including our own, we should celebrate that fact.

This article is based in large part on my Human Rights and the Search for Community *(in progress). Unpublished papers from this project, available on request, include* "Cultural Absolutism and the Nostalgia for Community," *and* "Ideologies of Social Exclusion in North American Society."

REFERENCES

Bidney, David. 1968. "Cultural Relativism," in *International Encyclopedia of the Social Sciences,* Volume III. New York: Macmillan.

Bunch, Charlotte. 1990. "Women's Rights as Human Rights: Toward a Re-Vision of Human Rights." *Human Rights Quarterly* 12: 486–98.

Cobbah, Josiah A. M. 1987. "African Values and the Human Rights Debate: An African Perspective." *Human Rights Quarterly* 9: 309–31.

Donnelly, Jack. 1989. *Universal Human Rights in Theory and Practice.* Ithaca, N.Y.: Cornell University Press.

Eisler, Riane. 1987. "Human Rights: Toward an Integrated Theory for Action." *Human Rights Quarterly* 9: 287–308.

Howard, Rhoda E. 1986. *Human Rights in Commonwealth Africa.* Totowa, NJ.: Rowman and Littlefield.

Pollis, Adamantia, and Peter Schwab, "Human Rights: A Western Concept with Limited Applicability," in Pollis and Schwab, eds. 1980. *Human Rights: Cultural and Ideological Perspectives.* New York: Praeger.

Renteln, Alison Dundes. 1990. *International Human Rights: Universalism versus Relativism.* Newbury Park, CA.: Sage.

Slack, Alison T. 1988. "Female Circumcision: A Critical Appraisal." *Human Rights Quarterly* 10: 437–86.

Teson, Fernando R. 1985. "International Human Rights and Cultural Relativism." *Virginia Journal of International Law* 25: 869–98.

NO

Vinay Lal

THE IMPERIALISM OF HUMAN RIGHTS

The notion of human rights is deeply embedded in modern legal and political thought and could well be considered one of the most significant achievements of contemporary culture and civilization. Certain classes of people in all societies have, from the beginning of time, been endowed with "rights" which others could not claim. The immunity that emissaries (now diplomats) from one state to another have always received constitutes one of the norms of conduct that has guided relations between states. Likewise, most cultures have had, in principle at least, intricate rules to govern the conduct of warfare. Civilians were not to be taken hostage as a military strategy; a soldier was not to be shot as he was surrendering; and so on.

Some of these customary modes of conduct are now enshrined in the law, transmitted on the one hand into "rights" that the citizen can claim against the state, and on the other hand into restraints on the state's agenda to produce conformity and contain dissent. The individual has been given a great many more rights, and—what is unique to modern times—never before have such rights been placed under the protection of the law. States are bound in their relations to their subjects by a myriad of international agreements and laws, including the Geneva Conventions, the International Covenant on Civil and Political Rights, the United Nations Charter, the Universal Declaration of Human Rights, and the U.N. Body of Principles for the Protection of All Persons Under Any Form of Detention or Punishment.

Moreover, it is only in our times that the "international community" seems prepared to enforce sanctions against a state for alleged violations of such rights. With the demise of communism, the principal foes of human rights appear to have been crushed, and the very notion of "human rights" seems sovereign. Should we then unreservedly endorse the culture of "human rights" as it has developed in the liberal-democratic framework of the modern West, indeed even as a signifier of the "end of history" and of the emergence of the New World Order? On the contrary, I would like to suggest several compelling reasons why, far from acquiescing in the suggestion that the notion of human rights is the most promising avenue to a new era in human relations, we should consider the discourse of human rights as the most evolved form of Western imperialism. Indeed, human rights can be viewed as the latest masquerade of the West—particularly America, the torchbearer since the end of World War II of "Western" values—to appear to the world as the epitome of civilization and as the only legitimate arbiter of human values.

To understand the roots of the modern discourse of "human rights," we need to isolate the two central notions from which it is derived, namely the "individual" and the "rule of law." It has been a staple of Western thought since at least the Renaissance that—while the West recognizes the individual as the true unit of being and the building block of society, non-Western cultures have been built around collectivities, conceived as religious, linguistic, ethnic, tribal or racial groups. As the *Economist*—and one could multiply such examples a thousand-fold —was to boldly declare in its issue of 27 February 1909, "whatever may be the political atom in India, it is certainly not the individual of Western democratic theory, but the community of some sort." In the West the individual stands in singular and splendid isolation, the promise of the inherent perfectibility of man; in the non-West, the individual is nothing, always a part of a collectivity in relation to which his or her existence is defined, never a being unto himself or herself. Where the "individual" does not exist, one cannot speak of his or her rights; and where there are no rights, it is perfectly absurd to speak of their denial or abrogation. On the Western view, moreover, if the atomistic conception of the "individual" is a prerequisite for a concern with human

rights, so is the "rule of law" under which alone can such rights be respected. In a society which lives by the "rule of law," such laws as the government might formulate are done so in accordance with certain normative criteria—for example, they shall be non-discriminatory, blind to considerations of race, gender, class, and linguistic background; these laws are then made public, so that no person might plead ignorance of the law; and the judicial process under which the person charged for the infringement of such laws is tried must hold out the promise of being fair and equitable. As in the case of "individual," the "rule of law" is held to be a uniquely Western contribution to civilization, on the two-fold assumption that democracy is an idea and institution of purely Western origins, and that the only form of government known to non-Western societies was absolutism. In conditions of "Oriental Despotism," the only law was the law of the despot, and the life and limb of each of his subjects was hostage to the tyranny of his pleasures and whims. In the despotic state, there was perhaps only one "individual," the absolute ruler; under him were the masses, particles of dust on the distant horizon. What rights were there to speak of then?

Having briefly outlined how the notions of the "individual" and the "rule of law" came to intersect in the formulation of the discourse of human rights, we can proceed to unravel some of the more disturbing and unacceptable aspects of this discourse. Where once the language of liberation was religion, today the language of emancipation is law. Indeed, the very notion of "human rights," as it is commonly understood in the international forum today, is legalistic. Proponents of the "rule of law," convinced of the uniqueness of the West, are not pre-pared to concede that customs and tra-ditional usages in most "Third World" countries have functioned for centuries in place of "law," and that even without the "rule of law" there were conventions and traditions which bound one person to respect the rights of another. We ex-pect rights to be protected under the law and the conformity of states to the "rule of law." Many obvious and commonplace objections to such a state of affairs come to mind. By what right, with what au-thority, and with what consequences do certain states brand other states as "out-law" or "renegade" states, living outside the pale of the "rule of law," allegedly oblivious to the rights of their subjects, and therefore subject to sanctions from the "international community?"

There is, as has been argued, one "rule of law" for the powerful, and an altogether different one for those states that do not speak the "rational," "diplomatic," and "sane" language that the West has decreed to be the universal form of linguistic exchange. It is not only the case that when Americans retaliate against their foes, they are engaged in "just war" or purely "defensive" measures in the interest of national security, but also that when Libyans or Syrians do so, they are transformed into "terrorists" or ruthless and self-aggrandizing despots in the pursuit of international dominance. The problem is more acute: who is to police the police? The United States claims adherence to international law, but summarily rejected the authority of the World Court when it condemned the United States for waging undeclared war against Nicaragua. More recently, the U.S. Supreme Court, in an astounding judgment barely noticed in the American press, upheld the constitutionality of a decision of a circuit court in Texas which, by allowing American law enforcement officers to kidnap nationals of a foreign state for alleged offenses under American law to be brought to the United States for trial, effectively proclaims the global jurisdiction of American law. As a noted Indian commentator has written, "We are thus back in the 15th, 16th, and 17th century world of piracy and pillage" (Ashok Mitra, "No Holds Barred for the U.S.," *Deccan Herald*, 3 July 1992). Were not the Libyans and Sandinistas supposed to be the pirates?

There are, however, less obvious and more significant problems with the legal-istic conception of a world order where "human rights" will be safeguarded. The present conception of "human rights" largely rests on a distinction between state and civil society, a distinction here fraught with hazardous consequences. The rights which are claimed are rights held against the state or, to put it an-other way, with the blessing of the state: the right to freedom of speech and ex-pression, the right to gather in public, the right to express one's grievances within the limits of the constitution, and so forth. The state becomes the guarantor of these rights, when in fact it is everywhere the state which is the most flagrant violator of human rights.

Not only does the discourse of "human rights" privilege the state, but the very conception of "rights" must of necessity remain circumscribed. The right to a fair hearing upon arrest, or to take part in the government of one's country, is ac-knowledged as an unqualified political and civil right, but the right to housing, food, clean air, an ecologically-sound en-vironment, free primary and secondary education, public transportation, a high standard of health, the preservation of one's ethnic identity and culture, and security in the event of unemployment or impairment due to disease and old age is not accorded parity. When, as in the United States, certain communities are in a systematic and calculated fashion deprived of the basic amenities required to sustain a reasonable standard of living, when an entire economy is designed on a war footing, does not that constitute a gross and inexcusable infringement of the "human rights" of those who are most disempowered in our society? Is it not ironic that in the very week this year when rebellious demonstrators in Thailand were being hailed in the Western media as champions of human rights, martyrs to freedom, and foes of tyranny, the insurrectionists in Los Angeles were contemptuously dismissed by the same media as "rioters," "hooligans," "arsonists," and "murderers?" No doubt some were just exactly that, but that admission cannot allow us to obfuscate the recognition that the action of the insurrectionists was fueled by a deep-seated resentment at the violation of their social, economic, and cultural rights.

Certainly there are organizations, such as the Minority Rights Group (London) and Cultural Survival (Boston), which have adopted a broader conception of "human rights," and whose discourse is as concerned with the numerous rights of "collectivities," whether conceived in terms of race, gender, class, ethnic or linguistic background, as it is with the rights of "individuals." But this is not the discourse of "human rights" in the main, and it is emphatically not the discourse of Western powers, which have seldom adhered to the standards that they expect others to abide by, and would use even food and medicine, as the contin-

uing embargo against Iraq so vividly demonstrates, to retain their political and cultural hegemony even as they continue to deploy the rhetoric of "human rights." Never mind that state formation in the West was forged over the last few centuries by brutally coercive techniques—colonialism, genocide, eugenics, the machinery of "law and order"—to create homogeneous groups. One could point randomly to the complete elimination of the Tasmanian Aboriginals, the extermination of many Native American tribes, the Highland Clearances in Scotland, even the very processes by which a largely Breton-speaking France became, in less than a hundred years, French-speaking. We should be emphatically clear that what are called "Third World" countries should not be allowed the luxury, the right if you will, of pointing to the excesses of state formation in the West to argue, in a parody of the ludicrous evolutionary model where the non-Western world is destined to become progressively free and democratic, that they too must ruthlessly forge ahead with "development" and "progress" before their subjects can be allowed "human rights."

The idea of "human rights" is noble and its denial an effrontery to humankind. But it is only as an imagined idea that we can embrace it, and our fascination with this idea must not deflect us from the understanding that, as an ideological and political tool of the West, and particularly of the only remaining superpower, "human rights" is contaminated. Perhaps, before "human rights" is flaunted by the United States as what most of the rest of the world must learn to respect, the movement for "human rights" should first come home to roost. As Noam Chomsky has written, people in the Third World "have never understood the deep totalitarian strain in Western culture, nor have they ever understood the savagery and cynicism of Western culture." Could there be greater testimony to this hypocrisy than the fact that inscribed on the marble wall of the main lobby at CIA headquarters in Virginia is this quotation from John (VIII: 32): "And Ye Shall Know the Truth/And the Truth Shall Make You Free?"

POSTSCRIPT

Are Human Rights Basic to Justice?

On the surface, the debate between Howard and Lal appears rooted as much in philosophy as criminology. Yet their attempt to link human rights with basic justice (or the lack of it) clearly shows the primacy of the issue for both criminology and criminal justice.

Lal says that the "idea of 'human rights' is noble and its denial an effrontery to humankind," but doesn't he seem to be throwing them out with his attack on how they are misused? Although Howard appears to be an advocate of human rights as a basis for justice, could her endorsement of a "weak" relativism lead to the intellectual sanctioning of abuses that one would not be able to associate with "justice"? For example, although it is illegal throughout India, the practice of suttee still occurs sometimes in rural areas. This is the custom of a Hindu widow willingly being cremated on her husband's funeral pyre as an indication of her devotion. Should Western scholars and others be concerned about this?

There is an enormous literature on human rights and justice in philosophy, ethnicity, and feminism, as well as in law and criminal justice. For a comparison of Canada's human rights policies with those of other countries, see *Ethnicity and Human Rights in Canada*, 2d ed., by E. Kallen (Oxford University Press, 1995). A good comparative discussion of victimology and justice is R. Mawby and S. Walklate's *Critical Victimology* (Sage Publications, 1995). For a radically different formulation of rights, see C. Young's *It's All the Rage: Crime and Culture* (Addison-Wesley, 1994). Also see N. Hooyman and J. Gonyea's *Feminist Perspective on Family Care: Policies for Gender Justice* (Sage Publications, 1995).

Several human rights concerns not directly addressed by Howard or Lal are examined in *Accountability for Human Rights Atrocities in International Law* by S. Ratner and J. Abrams (Oxford University Press, 1997); M. Kempton, "Review of *Human Rights Watch World Report 1997: Events of 1996*, by Human Rights Watch," *New York Review of Books* (March 27, 1997); and A. Foek, "Sweatshop Barbie: Exploitation of Third World Labor," *The Humanist* (January/February 1997). Rarely considered U.S. violations are discussed by T. Szasz in "Routine Neonatal Circumcision: Symbol of the Birth of the Therapeutic State," *Journal of Medicine and Philosophy* (April 1996). A summary of a recent conference can be found in "Conference Explores Rise in Reports of Hate Crimes," by M. Fletcher, *The Washington Post* (November 11, 1997). Another alleged rights violation is the topic of "Does Intersex 'Corrective' Surgery Do More Harm Than Good?" by W. McCroy, *Baltimore Gay Paper* (February 13, 1998).

ISSUE 19

Does the International Drug War Encourage Human Rights Violations?

YES: Eyal Press, from "Clinton Pushes Military Aid: Human-Rights Abusers Lap It Up," *The Progressive* (February 1997)

NO: Barry McCaffrey, from "Hemispheric Drug Control: Fighting Drug Production and Trafficking," *Vital Speeches of the Day* (May 1, 1997)

ISSUE SUMMARY

YES: Eyal Press, a writer and journalist, contends that expanding U.S. support of drug control in Latin America serves only to curry political favor with conservatives, take the focus off White House scandals, give the U.S. military something to do, and allow other countries' militaries to terrorize and repress their people.

NO: General Barry McCaffrey, director of the Office of National Drug Control Policy, argues that hemispheric drug control is a vital example of historical and economic linkages between North and South America to solve mutual problems, including drug production, distribution, consumption, and corruption.

Estimates of the cost of the war on drugs within the United States are at least $10 billion. The worldwide drug trade profits for organized crime, including governments participating in drug production and sales, are estimated to be between $600 billion and $1 trillion. Although recent claims by the *San Jose Mercury* that the CIA intentionally shipped drugs into the black and Hispanic communities of Los Angeles have been roundly discredited, there is no doubt that the CIA has participated for years in drug sales, coverups, and laundering. James Inciardi was one of the first criminologists to expose this activity.

Local and state police in several states have been arrested for bringing drugs into the United States through county airports, roads, and harbors, as well as for protecting dealers. Federal drug enforcers, formerly characterized as being "untouchable," are routinely caught participating in the international drug trade. These include FBI and DEA members.

In Latin America recent torture and murder cases have been linked to claims of police and army drug control. A police chief in the Mexico City area, for example, was charged in 1998 with torturing and decapitating a prisoner. Initially, claims were made that drug dealers were responsible. Now it appears that the murder by the officer was a result of drug profit disputes. In a rural, southern part of Mexico, in late 1997, 45 innocent civilians were slaughtered allegedly on the order of area politicians and police, some of whom had been trained by U.S. officials to control drug dealers but who apparently became (or were) heavy traffickers themselves.

In many villages in parts of Asia, Africa, and Latin America, the entire economy is based on drugs. This entails growing drugs, storing drugs, providing routes for transporting drugs, packaging drugs, and other economically based activities. Many of these same contributions to the drug trade are provided by some residents of U.S. inner-city projects, who exchange their services for local dealers' monies and protection (as well as personal supplies of drugs). Many of the richest and most powerful men and women in developing countries are enriched by drug trafficking. Newspaper accounts and a minority of criminologists have documented some of the leading banks, brokerage houses, and businesses in the United States that profit from drug laundering.

Some of the same U.S. military staff who trained Latin American soldiers to seek and destroy those thought to be Communists or Communist sympathizers also train police and soldiers to fight drugs. Ironically, U.S. personnel also participated in drug trafficking and protected other traffickers in order to raise money for almost any local thug who would promise to fight Communists. It appears that much of the U.S. government's initial involvement in the international drug war, which routinely precipitated human rights abuses, grew out of the cold war "idealism" that almost any rights abuses were acceptable if communism were kept in check. Later, the less noble objective—supporting drug chiefs (who were also military and police chiefs) as an easy route to profit and power—kicked in. In this historical context, some ask, how could human rights abuses *not* occur?

The issue is depicted by Eyal Press and Barry McCaffrey in the following selections. McCaffrey argues that the international war on drugs is benefiting (and being wholeheartedly participated in) by both South and North America. He feels that most leaders view drugs as a terrible problem and are working together to solve it. Press maintains that the so-called war, especially as fought by the Clinton administration, has another agenda. As you read these two selections, decide if there is any real evidence of human rights violations currently taking place as a consequence of efforts to control drugs internationally. Also consider the possibility that although governments fighting drug trafficking might have hidden agendas, good can still come out of such a fight if it reduces drug-related crime and suffering.

YES

Eyal Press

CLINTON PUSHES MILITARY AID: HUMAN-RIGHTS ABUSERS LAP IT UP

At midnight on December 31, 1999, the United States is due to evacuate Panama, removing thousands of troops and ceding control of the Panama Canal to its rightful owners after nearly a century of occupation. But the Clinton Administration is planning to keep the U.S. military in Panama anyway. The stated reason: to fight the drug war.

This past October [1996], U.S. Defense Secretary William Perry informed Latin-American defense ministers at a meeting in Argentina that the United States is negotiating with Panama's President Ernesto Pérez Balladeres to establish a multinational counter-drug center on Howard Air Base in Panama City. Thousands of U.S. troops will remain on the base to provide training and logistical support.

Heading these negotiations is John Negroponte, who served as U.S. ambassador to Honduras during the height of the contra war. Later in his career, while U.S. ambassador to Mexico, Negroponte pushed for heavy military involvement in the so-called drug war.

Now Negroponte is getting his wish. He and General Barry McCaffrey, the four-star general and Gulf War veteran whom Clinton named director of the Office of National Drug Control Policy in 1996, are committed to drawing the United States ever closer to the brutal militaries in the region. And Clinton is all for it.

Before his appointment as Clinton's drug czar, McCaffrey headed the Panama-based U.S. Southern Command, which for years has been at the forefront of military involvement in drug policy. It was McCaffrey who last summer proposed keeping 5,000 U.S. troops in Panama after 1999, a proposal made just as the Southern Command was launching "Operation Laser Strike," which sent hundreds of U.S. troops into the field to help police and military forces in Colombia, Bolivia, and Peru undertake a major counter-narcotics and crop-eradication operation. Before that, U.S. forces under McCaffrey's command provided the Colombian and Peruvian armies with sophisticated radar and surveillance equipment to track the flow and production of drugs in an operation known as "Green Clover."

Despite Republican charges to the contrary, Clinton has hardly been a dove in the drug war. In 1988, Ronald Reagan devoted $4.8 billion to anti-drug efforts. Clinton's latest budget calls for $15.1 billion, with two-thirds earmarked for repressive interdiction and law-enforcement efforts—the same skewed ratio set by Presidents Reagan and Bush.

Lately, Clinton's policy has gone from bad to worse. Beyond the proposed anti-narcotics base in Panama, Clinton is pressing for a series of measures that will augment the U.S. military's role throughout the hemisphere.

In fiscal year 1997, for example, the Administration requested $213 million for the International Narcotics and Law Enforcement account. These funds, which represent a $98 million increase from the previous year's allotment, will be used primarily to arm and train the military and police forces of Colombia, Peru, Bolivia, and Mexico. With barely a whisper from the media, Washington passed money to these forces by slashing $53 million from overseas-development programs specifically earmarked for children.

This fall, Clinton announced at the United Nations that the United States was sending an additional $112 million in military equipment—including helicopters, surveillance aircraft, patrol boats, troop gear, ammunition, training, and assistance—to the Colombian national police and the Colombian, Peruvian, Venezuelan, and Mexican militaries—forces that the Administration asserts "continue to deserve and need our support" in the battle against drugs. Eleven members of Congress promptly sent a letter to

Secretary of State Warren Christopher complaining that Clinton did not notify the proper Congressional committees before announcing this major transfer of weaponry.

Under the guise of the drug war, the Clinton Administration is bolstering repressive security forces responsible for human-rights abuses throughout much of Latin America. "We're looking at a tripling of U.S. military aid to the Andean region—a dramatic increase," says Colletta Youngers of the Washington Office on Latin America. "Beefing up extremely repressive forces in these countries will do nothing to cut off the flow of drugs, but it will lead to more human-rights abuses."

Youngers points out that drugs surfaced as a pretext just as the Cold War came to a close. "Since 1989, the drug issue has become the prime means for military-to-military relations" between the United States and the hemisphere's other armed forces, she says.

Senator Patrick Leahy, Democrat of Vermont, did manage to attach an amendment to the Foreign Operations bill that forbids U.S. assistance to military units that are known human-rights abusers. But "the amendment applies only to aid given under the International Narcotics Funding," says Robin Kirk of Human Rights Watch, who has documented the flow of aid to Colombian security forces. "It's a step in the right direction, but not broad enough."

In Bolivia, the United States has pressured the government to allow the army to participate in anti-narcotics programs despite reports of widespread abuses in the Chapare region, where most Bolivian coca is grown. Washington has also successfully pressed the Mexican military to involve itself in counter-

344 / 19. DOES THE DRUG WAR ENCOURAGE HUMAN RIGHTS VIOLATIONS?

narcotics, providing infusions of anti-drug training and equipment.

Even prior to this change, Mexico was using U.S. counter-narcotics weapons for repressive purposes. Tucked into a footnote of a recent General Accounting Office report on counter-narcotics is the following stunning admission: "During the 1994 uprising in the Mexican state of Chiapas, several U.S.-provided helicopters were used to transport Mexican military personnel to the conflict."

"Most Mexicans will tell you that the involvement of the military in this aspect of civilian life is very troublesome," says Eric Olsen of the Washington Office on Latin America. "This is happening in the states where the military is involved in counterinsurgency, such as Chiapas."

* * *

Besides fueling repression, the renewed drug war comes at an enormous cost to U.S. taxpayers while doing little to stop the flow of drugs. There is no serious evidence that securing the Pentagon's foothold in Panama and Latin America will reduce drug consumption in America. Since 1981, the United States has poured more than $23 billion into the fight against drug trafficking.

Despite enormous expenditures to stop drugs at the source, virtually the same amount of cocaine and heroin continues to flow into the United States. Last year Barry McCaffrey himself acknowledged as much, conceding that "the street price and availability of cocaine in the United States have not been demonstrably affected by the... counter-drug effort in Latin America."

In 1994, a Rand study commissioned by the U.S. Army and Office of National Drug Control Policy said that to achieve a 1 percent reduction in U.S. cocaine con-sumption, the United States could spend either $34 million on drug-treatment programs, or $783 million (more than twenty times more) on attempting to eradicate the supply of drugs at the source.

Why, then, has Clinton gone the expensive route? Not surprisingly, the primary motivation has been political: Clinton has found it far easier to win elections as a tough guy than by explaining the complexities of the issue. And for the Pentagon, the drug war yields a more tangible benefit, offering the military something to do now that the Cold War is over.

In an excellent exposé for the *Los Angeles Times*, reporters Mark Fineman and Craig Pyes outlined how much of the Pentagon's high-tech military equipment, designed for the Cold War, is now being deployed to track the flow of drugs. U.S. taxpayers are spending $1,500 per hour to operate the Navy's ROTHR system, a multimillion-dollar radar operation invented to help battleships locate Soviet aircraft cruising at high altitudes. Drug-war boosters point to 219 air interdictions in the Caribbean in the past three years, but meanwhile drug traffickers have shifted to using passenger planes that land, undetected, in Mexico and transfer the goods by truck.

On another front, U.S. Customs is planning to spend $30 million on a series of "Backscatter" X-ray systems that can purportedly detect drug shipments by bombarding trucks with radioactive particles. But the scanner, built to identify Soviet missiles in trucks, is patently incapable of locating the packages of heroin and cocaine routinely hauled over the border.

* * *

The fusion of drug and military policies finds its domestic application on the windswept plains of Fort Bliss, Texas; the remote mountain passes of Nogales, Arizona; the California desert; and the Rio Grande—all places where U.S. Special Forces scan the horizons using infrared radar systems and special map coordinates provided by the Army. Last year, according to an investigative report by Jim McGee of *The Washington Post*, more than 8,000 U.S. military personnel took part in 754 counter-drug missions on U.S. soil.

In Utah, soldiers assist the Drug Enforcement Agency with tapping telephones. In Key West, Florida, the government has erected a $13.5 million command center where military officers and federal drug agents work side by side.

The Pentagon's brazen insertion into domestic law enforcement violates the 1878 Posse Comitatus Act, which prohibits military involvement in searches and seizures. But, as one former official told *The Washington Post*, "it's been institutionalized."

Now that he's safely reelected, will President Clinton shift to a more enlightened policy? Don't count on it. At the start of his first term, Clinton acknowledged that the drug war waged by Presidents Reagan and Bush had failed. But the moment he heard criticism from the right, he adopted the very same strategies.

To reorient drug policy at this point, the President would have to push hard against a Republican Congress that is salivating over the Clinton scandals. He would also have to risk challenging, rather than accepting, the right's terms of debate on drug policy—terms that have emerged in large part because they make it so easy for elected officials of dubious moral stature to couch policy in the righteous language of a moral crusade.

NO

Barry McCaffrey

HEMISPHERIC DRUG CONTROL: FIGHTING DRUG PRODUCTION AND TRAFFICKING

Delivered to the 21st Regular Session of the Inter-American Drug Abuse Control Commission [CICAD], Organization of American States, [OAS], Washington, D.C., April 9, 1997

It is an honor to be here with the delegates from the thirty-one member states, including our own OAS Ambassador, Hattie Babbitt, and CICAD Executive Director David Beall. I'm glad to see many of my hemispheric colleagues, including Dr. Marino Costa Bauer, Peruvian Minister of Health, and President of the Peruvian Commission de Lucha Contra el Consumo de Drogas (CONTRADROGAS), Panamanian Attorney General Jose Antonio Sossa, Costa Rican Minister of Justice Juan Diego Castro Fernandez, and Mr. Danny Gill, Chairman of the National Council on Substance Abuse in Barbados. (Hemispheric relations in context.)

We are all encouraged by the positive direction of hemispheric relations. Civil strife and conflict are firmly in the past in Central America. Regional economic integration is developing an almost unstoppable momentum. All our nations are increasingly able to focus on domestic or regional issues as opposed to extra-hemispheric concerns. Perhaps this optimism has been best captured by the December 1994 Summit of the Americas in Miami and its continuing processes of consultation and cooperation. Now when we think of major cities, we frequently associate them with yet another important step toward integration and problem resolution; Buenos Aires, Belo Horizonte, Santiago—the site of next year's second Summit of the Americas—are examples. Our own U.S. role is guided by President Clinton's uplifting vision of mutually respectful relations that benefit all peoples. As you know, his special envoy to the Americas, Thomas F. McLarty, is playing a key role coordinating our government's engagement with the region.

When I speak to U.S. audiences about hemispheric drug control challenges and counterdrug cooperation with our North American, Central American, Caribbean, and South American neighbors and allies, I feel it is important to underscore that the increasingly important U.S. hemispheric relations do not revolve around any single issue. While drug policy concerns are critical to all of our nations, none of us should lose sight of the other realities that define the ways in which our peoples and governments interact. Indeed, the nations of the Americas are increasingly interlinked by history, culture, geography, and commerce.

More than 830 million people in the Western Hemisphere now live under democratic regimes. Collectively, our economies constitute a $13 trillion market. Indeed, intra-hemisphere commerce is already significant. The United States trades more with Brazil than with China; more with Venezuela than with Russia; more with Costa Rica—a nation of three million people—than with one hundred million Eastern Europeans; more with fourteen million Chileans than with almost a billion Indians. By the turn of the century, Latin America will have a $2 trillion economy, will trade more than $600 billion in goods and services, and our trade with the nations to our south will exceed our trade with Europe. One of President Clinton's priorities for his second term of office is to act on this reality by building on the successes of NAFTA [North American Free Trade Agreement] and the 1994 Miami Summit of the Americas.

DRUGS ARE A PRESSING INTERNATIONAL PROBLEM

Although no single issue dominates our hemispheric agenda, the overall problem of illegal drugs and related crimes represents a direct threat to the health and well-being of the peoples of the hemisphere. All of us here ... recognize that we cannot afford to let the demand for, and cultivation, production, distribution, trafficking, and sale of illicit narcotics and psychotropic substances interfere with the aspirations of our peoples. Illegal drugs inflict staggering costs on our societies. They kill and sicken our people, sap productivity, drain economies, threaten the environment, and undermine democratic institutions and international order. Drugs are a direct attack on our children and grandchildren. If we are to make inroads against this growing problem, we shall only do so collectively. We can make progress by formulating a common understanding of the problems posed by drug production, trafficking, and consumption and by developing cooperative approaches and solutions. That is exactly the vision spelled out in the CICAD Hemispheric Anti-Drug Strategy. If we act on this vision, we can prevent illegal drugs from darkening the dawn of a new millennium.

THE CONSEQUENCES OF DRUG ABUSE IN THE UNITED STATES

The consequences of illegal drug use have been devastating within the United States. We estimate that in this decade alone, drug use has cost our society more than 100,000 dead and some $300 billion. Each year, more than 500,000 Americans go to hospital emergency rooms because of drug-induced problems. Our children view drugs as the most important problem they face. Drugs and crime threaten all Americans, not just city residents, the poor, or minorities. Americans from every social and economic background, race, and ethnic group are concerned about the interrelated problems of crime, violence, and drugs. We fear the violence that surrounds drug markets. We abhor the effect it has on our children's lives. Americans are especially concerned about the increased use of drugs by young people. Today, dangerous drugs like cocaine, heroin, and methamphetamines are cheaper and more potent than they were at the height of our domestic drug problem fifteen or twenty years ago. In Arizona, ninety percent of homicides last year were related to methamphetamines. No nation can afford such devastating social, health, and criminal consequences.

DEMAND: THE ROOT CAUSE OF THE DRUG PROBLEM

No one should doubt that the demand for illegal drugs lies at the heart of the global drug problem. We in the United States are cognizant that we are a big part of the demand side of the drug equation. However, the percentage of our citizens that consumes drugs is not the central problem. Currently about six percent of our population, or twelve million Americans, use drugs—a fifty percent reduction from 1979's twenty-five million. Even the number of causal cocaine users is down seventy-five percent over the past decade. There are probably 600,000 heroin addicts in the United States. They represent but a fraction of the world's opium/heroin addicts and consume less than two

percent of the global heroin production capacity. A total of about 3.6 million Americans, or less than two percent of our population, is addicted to illegal drugs. This drug usage causes fourteen thousand deaths and costs $67 billion each year.

The problem is that American drug users have enormous quantities of disposable income. A crack addict in New York can afford a $350 a week habit or steal with relative ease $3,000 or more worth of property to maintain that habit. Indeed, Americans spend about $50 billion a year on illegal drugs. Of the estimated three hundred metric tons of cocaine smuggled into the United States every year, the wholesale value at U.S. points of entry is $10 billion. The retail value of that cocaine on our streets is $30 billion. These enormous sums are the reason criminal organizations dominate international traffic in illegal drugs, threaten our communities, and attack our institutions. All of us should recognize that the traffickers of cocaine, heroin, and the other drugs of abuse are actively seeking to develop new markets. If any country successfully reduces consumption of drugs that remain available, these drugs will find new markets. The new markets, along with the addicts and devastation that accompany them, will increasingly be found in those countries that produce the drugs and those through which they transit.

The U.S. National Drug Control Policy, recognizes this reality and prioritizes our efforts accordingly. Our number one goal is to prevent the sixty-eight million Americans under eighteen years of age from becoming a new generation of addicts. We find it unacceptable that drug use rates have doubled among our youth since 1992; we must and will reverse this trend. While we know that we can't arrest our way out of the drug problem, we will continue to uphold our severe drug laws. A million and-a-half Americans are now behind bars, many for drug law violations.

More than a million additional Americans are arrested for drug offenses every year. Incarceration is entirely appropriate for many drug-related crimes. There must be strong incentives to stay clear of drug trafficking, and prison sentences can motivate people to obey the law. Our challenge is to address the problem of chronic drug use by bringing drug testing, assessment, referral, treatment, and supervision within the oversight of the U.S. criminal justice system. We are doing so by increasing the number of drug courts that oversee treatment and rehabilitation for drug law violators and by validating ONDCP's [Office of National Drug Control Policy's] "Break the Cycle" concept. As a nation, we are optimistic that we can substantially reduce the demand for illegal drugs in the United States. One initiative we believe will help us in this effort is the $175 million-a-year anti-drug media campaign, which will be launched in the coming fiscal year.

DRUGS ARE A SHARED PROBLEM THAT MUST BE ADDRESSED BY ALL NATIONS

We recognize that domestic efforts by themselves cannot address what is fundamentally a global problem fueled by powerful, international criminal organizations. All our countries are affected by the drug problem, but not necessarily in the same ways. For some, the most pressing issue is drug consumption. For others, it may be drug-related violence and corruption. Some countries are affected by illicit production or trafficking. Other countries are beset by all these problems. No country is immune.

THE RESULTS OF HEMISPHERIC COOPERATION HAVE BEEN NOTABLE

Over the past years, countries in the Western Hemisphere have made strong efforts to curtail production of illicit drugs, their trafficking, and the laundering of drug moneys. Peru's bilateral and multilateral counterdrug cooperation has been notable. President Fujimori is committed to eliminating coca destined for illicit drug production. The joint U.S.-Peruvian air interdiction campaign forced down, seized and/or destroyed twenty-three narcotics aircraft in 1995. As a result, narcotics-related flights decreased by 47 percent compared to 1994. This campaign caused coca-base prices to fall to record low levels last year, providing a critical economic disincentive for campesino growers. We believe this drop was an important contributing factor in the Peruvian government's success in reducing coca cultivation by 18 percent last year. Brazil has drafted key money-laundering legislation and passed comprehensive legislation on regulation of precursor chemicals. The government of Panama has been an important supporting player in an increasingly sophisticated and effective regional effort to disrupt drug-trafficking patterns within South America and launch international anti-money-laundering initiatives. Our interdiction efforts in the so-called "transit zone" have been enhanced by eighteen bilateral cooperative agreements we have with a number of Caribbean states. In Colombia, Attorney General Valdivieso,

Foreign Minister Mejia, Minister of Defense Echeverry, Armed Forces Commander General Bedoya, and National Police Director General Serrano continue to oppose narcoguerrillas who are attacking the very institutions of democracy.

U.S.-MEXICAN COUNTERDRUG COOPERATION

By any measure, the United States and Mexico have made significant progress in our joint efforts to face up to the drug problem. Whether we speak of investigations of drug trafficking organizations, anti-smuggling projects, crop-eradication efforts, demand-reduction programs, or anti-crime legislation, our record of cooperation is substantial.

President Zedillo has made an obvious commitment to political, legal, and institutional reform and is dedicated to fighting drug trafficking—which he has identified as the principal threat to Mexico's national security. Under his leadership, Mexican drug seizures have increased notably, with marijuana seizures up 40 percent over 1994 and opium-related seizures up 41 percent. Cocaine, methamphetamine, and precursor chemical seizures also rose significantly.

No other nation in the world has eradicated as many hectares of illegal drugs as has Mexico. Our extensive counterdrug cooperation occurs under the rubric of the U.S./Mexico High Level Contact Group for Drug Control. This bilateral drug control policy group was established in March 1996 and has enabled us to advance our collective effort to thwart drug trafficking and the demand for drugs in both nations.

Our two great nations share many drug problems. However, we have resolved to address them forthrightly while affirming our commitment to the principles of international law, particularly those of national sovereignty, territorial integrity, and nonintervention in the internal affairs of other countries.

THE POTENTIAL FOR PUBLIC-PRIVATE SECTOR ANTI-DRUG COALITIONS

All of us recognize the vital contributions that national drug commissions can make in each of our nations. We also understand that central governments can't resolve every problem. It is worth recognizing some important programs already underway in different nations that promise to reduce social tolerance for illegal drug use. In Brazil, the recently established Associao Parceria Contra Drogas has launched a national anti-drug publicity campaign with substantial corporate and private-sector assistance. In Venezuela, the Alianza para una Venezuela sin Drogas has already increased public awareness of the drug problem. In Puerto Rico, the Alianza para un Puerto Rico sin Drogas has brought together political, business, community, and educational leaders from around the Island to form yet another effective anti-drug coalition. In May, the mayors of many of our cities will be gathering in Sao Paulo, Brazil, to discuss how municipal governments can build similar public private anti-drug ventures.

All of us should encourage and emulate these diverse initiatives. Drug use goes down when citizens, parents, educators, religious leaders, and local law enforcement come together to oppose illegal drugs.

MORE INTERNATIONAL COOPERATION IS NEEDED

As suggested by President Clinton's March 1997 report to Congress on the status of International Drug Trafficking and Abuse, international cooperation requires further strengthening. Illicit poppy cultivation for opium increased 11 percent globally from 1994 to 1995, doubling in one country since 1992. Ominously for the United States, our Drug Enforcement Agency estimates that Colombia was the source of 60 percent of the heroin seized in the United States last year. Ten years ago, there was no opium growing in Colombia. Many valiant Colombians have since died fighting this terrible drug trade. Many source-country governments face major threats to their democratic institutions from drug violence and corruption. Finally, all of us face a terrible threat from billions of dollars in illegal funds that distort our economic development and assault the integrity of our banking systems.

The time has come for all of us, as responsible governments, to understand that the world community cannot allow international criminal organizations to gain a foothold in any country.

The April 1996 meeting in Vienna of the U.N. Commission on Narcotic Drugs and the ECOSOC [Economic and Social Committee] Conference at the U.N. Headquarters in New York last June underscored the international consensus for cooperation that will: limit money laundering, control precursor chemicals, take action against institutions or companies facilitating the drug trade, develop procedures for boarding vessels suspected of carrying illegal drugs, and reduce demand for these substances.

THE UNITED STATES IS COMMITTED TO SUPPORTING INTERNATIONAL COUNTERDRUG EFFORTS

The United States government is absolutely committed to helping all nations achieve full compliance with the goals and objectives set forth by the United Nations in its 1988 convention. We will support regional and sub-regional efforts to address drug production, trafficking, and consumption. We will share information with our partners. We are prepared to assist in institution-building so that judiciaries, legislatures, and law-enforcement agencies successfully can counter international traffickers. We will support an international effort to stop money laundering. The magnitude of drug profits that filter through international financial institutions makes them conspicuous. Such sums are difficult to conceal from attentive bankers and governments working together. The U.S. government will continue working with our hemispheric partners to develop means of identifying and seizing illegal drug proceeds as they pass through banking systems.

WE MUST ALL REDOUBLE OUR COMMITMENT

The drug problem is a shared agony throughout this hemisphere. It affects us all differently. In the United States, drug abuse has enormous health consequences and also generates violent crime and unsafe streets. In Mexico, the problem is different. Geography and a common two thousand-mile border have drawn international drug trafficking organizations to that country as a route to the United States. In the Caribbean, small island nations with constrained resources have difficulty protecting their extensive coast lines. Cooperative action holds the promise of reducing trafficking through this transit zone. In Colombia and Peru, drug cultivation and production now provide resources to narcoguerrilla organizations. While the drug-abuse menace is a common problem for us all, it takes on different forms. All of us must guard against allowing drug-trafficking organizations from gaining a stranglehold on our economies, our families, or our democratic processes.

We are confident that we can continue making significant progress in the Western Hemisphere against drug production and trafficking. The U.S. 1997 National Drug Control Strategy affirms our commitment to helping reduce the availability of cocaine. We identify as a top international drug-policy priority support for the efforts of Bolivia, Colombia, and Peru in reducing coca cultivation. We are in the process of developing a regional initiative, the goal of which is nothing less than complete elimination within the next decade of coca destined for illicit cocaine production. The success of Peruvian drug-control efforts in reducing coca cultivation by 18 percent in the past year causes us to feel optimistic about our ability to achieve cooperatively this ambitious objective.

It is indeed an honor to address this meeting of the Inter-American Drug Abuse Control Commission of the Organization of American States—the world's oldest regional organization. The hemispheric cooperation that is fostered by the OAS has its roots in the ideals of Simon Bolívar, the liberator of northern South America, who envisioned the creation of an association of states in the Americas. His dream is alive as all Americans—North, South, and Central—come together to build a brighter future for this hemisphere.

POSTSCRIPT

Does the International Drug War Encourage Human Rights Violations?

This issue reflects several strands in end-of-the-century criminology and criminal justice. The increasing globalization of crime and crime control is one. Another is concerns with human rights and their violation. These include child exploitation in Asia; genocide in Europe, Asia, and Africa; biases against gender and racial minorities in the United States and elsewhere; and torture and brutal oppression in many Latin countries. To many, the alleged link between the latter and the drug problem in the United States is especially disheartening.

In the United States concerns about the drug problem include the issues of whether or not drugs should be legalized, how much of a connection there is between drugs and crime, and whether or not drug controls are applied fairly to different groups (e.g., whites and blacks). They also include direct policy concerns, such as which controls are the best: rehabilitation, increasing arrests, media campaigns, better training and support of police in preventing drugs from coming into the country, or assisting foreign governments in eradicating drugs.

The international implications of drug control brings globalization, human rights, and drugs and drug control together. In our zeal to reduce drug abuse, are we encouraging foreign officials to violate their citizens' human rights? Clearly, efforts to prevent the transportation of drugs into the United States reflects an emphasis on attacking the supply. Is this approach fair? Many Colombians, Mexicans, and others bitterly complain that the U.S. *demand* is the source of the drug problem. Indeed, there is a TV show in Mexico depicting the international drug problem from other countries' perspectives that ridicules U.S. behavior. Is America encouraging serious human rights violations? If so, is it worth it?

For an additional delineation of his position, see B. McCaffrey's "Prevention Programs Work," *Vital Speeches of the Day* (November 15, 1996). Sources that support Press include "Drug War Cowboys," in *The Mythology of Crime and Criminal Justice*, 2d ed., by V. Kappeler, M. Blumberg, and G. W. Potter (Waveland Press, 1996); "The American Crime Factory," in *Private Troubles and Public Issues: Social Problems in the Postmodern Era* by D. R. Simon and J. H. Henderson (Harcourt Brace, 1997); and "The Drug War: Violent, Corrupt and Unsuccessful," by J. McNamara, *Vital Speeches of the Day* (June 15, 1997).

CONTRIBUTORS
TO THIS VOLUME

EDITOR

RICHARD C. MONK is a professor of criminal justice at Coppin State College in Baltimore, Maryland, where he has been teaching criminology and criminal justice since 1993. He received his Ph.D. in sociology from the University of Maryland in 1978, and he has taught anthropology, sociology, criminology, and criminal justice at undergraduate and graduate levels at Morgan State University, San Diego State University, and Valdosta State College. His more recent work includes the forward for and a chapter in *Crimes of the Criminal Justice System* edited by Joel H. Henderson and David R. Simon (Anderson, 1994); "Some Unanticipated Consequences of Females Guarding Males," in *Subtle Sexism: Current Practice and Prospects for Change* edited by Nijole V. Benokraitis (Sage Publications, 1997); and the editors' introduction to "Police Training and Violence," a special issue of the *Journal of Contemporary Criminal Justice* (August 1996), which he coedited with E. Polk. In addition to editing this anthology, he edits Dushkin/McGraw-Hill's *Taking Sides: Clashing Views on Controversial Issues in Race and Ethnicity*, currently in its second edition.

STAFF

David Dean   List Manager
David Brackley   Developmental Editor
Juliana Poggio   Associate Developmental Editor
Rose Gleich   Administrative Assistant
Brenda S. Filley   Production Manager
Juliana Arbo   Typesetting Supervisor
Diane Barker   Proofreader
Lara Johnson   Design/Advertising Coordinator
Richard Tietjen   Publishing Systems Manager

AUTHORS

PAUL BUTLER is an associate professor at the George Washington University Law School.

FRANCIS T. CULLEN is Distinguished Research Professor of Criminal Justice at the University of Cincinnati in Cincinnati, Ohio.

DAVID N. DINKINS, former mayor of New York City, is a professor of public affairs and a senior fellow of the Barnard-Columbia Center for Leadership in Urban Public Policy in New York City.

EMILE DURKHEIM (1858–1917) was a French sociologist and one of the founders and leading figures of modern sociology. He was a professor of philosophy at the University of Bordeaux and a professor of sociology and education at the University of Paris.

RONALD DWORKIN is University Professor of Jurisprudence at Oxford University and a professor of law at New York University in New York City. He is the author of *Freedom's Law: The Moral Reading of the American Constitution* (Harvard University Press, 1996).

PATRICK FAGAN is William H. FitzGerald Fellow in Family and Culture Studies at the Heritage Foundation. He is a former executive director of the Free Congress Foundation and a former deputy assistant secretary of the U.S. Department of Health and Human Services.

BRUCE FEIN is a weekly columnist for the *Washington Times*.

JEFF FERRELL is an associate professor of criminal justice at Northern Arizona University in Flagstaff, Arizona. He is the author of *Crimes of Style: Urban Graffiti and the Politics of Criminology* (Garland, 1993).

W. BYRON GROVES (1953–1990) was an associate professor of humanistic studies at the University of Wisconsin–Green Bay.

MARK S. HAMM is a professor of criminology at Indiana State University in Terre Haute, Indiana. He is the author of *American Skinheads: The Criminology and Control of Hate Crime* (Praeger, 1993).

RICHARD J. HERRNSTEIN (d. 1994) was Edgar Pierce Professor of Psychology at Harvard University in Cambridge, Massachusetts, and a trustee for the Cambridge Center for Behavioral Studies. He coauthored, with James Q. Wilson, *Crime and Human Nature* (Simon & Schuster, 1985).

RHODA E. HOWARD is a professor of sociology at McMaster University in Hamilton, Ontario, Canada. She is the author of *Human Rights and the Search for Community* (Westview Press, 1995).

JAMES A. INCIARDI is director of the Center for Drug and Alcohol Studies at the University of Delaware in Newark, Delaware; an adjunct professor in the Comprehensive Drug Research Center at the University of Miami School of Medicine in Miami, Florida; and a member of the South Florida AIDS Research Consortium.

NOAM JUNGMAN is a member of the Israel Police in Jerusalem, Israel.

RANDALL KENNEDY is a professor at Harvard Law School. He is currently working on a book on race relations and the administration of criminal justice.

VINAY LAL is William R. Kenan Fellow of the Society of Fellows in the Humanities at Columbia University in New York City.

MICHAEL R. LEIPPE is a professor of psychology at Saint Louis University in Saint Louis, Missouri.

A. M. LEVI is a member of the Division of Identification and Forensic Science at Israel Police Headquarters in Jerusalem, Israel.

MICHAEL J. LYNCH is a professor in the Department of Criminology at Florida State University in Tallahassee, Florida. He is coauthor, with E. Britt Patterson, of *Race and Criminal Justice* (Harrow & Heston, 1991).

DENNIS R. MARTIN is former president of the National Association of Chiefs of Police in Arlington, Virginia.

EDWARD MARTONE is New Jersey director of the American Civil Liberties Union.

BARRY McCAFFREY is director of the Office of National Drug Control Policy (ONDCP) at the White House. He serves as the senior drug policy official in the executive branch and as the president's chief drug policy spokesman, and he is also a member of the National Security Council.

PAUL R. McHUGH is Henry Phipps Professor and director of the Department of Psychiatry and Behavioral Sciences at Johns Hopkins University School of Medicine.

EUGENE H. METHVIN is a Washington-based contributing editor to *Reader's Digest.* He has reported on the American criminal justice system for more than 40 years.

DANIEL PATRICK MOYNIHAN is the senior U.S. senator (D) from New York (1976–present, term ends 2001). He has held academic appointments at Cornell University, Syracuse University, and Harvard University.

CHARLES MURRAY is Bradley Fellow at the American Enterprise Institute and the author of *Losing Ground* (Basic Books, 1986) and *In Pursuit of Happiness and Good Government* (ICS Press, 1994).

OFFICE OF JUVENILE JUSTICE AND DELINQUENCY PREVENTION in the Department of Justice is congressionally mandated to lead the effort to address the public safety issues of juvenile crime and youth victimization. Its responsibilities include identifying effective strategies for addressing juvenile crime; coordinating, implementing, and supporting effective programs and encouraging innovative approaches; and providing technical assistance and training to essential components of the juvenile justice system. Shay Bilchik is the administrator.

EYAL PRESS is a writer and a frequent contributor to the *Progressive.*

JEFFREY REIMAN is William Fraser McDowell Professor of Philosophy at American University in Washington, D.C., and a member of the American Society of Criminology. He is the author of *Justice and Modern Moral Philosophy* (Yale University Press, 1992).

PAUL RUFFINS is a contributor to *Crisis* magazine.

JANELL D. SCHMIDT, supervisor of the Milwaukee County Child Protective Services, has worked with Lawrence W. Sherman on criminal justice research projects for the Crime Control Institute in Washington, D.C.

LAWRENCE W. SHERMAN is a professor of criminology in the Institute of Criminal Justice at the University of Maryland in College Park, Maryland, and president of the Crime Control Institute in Washington, D.C. His publications include *Policing Domestic Violence: Experiments and Dilemmas* (Free Press, 1992).

DAVID SHICHOR is a professor in the Department of Criminal Justice at California State University, San Bernardino.

EVAN STARK is an associate professor of public administration and social work at Rutgers University in Newark, New Jersey.

JOSH SUGARMANN, a former communications director of the National Coalition to Ban Handguns, is executive director of the New Right Watch, a nonprofit educational foundation that issues reports on topics dealing with the New Right in America.

THOMAS SZASZ is a psychiatrist, a psychoanalyst, and a professor in the Department of Psychiatry at the State University of New York's Upstate Medical Center at Syracuse, New York, where he has been teaching since 1956. His publications include *Our Right to Drugs: The Case for a Free Market* (Praeger, 1992).

CHARLES R. TITTLE is a professor of sociology at Washington State University in Pullman, Washington.

BOB TREBILCOCK writes frequently for *Redbook* magazine on news and social issues.

ERNEST VAN DEN HAAG is a distinguished scholar at the Heritage Foundation in Washington, D.C. He has contributed more than 200 articles to magazines and sociology journals in the United States, England, France, and Italy, and he is coauthor, with John P. Conrad, of *The Death Penalty: A Debate* (Plenum, 1983).

DAVID VON DREHLE is art editor for the *Washington Post.* His publications include *Among the Lowest of the Dead* (Times Books, 1995).

GARY L. WELLS is a professor in the Department of Psychology at Iowa State University in Ames, Iowa.

JULIA WILKINS is the author of two books on educating children, *Math Activities for Young Children: A Resource Guide for Parents and Teachers* and *Non-Competitive Motor Activities: A Guide for Elementary Classroom Teachers.*

JAMES Q. WILSON is James Collins Professor of Management and Public Policy at the University of California, Los Angeles, and chair of the board of directors of the Police Foundation. He is the author of *Bureaucracy: What Government Agencies Do and Why They Do It* (Basic Books, 1989).

JAMES D. WRIGHT is Charles and Leo Favrot Professor of Human Relations in the Department of Sociology at Tulane University of Louisiana in New Orleans, Louisiana. He is the author of 12 books, including 2 about the homeless, and over 140 journal articles, book chapters, essays, and reviews.

INDEX